Hannah Arendt
and the Meaning of Politics

Contradictions of Modernity

The modern era has been uniquely productive of theory. Some theory claimed uniformity despite human differences or unilinear progress in the face of catastrophic changes. Other theory was informed more deeply by the complexities of history and recognition of cultural specificity. This series seeks to further the latter approach by publishing books that explore the problems of theorizing the modern in its manifold and sometimes contradictory forms and that examine the specific locations of theory within the modern.

Edited by Craig Calhoun
New York University

Hannah Arendt
and the Meaning of Politics

Craig Calhoun and
John McGowan, editors

Afterword by Martin Jay

Contradictions of Modernity Volume 6

University of Minnesota Press
Minneapolis
London

Published by the University of Minnesota Press
111 Third Avenue South, Suite 290, Minneapolis, MN 55401-2520
Printed in the United States of America on acid-free paper

Library of Congress Cataloging-in-Publication Data

A catalog record for this book is available from the Library of Congress

ISBN 0-8166-2916-1 (hc)
ISBN 0-8166-2917-X (pb)

Contents

Acknowledgments

A conference is an action in public space made possible only by the collective efforts of many people. Most are not given the chance to disclose their distinctive personal identities or gain proper recognition for their performances. Organizers incur special debts, accordingly, that are very poorly discharged with the weak payment of mention in passages such as this one. The present case is no exception, though we are pleased to note that the importance of one crucial actor, Leah Florence, was recognized not only in public ritual but also in a variety of ways by nearly every participant in the 1995 conference on which this book is based, and repeatedly since then as we—and she—have labored to gather revisions in a timely fashion. Leah is the tremendously helpful administrative and editorial assistant to the Program in Social Theory and Cross-Cultural Studies, which sponsored the conference and the book. She is, of course, also a great deal more, and we are as grateful for her unofficial contributions to our collective lives as for her (under)paid work.

A number of other people also made special contributions to this venture. Most important, clearly, are those who presented papers or commentaries at the conference and revised them for publication in this book. Not only are their individual contributions strong, but they also joined in debate in a way that made each a contributor to the work of others and that made the event stimulating and engaging (and made the editorial process as nearly a pleasure as these things can be). We can only offer our thanks. (Jean Cohen, who participated actively and significantly in the conference, was unable to turn her oral remarks into a text in time for the publication of this book, and we greatly regret her absence.) Our thanks go also to the "audience" of University of North Carolina at Chapel Hill faculty, students, and guests who did much more than simply listen, helping both to create the occasion and to improve it with their remarks and interventions (even when the latter consisted of groans and laughter).

Paul Price played a crucial role from early in this project, assisting in our seminar, tracking down publications, and joining in debate. Several of our graduate students helped in substantial ways: preparing packets of papers, picking up participants at the airport, guiding them to dinner, making sure we had chairs on which to sit and (a crucial conference necessity) coffee to drink. For this help we thank Leslie Frost, Joe Gerteis, Adam McKible, and Jim Moody. These students were also among those who participated in the seminar we taught together on the work of Hannah Arendt, and their discussion, questions, and papers helped us to understand better both Arendt's works and the gaps in our own educations (which we have since labored to fill). We thank them for action as well as labor.

One of the Arendtian goals of action is to create lasting institutions and to renew them continuously through action. One institution close to our hearts is the Program in Social Theory and Cross-Cultural Studies, a small program at UNC that nonetheless looms large, we think, in local intellectual life. The program paid the bill for the conference and also provided its intellectual setting. We are grateful to the program and to the wide range of colleagues who make it work. The conference was also generously supported by the Institute for the Arts and Humanities, the Institute for Research in Social Science, and the Departments of English, History, Philosophy, Political Science, and Sociology. We are also grateful to another institution, the University of Minnesota Press, and especially our editor, Micah Kleit, who has been not only a pleasure to work with but also a valuable colleague. Last but not least, we thank our families—Pam, Salam, and Jonah; Jane, Kiernan, and Siobhan—who tolerated not just our work on this project but also years of reading groups, seminars, and late-night phone calls, and who often even encouraged us.

Introduction

Hannah Arendt and the Meaning of Politics

Craig Calhoun and John McGowan

Our public life today seems too often reduced to conflicts and nego-
tiations among competing interests, quarrels among those demanding
recognition for radically different identities, and assertions of allegedly
simple, timeless truths. Can these really give adequate meaning to the
idea of politics? Must politics be merely a matter of power relations,
or can it embody the realization of some of the higher and most distinctive potentials of human life?

No thinker has argued more passionately that politics should transcend the play of mere instrumental concerns than Hannah Arendt.
Brilliant, demanding, inspiring, original, and sometimes perverse, her
writings offer an important resource for theorists who would conceptualize a politics in which questions of meaning, identity, and value
take center stage. Arendt frequently frustrates, but her work is indis-
pensable for those who would learn how to take human plurality seriously, how to grasp public life not just as an occasion for choice but
also as an opportunity for different human beings to make a world in
common, and how to address the problems of not just suboptimal utility but also violence and evil.

In her contribution to the present volume, Kirstie McClure writes
nicely of addressing political issues "in the company of Hannah Arendt."
The phrase is useful in describing the task of this book as a whole. In

convening the conference on which this volume is based, we sought not so much to interpret or explain Arendt's work as to draw on the richness of this work in opening up various dimensions of the meaning of politics. Through both the event and the book our hope has been to nurture, in the company of Hannah Arendt, a political theory that gives a richer meaning to the idea of politics than has seemed common in recent years. Politics itself has been opened up in a variety of ways in recent years: movements as different as resurgent nationalism, gay liberation, and feminism have called forth remarkably powerful and creative politics of identity—some more attractive than others. Struggles have made public a wide range of topics historically kept private. One may argue about whether this is a good or a bad thing, but it is clearly transformative. So too, questions of the place of aesthetics in politics, of the creation of self versus the reflection of interests, and of the meaning of membership and migration have transformed contemporary politics. The resulting politics is broader and its meaning more complex than simple oppositions between liberalism and communitarianism, modernism and postmodernism, rational choice and cultural identity that have dominated much political thought. Arendt's work—like much of contemporary political activity—challenges us to a more basic rethinking of our political theory.

We editors and chapter authors have not eschewed close attention to Arendt's texts, to be sure, but exegesis has not been our primary goal. Several contributors have elsewhere published (or are about to publish) major works of exegesis and interpretation.[1] A great deal of important textual analysis and interpretation has also been published by others.[2] Our attempt has been to think with Arendt about the basic nature of politics and the problems of different strategies of political analysis. Four central concerns shape the chapters of this book, and we have approached them in the following order (though they do not neatly divide the book into parts, because many authors have addressed more than one concern): First, there is the issue of aesthetic self-presentation in politics. Second, perhaps most pervasive of all, there is the concern for judgment that led Arendt to her distinctive interpretation of Kant but that also motivated the unwritten third volume of *The Life of the Mind*. Third, Arendt sparks new thoughts on the nature and changing character of the public/private distinction. Finally, Arendt helps us think hard about the problems of violence and evil that too much recent political theory would rather leave to one side.

One of Arendt's favorite theoretical tactics was anamnesis, an attack on our forgetting of the heritage offered us by the past. She sought to bring back the resources offered us first by the Greeks, who forged classical political theory, and second by the American founders, who forged the modern conception of the people in action in creating the American Republic. Through a selective recovery of the resources offered by the history of political thought, she sought to reinvigorate our contemporary understanding of the possibilities of political life—and of the impoverishment that an apolitical life would mean. It is ironic, then, that in a short span of time Arendt herself should go through cycles of widespread forgetting and enormous popularity, a movement of anamnestic recovery.

In the 1950s and 1960s Arendt was among the most widely read philosophers and political thinkers in the world. By the 1970s and especially after her death in 1975, however, her work lost much of its prominence. Her influence remained significant through her students and colleagues, but her books ceased to be major objects of scholarly attention or to shape public debates. To many younger readers she seemed suddenly old-fashioned, out of sync with a world of renewed interest in Marxism, the rise of rational choice theory, several competing feminisms, multiculturalism, and postmodernism. Her eclipse was perhaps most complete—and most unfortunate—among parts of the left that were alienated by what had been made of her account of totalitarianism during the cold war and that were suspicious of her attempt to place political action beyond "mere" labor and to question the idea of making history. The embeddedness of her thought in classical scholarship and her allegiance to high culture against populist currents made her work seem distant in style as well as substance from the issues and approaches of the day.

As recently as 1990 it was rare to find Arendt's works taught among the basic modern theories for political scientists, sociologists, and philosophers. Her memory and her work remained current at the New School for Social Research and among a few other cognoscenti, but it remained a highly specialized taste. Arendt was never really obscure, but she was for a time not much read outside fairly specialized circles. But in fact, a resurgence—an anamnestic recovery—was already under way. A number of younger political philosophers had turned to Arendt's work for inspiration. Within three or four years, Arendt had firmly entered the canon of modern political theory. Not only was her work widely taught, but it also became one of the key reference points organizing debates. In sociology, though somewhat less prominently, her analyses came increasingly to inform a renewed interest in the meaning and significance of action and the relationship of action to agency. Instead of finding her work stylistically or substantively distant, students began to find it distinctively engaging.

Though the seeds of this resurgence had been planted in the 1980s, renewed interest in Arendt's work was remarkably swift. When we began, in 1993, to plan for a conference at the University of North Carolina on Arendt's work, Margaret Canovan's was the one really important recent book on Arendt, though we were shortly to be impressed by the discussion in Bonnie Honig's *Political Theory and the Displacement of Politics*.[3] A number of significant articles had appeared, of course, but we thought ourselves to be in the avant-garde. We were, in fact, merely riding the wave of the zeitgeist. By the time the conference was held in early 1995, at least a half dozen more books on Arendt had appeared, and as many more were on the way. Shortly after the conference, debate over the publication of Elzbieta Ettinger's *Hannah Arendt/Martin Heidegger* brought discussion of Arendt into the daily newspapers, though in an unfortunately personalistic way.[4]

The resurgence of interest in Arendt has come from many directions, but perhaps the single most important has been feminism.[5] Given Arendt's own resolute nonfeminism, it is especially interesting to see her work take a central place in feminist discourse. That Arendt was the most influential woman ever to write political theory would have guaranteed attention, but the level of engagement went far beyond such simple explanations.

In her lifetime Arendt was mainly ignored by feminists. In the years after her death, she was commonly considered by feminist authors as an example of a woman whose perceptions were distorted by her affiliations with dominant strains of masculinist thought. The result, in Mary Dietz's words, was that "the woman who is arguably the most influential theorist of action, participatory politics, and the public realm in the twentieth century appears to have had no discernable influence upon the second-wave feminist movement in either North America or Europe, in either its theory or its public, political practice."[6]

As Dietz notes, in the late 1980s and early 1990s an attempt to appropriate aspects of Arendt's thought for feminist theory gathered steam. The tendency, however, was for the literature to divide between critiques of Arendt's phallocentrism and claims that her work was more gynocentric than it appeared. The crucial concept for the latter point of view was natality. Arendt gained praise for placing in the forefront of political theory attention to a distinctively female experience and/or capacity—that of giving birth. (Although it could be argued that Arendt took seriously literally giving birth—or at least, being born—she was more interested in the metaphor of natality [Arendt's term, taken from Augustine, for the "new birth and beginning" afforded by action] as connoting the generally human capacity for creativity and novelty.)

The greater engagement with Arendt that is currently prominent in feminist theory, however, stems not so much from a simple appropriation as from a recognition that Arendt's importance for feminism is less as a theorist of gender than as a theorist of politics—the kind of politics that could take on new meaning for feminists.[7] This is prominent, for example, in Bonnie Honig's attempt to recover, with assistance from Arendt, an understanding of the indefinite openness of politics, its unpredictability. To take gender (among other possible ascriptions) as a matter of fixed identity prior to politics, Honig suggests, is to "close the spaces of politics." A self, in this sense, "is never exhausted by the (sociological, psychological, and juridical) categories that seek to define and fix it";[8] "A political community that constitutes itself on the basis of a prior, shared, and stable identity threatens to close the spaces of politics, to homogenize or repress the plurality and multiplicity that political action postulates."[9] Honig is critical of other aspects of Arendt's theory, such as what she sees as an excessive formalization of action (that anticipates Habermas's proceduralism) and an overly rigid public/private distinction. Nonetheless, the richness of Arendt's accounts of action in public space suggests an "agonistic feminism." Honig would perhaps go further in this direction than Arendt, but the most relevant point here is that Arendt's concept of politics, rather than gender, may hold the most promise for rethinking the practices and concepts of feminism—and, more generally, of identity politics.

The late 1980s and early 1990s saw a widespread crisis in critical imagination, partly—but only partly—because actual changes such as the end of the cold war outstripped theoretical projections. Many critical

visions that sought to expand the role of politics beyond mere instrumental contests about power found themselves running out of steam
or forced onto the defensive. In Reagan's America, Thatcher's Britain,
and Kohl's Germany, a variety of erstwhile radical critics of liberalism
found themselves defending what had once seemed a problematic liberal status quo of political and civil rights against an onslaught from
resurgent antipolitical economic liberalism and cultural conservatism.
The politics of expertise seemed ascendant against a politics of public
discourse at the same time that an anti-intellectual populism spread.
The collapse of Communist regimes throughout Eastern Europe and
the former Soviet Union further disoriented political discourse. Not
just the meaning of left and right but the meaning of politics itself
seemed uncertain. This was a problem for anyone concerned with
public life, of course; it was especially a problem on professional
grounds for political theorists and perhaps in even more basic ways for
feminists who observed the simultaneous dramatic growth of feminist
theory and its increasing separation from the feminist movement.

Ironically perhaps, this crisis of political culture came at the time
of the fullest incorporation of "identity politics" into political debate
and political theory. Attempts to introduce multicultural components
into college and university curricula spread almost as rapidly as cam-
pus chapters of the Young Republicans and evangelical Christian
groups. Theorists responded both by embracing much of the emphasis
on a politics of identity that had been brought to the fore by the "new
social movements" that had flourished in and after the 1960s, and by
discovering that identity politics was theoretically hydra-headed and
hardly a simple guide to thought or action. Did a concern for "identity" and "difference" mean, for example, an essentialist account of
what made the members of one category the same as each other and
different from those outside its boundaries? Or did it mean the endless, polymorphous production of new possibilities? Were claims to
"identity" claims on the broader community for recognition (as, for
example, Charles Taylor argued) or were they reflections of essentially
autonomous, self-subsistent collectivities?[10] These issues became basic
both to discourses about the political significance of gender, race, and
sexual orientation and to a more basic rethinking of the meaning of
politics itself.

Not least of all, the early 1990s saw the organization of much—
almost certainly most—debate in political theory organized around two

major oppositions: an argument between liberalism and communitarianism, and an argument over modernism and postmodernism. In other branches of political science, and in sociology and other social sciences, debates between "rational-choice" and cultural and historical explanations shared much with the liberal/communitarian and modernist/postmodernist clashes. These were clearly arguments with significance for the world of "practical politics," but in the work of many academic political theorists (and social and cultural theorists more generally) they became increasingly academic matters, themes on which to score points for professional advancement but detached from any engagement with broader publics. The postmodernist critique was perhaps the strongest challenge to academic orthodoxies; however, not only was it largely devoid of specific political purchase and implications, but also, many versions (though not quite all) challenged the idea that theory ought to have or aim at political purchase.

It was in this context that a renewed interest in the work of Hannah Arendt became not only attractive but also enormously revitalizing. It was not that adopting an Arendtian position seemed the way out to many theorists. Rather, it was that Arendt unsettled debates that were becoming arid and pedantic or that were stuck in political name-calling. As much as any other modern theorist, for example, she thematized a politics of performativity (with a significantly aesthetic dimension) in her idealization of the ancient Greek polis. Yet she was also strongly committed to a politics of communication. It was hard to put her neatly into the camp of Habermas against an aesthetic politics, yet it was impossible to deny her affinities with Habermas. Arendt helped theorists such as Honig develop a deconstructive approach to politics that was not apolitical. Conversely, she helped Habermasian liberal theorists such as Benhabib find a clearer place for politics of gender and difference within an associationist approach.[11] Similarly, here was arguably the most important female thinker of the twentieth century, yet she was certainly no feminist. Her work was full of themes, however, that were of great importance to later feminists. Above all, it seemed to unsettle many of the established oppositions in the existing discourse. For example, Arendt suggested that a false opposition had grown up between liberalism and communitarianism. Reading Arendt could invigorate and challenge each side in this debate as in many others.

Arendt's attraction grew, therefore, in direct proportion as thinkers were frustrated (or bored) by the seemingly forced choices: Are you a modernist or a postmodernist? committed to expressive identity politics or oriented to reasoned understanding through communication? liberal or communitarian? Those who wished to answer "both and neither" to each question found Arendt a great resource; those who remained on one side or the other found her challenging enough to require an answer. Part of the importance of Arendt's work in the 1990s, therefore, has been to help theorists try to think their way out of some divisions of the intellectual world that had become blinders in their views of the real world, and out of some academic arguments that had begun to grow stale. Arendt's work continues to stimulate and provoke in these ways. In addition, different responses to and extensions of Arendt have become influential ways of positioning work in the broad and intersecting fields of political theory, feminist studies, and social and cultural theory.

At the same time, Arendt's work is deep and rich enough that it has been able to sustain the interest of many and divergent inquiries. As the contributions to this book make clear, Arendt can inform very different views of the political world and understandings of public life. Her work is of central importance to current revitalizations of the classical republican tradition, helping theorists rethink ideas of moral virtue and political community. It is of equal importance to thinking through different forms of alienation in relationship to postmodernist critiques of conventional politics.

Perhaps most crucially, Arendt calls on us to recognize that human plurality is basic to the possibility and importance of politics. It is with this in mind that she argues against the temptation to short-circuit public life by asserting absolute truths. As important as mutual understanding is to her theory, it is crucial that mutual understanding be achieved through processes of communication that are never complete, and therefore that it never be approached as though it were analogous to scientific truth. Such truth, she argued (perhaps poorly conceiving the actual practice if not the political use of science) cuts off debate by demanding to be taken as final. What is crucial to political life is that public discussion continue indefinitely. Public discussion is a goal in itself, not merely a means by which to arrive at decisions. The public sphere exists to offer the occasion for self-revealing discourse as much as for achieving consensus or even reciprocal understanding.[12] The public life of classical Greece, she thus wrote, consisted "to an incredibly large extent of citizens talking with one another. In this incessant talk the Greeks discovered that the world we have in common is usually regarded from an infinite number of different standpoints, to which correspond the most diverse points of view. . . . In a sheer inexhaustible flow of arguments, Greeks learned to understand—not to understand one another as individual persons, but to look upon the same world from another's standpoint, to see the same in very different and frequently opposing aspects."[13] Moreover, she argued, "every claim in the sphere of human affairs to an absolute truth, whose validity needs no support from the side of opinion, strikes at the very roots of all politics and all governments."[14] Truth of this sort represented the force of necessity, not the possibility of freedom.[15] It concerned "man in his singularity" and accordingly was "unpolitical by nature."[16]

Politics, in such a conception, cannot be merely a matter of power, of divisions between ruler and ruled, or of distribution of economic goods. Politics has to be, among other things, a realm of self-creation through free, voluntary action undertaken in consort with and in relation to other people. The public realm in which politics takes place is above all else a space between people, created by their discourse and mutual recognition. This vision sets Arendt clearly against utilitarianism, with its sacrifice of public action and discourse to legislative and regulatory expertise. Utilitarianism's apparent answer to the problem of the meaning of politics turns out to be spurious: "The perplexity of utilitarianism is that it gets caught in the unending chain of means and ends without ever arriving at some principle which could justify the category of means and end, that is, of utility itself. The 'in order to' has become the content of the 'for the sake of'; in other words, utility established as meaning generates meaninglessness."[17] As important as the creation of political and legal institutions is, she could never imagine with Helvétius and Bentham that it is by means of good laws alone that virtuous people are made. Human beings so completely the creatures of external determination would cease to be capable of real action. But Arendt would have been sympathetic to aspects of the argument against natural goodness and innocence as well, affirming that "virtue—which perhaps is less than goodness but still alone is capable of 'embodiment in lasting institutions'" is the proper object of political arrangements.[18] Viable political institutions cannot be erected on the foundation of the supposedly natural goodness of humankind. That "the law is made for men, and neither for angels nor for devils," is thus the moral Arendt draws from her famous analysis of Melville's *Billy Budd* and uses in argument against Rousseau and Robespierre.[19] Politics that takes place among real people has to avoid perfectionism or risk not only impossibility but totalitarianism. As Maurizio Passerin d'Entrèves puts it,

> Arendt maintains that action has to transcend mere instrumental concerns for the sake of a political principle, but is fully aware that we can never eliminate them entirely. Her point is that politics should not be seen as just another kind of instrumental action or as a means to the pursuit of private advantage; it is the active engagement of citizens in all matters of public concern, the public discussion, deliberation, and decision-making with respect to issues affecting the political community (which may be local, national, or international).[20]

The importance of Arendt's political theory today lies partly in the fact that the heirs of Bentham and Rousseau are, in transformed guise, ascendant. A moment's glance at a journal such as *Political Theory* shows the extent to which an opposition between "liberalism" and "communitarianism" has come to organize debate. Yet these terms are somewhat misleading. Many communitarians—Charles Taylor and Robert Bellah, to name two—are in important senses "liberals."[21] They would defend a wide variety of "rights," including the protection of individuals from the tyranny of majorities and from governmental control. Their arguments are posed less against all liberalism than against the tendency of liberalism to fall into stronger or weaker versions of instrumental individualism and especially utilitarianism.[22] The communitarian position is more sharply a challenge to the kind of position Bentham espoused, especially when he asserted that "The community is a fictitious body, composed of the individual persons who are considered as constituting as it were its members. The interest of the community then is, what?—the sum of the interests of the several members who compose it."[23] Arendt can hardly support such a position. Like the communitarians, and like much of the tradition of moral republicanism and civic virtue, she has a strong commitment to an intersubjective and noninstrumentalist view of politics. But her account of public space is in important ways precisely not an account of community, and certainly not of community constituted by preestablished similarity among members.[24] Political action in public space is agonistic and focused on difference for Arendt in a way it seldom is for communitarians. Arendt suggests something important that is missing from, indeed occluded by, the typical "liberal/ communitarian" debates.

Arendt's work, in sum, is a splendid provocation as well as a vital resource. The essays in this book respond to Arendt's provocations as well as try to chart new courses that build on her writings. Each represents an attempt to think with, or on the basis of, or in reaction to Hannah Arendt on the subject of the meaning of politics. They all respond to problems located in the contemporary world and look with varying degrees of anxiety toward the future. They address in varying combinations the preceding issues, including crucially the challenge of rethinking the meaning of politics in a way that transcends the simple oppositions that have come to structure much political theory. The essays in this book use Arendt to revisit, reconfigure, and rethink any number of ways we currently understand the meaning of politics. What follows in this introduction is simply one account of how the assembled authors speak to one another; Martin Jay offers an alternative account in his afterword. The reader will doubtless be struck by themes that we and Jay have neglected, as well as Arendtian insights that might have been called upon to clarify, complete, complicate, or confound arguments made in this volume.

Much of the response to Arendt's work during her lifetime (if we exclude the Eichmann controversy) focused on her strict distinction between the political and the social, the public and the private. Since her death, commentators have been most fascinated (and this volume follows this trend to some extent) with her attempt to fashion a theory of political judgment. Eli Zaretsky and John McGowan return here to the earlier concern with Arendt's distinctive definition of the political. McGowan takes that definition as utopian, constructed to exclude the violence, terror, and evil that totalitarianism brought to the center of politics, thus destroying the freedom that Arendt insists is the very meaning and raison d'être of politics. To shift our political concerns from freedom to other goods is to ask of the political what it cannot deliver and to foster the kinds of frustration with the political that can lead to terror and totalitarianism. We should understand the Arendtian political, McGowan suggests, as an exemplary, idealistic purification presented to highlight the goods—relatedness, freedom to act, and freedom from terror—that we should look to the political to provide, rather than as an assertion of what the political actually is in the mixed and messy conditions of any actual state, even the city-states of the Greeks.

Zaretsky reminds us that an attack on the liberal wall between the public (political) and the private (economic) was a mainstay of the Marxist-inspired thinking that surrounded Arendt both in the Paris of the 1930s and the New York of the 1940s and 1950s. Hence, her separation of labor and work from action in *The Human Condition* is a direct repudiation of Marxist orthodoxy. Yet Zaretsky also sees *The Human Condition* as calling attention to another "private" sphere—the domestic, which Marxism neglected altogether. Just as *The Origins of Totalitarianism* revised Marxist accounts of the rise of imperialism and fascism with an insistence on the importance of nationalism, *The Human Condition* supplemented Marxist accounts of the bourgeois state with an insistence on the importance of meaning and identity. Alongside, yet distinct from, economic interest are motives deriving from drives for distinction, recognition, and uniqueness. In short, Arendt recognized the significance of what we now think of as "identity" issues, the fact that citizens look to the political not just (if at all) for regulated allocation of material resources, but also (and perhaps primarily) for meaning. For Zaretsky, Arendt should be paired with her exact contemporaries in the 1950s, E. P. Thompson and Raymond Williams, for highlighting the relevance of the "cultural, that is, . . . a realm of meaning" to the political. This emphasis changes our perspective on what holds a nation together (besides the compulsion of economic necessity or political force) and on the stakes for which citizens engage in political activity. Arendt believes that the advance of what is genuinely human depends upon making spontaneous activity possible, and she constructs the political for that work of protecting and advancing the possibility of action. In calling attention to the nation and to the domestic as sites of meaning-production and in focusing on political (as distinct from economic) goods, Arendt shadows forth themes crucial to contemporary feminism and other "new social movements."

Dana Villa's essay offers the fullest account in this collection of what might be called Arendt's version of identity politics. Villa argues that Arendt believes identity is only possible in "alienated" performance. Only where the self stages itself as "appearance" before others can its identity come into being. This constitution of identity in "the space of appearances" (a favorite Arendtian name for the political) has nothing to do with "authenticity" or the expression of a deep, true, or preexisting self. Instead, "Arendt interprets freedom as virtuosity precisely to keep the actor *in* the world, to frame her identity qua actor as coextensive with, rather than prior to, her actions"; "The unity (coherence of identity) of the agent is, then, not a given; rather, it is an *achievement*, the product of action." Only "entry into the public realm enables" this achievement. In Villa's reading, the public realm in Arendt is desirable *only* insofar as it provides a stage for virtuosity and distinction. He takes issue with Habermasian and communitarian readers of Arendt, who look to her comments on the public realm as support for their own projects of "recovering a robust, comprehensive, and unitary public sphere." Such attempts attribute to Arendt their own nostalgia (or fantasy). Villa's Arendt sees "the prospects for an authentic, comprehensive, and relatively permanent public sphere [as] just about zero": "It is not a question, therefore, of pretending that we can resurrect the agora or some approximation thereof by appealing to deliberation, intersubjectivity, or 'acting in concert.' What matters is our ability to resist the demand for 'functionalized behavior' and to preserve, as far as possible, our capacity for initiatory, agonistic action and spontaneous, independent judgment."

Villa gives us a fiercely individualistic Arendt, one he realizes must downplay certain Arendtian themes, such as "acting in concert." Furthermore, in claiming that "the autonomy or independence of judgment is to be maintained," Villa must strain against Arendtian descriptions of judgment as "thinking in company with others" to stress the Arendtian association of thinking with "withdrawal." This and other tensions within Arendt's musings on judgment occupy much of Anthony Cascardi's, Lisa Disch's, Kirstie McClure's, Richard Bernstein's, and Martin Jay's attention.

Cascardi sees Arendt as too Habermasian, as domesticating Kant by ignoring the disruption of imagination offered by the sublime in *Critique of Judgment*. Arendtian judgment is "representative thinking," the imaginative "visiting" that stirs one to envision something from the "standpoint of others." The success of this enterprise rests on the attainment or recovery or constitution of (these three are hardly equivalent, and which one we emphasize will strongly color our understanding of Arendt on judgment) "common sense," Kant's (and Cicero's) *sensus communis*. Cascardi is troubled by the omission of that which exceeds common sense, that which exceeds representation, the sublime. Arendt's omission scants the possibility of the transformative and thus is a step back from the productive tension, the unresolved "antinomy" of Kant's aesthetic writings: "Arendt's tendency to privilege the beautiful over the sublime must be seen as part of her larger passion to save politics from irrationalism." This assertion provides us with a very Habermasian Arendt, one at odds not only with the agonistic Nietzschean Arendt of Villa's essay but also with the romantic-existentialist Arendt of Martin Jay's classic essay and, to some extent, of his concluding remarks here. What Cascardi appears to neglect is Arendt's notion of "action," which in its spontaneity, incalculability, and novelty is analogous to (albeit more human and more representable, because it is tied to the words that immortalize deeds) the sublime. Not that Cascardi obliterates all tension from Arendt's work; he thinks that Arendt's rationalistic version of judgment "render[s] unintelligible the question of founding," while also acknowledging Arendt's continual engagement (particularly in *On Revolution*) with that question. (McGowan's essay provides an extended meditation on Arendt's accounts of founding.) It would not be extrapolating too far from Cascardi to think that he points toward a tension in Arendt between action and judgment. Whether this tension is productive or debilitating is, of course, another question altogether. Martin Jay begins his concluding remarks by claiming an almost total reversal from the Arendt who features action to the Arendt who features judgment, a capacity that resides in the spectator, not in the agent (who cannot, in this reading, know what she is doing). The relation of action to judgment (and vice versa) remains a vexed question for readers of Arendt, a question this volume poses but hardly answers.

Kirstie McClure examines the connection of judgment not to action but to opinion. Working from Arendt's contention that truth—because it compels assent—is irrelevant to, even destructive of, politics, McClure focuses on judgment as the process of public opinion formation, with a special stress on "process." The opinion is public not just because it is enunciated publicly and submitted to the response of others, but even more fundamentally because, working from Kant's stress on "publicity," Arendt argues that the "I" could not even form an opinion apart from the encounter with others. Whereas Villa has reminded us that for Arendt identity is produced only in the presence of others, McClure, following Kant and Arendt, avers "that even thinking, seemingly the most solitary of activities, depends on others—to deliver one's opinion in public was to 'communicate and expose to the test of others . . . whatever you may have found out when you were alone.'" Even prior to this communication of one's thoughts is the imaginative attempt to incorporate the viewpoint of others, that "enlarged mentality" requisite to judgment for Arendt. Only the invasion of the thinker's solitude by these others could render judgments and opinions possibly adequate to the world's "plurality."

By the same token, the novelty of action means that no judgment could ever be the final word. The problem with truth in the realm of human affairs is that it scants plurality and natality. As McClure emphasizes, opinion in Arendt is always in process and fallible. Opinion is not just formed in the imaginative attempt to take the standpoint of others into account, but it is also articulated more with the goal of keeping intersubjective talk going than in the interest of reaching a conclusion, of laying down the law. (This Arendtian commitment to the dialogic leads both McClure and Disch to bring Bakhtin into their discussions of Arendtian judgment.) Judgment is "an invitation to engagement rather than an appeal to truth," so that Arendt's public enunciation of an opinion in (to take the notorious example McClure uses) the Little Rock desegregation case "enact[s] her commitment to a form of public discourse" whose primary aims are "to get into community with others" (a Kantian phrase that both Arendt and McClure repeat) and the formation of opinion "forged through public examination," not a war waged from "fixed" positions. The necessity of others for this process means that adversarial debates aimed at subduing one side or the other destroys the very thing—an intersubjective place of exchange—one hopes to foster. To put this point in terms more suited to McGowan's and Kimberley Curtis's essays than to McClure's, plurality is a fundamental human condition and a fundamental good in Arendt, but plurality cannot be taken for granted; it must be nurtured and protected from behaviors that can overwhelm it, and the political takes its meaning primarily from its being the space where plurality appears, is enabled, is fostered, and is protected. The success of judgment, then, as a political process is measured more by its maintaining a vital political space than by any "results" or "conclusions" it generates.

We must be careful not to assimilate McClure's view too quickly with a communitarian focus on constituting a fully intersubjective public sphere. (Disch is probably closer to McGowan and Curtis on this point than is McClure.) For starters, McClure (like Villa) insists that Arendt simply assumes that the *sensus communis* is no longer available to us. Judgment in Arendt is a strategy necessitated precisely by this absence, not a strategy by which a common world can be reconstituted. (Admittedly, McClure, more than Villa, hedges on this point, as she seems to suggest that practices of judgment foster dialogues that are something like an attenuated public sphere—the best we can hope for, but better than nothing. In this diminished modernity, we can get the "odor of judgment" even if we are unlikely to get judgment itself.) Where McClure departs most from communitarian or Habermasian positions is in her disregard of agreement or consensus as the building block of community, preferring instead engagement, even (if we push a little at her own use of the Little Rock example) agonistic disagreement, provided the dialogue doesn't break down altogether. In refusing to focus on agreement, McClure can do justice to Arendt's insistence that the process of forging an opinion, even as it takes others' standpoints into account, still results in the formation of *one's own* opinion. She quotes Arendt: "[W]hile I take account of others when judging, this does not mean that I conform in my judgment to those of others. I still speak with my own voice and I do not count noses in order to arrive at what I think is right. But my judgment will no longer be subjective either."

It is worth noting, however, that the terminology of agreement is also present in Arendt's thoughts on judgment, both in her description of articulating an opinion as "the 'persuasive activity' of 'wooing' or 'courting' the agreement of others by appealing to the 'community sense'" and in one of her earliest statements of the problematic of judgment: "The power of judgment rests on a potential agreement with others, and the thinking process which is active in judging something is not, like the thought process of pure reasoning, a dialogue between me and myself, but finds itself always and primarily, even if I am quite alone in making up my mind, in an anticipated communication with others with whom *I know I must finally come to some agreement*. From this potential agreement judgment derives its specific validity."[25] Why I *must* come to agreement with these others and how I am to do so remain unclear. But Arendt ties "validity" directly to that "potential agreement."

McClure touches lightly on "validity." Insofar as she considers the validity of Arendtian judgment, she rests her case on the rhetoric of examples. Cascardi, Disch, and Bernstein also consider the force Arendt accords to examples and the force of Arendt's own examples. Clearly, Arendt stakes a lot on examples, although much is at stake in advocating judgment, persuasion, even epistemology, by example. There is the status of Arendt herself as an example to consider. McClure makes clear that she values the example of thinking and judging offered by Arendt's own practice more than she values the explicit accounts Arendt provides of thinking and judging. Others have found Arendt's life and work—her resolute, principled, and heroic resistance to the Nazis, her legendary integrity, the courage with which she presented her opinions in the Eichmann case, and other instances—exemplary. Recently, questions raised about Arendt's relation to Heidegger, particularly her willingness to be reconciled with him after World War II in spite of her knowledge of his involvement with the Nazis, have brought issues of character (as was true in the Eichmann controversy) to the fore in considerations of Arendt. It is an open question whether Arendt's own stress on examples lends support to a focus on character. To his credit, Richard Bernstein approaches the Heidegger-Arendt issues specifically in terms of Arendt's presentations of Socrates and Heidegger as exemplars of thinking. It is not Arendt's personal relationship to Heidegger that matters, but the forging of an opinion about Heidegger that aims to judge his significance as an example to oneself and others as we all attempt to engage in that process of thought and judgment for ourselves. Bernstein eventually finds the examples of Socrates and Heidegger insufficiently enlightening, both because the difference between the two exemplars (why did Socrates act with an exemplary integrity in difficult political circumstances, whereas Heidegger did not?) is never pinpointed and because the examples do not illuminate what Arendt "desperately wants to show," namely, "that thinking does have moral consequences—at least 'indirectly,' by liberating the faculty of judgment by which we judge 'this is right' and 'this is wrong' in moments of crisis."

McClure's process model of judgment and Disch's emphasis on communicability, not justifiability, as the criterion of judgment's success point us toward the intersubjective connections enabled by Arendtian judgment, not its content. Examples are pertinent precisely because they are all we have in the realm of what Kant calls "reflective judgments," those cases in which we must judge a particular instance in the absence of any universal category or rule under which to subsume it. At stake, then, in pursuing a rhetoric of examples is the conviction that particulars can do intersubjective work and establish public spaces in a manner different from and preferable to the kinds of political spaces generated by a focus on universals and agreement. Disch offers the most extended comparison of these two alternatives in her examination of Habermas's critique of Arendt. Disch, like McClure, shifts the focus away from claims to validity made by any political actor to the relations among actors established by communication itself. Both McClure and Disch quote Arendt's equation of speech with action, irrespective of content: "[F]inding the right words at the right moment, quite apart from the information or communication they may convey, is action." Disch glosses this passage: "Although we certainly do put words to use in communicative transactions, [Arendt's point is that] it is because of the unanticipated effect (peculiar to words) of saying the right word at the right moment that language precipitates new beginnings beyond the bounds of prior agreement." Disch, we might say, is committed to demonstrating the unity of Arendt's whole corpus, which involves not just finding in action the "transformative" principle Cascardi seeks but also interpreting Arendtian judgment as equally oriented toward transformation. Whereas McClure stresses opinion and process, Disch emphasizes the production of *inter-est*, of the "world" in Arendt's distinctive use of that term: "Arendt introduces the term *inter-est* to mediate between the extremes of pluralist fragmentation and communitarian fusion. It gives her a way to shift the locus of solidarity from the interiorities of political actors to the public realm." The process of judgment achieves not just opinion or dialogue but political solidarity, although "Paradoxically, . . . the commonality that sustains this version of political solidarity is not shared identity or truth" but distance. The Arendtian in-between "always fulfills the double function of binding men together *and* separating them in an articulate way."

In describing a commonality not based on agreement, Arendt offers a crucial resource to a later feminism that has been shaken by the difficulties and vicissitudes of identity politics. For Disch, Arendt provides a more useful way to think about what holds us together and what distances us from one another in heterogeneous democratic societies than does Habermas. Arendt underplays validity in favor of communicability: "I endow my views with 'communicability' by figuring out how to frame and word them 'in such a way that [others] understand,' regardless whether they concede validity to them." The Arendtian account of judgment can help us recover what was distinctive and worth preserving in feminist consciousness-raising of the early 1970s. Disch wants to use this Arendt-inflected reading of consciousness-raising (CR) both to intervene in feminist debates about the status of appeals to experience and to explore CR "as a model for participatory theory building and democratic politics." We might add that Disch's essay also serves as the "remembrance" of great deeds in words that is so crucial to Arendt's understanding of the distinction and "immortality" political agents aspire to achieve.

Disch looks for a specifically political benefit from the Arendtian process of judgment; she thinks that judgment can promote dialogue and *inter-est*, can establish and maintain the public realm, better than reliance on consensus or agreement can. It is precisely by eschewing justifiability and validity that Arendtian judgment can work its political wonders. Bernstein and Jay think such a version of judgment gives far too much away. The conflict in views here is most starkly posed by Disch's recalling for us that Arendt (in *Lectures on Kant's Political Philosophy*) "categorically separates judging from willing and then assigns morality to the will." For Disch, Arendt takes aesthetic judgment in Kant as a model of political judgment, one divorced from the determination of what is morally desirable or morally right and wrong. Hence, Arendt is faithful to the strict separation of thinking, willing, and judging found in the three Kantian critiques. Jay and Bernstein, on the other hand, focus on the inadequacies of Arendtian judgment as a means for reaching moral conclusions. They both insist that Arendt cannot get a morality from an aesthetics. (Bernstein faults Arendt for never even asking the question how, if at all, judgments of beautiful/ugly differ from judgments of right/wrong.) Either Arendt risks aestheticizing politics and thus comes to resemble the totalitarian politics she means to combat (this is Jay's suspicion) or she finds herself incapable of accounting for the very facts her work calls to our attention (this is Bernstein's view). Bernstein believes that Arendt is asking the right questions and that objections to Arendt's book about Eichmann have missed much of the point of her thoughts on the "banality of evil," but he thinks we must carefully consider just how far her answers get us. He argues that Arendt cannot sever judgment from morality after appealing to "thoughtlessness" and "the incapacity to judge" as explanations for the "evil" Eichmann did. Arendt herself insists that, in twentieth-century politics at least, moral and political content cannot be disentangled, because totalitarianism presents us with the "totality of moral collapse." Totalitarianism usurps what might previously have been a separate sphere, Bernstein asserts: "Arendt did not think that Eichmann . . . had 'closed his ears to the voice of conscience.' On the contrary, his 'conscience' was like an empty cipher that spoke with the voice of 'respectable society.'" The distance that enables individuality and autonomous moral decision making has collapsed in totalitarian society, and Arendt struggles to develop a model of "thoughtfulness" that would provide some kind of resistance to that collapse.

Bernstein concludes that Arendt does not provide a satisfactory model; what she gives us are examples that just don't explain enough, that don't provide guidelines adequate to our needs. Yet, paradoxically, it is Bernstein—who is much less taken with the power of examples than is either Disch or McClure—who recalls for us perhaps the most moving example invoked in all of Arendt's work. Arendt summons the example of "Anton Schmidt, a sergeant in the German Army who helped Jewish partisans . . . until he was arrested and executed by the Germans" as a counterweight to the example of Eichmann. The lesson Arendt draws from Schmidt "is that under conditions of terror most people will comply but *some people will not.* . . . Humanly speaking, no more is required, and no more can reasonably be asked, for this planet to remain a place fit for human habitation." Perhaps this is too thin a reed, too small a comfort, but it is all Arendt thinks she can offer, the "specific validity" of an example, not the necessary or universal validity of a rule. In the contingent world of plurality and freedom, the example shows that things *could* be this way, the counterexample that things *could* be that way (both ways will probably coexist, along with many other ways), and Arendt tells us that the vision of these alternate possibilities and the assurance that these possibilities will remain open even under the most terrible conditions are all we need to go on and all we can expect to be given to enable us to go on. Bernstein is moved but not convinced. He thinks we can (or, at least, believes we should strive to) construct a more solid defense against evil. And he thinks that Arendt herself felt the need for a more solid defense and attempted to fill that need in trying to develop an account of thoughtfulness and judgment that could guide decisions about right and wrong.

Kimberley Curtis's essay shifts the discussion in a rather different direction, toward Arendtian ontology, but in a way that reconfigures the issues raised in McGowan's, Disch's, Zaretsky's, McClure's, and Villa's essays. Curtis's Arendt believes that what ails us moderns is the fact that we have been "bequeathed" a "reality" so "thin and attenuated" that we no longer live in "a world stable and ordered enough to render . . . multiplicity . . . meaningful." Plurality, that prime Arendtian good, can coexist only with "a shared world." Like Disch on *interest*, Curtis is intent on stressing that Arendt calls upon us "to hold both agonistic and consensual moments of political life in a common, if tension-filled, frame . . . if we are to understand the deepest importance of Arendt's work to us." That importance rests, finally, on the ontological dimension of political action. Politics is the interaction that, as Villa indicates, generates the "reality" of our own distinctive identities but that also, Curtis adds, generates the "reality" of the common world that we occupy with others. But, as McClure, Disch, and Villa also stress, Arendt writes for moderns, those for whom "the known forms of tradition, authority, and religion [can] neither anchor our common world nor orient us ethically," a situation Curtis calls "postmetaphysical."

It is in the absence of "known forms" that Arendt turns to aesthetics. One direction that turn takes, of course, is an interest in Kantian judgment. But Curtis explores a different aesthetic moment in Arendt: her discussion of "tragic pleasure" in the speech she gave upon receiving the Lessing Prize in 1959. As Curtis limns the phrase, "tragic pleasure" has two components: it intensifies our awareness of reality and it teaches us the lesson of plurality, which is the lesson of our inability (as individuals, but also even as members of a single group or nation) to control that reality, to fashion it as we will. The "tragic" enters because we cannot shape the world to our needs or desires, but the "pleasure" comes from the fact that we get a world at all, a world of full and varied multiplicity, albeit by submitting to the confluence of varied actions, words, purposes, and selves that constitute, without directing, the real. Against tragic pleasure is set the "unbearable pain" of the totalitarian "rendering superfluous of human particularity," the pain that accompanies the destruction of the world, a destruction that is a protest against plurality. (See McGowan's essay for another description of "evil" in Arendt as the attempt to obliterate plurality.) Arendt's aesthetic "political theorizing [is] . . . an effort to cultivate our pleasure in the feeling of reality intensified through a constant attentiveness to the awe or wonder of human particularity."

Like Disch, McGowan, and McClure, but in a different key, Curtis emphasizes that only intersubjective interaction can generate the public realm that also allows difference, distinctiveness, and human particularity to exist. In Curtis more than in the other three, it is a question not so much of a public or political sphere in which different selves can meet and interact in their difference, as of the very reality of difference itself. Curtis brings home to us more dramatically than any of the other authors that for Arendt, the common world we share as public and political agents exists only as the result of the differences we reveal in our interactions. Thus, hard as it may be to grasp, we get commonality precisely and only by accentuating, cherishing, and producing ever more difference. Moreover, like Zaretsky, Curtis sees Arendt as radically shifting our sense of what politics is "for." Arendt's "ontological" concerns offer an important "incitement toward radical democratic political life" for "us brittle but not yet broken democrats." "Radical democratic participation" is important not only for *what* it might accomplish, but also for its ability "to sustain and intensify our awareness of reality." The agonistic and aesthetic (Villa's virtuoso performers) dimensions of Arendt's descriptions of political action follow from her "argument that our capacity to sense the real depends upon a mutual provocation between appearing beings." Together, politically, we create the world because we are unique—but only so long as we can cherish and care for that uniqueness and endure the limits plurality sets for us within the human condition. A rage against reality is a prominent feature of totalitarianism as Arendt understood it—and some version of that rage may explain the hesitant, ever-suspicious relation to politics in our own day.

Notes

1. See, for example, Richard Bernstein, *Hannah Arendt and the Jewish Question* (Cambridge: MIT Press, 1996); Lisa Disch, *Hannah Arendt and the Limits of Philosophy* (Ithaca: Cornell University Press, 1995); Dana Villa, *Arendt and Heidegger: The Fate of the Political* (Princeton: Princeton University Press, 1995); Susan Bickford, *The Dissonance of Democracy: Listening, Conflict, and Citizenship* (Ithaca: Cornell University Press, 1996); and John McGowan, *Hannah Arendt: An Introduction to Her Thought* (Minneapolis: University of Minnesota Press, in press).

2. Among the most recent important works are Margaret Canovan, *Hannah Arendt: A Reinterpretation of Her Political Thought* (Cambridge: Cambridge University Press, 1992); Jeffrey C. Isaac, *Arendt, Camus, and Modern Rebellion* (New Haven: Yale Uni-

versity Press, 1992); and Maurizio Passerin d'Entrèves, *The Political Philosophy of Hannah Arendt* (London: Routledge, 1994). See also Philip Hansen, *Hannah Arendt: Politics, History, and Citizenship* (Stanford: Stanford University Press, 1993); Michael G. Gottsegen, *The Political Thought of Hannah Arendt* (Albany: State University of New York Press, 1994); and Seyla Benhabib's *The Reluctant Modernism of Hannah Arendt* (London: Sage Publications, 1996). Among earlier works, George Kateb's *Hannah Arendt: Politics, Conscience, Evil* (Oxford: Martin Robertson, 1984) stands out, along with several essays by Ronald Beiner. Elisabeth Young-Bruehl's biography, *Hannah Arendt: For Love of the World* (New Haven: Yale University Press, 1982), is, of course, also an important work of intellectual interpretation.

3. Canovan, *Hannah Arendt*; Bonnie Honig, *Political Theory and the Displacement of Politics* (Ithaca: Cornell University Press, 1993).

4. Elzbieta Ettinger, *Hannah Arendt/Martin Heidegger* (New Haven: Yale University Press, 1995). See Alan Ryan, "Dangerous Liaison," *New York Review of Books*, January 11, 1996, pp. 22–26, for a sensible review of what he calls Ettinger's "brief, breathless, and soap-operatic account of Arendt's relationship with Heidegger" (p. 22).

5. See Bonnie Honig, ed., *Feminist Interpretations of Hannah Arendt* (University Park: Pennsylvania State University Press, 1995), especially the excellent review essay "Feminist Receptions of Hannah Arendt," by Mary G. Dietz, pp. 17–50.

6. Dietz, "Feminist Receptions," p. 18.

7. Dietz acknowledges much of this but also suggests that "*The Human Condition* carries a far more provocative gender subtext than most feminists have noticed to date. . . . Arendt not only thematizes gender as a dominant category of modernity; she also displaces it through an action concept of politics" (ibid., p. 29).

8. Honig, "Towards an Agonistic Feminism," in Honig, *Feminist Interpretations*, p. 149.

9. Ibid., p. 159. Honig's argument clearly applies to a variety of claims to a politics based on already-settled identities besides gender—not least of all nationality.

10. See Amy Gutman, ed., *Multiculturalism: Examining the Politics of Recognition*, rev. ed. (Princeton: Princeton University Press, 1994); and Craig Calhoun, ed., *Social Theory and the Politics of Identity* (Cambridge, Mass.: Blackwell, 1994).

11. See Honig, "Towards an Agonistic Feminism"; Dana Villa's contribution to the present volume; Seyla Benhabib, "Feminist Theory and Hannah Arendt's Concept of Public Space," *History of the Human Sciences* 6, no. 2 (1993): 97–114; and Benhabib, "Models of Public Space: Hannah Arendt, the Liberal Tradition, and Jürgen Habermas," in *Habermas and the Public Sphere*, ed. Craig Calhoun (Cambridge: MIT Press, 1992).

12. See the helpful discussion of Arendt's "expressive" and "communicative" approaches to action—and the sometimes fruitful, sometimes confusing tension between them—in chapter 2 of d'Entrèves, *Political Philosophy*.

13. Hannah Arendt, "The Concept of History," in *Between Past and Future* (New York: Penguin, 1961), p. 51. See also her *The Human Condition* (Chicago: University of Chicago Press, 1958), pp. 22–28.

14. Hannah Arendt, "Truth and Politics," in *Between Past and Future*, p. 233.

15. Hannah Arendt, *On Revolution* (New York: Penguin, 1963), pp. 53–54.

16. Arendt, "Truth and Politics," p. 256.

17. Arendt, *The Human Condition*, p. 154.

18. Arendt, *On Revolution*, p. 84.

19. Ibid.

20. D'Entrèves, *Political Philosophy*, p. 89.

21. This could not so easily be said of the neo-Aristotelians, such as MacIntyre.

22. The slippage from broader forms of liberalism toward utilitarian-instrumental conceptions is all the more pronounced outside academic political theory and where political science interacts most closely with actual politics—for example, in the discourse about constitutional reforms and democratization in Eastern Europe.

23. Jeremy Bentham, *Introduction to the Principles of Morals and Legislation* (London: Athlone Press, 1970), p. 12.

24. This is also the focus of one of Arendt's key differences from Heidegger. Appropriating his ideas of "world," "space," and "disclosure," she sharply challenged the value of "being at home" in the world and the potential illusions of feeling too much at home in a particular image of the world. As Margaret Canovan rightly remarks, "Arendt's distinctive adaptation of his [Heidegger's] position lies in her claim that the space in which reality appears is the public and political space which plural human beings forge among themselves, and, in other words, that what is required for the disclosure of reality is a free politics that is the opposite of the regime to which Heidegger gave his support" (*Hannah Arendt*, p. 112).

25. Arendt, *Between Past and Future*, p. 220; emphasis added.

Part I

One

Aesthetic Foundations of Democratic Politics in the Work of Hannah Arendt

Kimberley F. Curtis

> *... to write across the chalkboard, putting up there in public words you have dredged, sieved up from dreams, from behind screen memories, out of silence—words you have dreaded and needed in order to know you exist.*
>
> *I mean all the times when people have summoned language into the activity of plotting connections between, and making distinctions among, the elements presented to our senses.*
> Adrienne Rich, What Is Found There

> *... we could scarcely be silent without being tormented by the damning thought that speaking might have saved us.*
> Thucydides, History of the Peloponnesian War

The outpouring in recent times of conference panels and individual essays as well as journal articles and books devoted to the work of Hannah Arendt has been enormous. Taken together, these efforts seem to suggest a shared sense that in her work there is something of great import for us. Although I cannot speak with certainty about what this import is for others, I believe that the deepest currents of her work kindle our contemporary souls in profoundly similar ways. At its most general level, this essay is about that kindling.

To put the matter succinctly, Arendt is our poet of political life. She distills that life, condenses it, and offers us an idiom for its deepest impulse, an impulse itself essentially poetic. Adrienne Rich puts it best when she calls it "The impulse to enter, with other humans, through language, into the order and disorder of the world" (1993, 6). Arendt promises, too. She promises, as we enter public life in speech and through deed, that our being in space and time will be confirmed with a potency only to be tendered there.

This appeals to us, allures us, for we feel ourselves, in this regard, to be fragile—brittle, if not already broken. If we return to the troubling work of Hannah Arendt again and again, it is perhaps for reassurance of an ontological kind. But it is also for the incitement toward a democratic way of life that her political idiom inspires in us. My purpose in this essay is to articulate the relationship between this ontological reassurance and this incitement toward democratic political life. I will do so by elaborating the aesthetic foundations of Arendt's work as they speak to the practice of politics as an essentially democratic undertaking. In our post–cold war world, where increasingly democracy has become synonymous with capitalism and markets, we are in great need of work that deepens and stimulates our ethical imaginations toward radical democratic practices. I will try to argue here the way in which Arendt's aestheticism does just this.

It is, of course, precisely this issue of the ethical content of Arendt's aesthetic theorization of political life that has caused unease among her contemporary critics.[1] In an early debate (which occurred during Arendt's lifetime) between Lionel Abel and Daniel Bell, the concern centered on Arendt's portraits of Adolf Eichmann and the actions of the Jewish councils during Nazi rule. Abel charged that in both cases Arendt's analysis was guided by aesthetic considerations at the expense of moral and even political actualities (Abel 1963). Bell responded that Abel had mistaken Arendt's adherence to a single standard of universal order—that is, her concern with justice in this sense—for aesthetic judgment. It is this adherence that gives her writing a tone of coldness, Bell argued, not aesthetic considerations. However, because they both "derive from a singular preoccupation and are also separate from morality and also have a formal quality" (Bell 1963, 418), Bell concedes that though Abel's is a cruel mistake, it is a comprehensible one. Argument centered, in this case, on whether Arendt had breached a boundary that should not be breached.

In another early article, Martin Jay sustains the clear-cut distinction between aesthetics and ethics and sounds a theme that continues to trouble readers of Arendt. Jay argues that Arendt's "aestheticization of politics," by which he means the disjuncture she makes between political and "any rational, utilitarian, historical and social foundation," makes her greatest affinity to the political existentialists of the prewar years, especially to the decisionists (1978, 353). In this context he goes on to intimate that in succumbing to the "dangerous charms" of the political existentialists, who "have been seen by most historians as having prepared the way for fascism" (351), Arendt's aestheticization of political life shares elements of fascist political ideology. More recently and in a more sustained, less certain vein, George Kateb has explored the parallels between Arendt's work and fascist thought. His objection to Arendt's work—insofar as her conception of action is, at best, amoral and, at worst, probably immoral—is closely bound to her aestheticization of political life (1984, 28–44).

The aesthetic antirationalism of Arendt's political theorizing is the subject of a somewhat different, more recent set of debates regarding her conception of political action and her public realm theory. This is a debate between those who embrace a consensual communicative politics, on the one hand, and those who argue for an agonistic performative politics, on the other. Although for both, Arendt's work is a crucial contribution to revitalizing the distinction between *praxis* and *techne* and thus to restoring to political life its distinctive and emancipatory potential, the consensualists tend to appropriate Arendt's public realm theory for their consensual-universalist ends (Habermas 1977), ignoring or rejecting Arendt's agonistic aesthetic account of action in which "immoral and political greatness, heroism, preeminence are revealed, displayed, shared with others" (Benhabib 1992, 178). The agonists, by contrast, appropriate just this aspect of Arendt's work, namely, the ideal of "agonisitic subjectivity" (Villa 1992b), the embrace of political life as uniquely individuating through the "self's agonal passion for distinction" (Honig 1993, 80). This theorization of political life is held to be crucial, as it represents the greatest hope against the contemporary forces of normalization, subjectification, and the effects of a total will to mastery. This position finds precisely *in* Arendt's aestheticization of political life a strong emancipatory moment. Substantial differences regarding what politics can and ought to be govern this debate, ranging at the extremes from a form of communicative rationality to episodic eruptions of resistance in a darkened, fragmented world. And so Arendt's work is purified to serve the respective hopes and dreams that animate each position within the confines of the present. I have no quarrel with this use of Arendt's work—it is at the center, explicitly or implicitly, of all political theorizing. Still, I think attention to the ethical concerns that animate her political theorizing suggests that to hold both agonistic and consensual moments of political life in a common, if tension-filled, frame is crucial if we are to understand the deepest importance of Arendt's work to us.

Before turning to my elaborations of her work, I want to give a caveat, namely, that I do not wish to engage in too much purification of my own. I have indicated that Arendt's work is troubling, and much of that trouble turns around her aestheticization of political life *at the expense of* a theorization of everyday political life. Very recently Mary Dietz, enormously sympathetic to the power of Arendt's theorization of politics as "a kind of theater where freedom can appear" (Arendt 1954, 154), has argued, nonetheless, that Arendt's public realm theory is "vulnerable to charges of aestheticism, sentimentalism, and self-defeat" (1994, 880). Moreover, Arendt's theory has no "action-coordinating concept that appreciates the purposeful nature of human struggle as politics" (873). Hence, what counts as politics is far too narrow and, even more to the point, neither celebrates nor inspires a kind of measured application of our imagination and our cognitive skills to the problem of "what is to be done." Dietz's argument is subtle and important. As she puts it, Arendt's theory is vulnerable to charges of aestheticism "not because it rescues theatrical performance in the face of reductive and routinizing life processes but because it celebrates the 'practical purposelessness' of speech and action and the transcendence of 'mere productive activity' in politics *as it does so*" (880; emphasis added).

Dietz is, I think, quite right, and she sets forth a challenge to those of us inspired by Arendt's agonal, theatrical account of public life—namely, to theorize the public sphere as a place vital because of both its performative and its cognitively purposeful activities. I will not so theorize here, but I will attempt to more thoroughly elaborate the ethical power of Arendt's theatrical account of action, for as much as Dietz is right regarding Arendt's theoretical shortcoming with respect to the cognitive-purposive activities in political life, Dietz's own work is equally (and, to her credit, self-admittedly) vulnerable to charges of insufficiently theorizing how to limit ethically the "methodical politics" of means/ends she advocates. She is, I think, right to suggest that the condition of plurality itself provides the common ethical dimension to both moments of political life. Let me now approach the effort to illuminate more thoroughly that ethical dimension and, thereby, the importance of Arendt's preoccupation with the theatrical, aesthetic moment of political life.

Preliminaries

In a speech delivered in 1959 to the Free City of Hamburg on the occasion of accepting the Lessing Prize, Hannah Arendt recalled the Greek doctrine of the passions. Before this all-German audience just fourteen years after the war had ended, she distinguished between passions that are truly pleasant and those that are evil, on the basis of the *amount of reality* a given passion transmits, as distinct from the *force* with which that passion affects the soul. Evil passions may be felt keenly, sharply; they may overwhelm us with their force. But those that are truly pleasurable have the capacity to intensify our awareness of reality, to make our sense of the real fuller, deeper (Arendt 1955, 6).

To such an audience the political-moral lesson must have been clear, not only to those enthusiasts of National Socialism, for whom the thrill of being submerged in a movement of world-historical importance had, at least initially, allured them, but also to those who had been, as Arendt called them, "inner emigrants" during the war, those who exiled themselves from the unreality of a world grown too brutal, to an interior life certainly more sane but only apparently more real. The lesson in both cases was a sharp reminder that however intense or real our feelings and our inner life may seem, however poignant and piercing, a full sense of reality is possible only in a world capable of supporting, sustaining, and stimulating multiple and conflicting voices and strivings.

What makes such a world possible? In Lessing, Arendt found part of the answer, for he was, in her view, a partisan for such a world. His partisan activity took the form of "scattering into the world" what he referred to as "*fermenta cognitionis*": thoughts designed both to strengthen the position of opinions so embattled that their very existence as an angle on the world was at risk, and to stimulate the emergence of new opinions (Arendt 1955, 8). Lessing was a polemicist for the multidimensionality of the world of discourse. The passion that drove and sustained his partisanship was an openness, a real gladness in the recalcitrant and plural quality of the world, and the pleasure he felt that so attracted Hannah Arendt was that induced by tragedy. Thus, "tragic pleasure" (6) born of a passion for agonism of the type Lessing practiced was a pleasure, Arendt told her audience, of which "we" are very much in need.

But, it seems, Lessing could help us only so much, for the drama that engages us as a "we" is, let us say, more dramatic, more difficult to face, more difficult to perform. However much we succeed in feeling this pleasure by scattering our *fermenta cognitionis* in the manner of Lessing, our sense of reality will remain thin and attenuated without a world stable and ordered enough to render the multiplicity of Lessing's *fermenta* meaningful—to make it more than a playful (but perhaps not too fun) game of profusion that thrives on disruptions in the order of reason, on instabilities, on paralogy.[2] Yet it is our fate not to have been bequeathed such a world. Our drama is distinctively marked by a postmetaphysical condition in which the "pillars of truth" that have in the past served variously to secure such a world no longer have effective force. Neither God's commandments historically revealed, nor *ius naturale*, nor the self-evident truths of reason can serve as the transmundane sources of authority, sources whose eternity and permanence, until the nineteenth century, gave relative permanence to positive law, thereby enabling it to serve—its own changeability notwithstanding—as a stabilizing factor for the "ever-changing movements of men" (Arendt 1958, 462). Without such eternal "pillars" we seem unable to give form and coherence to something stable enough to call a shared world. And without such a world, all that multiplicity will vanish like a phantom, wasted into the stream of meaninglessness, our sense of human reality wasted with it.

Does Arendt's response to this terrible paradox she so relentlessly articulated—of needing a shared world to render our *fermenta* meaningful, yet simultaneously lacking the resources necessary for its constitution or securement—leave us at this impasse? Are we doomed to an attenuated and politically dangerous sense of the real? Convinced that the known forms of tradition, authority, and religion could neither anchor our common world nor orient us ethically any longer, where did Arendt turn, and where was she most suggestive with respect to our postmetaphysical drama?

Arendt's thought, like that of many in the twentieth century, takes an aesthetic turn. By this I refer to two things. On the one hand, I refer to her account of action in the public realm. It is this account that has provoked the most sustained concern, because of its purported immorality. Formulations such as the following exemplify this troubling moment of Arendt's work: "Unlike human behavior . . . action can be judged only by the criterion of greatness because it is in its nature to break through the commonly accepted and reach into the extraordinary. . . . Pericles knew full well that he had broken with the normal standards for everyday behavior when he found the glory of Athens in having left behind 'everywhere everlasting remembrance (mnemeia aidia) of their good and evil deeds.' The art of politics teaches men how to bring forth what is great and radiant" (1958, 205–6). On the other hand, Arendt's aestheticism refers to her thoughts on political judgment. Indebted to Kant's theory of aesthetic judgment, they hinge upon the artistic transfiguration of the judge qua storyteller, who saves from time's ruin the "great and radiant" but otherwise futile particular exertions of human speech and deed. Arendt's aestheticism, in both respects, emerges from a fascination with the potent triangle of relationships between human particularity, beauty, and permanence. My focus in this essay bears most on this first aspect of her aestheticism, as I develop her ontology and attempt to illuminate the profoundly ethical concerns animating her theorization of political life. A complete argument regarding the aesthetic foundations of democratic politics in Arendt's work would have to address as well, of course, the second aspect of her aestheticism to which I have referred.

Our Ethical Horizon

I do not believe that either the ethical power or the political relevance of Arendt's aestheticism can be properly assessed without engaging the claim that is, in my view, the defining and driving force of her political theorizing, namely, that the "horizon of experience" that frames our central ethical problems is and remains the totalitarian form of rule in which "unbearable pain," as she once put it, has come to be, more than killing and death, the worst, most terrifying possibility, the worst evil (1955, 127). The pain that cannot be borne is that which we feel at the radical rendering superfluous of human particularity. In the camps, and to a lesser extent more generally under totalitarian conditions, human beings were reduced to "living corpses"; all human particularity was extinguished. The point here is not that this was, historically speaking, the first time genocide was practiced, but rather that for the first time making human particularity superfluous became a political *ideal*.[3] For the first time, extinguishing the human condition of plurality—the fact that "we are all the same, that is, human, in such a way that nobody is ever the same as anyone else who ever lived, lives, or will live" (1958, 8)—became a political ideal.

The implicit contention, then, underlying Arendt's work is that it is this historical moment that remains the experiential horizon of our deepest ethical challenges in our practical as in our philosophical lives, not only (nor even perhaps primarily) because it stands, as it does, as the highest manifestation of evil, but also because meditation on the essence of its evil now so "brightly" illuminates our world more generally.[4] We live in a world—nontotalitarian for the most part—that seems nevertheless increasingly designed to render human particularity superfluous.[5] And though Arendt contends that this is a pain worse than death, as her preceding discussion of pleasure makes clear, she is highly aware that in a world designed to eradicate human particularity, the assumption that people will feel this pain can by no means be relied upon. As the totalitarian experiments demonstrated, the human being is a conditioned, shockingly malleable thing capable of feeling pleasure in a disturbing multitude of ways.

The deepest casualty of the world Arendt describes is our sense of reality.[6] In this our new world, inaugurated by the totalitarian experiments, our ethical challenges take on a novel, elemental quality: namely, how to take in and remain provoked by the real, how, as she puts it in numerous and diverse places in her work, to remain "fully alive." This, I suggest, is what Arendt implicitly contends is the primary ethical dilemma of our time.[7] And it is this to which her aestheticism forms a concerted response. Our paramount challenge, ethically speaking, is how to save human particularity—how to create a world in which it can appear and flourish, and how to cultivate our passion for it.[8]

I suggest we understand Arendt's political theorizing, as well as her moralizing on that day in 1959 with the free citizens of Hamburg, as an effort to cultivate our pleasure in the feeling of reality intensified through a constant attentiveness to the awe or wonder of human particularity.[9] Her theory is a kind of pedagogy about the wonder of the human condition of plurality. A many-sided pleasure, this awe or wonder is perhaps best elucidated by the Greek term *deinon* as used in the opening line of the second choral ode in *Antigone*. It reads, "There are many *deinon* things, but not one of them is more *deinon* than the human being."[10] That which is *deinon* inspires wonder and awe because it is somehow strange, unsuspected, and thus causes fear. As Martha Nussbaum puts it, "One is surprised by it, for better or worse [and thus] this opening of the Chorus' ode on the human being is a deeply ambiguous praise" (1986, 52). Still, praise it is—praise for the spectacular appearances of the being we call human—and as such it expresses the tragic sensibility to which, following Arendt's discussion of Lessing, I will refer as the aesthetic sensibility of tragic pleasure.[11] It is a sensibility that goes, of course, directly and uncompromisingly against the aesthetic sensibility undergirding Western metaphysical thinking.

This effort to re-sacrilize, if you will, our feeling for human particularity, to teach us to feel quickened and awed and pleasured by it through the cultivation of a specific aesthetic sensibility, is rooted in an ontology that is profoundly democratic in nature. That is to say, as I will argue in more detail momentarily, our sense of reality is actually sustained by the "infinitely improbable" appearance of the particularity of each human being. In "What Is Freedom?" Arendt describes this relationship between the "miracle" of human particularity and our sense of reality: "It is in the very nature of every new beginning that it breaks into the world as an 'infinite improbability,' and yet it is precisely this infinitely improbable which actually constitutes the very texture of everything we call 'real'" (1954, 169). Thus, Arendt's theory suggests that we are in need, again and again, of the appearance of the "infinitely improbable" if we are to have a full sense of the real. It is this need that leads her to a theorization of action in the public realm, not nostalgia for Greek and Roman polis life,[12] for it is a central contention on her part that the reality-engendering and reality-confirming capacities of life in the public realm are the highest.[13] It is for this reason also that the public-political realm is, *for us* in our postmetaphysical condition, of unmatched importance to protect and create.[14]

The Arendtian contention, then, is that, in the most elemental sense, we need a vigorous and diverse public and democratic life not to attain individual glory, nor to win immortality and defeat a nauseating futility (Kateb 1984), nor to "mak[e] the world beautiful" so as to redeem appearances (Villa 1992a; see also Parekh 1981), nor, to be sure, to act in concert (Habermas 1977; Benhabib 1992), nor simply for the sake of sheer survival. Rather, we need a vigorous, diverse public realm and multiple arenas for radical democratic participation to sustain and intensify our awareness of reality. This is a profoundly ethical need, in the sense that without such an awareness we can neither belong well to a world of others nor care for them well. Indeed, implicit in Arendt's humanism—nonessentialist, qualified, and tentative though it is[15]—is the contention that whether we are, in fact, to have being as *humans* in any specific sense at this point in our history will depend upon our capacity to belong to and care for each other in such a way as to make our sense of the real fuller and deeper. I think it is this which proves so moving to us brittle but not yet broken democrats, and this despite Arendt's own considerable reservations about the extent to which radical democracy is possible today,[16] despite her failure to theorize adequately politics as an everyday, purposeful activity,[17] and despite her almost complete lack of theoretical tools with which to identify issues of social and economic equality as political.[18] Despite all of this, there is, nonetheless, an important incitement toward radical democratic political life rooted in her ontological concerns and in her aestheticism.[19]

Thus, it is by no means unmediated pleasure at the *deinon* quality of human particularity, nor is it just any quality of vitality or feeling of being alive at which Arendt's aestheticism aims. Were this so it would be of interest only as danger. Rather, her aestheticism is mindful, indeed driven, by the needs for a world sufficiently common that human particularity and human plurality can be cherished and saved, and for a world whose texture of realness has the particular quality of fullness, as opposed to force.

Before further elaborating these contentions by turning to engage directly with the aesthetic nature of Arendt's ontology, I want to note her interpretation of Nietzsche's proclamation regarding the end of traditional metaphysics. Whereas Nietzsche proclaimed, "God is dead," Arendt more delicately reframed our condition thus: "the *traditional* thought of God is dead" (1971, 10; emphasis added). By this she meant that we no longer are able to sustain belief in the existence of an otherworldly realm of truth and harmony in such a way that it can be *politically* meaningful. She wrote, "I have clearly joined the ranks of those who for some time now have been attempting to dismantle metaphysics, and philosophy with all its categories, as we have known them from their beginning in Greece until today. Such dismantling is possible only on the assumption that the thread of tradition is broken and that we shall not be able to renew it" (212). Ours is a position that is at once new and also a return to a beginning which Arendt captures by culling the *experience* behind the central story of beginnings in the West—"we know only 'male and female created he them'—that is, from the beginning this plurality poses an enormous problem" (1979, 313). Today, as once before, we stand nakedly in the plural, naked because the doctrines and traditions of meaning that have clothed and "civilized" this awesome plurality have collapsed, leaving us with, as Arendt puts it, "the elementary problem of human living-together" (1954, 167).

It is from this apparently utterly unstable situation forced upon us, in Arendt's view, by modern events, that she takes her bearings. That is, our condition of naked plurality becomes, for Arendt, the beginning of all ethical reflection. Of much importance to note here is that despite the end of faith in a metaphysical order, despite our return to the state of being "newborns," as Nietzsche put it, it is not with *nothing* we are left. Indeed, Arendt critically muses, "To talk about nihilism in this context is perhaps just unwillingness to part company with concepts and thought-trains that actually died quite some time ago" (1971, 12). We are, then, not "groundless"; Arendt does not use this metaphor, which by now rises so naturally to postmodern lips. Instead she uses the metaphor "thinking without a bannister": "That is, as you go up and down the stairs you can always hold on to the bannister so that you don't fall down. But we have lost the bannister. That is the way I tell it to myself. And this is indeed what I try to do" (1979, 336–37). She is suggesting that, far from being groundless, what we have is indeed the ground. And from the beginning Arendt accepts this ground, bannisterless though it be, as the starting point for reestablishing bearings, arguing in a strikingly positive formulation, "plurality is the law of the earth" (1971, 19).[20]

Ontology of Display

"In this world which we enter, appearing from a nowhere, and from which we disappear into a nowhere, Being and Appearing coincide. . . . Nothing and nobody exists in the world whose very being does not presuppose a *spectator*. . . . Not Man but men inhabit this planet. Plurality is the law of the earth" (1971, 19). In these few lines, which constitute the essence of the first paragraph of the opening chapter of *Thinking*, the ethical-aesthetic texture of what I will call Arendt's ontology of display is laid forth. Arendt's basic approach to the nature of reality is phenomenal, and the central metaphor that carries the weight of her phenomenological conception is the theater. Like the reality created on the stage, things and creatures of the world are appearing in nature such that what appears is "meant to be" perceived—seen, heard, touched, tasted, and smelled —by sentient creatures.[21] Furthermore, without this perceptivity, without sentient spectators "able to acknowledge, recognize and react to what is . . . meant for their perception" (19), nothing is. Hence, plurality is the "law of the earth" in the sense that for anything to be at all, the basic unit of plurality—actor-spectator or thing-sentient creature—is presupposed. Plurality brings into being "what is."

As creatures who both themselves appear and perceive others, who are both, in this sense, objects and subjects, all sentient beings are "fit for" this world in which Being and Appearing coincide.[22] Critical to this sense in which things are fit for the world is Arendt's suggestion that we cannot make sense of the enormous richness of what is presented to the senses in functional terms alone, as, for example, the need of the organism for self-preservation or reproduction. When it comes to appearance, there is a "sheer functional superfluity" in what is displayed (1971, 27). Experience intuitively confirms such claims even at the simplest level of life, as when we cast our eyes along the edge of the sea and light upon the almost fluorescent orange of the starfish clinging to dark rock and find, as we kneel for a closer look, that we quickly pass over its pale purple sister as we are drawn toward the delicate translucence of the sea anemone's emerald fingers and still on, to marvel at the bloodred urchin's prickly spines. What can such colors be *for?* we wonder. Arendt suggests we not seek an answer to this question in a functional direction alone, or even primarily. To do so is to reduce the richness of "what is" in the manner of a philistine whose hallmark is, as she puts it in another work, "an inability to think and to judge a thing apart from its function or utility" (1954, 215). Our experience of the surface profusion of the world invites us to understand it at a fundamental level in terms of display.

We find a more active sense to this display quality of the sentient world in higher animals, reaching its climax in humans. In these higher forms of life, Arendt argues, we can speak of what she calls the "urge to self-display" (1971, 29). Here Arendt follows the fascinating work of Swiss biologist and zoologist Adolf Portmann in suggesting that there is a spontaneous impulse to show or exhibit the self, a response to "the overwhelming effect of being shown" (21). She writes, "[W]hat-*ever can see wants to be seen, whatever can hear calls out to be heard, whatever can touch presents itself to be touched*" (29; Arendt's emphasis). Here too Arendt's theatrical metaphor carries her meaning. Just as the actor, onstage before the eyes of all, feels the thrill of being seen and responds spontaneously to it by excelling, so too higher forms of life are possessed by an urge to self-display—not to express some inner authenticity but to make their presence felt, to be recognized and acknowledged "as an individual" (29). Here Arendt tries to articulate what she calls "the expressiveness of an appearance," which is different from the commonsense notion that when we express something, it is something inner that is "pressed out" (30). This urge to display and self-display, which is the very essence of things in an appearing world, by contrast, expresses itself; it makes an effort to shine forth, to excel in its particularity before others. Thus, inasmuch as things appear, they demand recognition, long for reaction, desire to be countenanced.[23]

It is in this sense too that we should understand Arendt's thought that plurality is the law of the earth. That is, sentient creatures, according to their complexity, possess an active response to being perceived—in the form of an impulse to distinguish themselves. Thus "what is" is constantly contributing to and bringing forth the wild, spectacular quality of the world.

Here, then, to summarize, we find an ontology of display that suggests that reality in an appearing world such as ours is something born out of a highly charged mutual sensuous provocation between actors and spectators that is essentially aesthetic in nature. All living creatures are, in this respect, linked together in a continuous though developmentally differentiated whole. Arendt uses the language of "impulse," "urge," and "spontaneity" to underline the mysterious "given" quality to this conception of the nature of "what is." When we speak of this nature, we speak of a universe alive with yearning to sense and be sensed, a universe that perpetually gives birth to its own plurality and profusion.

Yet there is discontinuity between the nonhuman natural and the human world as well, for "purely" natural things "emanate" this profusion; "[they have] no choice but to show whatever properties a living being possesses" (1971, 36). Against this backdrop of emanation, humans prepare and make this profusion "fit for" the world of appearance. In humans the urge to make our presence felt through self-display is manifest in the effort "to present [ourselves] in word and deed and thus indicate how [we] wish to appear, what in [our] opinion is fit to be seen and what is not" (34).[24] That is to say, we present our response, our take on the world. In this way humans bring forth the plurality of the earth in a unique way, and it is this which marks the radical discontinuity of the human species with the rest of the natural world. I think we conceive of this relation best as a continuity out of which discontinuity arises, as a "difference in identity," to use a phrase Arendt coins in another context (187).

This ability to present ourselves is, of course, Arendt's way of saying that humans alone have the ability to be free. And the way Arendt theorizes this freedom appears indeed to rely upon this ontology of display.[25] That is to say, our capacity to take undetermined action, to begin something new, is rooted in the unprecedented fact of our own naked appearance in an already existing world. It is rooted in the human condition of natality. Having the quality of the miraculous, appearing from a "nowhere," statistically improbable and without model, our capacity for action is a "response" to this unprecedented fact of our birth (1958, 177). That is, it is a response to the unprecedented both that we feel ourselves to be and that others perceive us to be. So this sensuous provocation, this active urge to self-display, is also the engendering root of our own capacity for freedom. As Arendt somewhat mystically but compellingly puts it, "Because he is a beginning, man can begin; to be human and to be free are one and the same" (1954, 167).

Hence, the capacity to begin, through which we undergo a kind of "second birth" by "confirm[ing] and tak[ing] on the naked fact of our original appearance" (1954, 176–77), is distinctive to humans. Yet we should be quick to note that this does not mean that humans create themselves. Arendt does not share the Hegelian-Marxian vision of the power of the human will. Her dissent is rooted partly in her insistence on "the sheer thereness of being" (1971, 37), by which she means the elemental fact that the world long preceded our appearance and will long outlast our disappearance, but even more it is rooted in the fact of plurality itself. By this I mean, in this context, that because we exist only in the plural in an appearing world, the only mode through which things can be acknowledged is in the way they seem. Here again, the metaphor of the theatrical stage carries Arendt's meaning. That which appears is common to all in its sheer thereness, yet it is observed by spectators each of whom occupies a slightly different "seat." As the fundamental mode of appearance, Arendt argues, it-seems-to-me (*dokei-moi*) means that everything that appears, whether it chooses or not, acquires a kind of "disguise" that inevitably thwarts our ability to control the effect of our self-presentation on others, as well as our ability to know others in any definitive sense. Here the point is that disguise is an inadvertent, inevitable accompaniment of every appearance in a world of plural others. Arendt makes an additional point regarding disguise, namely, that as we reveal or display ourselves, we actively choose also to conceal. She quotes Merleau-Ponty affirmatively in this context: "No thing, no side of a thing, shows itself except by actively hiding the others" (1971, 25).

There is, thus, a recalcitrant quality to our experience of the world in which plurality reigns. In our eliciting self-presentation, we suffer, we might say, a beautiful vulnerability. That is to say, our perception of the world (which is always the substance of our self-presentation), as much as it is uniquely our own, is profoundly disputable, profoundly and endlessly provoking. Arendt's conception, then, of this effort at self-presentation (which she calls "glory" in her "Greek" works), is not a unidirectional, megalomaniacal urge to be admired by others. Rather, although clearly an urge to be acknowledged and a hope of being praised, this urge at the center of the being of "man" is, in its very essence, "world open and communicative" (1958, 168). As the reference for the actor on a stage is always a specific audience, so too our efforts at self-presentation always "play" to a specific community.[26] Intrinsic to our effort at self-presentation is a deliberate responding to and moving toward the plural world of others. We offer ourselves—that is, our take on the world—in eliciting presentation, and we depend upon our world's perceptivity, upon others' own urge, in turn, to make their presence in the world felt through self-display. Thus, the very quality and character of our particularity emerges in the interstices of the human world and perpetually evades transparent knowledge and control—that of others as well as our own. We are essentially, in this regard, nonsovereign beings, for we are dependent upon the responsiveness of others and upon our ability to provoke them for the appearance of our specific individuality. (That our urge for self-presentation might result in many forms of distortion is an enduring feature of an appearing world. It points to the fragility and vulnerability of all our efforts to offer ourselves to the world. The only antidote for it is the publicity of the world itself.)

What I have argued thus far in interpreting Arendt's formulation "plurality is the law of the earth" is that the engendering ground of the real is the mutual provocation that occurs between appearing beings whose sensual apparatuses, desires, and urges "fit them," as spectating subjects and observed objects, for the phenomenal world. "We exist only in the plural" (1971, 99); that is, the specific reality of appearance is only in the plural, and that wild, spectacular plurality, as our individual reality, itself is engendered through a kind of mutual sensuous provocation that is aesthetic in nature.[27] My argument here is not meant to oppose the argument that intersubjectively formed cognitive interests are also important in engendering the plurality of the human world. Arendt, to be sure, speaks of the fact that we humans alone make our presence felt by exercising "deliberate choice" about how we wish to appear, and, as I have indicated, speech is our primary means of doing so. My point is that we do not cognitively decide to "make our presence felt." The way Arendt theorizes this phenomenon is nearer to an aesthetic-existential drive that manifests itself in the world in multiple forms, among which are, importantly, cognitive-purposive aims.[28] Conceptually speaking, the urge to make our presence felt and to feel that of others—what I have referred to as mutual aesthetic provocation in which we, being responsive to an appearing world, offer ourselves in an eliciting display—is the prior ground, the *conditio sine non* for engendering the plurality of the human world, for the reality of human particularity itself. This, then, is the first elemental link between the aesthetic ground of Arendt's account of reality in our appearing world and the ethical concerns that govern her political theorizing.

Yet Arendt also argues, "Reality in a world of appearances is first of all characterized by 'standing still and remaining' the same long enough to become an object for acknowledgment and recognition by a subject" (1971, 45), and "[E]very living thing depends on a world that solidly appears as the location for its appearance" (21–22). In what sense does Arendt think this "solidly" and this "standing still and remaining" are the same? Here the question is not how appearances are, in the first instance, engendered at all, but rather how the reality of their thereness is confirmed, guaranteed. The problem we are concerned with is our "sensation of reality," our feeling for the realness of ourselves and the world writ large.

In an appearing world the reality of what we perceive, Arendt argues, is guaranteed by its "worldly context" (50), by which she means, at the most general level, what we share in common. Thinking of this in the most basic of ways, all sensuous creatures, "despite or amidst the surprising diversity of the world's appearances and the astounding diverseness of sense organs among animal species," have "appearances as such in common," as well as the elemental fact of their specific coming and going (20). We share, as Arendt puts it, a common stage (21). Yet this fact of sharing the same stage does not in itself impart a sensation of reality, does not in itself feel solid and sufficiently identical with itself to confirm our sense of it and of our own reality. Such confirmation depends, on the one hand, on a sixth sense, which guarantees that my utterly different five senses sense the same object and which makes my sensing of the object communicable to others, and, on the other hand, on what Merleau-Ponty has called "our perceptual faith" (46). In describing this faith Arendt writes, "[O]ur certainty that what we perceive has an existence independent of the act of perceiving, depends entirely on the object's also appearing as such to others and being acknowledged by them" (46). But this formulation may be misleading. What does Arendt mean when she says that our sensation of an object's reality depends upon its also appearing "as such" to others? What meaning should we ascribe to the "as such"? It is certainly not "as identical." Precisely to the contrary, our perceptual ability to transcend the subjectivism of our own seeing and thus to gain a sensation of the object's reality depends upon the perceptual acts of distinct others. In an important passage in "The Concept of History," in the context of less ontological considerations, the point, I think, becomes clear: "[T]he Greek learned to exchange his own viewpoint, his own 'opinion'—the way the world appeared and opened up to him (δοκεῖ μοί, "it appears to me," from which comes δόξα, or "opinion")—with those of his fellow citizens. Greeks learned to *understand*—not to understand one another as individual persons, but to look upon the same world from one another's standpoint, to see the same in very different and frequently opposing aspects" (1954, 51; Arendt's emphasis).[29] The point here is that our ontological assurance in the act of perception depends on the perceived thing taking on a certain kind of objectivity, an objectivity that can be won only if our perception is embedded in the multiplicitous perspectival quality all things acquire in an appearing world.[30]

When Arendt thus argues that our sensation of reality depends upon a world shared in common, a world that "solidly appears" and becomes the "location" in which appearances can "stand still and remain the same," this is a solidity and a sameness born, in the first instance, through the responses and provocations of witnessing spectators and sensuous actors for whom the spectacular display quality of the appearing world is paramount. The crucial point here is that our capacity to experience a world in common, to constitute a certain worldly solidity, is utterly dependent upon the engendering ground of plurality itself, upon the aesthetic provocation of multiple, distinct appearing beings. If we can locate the common world at all, therefore, it is paradoxically to be found only where this provocation flourishes.[31] And although aesthetic provocation is not a sufficient ground for our ability to experience a world in common and thus to have a sensation of reality, it is a crucial dimension of that ability.[32] As such, because the existence of a world in common is a precondition for any appearing thing to be confirmed in being as such—and here, of course, it is human particularity that is our first concern—this relationship between aesthetic provocation and the possibility of a common world forms the second elemental link between Arendt's account of reality in our appearing world and the ethical concerns that govern her political theorizing.

If, then, we look carefully at Arendt's account of reality in an appearing world, what we see is the argument that our capacity to sense the real depends upon a mutual provocation between appearing beings that is aesthetic in nature. Both our ability to engender or actualize the plurality of the human condition and our ability to give human experience some degree of permanence by establishing a minimal sense of a common world depend upon the vitality of this mutual aesthetic provocation. We are, then, in great need of our mutual sensual yearning for each other in this sense.

This need appears even more clearly when we very briefly consider the other aspect of Arendt's ontological reflections that I have held in abeyance until now—necessity. I have postponed exploring necessity in the effort both to highlight the aesthetic texture of Arendt's ontology and to unfold the strength of the case she makes for the onto-logical nature of plurality. Necessity, which subjects us all, is equally important to Arendt's conception of "what is." From this angle, being is conceived as a relentless cycle of compelling, multiplicitous needs bounded on one side by appearing (birth) and on the other by disap-pearing (death). Here the world is one of intense functional necessity in which natural beings are driven by survival itself, in which the very beat of life wells out of the crush to survive, not out of the incitements of display. Nature, as the life process, presses inexorably on all living things, its mode compulsion and often violence. It is independent of will and neither progresses nor regresses. It has no temporality; it is the realm of "being-forever" (1954, 28), endlessly turning, ever recurring in its relentless fertility. Here, in some basic sense, everything is the same insofar as all things are coerced by a profusion of incoherent and conflicting drives and needs in the service of the life process.

Arendt's ontological reflections revolve, thus, around the para-doxical tension that "what is" is something born of the driving, coer-cive cycles of the life process and something, overflowing with sensu-ous profusion and diversity, that perpetually brings itself before itself, that is, brings itself into being. Yet the substantiality of our ability to sense the reality of necessity has, in significant degrees, receded. To an unprecedented extent in the twentieth century, those of us in a position of privilege are now faced with having to choose to be present to the reality of necessity. That is, our experience of necessity has come to de-pend greatly upon aesthetic provocation between actor and spectator. If we, for example, think of a whole slew of problems associated with modern technology that have become political problems of the first order (e.g., nuclear waste, genetic engineering, ozone depletion, water degradation), it becomes clear that our dominant social forms, ideas, and practices are intimately bound, to a novel extent, to denying the factuality of necessity. All of these problems point to the need to grant prior ontological status to the plural unit of actor-spectator without whose testimony the sheer factuality of the world—both socially and naturally understood—is in danger of nonbeing. They point to this need, that is, only if we theorize our experience in light of our new-found capabilities. The power of Arendt's ontological reflections here resides in her insistence that "there is a there there" that we must not submit to but encounter. To deny this "there" is to risk blindly paying a price. At the very least, Arendt argues for a deliberate judgment.[33]

Arendt's ontological reflections point to a newfound fragility of our capacity to sense reality, to be present to "what is" under post-metaphysical conditions. And this is, of course, of profound concern, because the first requirement of all ethical discernment is to be present to "what is," in all its compulsion and profusion. We have neither *physis* nor an *ens creatum*; what we have is aesthetic provocation under conditions of plurality. But even this is far from secure, for what I have been suggesting we find in Arendt's work is an account of how our sense of the real is engendered in an appearing world, not that the real is a natural constant as such. She theorizes this aesthetic provocation, and the initiative to which it is tied, in the following way: "[It] may be stimulated by the presence of others but never conditioned by them" (1958, 177). So, although it is a feature of ourselves as appearing beings that, Arendt believes, can never be conditioned away absolutely, its effective force in our lives is extremely mutable, subject to varying conditions, institutions, sensibilities, practices. This means, of course, that our sense of the real is likewise mutable. And it is Arendt's contention that our own historical conditions dangerously attenuate the effective force of aesthetic provocation and have done so explicitly and increasingly since the onset of the modern age. "Modern sensibility," she says, "is not touched by obscurity" (1963b, 70).

Our need, as I have suggested, is to cultivate our tragic pleasure— our pleasure in the feeling of reality intensified through the presence of particular others and through the recalcitrant and plural quality of the world thus engendered. We need strong particular others, by which I mean people in love with and stirred by Lessing's tragic. This need, Arendt suggests, makes us uniquely vulnerable to the presence or absence, strength or weakness of public-political life. Indeed, our need should propel us toward the publicity of the public realm, for although Arendt clearly recognizes that all forms of human togetherness give us some sensation of reality, insofar as self-disclosure or the unique particularity of appearing beings is implicit in everything one says and does (1958, 179), the potential for intensifying our awareness of reality, making it fuller and deeper, is greatest in the merciless brightness of the public realm. This is because political association of this kind constitutes the widest possible way to be seen and heard and to see and hear (50), and thus to let most fully appear the "living essence" of each unique, particular person as he or she, in word and deed, countenances the world and elicits, in turn, the world's own countenance.[34]

For Arendt this is the highest level of the political (1954, 263), and the pleasure in this kind of human togetherness—its merciless brightness and formality notwithstanding[35]—forms the deepest impulse for it. The questions remaining, of course, are many: What are the preconditions for the growth and development of vigorous, multiple publics? What is the role of social and economic inequality? And so on. With questions such as these, though Arendt is not silent, her work is not of great help. Still, if she is right about the way we need each other, then we can read our present organization of life (political, social, economic, and intimate practices) critically in terms of our need for strong particular others to intensify our awareness of reality. We can yearn for radical democratic practices not only out of calculating self-interest, nor because they allow citizens access to a sphere in which interests can become enlightened, nor out of a sense of justice, but because our very ability to have a sense of the real is at stake. And this is of utmost importance, as it is the precondition of our ability to belong to each other, to care for our lives together, and, finally, to act deliberately together.

Notes

I am very grateful to the participants in the conference "Hannah Arendt and the Meaning of Politics," at the University of North Carolina at Chapel Hill in early 1995, where I first presented a version of this work. I especially thank Susan Bickford for her engaging comments and keen interest in this project. My thanks also to Romand Coles who gave the essay a very challenging postconference read that has sharpened my thoughts and, I hope, the work as well.

1. In light of this fact, it is remarkable that a good deal of Arendtian scholarship barely mentions Arendt's aestheticization of political life (see Canovan 1974 and Bradshaw 1989). Other scholars of her work set her aestheticization of political life at the center of their inquiry, but either they fail to develop their initially bold assertions about the relationship between politics and aesthetics (Parekh 1981) or they stop short in fear of what they hold to be the amorality of Arendt's aestheticism (Dossa 1988).

2. I am paraphrasing here the work of Jean-François Lyotard (1984, 1985).

3. Berel Lang develops this point briefly but succinctly in his essay "Hannah Arendt and the Politics of Evil" (see 1994, 50–51). For Arendt's most concentrated articulation of this point, see 1951, 456–57.

4. Arendt's most sustained analysis of the historical conditions and developments in the modern age that contribute to this possibility is to be found, of course, in *The Human Condition* (1958).

5. Our most trenchant theorists of the world in this regard are, in addition to Arendt, I think, Max Weber, Michel Foucault, and Friedrich Nietzsche.

6. I use the term "reality," as does Arendt, in a very elemental sense, referring to our ability to take in or countenance "everything that happens on earth" (1951, xxx). That is to say, it refers to our capacity to experience, to feel the impact of what comes to

pass. The frame of reference remains, for Arendt, the emancipation from reality that she thought totalitarian ideology, together with totalitarian practices of terror, made possible. See especially her final chapter, "Ideology and Terror, " in 1951.

7. Indeed, what most struck Arendt about Adolf Eichmann, the most famous representative of our time in this regard, was his "remoteness from reality" (1963a, 288).

8. Although I cannot argue it here, I think Arendt attempts to cultivate this passion through both the content and the form of her political theorizing.

9. Arendt's entire critique of the modern age is concerned with the loss of the world and the radical subjectification of existence that accompanied that loss. The terrible assault on our sense of reality that this represented in her view remains her deepest concern.

10. I am following both the translation and the insightful discussion of *Antigone* and "things *deinon*" in Nussbaum 1986.

11. George Kateb has suggested that Arendt's humanism is undergirded by what he calls "a non-aesthetic sense of beauty" that is rooted in a fundamental gratitude for the way things are. In explicating this he writes, "[I]f what there is, is to be seen and felt, not as beautiful but as worthy of the emotions aroused by beauty and not merely used or changed or despised because unusable or unchangeable, then the person must begin and end in gratitude. Things as they are do not need to be beautiful to be beautiful" (1984, 166–67).

12. Indeed, if we centralize Arendt's ontological concerns, it becomes clear that it was the Greeks' and Romans' passion for reality that made their political understandings of vital interest to her. It is this passion, I should add (though I cannot develop the point here) that made their delimitations on the public-political world of keen interest to her as well. This is particularly true of her interest in Aristotle and Cicero, but by no means is it limited to their work (see especially the chapter "Labor" in 1958).

13. What Arendt meant by the public realm can be partially elucidated by reference to recent work by Nancy Fraser, who makes a very convincing case that our normative ideal should be multiple publics, in contrast to a single, overarching institutionalized space. It is toward this ideal that Arendt's ontology and her celebration of council politics overwhelmingly point. However, these dimensions of her work stand in irresolvable tension with other parts of her theoretical work, parts that badly limit our conceptual license to imagine multiple publics. I have in mind most particularly her rigid distinction between public and private life and between the social and political realms. Hence, her ontology and her celebration of council politics suggest a far more radically democratic politics than do these central distinctions of her explicitly political theorizing. The paradox remains, however, that these limiting distinctions *at the same time* clear conceptual space for the crucial phenomenon she was trying to theorize, namely, the peculiar capacity of political life to intensify our awareness of reality. Ironically, it is this very capacity that stirs our ethical imagination toward radical democracy (see Fraser 1992).

14. In this sense our situation stands in sharp contrast to other historical periods—for example, to the world of medieval Christian peoples, for whom "what is" was an *ens creatum*, or to the ancient Greeks, for whom *physis* was the ontological ground.

15. Here I am in full agreement with Jeffrey Isaac's arguments about the humanistic foundations of Arendt's political theorizing (1989, 63–68; see also Curtis 1995).

16. See, for example, Arendt's speculative reflections at the end of *On Revolution* as to whether a political elite, self-selected from an open public sphere on the basis of their demonstrated concern for public more than for private life, might be a more realistic way of saving public life from the corrosion of private individuals than is universal representative democracy (1963b, 277–81).

17. For the best argument about the theoretical and practical deficiency in Arendt's work, see Dietz 1994.

18. For such critiques see Pitkin 1981, Benhabib 1992, and Bakan 1979.

19. Arendt's endorsement of radical democracy takes explicit form, of course, in her celebration of the public sphere created by council politics, the student antiwar movement, and the Civil Rights movement, and even, though in accommodated form, in her advocacy for global federalism.

20. Compare this formulation from her final work with the following call from the preface to *The Origins of Totalitarianism*, her first published work: "[H]uman dignity needs a new guarantee which can be found only in a new political principle, in a new *law on earth*, whose validity this time must comprehend the whole of humanity while its power must remain strictly limited, rooted in and controlled by newly defined territories" (1951, xxi; emphasis added).

21. That Arendt's ontology is thought to counter directly the problems that, in her view, define the modern age is clear from the following quotation. Speaking about Cartesian doubt, she writes:

> It now turned out that without confidence in the senses neither faith in God nor trust in reason could any longer be secure, because the revelation of both divine and rational truth had always been implicitly understood to follow the awe-inspiring simplicity of man's relationship with the world: I open my eyes and behold the vision, I listen and hear the sound, I move my body and touch the tangibility of the world. If we begin to doubt the fundamental truthfulness and reliability of this relationship, which of course does not exclude errors and illusions but, on the contrary, is the condition of their eventual correction, none of the traditional metaphors for suprasensual truth—be it the eyes of the mind which can see the sky of ideas or the voice of conscience listened to by the human heart—can any longer carry its meaning. The fundamental experience underlying Cartesian doubt was the discovery that the earth, contrary to all direct sense experience, revolves around the sun. The modern age began when man, with the help of the telescope . . . learned that his senses were not fitted for the universe. (1954, 54–55)

22. Arendt's claim in this context may need clarification, namely, that the only reality there is in an appearing world is that which appears to the senses. The philosophical idea of being is just that: a thought-thing (1971, 51). It is one of the metaphysical fallacies, as Arendt refers to them, that philosophers have concluded from the sheer activity of the invisible thinking process that "there exist 'things in themselves' which in their own intelligible sphere, *are* as we 'are' in a world of appearances" (44). This is not to say that thinking is nothing, but rather that reality is not one of the properties of thinking.

23. It is easy to misunderstand Arendt here as having an expressivist theory of action that relies on the notion of some essential kernel of truth buried deep within the self that is *pressed out* through the theatrical self-display in speech and deed. Arendt distinguishes between two meanings of the term "self-display," and it is crucial to understand that she relies on the first meaning of the term. She writes, "The word 'self-display,' like the German *Selbstdarstellung*, is equivocal: it can mean that I actively make my presence felt, seen, and heard, or that I display myself, something inside me that otherwise would not appear at all" (1971, 29). I say the first meaning is crucial because it depicts the self's urge to make its being felt *in the world*.

24. Although, for humans, language is the crucial medium through which this sensuous provocation that engenders the real makes itself manifest, all language is, in this regard, by no means of a piece. Indeed, Arendt's reflections on speech might be understood as directed toward a revitalization of the sensuous richness of speaking in its capacity to make real what occurs. She relates the wonderful story in which a man tells Demosthenes how terribly he has been beaten. Demosthenes replies, "But you suffered nothing of what you tell me." Upon hearing this, the man raises his voice and cries out, "I suffered nothing?" "Now," says Demosthenes, "I hear the voice of somebody who was injured and who suffered" (from Plutarch's *Lives*, quoted in Arendt 1958, 26). Demosthenes' forthright denial upon hearing the man drolly recount his hair-raising story speaks of the extent to which language can become drained of its evocative, engendering potentiality. The same thing is true, of course, of the written word.

25. This ontological work receives no sustained elaboration until Arendt's final work, *The Life of the Mind*, but, as is evident in her account of action, the aesthetic provocation that governs free beings under the earthly condition of plurality and through which that very plurality and diversity is engendered is already the unsaid ground.

26. Lest this sound too much like Rousseau's active and restless "artificial men" who, tyrannized by their passion for the esteem of others, have become emptied of any feeling of their own substantiality, we should note the way Arendt thematizes this deliberately chosen "playing." She suggests that many of our choices (of how to play) are determined by the culture in which we live; that is, we choose them to please others. We are also inspired by the effort to please ourselves or, alternatively, by the effort to persuade others to be pleased by what pleases us. Virtue, in any case, as well as the substantiality of the self, is constituted through a "promise to the world, to those to whom I appear, to act in accordance with my pleasure" (1971, 36). As is evident from these multiple ways in which we experience pleasure, such a promise entails complex considerations, but the salient point in this context is that the specific community by which we wish to be countenanced also importantly includes the self; our provocation with and in the world is always a response to our own appearingness as well. The extent to which Arendt conceptualized a kind of autonomy for the self is best explored in her reflections on thinking (see 1971). Her conception of the self is, however, complex. For a reading that fruitfully exaggerates its multiplicitous character, see Honig 1993.

27. This provocation is agonistic but certainly not essentially egoistic, as it is born amid an enormous yearning for and vulnerability to the sensuous provocation of others.

28. These cognitive-purposive interests are complex and crucial, and their formation, content, and socioeconomic preconditions must be theorized, a task beyond the focus of this essay.

29. For a very similar formulation, see Arendt 1958, 57.

30. This objectivity is to be understood, of course, in strict contrast to the "eunuchic" objectivity governing the social sciences (Arendt 1954, 53).

31. This paradoxical insight usually implicitly, but sometimes explicitly, informs much of the vital work of women of color in the debate about whether and in what sense we can speak about a common world of women. From this vantage point the effort of many white women to substantiate the claim to women's common world by reference to some shared experience or condition qua identity in fact corrodes the kind of dialogue through which the common world of women might possibly emerge (see Lorde 1984; hooks 1989; and Reagon 1983). For fascinating dialogue between white women and women of color that bears directly on this issue, see Mohanty and Martin 1986; and Pratt 1984.

32. As I have already noted, I am not here concerned with the second moment of aestheticism in Arendt's work: her thoughts on political judgment, in which she is most
concerned with the relationship between beauty and permanence, and political judgment and particularity. An elaboration of these issues is absolutely central to a full account of her understanding of the common world and would anchor somewhat more
firmly—but in no way absolutely—the parameters of the common.

33. See my article "Hannah Arendt, Feminist Theorizing, and the Debate over New
Reproductive Technologies" (in Curtis 1995), where I discuss the implications of such
denial for certain key capacities and experiences tied to our capacity to be citizens in a
democratic polity.

34. In this focus on our sensation of reality, we should not overlook the fact that
there are a great many worthy and essential experiences that do not intensify our awareness of reality in the manner of fullness but that, nonetheless, are important to our being
human, love being perhaps the strangest (1958, 50). To meditate on this is to realize the
specificity of the reality-intensifying capacities of political togetherness as Arendt attempts to theorize them.

35. Indeed, Arendt is quick to acknowledge that no one can remain in public light
for long, and that one of the preeminent political virtues is courage.

Works Cited

Abel, Lionel. 1963. "The Aesthetics of Evil: Hannah Arendt on Eichmann and the
  Jews." *Partisan Review* 30, no. 2:211–30.
Arendt, Hannah. 1951. *The Origins of Totalitarianism*. New York: Harcourt Brace
  and World.
———. 1954. *Between Past and Future*. Harmondsworth: Penguin.
———. 1955. *Men in Dark Times*. New York: Harcourt Brace Jovanovich.
———. 1958. *The Human Condition*. Chicago: University of Chicago Press.
———. 1963a. *Eichmann in Jerusalem: A Report on the Banality of Evil*. New York:
  Viking Press.
———. 1963b. *On Revolution*. Harmondsworth: Penguin.
———. 1971. *Thinking*. New York: Harcourt Brace Jovanovich.
———. 1979. "On Hannah Arendt." In *Hannah Arendt: The Recovery of the Public
  World*, edited by Melvyn Hill. New York: St. Martin's Press.
Bakan, Mildred. 1979. "Hannah Arendt's Concepts of Labor and Work." In *Hannah
  Arendt: The Recovery of the Public World*, edited by Melvyn Hill. New York: St.
  Martin's Press.
Bell, Daniel. 1963. "The Alphabet of Justice: Reflections on Eichmann in Jerusalem."
  Partisan Review 30, no. 3:417–29.
Benhabib, Seyla. 1992. "Models of Public Space: Hannah Arendt, the Liberal Tradi-
  tion, and Jürgen Habermas." In *Habermas and the Public Sphere*, edited by Craig
  Calhoun. Cambridge: MIT Press.
Bradshaw, Leah. 1989. *Acting and Thinking: The Political Thought of Hannah Arendt*.
  Toronto: University of Toronto Press.
Canovan, Margaret. 1974. *The Political Thought of Hannah Arendt*. London: J. M. Dent.
Curtis, Kimberley. 1995. "Hannah Arendt, Feminist Theorizing and the Debate over
  New Reproductive Technologies." *Polity 28*, no. 2: 159–87.
Dietz, Mary. 1994. "'The Slow Boring of Hard Boards': Methodical Thinking and the
  Work of Politics." *American Political Science Review* 88, no. 4:873–86.

Dossa, Shiraz. 1988. *The Public Realm and the Public Self: The Political Theory of Hannah Arendt*. Waterloo, Canada: Wilfred Laurier University Press.

Fraser, Nancy. 1992. "Rethinking the Public Sphere: A Contribution to the Critique of Actually Existing Democracy." In *Habermas and the Public Sphere*, edited by Craig Calhoun. Cambridge: MIT Press.

Habermas, Jürgen. 1977. "Hannah Arendt's Communicative Concept of Power." *Social Research* 44:3–24.

Honig, Bonnie. 1993. *Political Theory and the Displacement of Politics*. Ithaca: Cornell University Press.

hooks, bell. 1989. *Talking Back*. Boston: South End Press.

Isaac, Jeffrey. 1989. "Arendt, Camus, and Postmodern Politics." *Praxis International* 9:48–71.

Jay, Martin. 1978. "Hannah Arendt: Opposing Views." *Partisan Review* 45, no. 3:348–80.

Kateb, George. 1984. *Politics, Conscience, Evil*. Totowa, N.J.: Rowman and Allenheld.

Lang, Berel. 1994. "Hannah Arendt and the Politics of Evil." In *Hannah Arendt: Critical Essays*, edited by Lewis P. Hinchman and Sandra K. Hinchman. Albany: State University of New York Press.

Lorde, Audre. 1984. *Sister Outsider*. Trumansburg, N.Y.: Crossing Press.

Lyotard, Jean-François. 1984. *The Postmodern Condition: A Report of Knowledge*. Translated by Geoff Bennington and Brian Massumi. Minneapolis: University of Minnesota Press.

———. 1985. *Just Gaming*. Translated by Wlad Godzich. Minneapolis: University of Minnesota Press.

Mohanty, Chandra, and Biddy Martin. 1986. "Feminist Politics: What's Home Got to Do with It?" In *Feminist Studies/Critical Studies*, edited by Teresa de Lauretis. Bloomington: Indiana University Press.

Nussbaum, Martha. 1986. *The Fragility of Goodness: Luck and Ethics in Greek Tragedy and Philosophy*. Cambridge: Cambridge University Press.

Parekh, Bhikhu. 1981. *Hannah Arendt and the Search for a New Political Philosophy*. Atlantic Heights, N.J.: Humanities Press.

Pitkin, Hannah. 1981. "Justice: On Relating Public and Private." *Political Theory* 9:327–52.

Pratt, Minnie Bruce. 1984. "Identity: Skin, Blood, Heart." In *Yours in Struggle*, edited by Elly Bulkin, Minnie Bruce Pratt, and Barbara Smith. Brooklyn, N. Y.: Long Haul Press.

Reagon, Bernice Johnson. 1983. "Coalition Politics: Turning the Century." In *Home Girls: A Black Anthology*, edited by Barbara Smith. New York: Kitchen Table: Women of Color Press.

Rich, Adrienne. 1993. *What Is Found There*. New York: W. W. Norton.

Villa, Dana. 1992a. "Beyond Good and Evil: Arendt, Nietzsche, and the Aestheticization of Political Action." *Political Theory* 20:275–309.

———. 1992b. "Postmodernism and the Public Sphere." *American Political Science Review* 86, no. 3:712–20.

Two

The Odor of Judgment: Exemplarity, Propriety, and Politics in the Company of Hannah Arendt

Kirstie M. McClure

> *How wrong it is to cite the Romans at every turn. For any compari-*
> *son to be valid, it would be necessary to have a city with conditions*
> *like theirs, and then to govern it according to their example. In the*
> *case of a city with different qualities, the comparison is as much out*
> *of order as it would be to expect a jackass to race like a horse.*
>
> Francesco Guicciardini

Guicciardini's *Ricordi* are studded with moments of impatience at his contemporaries' reverence for the ancients, an impatience that extended to his friend Niccolò Machiavelli, among others. At stake in such rebukes, however, was not simply the question of comparative empirical accuracy, but the relationship between past and present presupposed by Renaissance conventions governing the invocation of historical exemplars as guides to action in the present. Against the idea that great deeds of the past served as imitable instances of a general rule, Guicciardini counterposed, by reference to the complexity of situational detail, an irreducible historical distance. "To judge by example," he insisted, "is very misleading. Unless they are similar in every respect, examples are useless, since every difference in the case may be a cause of great variations in the effects."[1] While not yet Ranke's things *wie es eigentlich gewesen,* Guicciardini's view of historical writing can be read as sufficiently anticipatory to place him at the inception of modern historiography.[2]

By most modern historiographical standards, not simply as up-held by professional historians but as assimilated into far broader registers of contemporary intellectual culture, Hannah Arendt's recourse to historical examples is no less mistaken than Machiavelli's. Call it her Hellenism or republicanism or nostalgia for the polis, find it in her neglect of causality or her inattention to context or her reverence for foundings, summarize it philosophically as her "antiquated concept of theoretical knowledge"[3]—the various modalities through which Arendt articulated a relation between past and present are anything but modern. Arendt was well aware of this fact, as her remarks on "our modern concept of history" and "modern historians" amply indicate.[4] But Arendt, like Machiavelli, took historical reflection to be something other than an account of the past "as it really happened." The "objectivity" required by the latter, "the 'extinction of the self' as the condition of 'pure vision' (*das reine Sehen der Dinge*—Ranke) meant the historian's abstention from bestowing either praise or blame."[5] Whatever else may be said of Arendt's recourse to history, it is clear that she, no less than Machiavelli, abstained from that abstention. Like Machiavelli, too—although her own exemplar was Kant, from whose third critique she took the phrase—for Arendt "examples are the go-cart of judgments," the worldly particulars that elicited the "specifically political ability" of judging.[6] Though neither of them put it so bluntly, both might have suggested that Guicciardini was off the mark. The point of their use of exemplarity was not, as he imagined, to expect a modern jackass to run like an ancient horse, but to caution modern horses not to act like jackasses.

In a different context I would be tempted to pursue the historical resonances of Renaissance rhetorical controversies in Arendt's use of exemplarity. But our concern in this volume—*Hannah Arendt and the Meaning of Politics*—points in more contemporary directions. I begin with this intimation of an affinity between Arendt and Machiavelli, nonetheless, to mark something of the sensibility that informs what is to follow. A scholar neither of Arendt nor of "the tradition of German philosophy" that she said she could be said "to have come from,"[7] I have engaged her work as a visitor in a place that is, by way of professional formation, not my own. My perspective on her "thought-trains" is not that of a regular passenger familiarly seated in their interior compartments, but that of a hobo slung in the undercarriage, discomfitingly close to the steely rush of their wheels. In this essay, then, I shall be concerned less with Arendt's use of exemplarity per se than with the ways in which this inflects her rendering of judgment as "one of the fundamental abilities of man as a political being."[8] As the phrase "rendering of judgment" all too weakly implies, what I mean to examine is Arendt's judging of judgment—not, I should add, in the service of clarifying her "theory" of such things, but in the hope of suggesting something of the political edge of her unfinished reflections on judgment. Along the way, I shall pursue this question of exemplarity a bit further, then turn to Arendt's "thinking in company." Toward the end, in the hope of keeping the political stakes of her judging in view, I shall consider the controversy sparked by her responses to Little Rock as an exemplary instance of the political character of her understanding of judgment.

The Double Movement of Exemplarity: From Machiavelli to Arendt

Let me begin by returning briefly to Guicciardini's rebuke, for it is arguably the case that Guicciardini's critical brush painted too broadly, that he mistook Machiavelli's use of Roman examples as too securely inhabiting the conventions of the day.[9] This, at least, is suggested by some recent Renaissance scholarship. Timothy Hampton, in particular, has called attention to a curious detail in Machiavelli's own account of the matter in *The Prince*.

Admonishing his reader not to "marvel" at his forwarding of "very great examples," Machiavelli notes that individuals "almost always" follow paths laid down by others, "proceeding in their actions by imitation." Strict imitation, however, is not necessarily possible. "Not being always able to follow others exactly," he observes, "nor attain to the excellence of those he imitates, a prudent man should always follow in the path trodden by great men and imitate those who are more excellent, so that if he does not attain their greatness [*virtù*], at any rate he will get some odor of it." "What exactly," Hampton asks, "is the odor of *virtù*?"[10] The dilemma becomes more complex still as Hampton, drawing upon the work of J. G. A. Pocock, observes that Machiavelli offers not a unitary model for princely emulation, but a "gallery of specimen types of innovation" extending from great founders and classical legislators to their more or less successful latter-day imitators.[11] Were this not difficult enough (and here Hampton finds support from Victoria Kahn), the problem is compounded further by Machiavelli's recommendation that elements of two or more exemplars may be combined—mixed and matched, as it were, without regard to historical context, into an ensemble—to meet the challenge of particular configurations of contemporary circumstances.

In effect, while Guicciardini's insistence upon comparative detail limits (if not, indeed, precludes) the imitability of historical exemplars, Machiavelli's attention to detail displaces conventional notions of exemplarity with an innovation of his own. Each writer, in other words, refuses the political use of exemplarity as rule following. But Machiavelli's refusal reinvents "exemplarity" as a recombinative distillation of past particulars, a distillation within which historical reflection provided neither rules nor prescriptions but exercises of imaginative engagement with the vicissitudes of political action. "A reading of history," as Hampton observes, in this context becomes "a test of judgment" even as it undermines the pragmatics of strict imitability.[12] To put it differently, Machiavelli's innovation may find its power less in the citation of historical referents as historical *models*—that is, in framing past actions as embodiments of rules for the present—than in the exemplarity of the historian's judgment itself, in Machiavelli's own critical practice of rationing praise and blame across a range of instances. What is to be imitated, then, is not the deeds of the past "as they really were," but rather the author's perspicuity in choosing and weighing examples, for this choosing and weighing itself serves as an exemplar of the proprieties of political judgment.[13]

Machiavellian exemplarity, from this perspective, thus operates on two levels. On the one hand, and most obviously, in referential terms it pertains to the representation of specific actions; on the other hand, it resides in the judgments that select such instances and allocate to them their due portions of honor and criticism. While the first operation evokes for the reader the images of particular deeds and doers, drawing on times that are not-now or places that are not-here, the second engages her imaginatively, here and now, in the practice of distinguishing fame from infamy, of discriminating between the admirable and the ordinary, of separating the noteworthy from the notorious—in the practice, that is, of judging the risks and responsibilities of political action. If the "odor of *virtù*" resides in enactments of political good sense, then the practice of exemplary reflection that informs such performances can be understood as something other than an incitement to political glory. Encouraging a taste for politics through accounts of worldly doings, the exemplarity of a writer's differential allocation of praise and blame encourages the development of a capacity for political judgment. In this respect, broadly speaking, the double movement of exemplarity aims to animate what could be characterized as the formation of "political taste."

Thinking in Company

As Machiavelli invites his readers to "the odor of *virtù*" through exemplary reflection on select examples, so Arendt draws hers to "the odor of judgment" in a similar fashion. In this regard Machiavelli's famous description of his habit, taken on in forced exile from the world of action, of retiring to his books to converse with the great, finds a parallel of sorts in Arendt's representation of thinking in company. "Our decisions about right and wrong," she observed, "will depend upon our choice of company. . . . And this company [in turn] is chosen through thinking in examples, in examples of persons dead or alive, and in examples of incidents past and present."[14] For Machiavelli this company included the words and deeds not only of political actors but also of historians and poets and rhetoricians, both ancient and modern. For Arendt such company included both greater and lesser icons of the Western philosophical "tradition," the invention of which as an image of unbroken continuity punctuates the centuries that separate her from Machiavelli.[15] But it also embraced a host of literary and cultural figures (Dante, Shakespeare, Lessing, Goethe, Varnhagen, Rilke, Dinesen, Benjamin, and Brecht, among others), as well as a handful of political actors and writers (Machiavelli, Robespierre, Adams, Jefferson, Tocqueville, and Luxemburg, to note but a few). Whether Arendt spoke of authority or revolution, of the modes of the *vita activa* or the life of the mind, that speaking without exception proceeds both directly and indirectly by way of engagement with something like an ad hoc committee of this company.

Such engagements on Arendt's part, though they arose after the solidification of "the tradition" that stands between her and the Renaissance, carried the burden of discontinuity, so convinced was she that that tradition had been ruptured. As a consequence, her committees bear the mark of the untimely, of being convened somehow out of time, even on those numerous occasions when her reflections take the form of a conventionally chronological narration. The pastness of her committees' thinking no longer being part of a tradition, their ad-hocness itself testifies to their deficit of authority. In this respect, at least, Arendt's description of Benjamin's use of quotations may capture something of her own practice of thinking in the company of exemplary thinkers:

> Insofar as the past has been transmitted as tradition, it possesses authority; insofar as authority presents itself historically, it becomes tradition. Walter Benjamin knew that the break in tradition and the loss of authority which occurred in his lifetime were irreparable, and he concluded that he had to discover new ways of dealing with the past. In this he became a master when he discovered that the transmissibility of the past had been replaced by its citability and that in place of its authority there had arisen a strange power to settle down, piecemeal, in the present and to deprive it of "peace of mind," the mindless peace of complacency.[16]

Extracted from their original context, Benjamin's quotations were at once fatal to illusions and, in an odd sense, preservative in that their citation might ensure the survival of something from the past, if "for no other reason than it was torn out of it."[17] Similarly apt is Arendt's at once admiring and haunting description of Benjamin's "gift of *thinking poetically*":

> [T]his thinking, fed by the present, works with the "thought fragments" it can wrest from the past and gather about itself. Like a pearl diver who descends to the bottom of the sea, not to excavate the bottom and bring it to light but to pry loose the rich and the strange, the pearls and the coral in the depths and to carry them to the surface, this thinking delves into the depths of the past—but not in order to resuscitate it the way it was and to contribute to the renewal of extinct ages. What guides this thinking is the conviction that although the living is subject to the ruin of time, the process of decay is at the same time a process of crystallization, that in the depth of the sea, into which sinks and is dissolved what was once alive, some things suffer a "sea-change" and survive in new crystallized forms and shapes that remain immune to the elements, as though they waited only for the pearl diver who one day will come down to them and bring them up into the world of the living.[18]

Arendt, too, was drawn to the poetic, as she was drawn to the practice of surfacing thought fragments from the past into the world of the living. But she hardly shared Benjamin's aspiration to assemble a montage of quotations so perfect as to eliminate the need for commentary. Such self-effacement was not her style.[19] To the contrary, her engagements with the "pearls and coral" that she extricated from the ruins of "the tradition," no less than Machiavelli's engagement with Livy, occasioned not the revelation of essences but a dialogue, moments of agreement and qualification, appropriation and rejection that could, and often did, go on at great length. Arendt's thinking in company, in this respect, is a thinking-in-response—in Bakhtin's terms, an "answer-word" to another's utterance that is itself, as a public utterance, directed to the "answer-words" of still others—that differs quite radically from the complacency that typically inhabits the notion of "conversation." Here, too, in reading Arendt I think we can discern the double movement of exemplarity. As thought-deeds, her interlocutors' fragments are treated like Machiavelli's exemplary actions: they are compared and elaborated, questioned and qualified; they are held accountable to distinctions not their own. They are, in a word, judged. At the same time, the pearls and coral that emerge through this process are also brought into conjunction with their contemporary analogues, juxtaposed and conjoined along axes of similitude and difference that make sense only from the perspective of the present. According them honor in some respects, criticism in others, Arendt's manner of proceeding in such judgments itself enacts a certain decorum or propriety, and in so doing dons the mantle of exemplarity.[20]

To speak of Arendt in these terms is to suggest that the question of judgment, so commonly represented as an outgrowth of her account of Eichmann, is, as it were, written into her work from the outset, long before she explicitly thematized the relationship between thinking and judging as a phenomenon demanding reflection. The singularity of her public judgments, as her biographer indicates, was already well in evidence with her dissertation on Augustine, which was reviewed "not at all favorably."[21] The issue of judgment is no less present in her opinions on Little Rock or Eichmann or Watergate or "the conquest of space." The "keyword" here, though, to borrow Raymond Williams's term of art, is *opinion*. To have an opinion, in Arendt's lexicon, was not, as it is for modern survey research, a matter simply of responding to a question or registering one's "feelings" on an imaginary thermometer of differential affect. Rather, it was a consequence of judgment. By the same token, the public deliverance of one's opinions, be it in speech or writing, in Arendt's view of such things bore little resemblance to the conventions of subjective enunciation that elicit either a conventional nod of agreement or the equally conventional sign of its refusal, "That's just your opinion." Instead—crediting Kant with the discovery that even thinking, seemingly the most solitary of activities, depends on others—to deliver one's opinion in public was to "communicate and expose to the test of others . . . whatever you may have found out when you were alone."[22]

The portion of Arendt's lecture on Kant from which the preceding observation is drawn aptly instances the ways in which her "thinking in company" is inflected by what I have called the double movement of exemplarity. According Kant's notion of "publicity" exemplary status, she praises his equation of "the public use of one's reason" with "the freedom to speak and write."[23] At the same time, in criticizing his restriction of this freedom to the "scholar" or "world citizen," she distances it from what she deems extraneous or problematic.[24] Having thus relieved her Kantian coral of matters better left behind, she transports it to the present, allowing its color to contrast with a contemporary commonplace by discriminating between the presuppositions of the latter and the sense she distills from her fragmentary prize:

> Freedom of speech and thought, as we understand it, is the right of an individual to express himself and his opinion in order to be able to persuade others to share his viewpoint. This presupposes that I am capable of making up my mind all by myself and that the claim I have on the government is to permit me to propagandize whatever I have already fixed in my mind. Kant's view of this matter is very different. He believes that the very faculty of thinking depends on its public use; without "the test of free and open examination," no thinking and no opinion formation is possible. Reason is not made "to isolate itself but to get into community with others."[25]

No less than in Machiavelli's reportage of past deeds, the movement of exemplarity in Arendt's engagement with Kant here operates on two levels. The first level—the referentiality of the thought-deeds that are Kant's writings—from this perspective serves as the occasion for the second, or, better, it provides the vehicle through which the second takes its public form. Fragments of Kant's texts, in other words, are crystallized into examples, not as models to be internalized as one's own but as "go-carts" for judgment. Scrubbed by critical scrutiny, an admired element—Kant's defense of freedom of thought and speech—

is set alongside an analogous example of common belief. In effect, that which would otherwise go without saying—here, the contemporary notion that opinion is something *brought to* public debate—is cast into relief through its contrast to the notion of opinion as something *forged through* public testing. In the process, the commonplace emerges not only as something that could be other than it is (an obvious point in any case for a world in which "opinion" is taken to be utterly subjective), but also as something that, under the pressure of coralline comparison, discloses apposite images of public discourse.

That Arendt favors one of these images is fairly clearly the case. And yet, what is urged upon the reader here is not simply a matter of unsettling the taken-for-grantedness of a common view (though this is at least part of the point); much less is it the replacement of that common opinion with a philosophical truth drawn from Kant. Even Kantian coral, as it turns out, is in the end but a crystallized opinion, as the closing remarks of the lecture suggest. Kant's defense of freedom of speech and thought is "noteworthy," for although he agrees with philosophers that "thinking is a 'solitary business,'" he links it with the presence of others. "It is by no means true that you need or can even bear the company of others when you happen to be busy thinking," Arendt continues, "yet, unless you can somehow communicate and expose to the test of others, either orally or in writing, whatever you may have found out when you were alone, this faculty exerted in solitude will disappear." Citing another of her exemplary thinkers, the lecture ends in a way that refuses even Kant's coral the status of general validity: "In the words of Jaspers, truth is what I can communicate. Truth in the sciences is dependent on the experiment that can be repeated by others; it requires general validity. Philosophic truth has no such general validity. What it must have, what Kant demanded in the *Critique of Judgment* of judgments of taste, is 'general communicability.' 'For it is a natural vocation of mankind to communicate and speak one's mind.'"[26]

This, of course, is what Arendt has been doing all along—communicating and speaking her mind—and it is precisely in this that the second operation of exemplarity finds its worldly face. From example to example, through comparison, qualification, distinction, and elaboration, Arendt rations admiration and criticism across a range of instances, but what she urges upon her interlocutors is not "think what I think" but "think thusly." What is exemplary, in other words, is not her "thoughts" but her thinking. By thinking in company, by comparing, qualifying, distinguishing, and elaborating, and by communicating and speaking one's mind in turn, one can begin thinking in accordance with a similar decorum. This, of course, cannot restore the tradition to authority or culminate in truth. Nor does such thinking attain the excellence of pearls and coral. Uncrystallized by the "sea-change" of time, it remains vulnerable to the elements of living contestation. But it might, nonetheless, get the odor of judgment.

Judging in Public

Arendt, as we know, was a thinker who thought about thinking. Yet, were I simply reading this rather than writing it as well, my impatience at this point would be palpable. Like writing about writers writing, thinking about Arendt's thinking about thinking courts the arcane. In a sense the objection is valid, for nothing in the foregoing directly engages the question of Arendt and "the meaning of politics." But in regard to a thinker for whom thoughtlessness accompanied the greatest of modern political disasters, the objection itself runs afoul of one of Arendt's most prominent thought-trains. With her characteristic admixture of the strikingly acute and the flatly matter-of-fact, she asked, "Could the activity of thinking as such, the habit of examining whatever happens to come to pass or attract attention, regardless of results and specific content, could this activity be among the conditions that make men abstain from evil-doing or even 'condition' them against it?"[27] In part, but only in part, this was a question that pertained to the political potential of conscience.[28] Beyond this, however, it was also a question of political judgment, which Arendt, to the distress of some, took to be distinct from the operation of conscience, as well as separable from such motivations as pity or compassion.[29]

As a public intellectual, Arendt's own political judgments frequently ignited controversy. The furor that greeted her account of the Eichmann trial is, in this regard, but the most prominent instance of a more general phenomenon. Indeed, though the narrowness of its public makes it an odd form of testimony, the burgeoning scholarly literature on her work bears witness to the fact that her judgments are still regarded as worth arguing with. And yet, my impression is that her "Reflections on Little Rock" represents something of an exception to this, as if the now nearly four decades of political experience since its publication had rendered it obsolete.[30] From the standpoint of the present, Arendt's account of the political dilemmas of Little Rock is perhaps embarrassing in its opposition to the federally enforced integration of public education. This was not, of course, an opposition to integration as a project for "like-minded citizens," but her opinions nonetheless remain disturbing.[31] Arendt's judgment here, if remembered at all, might best be remembered as a misunderstanding explicable by reference to her experience as a German Jew.[32] Alternatively, in theoretical rather than biographical terms, her acknowledgment of "discrimination" as a constituent feature of the social—and hence utterly legitimate in its own domain—might be memorable in a cautionary sense, that is, as a sort of discomfiting reminder of the dilemmas attending her delineation of the realms of the political, the social, and the private.[33]

But there is another way of engaging Arendt's responses to the events in Little Rock, another way of reading that views them neither as a regrettable political lapse nor as one among other textual remnants of her "philosophy," but rather as a portion of what she referred to as "the common world," the object-world that relates and separates human creatures in their manifold particularity. "Thinking," as she put it, "because it can be remembered, can crystallize into thought, and thoughts, like all things that owe their existence to remembrance, can be transformed into tangible objects which, like the written page or the printed book, become part of the human artifice."[34] Considering her "Reflections" in this light, we might begin to engage its political character not by slotting it contentwise into one or another readymade category ("conservative," "elitist," or "racist" here are obvious, if tendentious, options), but by regarding it as a thought-deed, as an enactment of public judgment that by virtue of its printed form has become available to us, here and now, as a part of "the world." Put somewhat differently but still drawing on Arendt's own lexicon, we might regard her reflections as instances of the sort of public speech that she described as "coeval and coequal, of the same rank and the same kind" as political action.[35] To do so, at least as Arendt construed the kind of political action that manifests itself in speech, would be to view her reflections less in terms of the content of their arguments than "more fundamentally" as an example of "finding the right words at the right moment, quite apart from the information or communication they may convey."[36]

In light of the controversy Arendt's remarks occasioned, it might be difficult to imagine how they could be conceived as a matter of "finding the right words at the right moment"—indeed, one of her original respondents deemed them "neither relevant nor opportune."[37] In reading her initial critics, however, it is nonetheless possible to distinguish at least three senses in which hers were not "the right words," the combination of which, viewed from the distance of the present, might suggest that they may have been the right words to the extent that they were perceived as the wrong ones. Most obviously, of course, for her critics those words came to the wrong conclusions. But further, in a sense that only seems to be literal, they were not "the right words" in that they were perceived to make no sense. Thus construed, many of Arendt's words were not simply not "the right words" in the sense that they supported the wrong conclusions; rather, they were not "the right words" because they deployed "false" or "implausible" or "vague" distinctions, because they forwarded "superficial" or "nonsensical" notions, because they instanced "strange" conceptions, "strange" pleas, and "strange" concerns, as well as "perverse" usages of common terms. Were this not damning enough, they were not "the right words" because, in place of the "basic facts of sociology and history," they offered "metaphysical mumbo-jumbo," a "decrepit metaphysics" blended with "even more decrepit non-facts."[38]

The differences here between Arendt and her critics might be cast in terms of her later distinction between two understandings of "opinion"—that is, between opinion as something forged through public examination, and opinion as something brought to public debate—and their apposite images of public discourse. That Arendt's opinions on Little Rock were contingent judgments, open to change or elaboration in the crucible of public testing, is supported in the first instance by the "preliminary remarks" that opened the original essay. There she acknowledged a friend's "just criticism" that she failed to take adequate account of the historically central political role of educational institutions in the United States.[39] Further, although to my knowledge her rethinking of the matter was not available to a broad public until after her death, she conceded, in a letter responding to Ralph Ellison's criticism, that she had misjudged the meaning of black parents' behavior in the situation.[40] At both moments, as if enacting Kant's claim that reason is made "to get into community with others," Arendt's judgments of the matter bear the mark of change, but—and precisely to this extent—they also enact her commitment to a form of public discourse rather different from that intimated in the writings of her initial critics.

To note this is not a matter of excusing or apologizing for Arendt's initial judgments, for the observation points to more substantive political and theoretical concerns than the question of Arendt's personal character. If anything today remains striking about her critics' insistence that her words were not "the right words," it is the extent to which that insistence subscribes to a markedly different understanding of public debate. Taking her reflections as the expression of an erroneous and unacceptable opinion that they were being urged to share, her critics' persistent reception of her words as "vague," "perverse," "strange," "odd," "misguided," and the like suggest nothing so clearly as a refusal to regard those words as anything but alien. What she treated as a process of forging opinions, they enacted as a war of words, a war in which her words were like broadcasts from an enemy transmitter, as if she had "made up her mind all by herself" and was simply "propagandizing what had been fixed there." And what they took to be fixed there, they rejected as out of the question.

But aside from testifying to the acuity of Arendt's distinction between two understandings of "opinion," these observations suggest a third sense in which Arendt's words on Little Rock were not "the right words," a sense in which, here in the United States of the mid-1990s, they might appear retrospectively as "the right words at the right moment" precisely because they were perceived in the late 1950s as so wrong. Again, lest I be misunderstood, this is not a matter of the specific content of her original judgments, for the propriety of "right words," on Arendt's account, was something separable from the information conveyed by their arguments. What she called "great words" were not to be taken as great because they expressed great thoughts. Instead, epitomizing the issue through a Sophoclean pearl, "great words, counteracting [or paying back] the great blows of the overproud, teach understanding in old age."[41] What is at issue here, then, nearly four decades after these essays were originally published, is not only the disparity between two images of public debate but also the ways in which this disparity emerges, between Arendt's and her opponents' essays, as apposite exemplars of the "decorum" or "proprieties" of political judgment. As her critics judged Arendt's reflections, so too did they judge the world—and in light of that judgment, both were out of order in a similar way.

In these terms, what is common to Arendt's original critics—despite their differences of substantive argumentation, tone, and style—is a practice of judgment that proceeds by incorporating the particularities of Little Rock under a general principle, the principle of equality, as a moral rule. As Sidney Hook framed the issue, at stake was a matter of human rights as such. Distinctions between public and private, between the political, the social, and the personal, were irrelevant: "the moral question is primary and it cuts across all categories."[42] "As moral creatures," he observed, "we are called upon to apply appropriate rules of equality, and, where differences are relevant, rules of equitable inequality in the light of some shared ideal."[43] The only relevant difference, in Hook's view, was individual merit or personal distinction. Spitz concurred. The "real issue" for him was "the choice between two constitutional values—liberty and equality."[44] Accepting that social differences, "and hence inequalities, of some kind must always exist," Spitz sought "a rational basis for such differences." This, in his view, was simply a "measure of equality of opportunity" that would start "the race on equal terms," allowing individuals "to discover and to display their true worth" and to "show in what respects they are truly unequal." Anything short of this was "an argument for artificial, and therefore false, inequality." Tumin, finally, speaks simply of "the equalization process" as a matter of fact. Evidence of obstacles to and encouragements of its worldly progress was scientifically ascertainable by the best opinion polls, but its universal value was self-evident.[45] Enacted rather than argued, the proprieties of political judgment that govern these responses are taken as a matter of course. Their basic dicta might be loosely summarized as follows: logic arbitrates meaning, principle precedes prudence, general rules command particular circumstance.

By contrast, the proprieties of judgment underlying Arendt's reportage—proprieties partially glimpsed in her reply to her critics—foreground attentiveness to the particularity of the particulars of Little Rock, to their status, that is, as examples: "The point of departure for my reflections was a picture in the newspapers, showing a Negro girl on her way home from a newly integrated school; she was persecuted by a mob of white children, protected by a white friend of her father, and her face bore witness to the obvious fact that she was not precisely happy. The picture showed the situation in a nutshell because those who appeared in it were directly affected by the Federal Court order, the children themselves."[46] With this beginning, Arendt describes a process of imagining herself, as it were, into the picture and the series of questions she pursues along the way: "What would I do if I were a Negro mother?" "What would I do if I were a white mother in the South?" "What exactly distinguishes the so-called Southern way of life from the American way of life with respect to the color question?"[47] The original essay takes up these things in a different order, opening with remarks engaging the third question and its relation to America's place in the world, then using a discussion of the photograph as a transition from specifically American political concerns, both historical and constitutional, to a series of more abstract reflections on "society" and "the body politic," as well as on the relationships between the political, social, and private realms as Arendt construed them.

Fugue-like, Arendt's account unfolds, repeating its opening themes in multiple variations across a series of topical as well as temporal domains. Her "argument," in this respect, is disclosed through narration rather than developed through logic, and its presentation persistently eludes reduction to premises, derivations, corollaries, and the like. Indeed, to take her critics at their word, what was most irritating about her reflections was their tendency to violate what a reader reading for logic expects of them. Hence, perhaps, the epithet "Arendt-type logic," for what that critic regarded as her defiance of "elementary logic" had to do, for another, with her myriad refusals of clear definitional lines. For the latter critic, Arendt's characterization of "society" as "that curious, somewhat hybrid realm between the public and the private" deserved little more than denial: "There is," he affirmed, "no such thing."[48] Here, as elsewhere, it is difficult to avoid the impression that the political differences between Arendt and her critics run quite beyond the questions of federal policy that occasioned their initial articulation. So too, however, in their enactment of incommensurable modes of public discourse, do they exceed what might be called questions of philosophical justification or theoretical approach, though this is doubtless one terrain on which the political distance between them takes shape. If, from the standpoint of the present, Arendt could be said to have found "the right words at the right moment," perhaps this running beyond and exceeding might suggest how that could be so.

Reducible to differences of neither opinion nor method, the clash between Arendt and her critics might appear as a collision of worlds. But to cast the conflict in these terms would be to affirm her critics' perception of her thinking as alien; likewise, to choose her side in what they construed as a war of words is to remain within that imagery. To consider the differences at issue as different proprieties of political judgment, on the other hand, is to consider the controversy as a moment that discloses alternative enactments of political decorum. By decorum here I mean not methods of judging but habits of thought, one might even say customary ways of thinking. This is not a matter of endorsing "custom" as a traditional way of doing things, but a matter rather of attending to the customs and conventions that undergird ways of thinking. The common world presupposed by both Arendt and her critics is a world that is fundamentally posttraditional, but a world in which the substantive claims of custom and tradition have been divested of authority is a world of questions, and in a world of questions the question how to think takes on a singular significance.

The dissolution of tradition and the disruption of customary ways of doing things, however, is by no means peculiar to late modernity. Arendt, in any case, would doubtless note the Greek turn to philosophy and the subsequent contestation between philosophical schools as a case in point. The same could be said of late Renaissance turns to "method" and the diverse contestations this entailed, as it could also be said of nineteenth-century turns, in what were becoming the human sciences, to "theory" and its attendant divisions. Historically considered, however, this series of turns is not a matter of successive displacements but of layering, of mutual imbrications and interactions. Philosophy, method, and theory emerge in multiple combinations and relations, themselves engendering new permutations over time. What Arendt refers to as the rupture of traditional ways of thinking, from this perspective, has to do with the ways in which customary ways of thinking—themselves forged through the successive crises modernity spawns for customary ways of doing—have been thrown into disarray by the continuing challenges of the twentieth century. In this regard, far from navel gazing on the part of those who think too much about thinking, the current proliferation of metamethodological and metatheoretical debates are themselves signs of the extent to which the conventions governing "theory" and "method" as intellectual disciplines have come to suffer the fate modernity demands of all traditions. In effect, the proprieties of political judgment discernible in the responses of Arendt's critics—logic arbitrates meaning, principle precedes prudence, general rules command particular circumstances—are among the habits of thought whose authority has become a question.

Politics, Decorum, and the Odor of Judgment

The third part of Arendt's triptych of mental activities, the "Judging" volume of her *Life of the Mind*, was never written. First broached in "The Crisis in Culture," then continued in her lectures on Kant, her initial formulations of its concerns identify Kant's critique of aesthetic judgment as one of the centerpieces of his, to her mind, unwritten political theory. Again, it may seem, we court the arcane—indeed, what could be more so than to speak of an unwritten book about an unwritten book? To note a linkage between judgment and decorum or propriety, however, is to call attention at the outset to the ways in which any distinction between the arcane and the pertinent, between what is seemly or appropriate and what is inappropriate or unseemly, is itself the manifestation of a certain decorum. But rather than reconstruct Arendt's theory of judgment, I propose to consider Arendt's responses to Little Rock retrospectively in light of her later investigations of judging, for it is there that the proprieties of judgment briefly sketched in her reply to her critics find more extensive articulation.[49]

Arendt, to be sure, does not speak of decorum, but its *politique* chords resonate throughout those portions of her Kant lectures that engage his account of aesthetic judgment. Her discussion, in particular, of his subordination of genius to taste is more than suggestive, for the pearl that surfaces to open the question of the *sensus communis* is nothing less than a passage from Cicero's classic treatise on political speech, *De Oratore*. Assimilating the relationship between actors and spectators to that between artistic geniuses and their critics, Arendt identifies the faculty of judgment as the faculty they hold in common, then marshals Cicero to the point:

> For everybody discriminates [*dijudicare*], distinguishes between right and wrong in matters of art and proportion by some silent sense without any knowledge of art and proportion: and while they can do this in the case of pictures and statues, in other such works, for whose understanding nature has given them less equipment, they display this discrimination much more in judging the rhythms and pronunciations of words, since these are rooted [*infixa*] in common sense, and of such things nature has willed that no one should be unable to sense and experience them [*expertus*].[50]

Cicero goes on, she points out, "to notice that it is truly marvelous and remarkable 'how little difference there is between the learned and the ignorant in judging, while there is the greatest difference in making.'"[51]

What Arendt doesn't discuss is that Cicero's orator is not talking about pictures and statues but delivering an account of rhetorical decorum, and a number of his surrounding discussions are by no means impertinent to Arendt's own concerns with Kant. The observation of stylistic proprieties, for instance, is a question not of regulation by rules but of the cultivation of practices the seemliness of which in any particular case tends to be differentiated by time and place, by audience and occasion, or by other circumstances. One's choice of style in such instances, however, no less than one's choice of words, is neither above nor beyond common language:

> [T]he vocabulary of conversation is the same as that of formal oratory, and we do not choose one class of words for daily use and another for full dress public occasions, but we pick them up from common life as they lie at our disposal, and then shape and mould them at our own discretion, like the softest wax. Consequently, at one moment we use a dignified style, at another a plain one, and at another we keep a middle course between the two; thus the style of our oratory follows the line of thought we take, and changes and turns to suit all the requirements of pleasing the ear and [moving the soul] of the audience.[52]

Such things as rhythm and meter, interval and division, might be rigorously analyzed and formalized as rules for poets or musicians. For the arts of political speech, however, one need not worry too much about such formalizations. Rooted in the quotidian usages of a time and place, the requisite things "will turn up in one's prose of their own accord"; they "will fall in and report themselves as present without being summoned."[53] Indeed, it is because its materials are drawn from the terms and accents of common life that oratory has the capacity to move "the unlearned crowd when it forms the audience."[54] But what lends such speech its power also suggests its bounds. Although one's skill in the use of words may be sharpened by rhetorical training and augmented by broad education, such speech remains embedded in a series of largely tacit understandings of appropriateness dispersed across the common life that both speakers and audiences are presumed to share.[55]

Although the preceding topics culminate in Arendt's Ciceronian pearl—that the faculty of judgment is rooted in common sense—what follows that pearl is of interest also. Now analogizing the orator to the poet or thespian, Cicero notes that though few of their auditors grasp the rules of poetry, "yet all the same if only a slight slip is made . . . the [entire] audience protests."[56] Similarly, confronted with discrepancies in actors' pronunciation, "the ordinary public drives them off the stage." As Cicero has it, the reason there is so little difference between the learned and the ignorant in judging is that such art, arising from the nature of speech, would "be deemed to have failed if it had not a natural power of affecting us and giving us pleasure." As his examples suggest, however, to the extent that proprieties are transgressed, such performances can displease as well. Further, and of no small political moment, the pleasure or displeasure they elicit has to do not simply with what a speaker says but also with the extent to which such utterances are found appropriate to the circumstances and occasion at hand. Quite aside from content, then—which itself may be more or less agreeable—different sorts of occasions demand different sorts of speech, and this too is an aspect of decorum tacitly governed by common sense. For guidance regarding such proprieties, however—aside from general admonitions that one's words suit the moment—"it does not seem possible to lay down any rules."[57] Instead, Cicero observes, "while the ability to do what is appropriate is a matter of trained skill and natural talent, the knowledge of what is appropriate to a particular occasion is a matter of practical sagacity [*deceat prudentiae*]."[58] In short, the conformity of political speech to the variegated demands of decorum can be taught, but the determination of what decorum might require or permit in any specific instance is a matter of prudential judgment, a judgment that rests only on the sort of tacit knowledge that characterizes one's participation in ongoing cultural practices.[59] Like beauty, in the end, decorum lies in the eye of the beholders, but their pleasure or displeasure in particular performances remains "rooted in common sense."

By elaborating Cicero's broader discussion of these matters, I do not mean to imply that Arendt's reading of Kant proceeds in "Ciceronian" terms. She was too doubtful of the possibility of resuscitating the thought of extinct ages to find such a project attractive, and too committed to Lessing's notion of *selbstdenken* to find it desirable. Instead, having glimpsed something of the thematic constellation that surrounds her Ciceronian pearl, I think we might glimpse as well some of the more extensive conceptual resonances that could prompt its appearance in a political reading of Kant's aesthetic judgment. Written long before the modern confinement of "propriety" to the realm of manners and "good society," long before the migration of "decorum" into the critical vocabulary of art and literature, Cicero's articulation of these terms as fundamental to political speech is an exemplary contrast to Kant's treatment of "the sense of decorum" as a question of aesthetics.[60] Yet, with regard to the rooting of decorum in common sense, as well as to the linkage of its observation with pleasure and its violation with displeasure, Cicero's broader ensemble of concerns lingers like a distant echo in Kant's notion of taste. And, I think unsurprisingly, it is precisely these aspects of Kant's critique that Arendt takes up as pivotal to his "unwritten political philosophy." In keeping with her practice of thinking in company, this long leap from republican Rome to eighteenth-century aesthetics crystallizes what she took as a distinctively modern dilemma—the dilemma of political judgment in a world unloosed from the moorings of tradition and custom, a world in which distinctions between right and wrong no longer went without saying. What Cicero contributes to this crystallization is an emphatically political twist on the connection between decorum and common sense, while Kant provides an account of the significance of reflective judgment in the operations of common sense and an insistence on the communicability of such judgments. What emerges through their juxtaposition might be regarded, perhaps, less as a "theory of judgment"—that is, less as an account of what judgment *is*—than as an exemplum or narration of how judging might best proceed in a world bereft of bannisters. Here, finally, on the wind of Arendt's writing, we might discern the odor of judgment.

It will be useful here to recall Arendt's description of her initial engagement with the events in Little Rock: "The point of departure for my reflections was a picture in the newspapers, showing a Negro girl on her way home from a newly integrated school; she was persecuted by a mob of white children, protected by a white friend of her father, and her face bore witness to the obvious fact that she was not precisely happy. The picture showed the situation in a nutshell because those who appeared in it were directly affected by the Federal Court order, the children themselves."[61] Following this, Arendt recounted a number of questions that hinged on putting herself, via imagination, "in the place" of others—that is, in the South—and considering what she would do as a black mother, then what she would do as a white mother in that particular context. Finally, and apparently after the first answers developed, she asked what distinguished between "the so-called Southern way of life" and "the American way of life" with regard to the question of race. She characterized the account that emerged through this process as a repetition of the "essential points" of her original article "on a different, less theoretical level."[62]

Regarded in light of Arendt's later accounts of judging, this description encapsulates as a written memory what is elaborated in the lectures on Kant's aesthetics as the "two mental operations involved in judgment." First is "the operation of the imagination," in which one judges things not actually present—things "removed from one's outward senses" that as images or representations nonetheless become objects for one's "inner senses." Through such representation the "operation of imagination prepares the object for 'the operation of reflection.' And this second operation—the operation of reflection—is the actual activity of judging something."[63] Further, and again resonant with Arendt's treatment of Kant, specific acts of imagination narrated in the reply instance her notion of "impartiality" as a practice of "enlarged thinking." Through imaginative thinking from the standpoints of others—literally, that is, from "the place where they stand, the conditions they are subject to"—"enlarged thinking" generates a series of comparative reflections "on the particular conditions" of those standpoints, reflections that enable one, finally, "to arrive at one's own 'general standpoint.'" This "general standpoint," however, emerges neither as a claim to truth nor as a claim to "know" what the other thinks or feels, but rather as an articulation of one's *doxa*, one's opinion, as to the generalities pertinent to the case at hand.[64]

The activities Arendt here recounts as judging find condensed articulation elsewhere as well. Indeed, in "Truth and Politics" they are identified with the representative character of specifically *political* thinking as a process of forming opinions:

> I form an opinion by considering a given issue from different viewpoints, by making present to my mind the standpoints of those who are absent; that is, I represent them. This process of representation does not blindly adopt the actual views of those who stand somewhere else, and hence look upon the world from a different perspective; this is a question neither of empathy, as though I tried to be or to feel like somebody else, nor of counting noses and joining a ma-

jority but of being and thinking in my own identity where I am not. The more people's standpoints I have present in my mind while I am pondering a given issue, and the better I can imagine how I would feel and think if I were in their place, the stronger will be my capacity for representative thinking and the more valid my final conclusions, my opinion.[65]

The impartiality associated with such "opinion"—what in the Kant lectures appears as "one's own general standpoint"—is a matter of degree rather than an achieved condition. Generated by enlarged or representative thinking, it is not a position of neutrality, not a "higher standpoint" with a claim to settle matters in dispute, but an exertion of imagination that demands leaving one's private interests behind.[66] Enlarged thinking "means that one trains one's imagination to go visiting," that one abstracts from the contingent circumstances of personal profit or advantage—but for Arendt the "impartiality" approached by such thinking is at best no more than "a viewpoint from which to look upon, to watch, to form judgments."[67]

Thus construed, judging appears as a sort of mental practice, a mode of intellectual self-discipline or self-formation that enables one to assess the particulars of the world, its words and deeds, its events great and small, without subsuming them under general rules. But Arendt's rendering of judgment goes beyond this by complicating it—specifically, by implicating the judging subject not simply in the affirmation but in the production and reproduction of a common world. On the one hand, from the standpoint of the public world, the assessments and opinions arrived at through reflective judgment are only the first step. As we noted earlier, from Arendt's perspective judging, like reasoning, is not self-sufficient but is meant "to get into community with others."[68] Or, as she put it in another place, "judging . . . realizes thinking, makes it manifest in the world of appearances, where I am never alone."[69] Merely having an opinion differs little from having a fantasy; without worldly involvement with others, without communication in speech or writing, such opinions never find validation through the exposure of public testing. On the other hand, although Arendt indeed identified "the actual activity of judging something" with "the operation of reflection," this was but the second of two mental operations involved in judgment. Reflective judgment doesn't stand on its own, for its objects are "prepared" by a preceding operation, "the operation of imagination." While the first of these complications points back to Arendt's conception of public discourse, the second points elsewhere, to the workings of "imagination" in the activities of the judging self. It is the latter of these that will concern me here.

We briefly considered imagination in relation to representative thinking when, in the Little Rock example, we noted Arendt's description of imagining herself into the South, first as a black mother, then as a white mother. But there is a prior and quite noteworthy aspect of imagination in Arendt's treatment of judging, and that is her account of what is entailed by imagination's capacity to "make present what is absent" through representation.[70] Imagination, in this account, transforms worldly objects of perception into images and representations. Any particular image, however, elicits not simply reflection but an effect analogous to that elicited by objects of the "discriminatory" or "private" senses of taste and smell—an "it-pleases-or-displeases-me" that Arendt, speaking of those "private" senses, describes as "immediate and overwhelming." In short, it "arouses one's pleasure or displeasure." This effect is not yet the activity of judging but is its preliminary preparation. Through representation, Arendt suggests, "the operation of imagination has made the absent immediately present to one's inner sense, and this inner sense is discriminatory by definition." The immediate "it-pleases" or "it-displeases" registers a choice, but, she continues, "this choice is itself subject to still another choice: one can approve or disapprove of the very fact of *pleasing*."[71] One's feelings of pleasure or displeasure in the images of imagination, in other words, are themselves subject to approbation or disapprobation in the activity of reflection.[72]

The question this raises for Arendt is how one is to choose between approbation or disapprobation. Here, one might say, in the theater of one's mind, reflective judgment regards the pleasure or displeasure elicited by an image rather like Cicero's audience views a performance—that is, as something that confirms or violates the "common sense" of propriety or decorum. This drama, however, remains private, as if the modern discovery of subjectivity had not only driven decorum inward, into the interiority of individual consciousness, but also transformed it from the presumptive immediacy of a common response into a question that the judging self must put to itself. That one's pleasure or displeasure in an image reports itself without being summoned is here neither a marker of one's community sense nor a confirmation of propriety. Rather, as an object of reflective judgment, it is an occasion for reflective examination, an occasion for considering the extent to which one's immediate response is an appropriate response to the particular image that incited it. The criterion Arendt advances to guide these considerations is "communicability or publicness," and the basis for deciding what is or is not communicable is what, in Arendt's lexicon, has to do with "common sense."[73]

Common sense in this context, however, is not a preexisting standard. It is not antecedent to judgments, not something applied rulelike to organize or govern a particular, but something *appealed to:* as an "extra sense . . . that fits us into a community," it is what judgment "appeals to in everyone."[74] Something unusual has happened here, as if Cicero's "practical sagacity"—that is, the sense of what might be appropriate to a particular occasion—has reappeared, in the interiority or privacy of the judging subject, in the process of judging the communicability of one's feelings. As an element of the activity of reflection, however, such sagacity is assisted by the practice of "enlarged thinking," and in this regard Arendt's rewriting of *deceat prudentiae* constitutes an inward preparation for the sort of public enunciation tapped by Cicero's usage of the phrase. Imaginatively visiting the place of others, one checks one's initial pleasure or displeasure in an image by considering it from the standpoints of places where one is not, and in so doing attempts to distance one's political judgments from the involuntary immediacy of the it-pleases-or-displeases-me. The latter, "which as a feeling seems so utterly private," is transformed by reflection into something that is "open to communication." Again, what emerges from this process is one's own opinion, but its communicability has nothing to do with the expectation that that opinion is a finished product, much less that it conforms either to a preexisting cultural consensus or to the weaker standard of majority opinion. Refusing the posture of truth, it also does not pose itself as something that anyone who thinks rightly, be they few or many, must find compelling. Rather, its communicability is revealed in the activity of its public articulation—that is, in the "persuasive activity" of "wooing" or "courting" the agreement of others by appealing to the "community sense."[75]

Drawing these various observations together, we might characterize Arendt's writings on Little Rock as one prominent public face of this process of judging. As an exemplar of the proprieties of judging that she identified with political thinking, their claim on the reader is an invitation to engagement rather than an appeal to truth. In effect—

and here recalling Arendt's linkage of opinion to a very specific mode of public discourse—these writings present themselves as an attempt "to communicate and expose to the test of others" what she discovered in the solitude of thought. Given what we've seen of her critics' responses, that attempt clearly failed; but the question to be asked here and now, I think, is what to make of this fact. It is, of course, possible to read that failure through the lens of Arendt's biography. Her opinions on Little Rock, so construed, reflect her childhood relationship to her mother as a favored image of the family, her experience of racial prohibitions in German marriage laws, as well as her self-confessed unfamiliarity with the American South, and her inability to understand racial prejudice in the United States more generally. But although such considerations quite plausibly identify personal and cultural sources for the content of Arendt's views, they leave unaddressed the intensity with which her reflections were repudiated by her contemporary interlocutors. Neither the factual claim that Arendt's views were different from some or most or even all others at the time, nor the inference that her views were reflections of her life, accounts for the extent to which they were publicly regarded as so thoroughly unacceptable.

By considering the chasm between Arendt and her critics as a distance enacted by disparate proprieties of political judgment, the apparent incommunicability of her opinions can be transposed into a different sort of question. To the extent that decorum operates through tacit understandings of what is fitting or appropriate—to the extent, that is, that its expectations tend to go without saying—its proprieties become most noticeable only in their violation. Viewed in these terms, what I've described as a clash between apposite images of public debate and alternative proprieties of judgment appeared as an event in public discourse, an event in which Arendt's violation of proprieties was met with visceral protestations of displeasure, and an event, finally, that on the part of her critics manifested itself not only as a refusal of her thoughts but as a refusal of her way of thinking as well. Both, from the critics' perspective, were equally out of order. In this light the question is not why Arendt's opinions were out of order but what sort of order they were perceived to transgress. Here, we might say, the issue is not her difference from her respondents but the difference between them.

Political judgment, for Arendt's critics, was a matter of applying rules and principles to particular cases. In the case of Little Rock, this entailed the application of the rule of equality, either as a universal moral principle or as a basic constitutional value. Politics, so understood, is a department of morality and law, whereas "society" is the "matter" to be formed and organized in accordance with the proper principles. Political argument, in this view, is a process of reasoning from principles, a process requiring clear definitions and consistent logic. In terms of these expectations, Arendt's thinking from examples, her attention to particulars, her tacking back and forth across indistinct distinctions, and her reliance on narration could only seem perverse. But if Arendt's public judging appeared bizarre to her critics, their posture from her point of view was both familiar and problematic. As she put it some years before the Little Rock controversy, "[W]herever common sense, the political sense par excellence, fails us in our need for understanding, we are all too likely to accept logicality for its substitute, because the capacity for logical reasoning is also common to us all."[76] The distinction between common sense and logic, however, carries in its train a distinction between understanding and logical reasoning that, in Arendt's lexicon, was nothing if not politically fraught. Common sense, she noted, presupposes a common world "into which we all fit and where we can live together because we possess one sense which controls and adjusts all strictly particular sense data to those of all others." Recast in terms of her later concern with judgment, common sense is that public political sense which emerges and evolves through public discourse to orient its participants to the world they have in common. "Logic," on the other hand, "and all self-evidence from which logical reasoning proceeds can claim a reliability altogether independent of the world and the existence of other people." As a decorum governing public communication, its disregard for the particularities of the common world leaves the ordinary sensibilities of its actual members behind, and its "chief political characteristic is . . . a compulsory power of persuasion."

In light of this distinction, if Arendt's opinions on Little Rock still remain arguable, the proprieties of her judging nonetheless bear the mark of exemplarity. One may well disagree with those opinions. Some might—as Ralph Ellison did—contest the extent to which her "enlarged thinking" sufficed in the particular instance to generate politically adequate interpretations of the meanings others attached to their actions. But, by the decorum of Arendt's political judgment, such disagreement is precisely the point. Indeed, on her account it is the very stuff of political discourse. What she referred to as getting "into community with others" was not a matter of conforming to a common mind; much less was it a matter of submitting to the self-evident truth of a disembodied reason and of making the world over in its image. In the words of her "Reflections," whatever one might think of the information they convey, the odor of judgment still lingers. Counteracting the pride of logic and recommending themselves to the understanding of a later age, her words were in this regard perhaps the right words after all.

Notes

In addition to benefiting from the challenging conversations among the participants at the conference for which this essay was initially prepared, I am indebted to others as well. Though the writing of the essay eventually led elsewhere, George Kateb's criticisms of Arendt's account of conscience in political judgment provided its original incitement. Discussions with Bonnie Honig and Linda Zerilli helped refine my focus on exemplarity, and Richard Flathman's comments on an early draft provoked further thought on the question of propriety. On questions of Ciceronian rhetoric, Renaissance exemplarity, and Latin translation, Nancy Streuver has been both invaluable in print and generous in person.

1. Francesco Guicciardini, *Maxims and Reflections (Ricordi)*, trans. Mario Domandi (Philadelphia: University of Pennsylvania Press, 1965), 69 (no. 110).

2. Felix Gilbert, *Machiavelli and Guicciardini: Politics and History in Sixteenth-Century Florence* (New York: Norton, 1965), 300–1.

3. Jürgen Habermas, "Hannah Arendt's Communications Concept of Power," *Social Research* 44 (1977): 23.

4. Hannah Arendt, "The Concept of History," in *Between Past and Future* (New York: Viking-Penguin, 1968), 48–49.

5. Ibid., 49.

6. Hannah Arendt, *Lectures on Kant's Political Philosophy*, ed. Ronald Beiner (Chicago: University of Chicago Press, 1982), 76; and Arendt, "The Crisis in Culture," in *Between Past and Future*, 221.

7. Hannah Arendt, "'Eichmann in Jerusalem': An Exchange of Letters between Gershom Scholem and Hannah Arendt," *Encounter*, January 1964, 53.

8. Arendt, "The Crisis in Culture," 221.

9. Throughout these remarks, I am indebted to Timothy Hampton's *Writing from History: The Rhetoric of Exemplarity in Renaissance Literature* (Ithaca: Cornell University Press, 1990); Victoria Kahn's *Rhetoric, Prudence, and Skepticism in the Renaissance* (Ithaca: Cornell University Press, 1985); and Nancy Streuver's *The Language of History in the Renaissance* (Princeton: Princeton University Press, 1970).

10. Hampton, *Writing from History*, 66. The preceding passages open the sixth chapter of Machiavelli's *The Prince*. The translation is Hampton's.

11. J. G. A. Pocock, *The Machiavellian Moment: Florentine Political Thought and the Atlantic Republican Tradition* (Princeton: Princeton University Press, 1975), 180, cited in Hampton, *Writing from History*, 67.

12. Hampton, *Writing from History*, 69.

13. As Victoria Kahn puts it, for Machiavelli "the point . . . is not that the reader

should imitate any single example of the text . . . , but rather that he should imitate the author's judgments of decorum." There is, she argues, "a pedagogical claim" and the "conviction that it is possible, however indirectly, to educate the judgment" (*Rhetoric, Prudence, and Skepticism*, 187).

14. From Arendt's closing lecture in a course titled "Basic Moral Propositions," quoted in Ronald Beiner, "Interpretive Essay," in *Hannah Arendt: Lectures on Kant's Political Philosophy* (Chicago: University of Chicago Press, 1982), 113.

15. For a discussion of the anxieties attending Renaissance thinkers' impressions of the gulf between the ancient world and their own, see Thomas M. Green, *The Light in Troy: Imitation and Discovery in Renaissance Poetry* (New Haven: Yale University Press, 1982).

16. Hannah Arendt, "Walter Benjamin," in *Men in Dark Times* (New York: Harcourt Brace Jovanovich, 1955), 193.

17. Ibid.

18. Ibid., 205–6.

19. I am aware of no better example of this than Arendt's response to Scholem's criticisms of *Eichmann in Jerusalem*. "What confuses you," she writes, "is that my arguments and my approach are different from what you are used to; in other words, the trouble is that I am independent. By this I mean, on the one hand, that I do not belong to any organization and always speak only for myself, and on the other hand, that I have great confidence in Lessing's *selbstdenken* for which, I think, no ideology, no public opinion, and no 'convictions' can ever be a substitute. Whatever objections you may have to the results, you won't understand them unless you realize that they are really my own and nobody else's" ("'Eichmann in Jerusalem,'" 55).

20. Arendt's view of those who refused the proprieties of such "thinking in company" is succinctly captured by the terms of her refusal to engage Melvin Tumin's criticism of her "Reflections on Little Rock": "Mr. Tumin," she notes flatly, "has put himself outside the scope of discussion and discourse through the tone he adopted in his rebuttal" (see "A Reply to Critics," *Dissent*, spring 1959, 179). Tumin's commentary, titled "Pie in the Sky" and published with her original article (*Dissent*, winter 1959), indeed is distinctive in its capacity to blend the splenetic with the sanctimonious under the sign of the "basic facts of sociology and history" (65).

21. Elisabeth Young-Bruehl, *Hannah Arendt: For Love of the World* (New Haven: Yale University Press, 1982), 75. Indeed—and suggestive of the perils of admonishing modern horses—Young-Bruehl goes on to observe that "Arendt began her publishing career as she ended it forty years later—as a burr under scholarly saddles" (75).

22. Arendt, *Lectures on Kant's Political Philosophy*, 40.

23. Ibid., 39.

24. Ibid.; see also 55–60. A more extensive account of world citizenship appears in Arendt's essay "Karl Jaspers: World Citizen?" in *Men in Dark Times*, 81–94.

25. Arendt, *Lectures on Kant's Political Philosophy*, 39–40.

26. Ibid., 40.

27. Hannah Arendt, *The Life of the Mind*, ed. Mary McCarthy (New York: Harcourt Brace Jovanovich, 1978), 5.

28. Hannah Arendt, "Thinking and Moral Considerations," *Social Research* 38 (autumn 1971): 417–46.

29. For the issue of conscience, see Arendt's "Civil Disobedience," in *Crises of the Republic* (New York: Harcourt Brace Jovanovich, 1972), 51–102; regarding pity and compassion, see her *On Revolution* (New York: Penguin, 1965), especially chapter 2, "The Social Question." For a searching criticism of Arendt's insistence on distinguishing

political judgment from such things, see George Kateb, *Hannah Arendt: Politics, Conscience, Evil* (Totowa, N.J.: Rowan and Allanheld, 1984).

30. Two exceptions to this are Ann Norton, "Heart of Darkness," and Jean Bethke Elshtain, "Political Children," both in *Feminist Interpretations of Hannah Arendt,* ed. Bonnie Honig (University Park: Pennsylvania State University Press, 1995).

31. In "A Reply to Critics," Arendt imagines what she would do if she were a white mother in the South: "If . . . I were strongly convinced that the situation in the South could be materially helped by integrated education, I would try—perhaps with the help of the Quakers or some other body of like-minded citizens—to organize a new school for white and colored children and to run it like a pilot project, as a means to persuade other white parents to change their attitudes" (180).

32. See Young-Bruehl, *Hannah Arendt,* 309–18; or Margaret Canovan, *Hannah Arendt: A Reinterpretation of Her Political Thought* (Cambridge: Cambridge University Press, 1992), 243.

33. Although their comments were not directed to Arendt's reflections on Little Rock in particular, a number of writers have noted more broadly the instability of these distinctions in her work. See, for example, Hannah Pitkin, "Justice: On Relating Public and Private," *Political Theory* 9 (1981): 327–52; Norma Maruzzi, "The Social Question, the Mask, and the Masquerade," in "Speaking through the Mask: The Construction of the Body in the Political Thought of Hannah Arendt" (Ph.D. diss., Johns Hopkins University, 1990); Bonnie Honig, "Toward an Agonistic Feminism: Hannah Arendt and the Politics of Identity," in *Feminists Theorize the Political,* ed. Judith Butler and Joan Scott (New York: Routledge, 1992); and Seyla Benhabib, "Models of Public Space: Hannah Arendt, the Liberal Tradition, and Jürgen Habermas" and "Judgment and the Moral Foundations of Politics in Hannah Arendt's Thought," both in *Situating the Self: Gender, Community, and Postmodernism in Contemporary Ethics* (New York: Routledge, 1992).

34. Hannah Arendt, *The Human Condition* (Chicago: University of Chicago Press, 1958), 76.

35. Ibid., 26.

36. Ibid. Leading into this account, Arendt offers the exemplar of the Homeric Achilles as "the doer of great deeds and the speaker of great words," a reference, it should be noted, to Homer's *poetic representation* of Achilles. As is so often the case in her work, this "pearl" is then juxtaposed to a modern analogue, which in turn is subjected to a heightened contrast through the citation of a further pearl, here a passage from Sophocles: "In distinction from modern understanding, such words were not considered to be great because they expressed great thoughts; on the contrary, as we know from the last lines of *Antigone,* it may be the capacity for 'great words' (*megaloi logoi*) with which reply to striking blows that will eventually teach thought in old age." The failed syntax here is clarified by the attending note: "The literal translation of the last lines of *Antigone* (1350–54) is as follows: 'But great words, counteracting [or paying back] the great blows of the overproud, teach understanding in old age'"(25).

37. David Spitz, "Politics and the Realms of Being," *Dissent,* winter 1959, 65.

38. Appreciating the possibility that readers might regard such a series as hyperbolic, what follows is a list of the specific phraseologies from which this summation was gleaned. In ibid., David Spitz contributes an extensive list of Arendt's "wrong words": "Her notion of what constitutes a valid political principle . . . testifies more to her sense of misguided courage than it does to her power of insight" (56–57); her "distinction between the political, the social, and the private life . . . collapses as soon as we attempt to specify those acts which affect *only* the individual" (57); she proliferates Mill's "artifi-

cial and false" distinctions (58); and she has a "superficial" notion of federalism, also
described as "fictional" or "nonsense" (59). Spitz also singles out Arendt's "perverse
use" of the terms "liberty" and "equality" (60), her "odd notion of freedom, not to
speak of human values"(61), her "specious idea of freedom" (61), and her "strange conception of the mob," "strange plea for natural inequality," and "strange concern for diversity" (62). In Spitz's view, she also misunderstands the distinction between "the political as distinct from the philosophical arena" (63). Melvin Tumin opens his "Pie in the
Sky" with the observation that Arendt's essay is "a horrible joke," a collection of "metaphysical mumbo-jumbo" with a "disregard for basic facts of sociology and history"
(65). It represents "some new Arendt-type logic" with "no affinity for evidence and
proof" (66); "How could she have written this?" he asks. Noting what he takes as obvious and multiple contradictions, he says she is "of three minds" on whether racial differences can be "eradicated," all of which rest on no more evidence than "an Arendt-
type force . . . of conviction" (67). Her words showing "minimal respect for the facts,"
"the best with which we can credit [her] is . . . ignorance" (68). She has, he continues, a
"curious" way of reading newspapers and diagnosing trends (68). It is "strange that she
should use public opinion polls to inform herself . . . but not strange that she should use
the worst polls and misinterpret them through exaggeration," and all this misunderstanding and exaggeration appears "in true Arendt style" (69). Her "ignorance of facts"
serves "the interest of shoring up her decrepit metaphysics with even more decrepit non-
facts"; we cannot be "expected to take her distinctions between the public and private
domains of life seriously," nor can we take her "conceptions of the separate terrains and
domains of society seriously. They lead to conclusions which simply defy logic and elementary human decency" (70). When the *Commentary* editorial board refused to print
Arendt's "Reflections" in 1958, Sidney Hook recast his original critique in more general
terms, excising direct reference to Arendt's original. Yet though her name never appears
in his "Democracy and Desegregation" (*The New Leader*, April 21, 1958), a good deal
of it is still clearly directed at her, for instance, his criticism of the failure to distinguish
between "prejudice" and "discrimination" (5) and to understand the difference between
"discriminating against" and "discriminating between" (12), as well as his claim that
"vague distinctions between the political, the public, the social, and the personal or private" have "everything mixed up" (11). This, in my view, is a reasonable selection of the
instances in which Arendt's three initial critics made a point of refusing her words.

    39. Hannah Arendt, "Reflections on Little Rock," *Dissent*, winter 1959, 46.

    40. The account is provided by Young-Bruehl, *Hannah Arendt*, 316–17.

    41. Arendt, *The Human Condition*, 25 n. 8. The continuation of this note offers an
additional example of the "ancient connection between speech and thought from which
our notion of expressing thought through words is absent": "An anecdote, reported by
Plutarch, may illustrate the connection between acting and speaking on a much lower
level. A man approached Demosthenes and related how terribly he had been
beaten. 'But you,' said Demosthenes, 'suffered nothing of what you tell me.' Whereupon
the other raised his voice and cried out: 'I suffered nothing?' 'Now,' said Demosthenes,
'I hear the voice of somebody who was injured and who suffered'" 26 n. 8.

    42. Hook, "Democracy and Desegregation," 10.

    43. Ibid., 12.

    44. Spitz, "The Realms of Being," 60.

    45. Tumin, "Pie in the Sky," 67.

    46. Arendt, "A Reply to Critics," 179.

    47. Ibid., 179, 180, 181, respectively.

    48. "There is no such thing as society constituting 'a somewhat hybrid realm' be-

tween the political and the private. The political and the private are not distinct and separate entities; nor do they exist apart from society; they are intrinsically and inextricably a part of society" (Spitz, "Realms of Being," 58).

49. Others have offered interpretations of this theory, most notably Maurizio Passerin d'Entrèves in chapter 3 of *The Political Philosophy of Hannah Arendt* (New York: Routledge, 1994); and Benhabib, "Judgment and the Moral Foundations."

50. Arendt, *Lectures on Kant's Political Philosophy*, 63-64, quoting Cicero, *De oratore* 3.195. Arendt's translation here, which is probably her own, differs subtly but not insignificantly from E. W. Sutton's (Loeb Classical Library [1942; reprint, Cambridge: Harvard University Press, 1992]), most notably by rendering *tacito quodam sensu* as "some silent sense" rather than Sutton's unduly modernized "some subconscious instinct," and by rendering *sunt in communibus infixa sensibus* as "rooted in common sense" rather than Sutton's "rooted deep in the general sensibility." In both cases her phrasing is considerably less psychologizing. I am grateful to Nancy Streuver and Salvatore Camporeale for consultation regarding Latin translations.

51. Arendt, *Lectures on Kant's Political Philosophy*, 64.

52. Cicero, *De oratore* 3.177-78. Sutton's rather anachronistic rendering of *animorum motum* as "influencing the mind" misses the Aristotelian tenor of Cicero's phrasing.

53. Ibid., 3.191, 194. On Cicero's image of the ideal orator, developed in this work at 1.45-73, the arts of political speech required as well the cultivation of a broader culture, including philosophy.

54. Ibid., 3.195.

55. Hence Cicero's criticism of Stoics: not only are their philosophical positions out of keeping with political life, but

> even the style of their discourse, though possibly subtle and undoubtedly penetrating, yet for an orator is bald, unfamiliar, jarring on the ear of the public, devoid of clarity, fullness and spirit, while at the same time of a character that makes it quite impossible to employ it in public speaking; for the Stoics hold a different view of good and bad from all their fellow citizens or rather from all other nations, and give a different meaning to "honour," "disgrace," "reward," "punishment"—whether correctly or otherwise does not concern us now, but if we were to adopt their terminology we should never be able to express our meaning intelligibly about anything. (Ibid., 3.66)

56. Ibid., 3.196, 197 (*theatre tota reclamant,* in Sutton, is "protests to a man").

57. Ibid., 3.211.

58. Ibid., 3.212.

59. For Richard Lanham, decorum in this sense "becomes not only a rhetorical criterion but a general test of acculturation." See his *Handlist of Rhetorical Terms*, 2d ed. (Berkeley: University of California Press, 1990), 46. Whatever purchase this might have on Cicero's perspective, Arendt's distinction between action and behavior might complicate the matter by virtue of its emphasis on the beginning of something new.

60. Immanuel Kant, *Critique of Judgment*, trans. J. H. Bernard (New York: Hafner, 1951), 135 (no. 40). In keeping with his distinction between the realms of science, aesthetics, and morality, Kant begins here with a differentiation between commonplace notions of "a sense of truth," "a sense of decorum," and "a sense of justice."

61. Arendt, "A Reply to Critics," 179.

62. Ibid.

63. Arendt, *Lectures on Kant's Political Philosophy*, 68.

64. Ibid., 44–45. As Arendt notes, this "is not the generality of the concept" under which one can subsume specific instances, but is, "on the contrary, closely connected with particulars, with the particular standpoints one has to go through" to achieve "one's own 'general standpoint'" (44–45).

65. Arendt, "Truth and Politics," in *Between Past and Future*, 241. Recalling Gaya-tri Spivak's interesting discussion of two senses of "representation," I take it that in imaginatively "representing" the standpoints of others, Arendt means to "re-present" (*darstellen*), to show or depict in her own identity how the world would look from those positions, not to "represent" (*vertreten*), to substitute or stand proxy for those who or-dinarily inhabit them. See Gayatri Spivak, "Can the Subaltern Speak?" in *Marxism and the Interpretation of Culture*, ed. Cary Nelson and Lawrence Grossberg (Urbana and Chicago: University of Illinois Press, 1988), esp. 275–79.

66. Arendt, *Lectures on Kant's Political Philosophy*, 42–43; and "Truth and Politics," 242.

67. Arendt, *Lectures on Kant's Political Philosophy*, 43–44.

68. Ibid., 39–40.

69. Arendt, "Thinking and Moral Considerations," 446.

70. Arendt, *Lectures on Kant's Political Philosophy*, 65. My discussion draws on 64–65 of this text.

71. Ibid., 69.

72. Arendt's displeasure, we might say, remains palpable in her reference to the *Life* photograph, particularly in her description of the black student as "persecuted by a mob of white children" ("A Reply to Critics," 179).

73. Arendt, *Lectures on Kant's Political Philosophy*, 69.

74. Ibid., 70, 72.

75. Ibid., 72. In Arendt's lectures for courses at the New School and Chicago, this shift from the feeling of pleasure or displeasure in an image to the approbation or dis-approbation entailed in judging is connected with enlarged thinking as a move beyond subjectivity:

> Suppose I look at a specific slum dwelling and I perceive in this particular building the general notion which it does not exhibit di-rectly, the notion of poverty and misery. I arrive at this notion by representing to myself how I would feel if I had to live there, that is, I try to think in the place of the slum-dweller. The judgment I shall come up with will by no means necessarily be the same as that of the inhabitants, whom time and hopelessness may have dulled to the outrage of their condition, but it will become for my further judging of these matters an outstanding example to which I refer. . . . Furthermore, while I take account of others when judging, this does not mean that I conform in my judgment to those of others. I still speak with my own voice and I do not count noses in order to arrive at what I think is right. But my judgment will no longer be subjective either. (*Lectures on Kant's Political Philosophy*, "Inter-pretive Essay," 107–8 and n. 35, quoting Arendt's "Some Ques-tions of Moral Philosophy" [lecture delivered at the New School, March 24, 1965]; also in "Basic Moral Propositions" [lecture de-livered at the University of Chicago], Hannah Arendt Papers, con-tainer 40, p. 024648, Library of Congress)

76. Hannah Arendt, "Understanding and Politics," *Partisan Review*, July–August 1953, 387. The following passages are from this source as well.

Three

Propriety and Provocation in Arendt's Political Aesthetic

Susan Bickford

Kirstie McClure and Kim Curtis intend to reclaim the specifically political and ethical components of Hannah Arendt's "aesthetic turn." Their essays work on multiple levels: they tell us what we can learn from Arendt's thinking about aesthetics, and they also display a certain kind of artistry, or aesthetic judgment, in their very composition. Further, these two essays share a substantive insight, which is that the aesthetic orientation for Arendt is characterized by a particular quality of relatedness to others. McClure addresses this in terms of judgment; Curtis, in terms of action. Their work enables us to think about human interaction under conditions of plurality without falling into that curious but common opposition of the performative and the communicative aspects of such interaction.

McClure argues that we can learn about the political meaning of Arendtian judgment by bringing together Arendt's explicit writings on judgment with an example of one of Arendt's own political judgments. McClure has not only written about Arendt's method of exemplary reflection, then, but her essay in fact provides us with an example of it—and this time the exemplar is Arendt herself. McClure suggests that we understand the controversy between Arendt and her critics about her "Reflections on Little Rock" as a clash between different understandings of the character of public discourse and between different "proprieties" of political judgment. Let me briefly review the distinction that McClure identifies. Arendt's critics treated public discourse as the clash of firm and fixed opinions, what McClure calls a "war of words." The kind of judgment they regarded as appropriate—the propriety they followed—was one that interpreted specific events through the lens of general principles and communicated them through logical argumentation; in McClure's summary, "logic arbitrates meaning, principle precedes prudence, general rules command particular circumstance." Conversely (or, as her critics perceived it, perversely), Arendt's own "propriety of judgment" involved attentiveness to particulars, thinking from examples and from the standpoints of specific others.

McClure shows us that, in a variety of mutually reinforcing ways, Arendt's image of public discourse and judgment was the result of her commitment to a crucial aspect of the human condition: the togetherness of many distinctive humans. It is this commitment that underlies both Arendt's performance of exemplary thinking and her analysis of "opinion." Arendt's own judgments, McClure argues, were made through the double movement of exemplary thinking: choosing and critically culling insights from an exemplar, and then using the resulting illumination to scrutinize contemporary events and assumptions. Arendt's purpose in publicly performing this movement is itself dual: to say what she thinks and to urge others to "think thusly" in making judgments.

Exemplary thinking thus involves a kind of traveling, which has its parallel in the concept of "going visiting" that Arendt invokes in her discussion of opinion formation, or judgment. Opinions rely on communicability, or publicity. No opinion formation is possible, Arendt says, without what Kant called the "test of free and open examination." Opinion formation thus involves considering how we might provide communicable reasons for our judgment. And we figure that out by "going visiting": imagining ourselves in the positions of those others to whom we want to give an account. Such an account is intended "not to prove, but to be able to say how one came to an opinion and for what reasons one formed it."[1] The double movement of exemplary thinking is roughly echoed in the two acts of judgment: imagination, which elicits discrimination, the "it-pleases-or-displeases-me"; and reflection, in which we figure out whether we approve of our pleasure or displeasure through making present in our minds the "standpoints" of others.

By probing Arendt's specific understanding of opinion, McClure highlights what I think is one of the most fruitful political and theoretical resources Arendt's work offers us. Contemporary complaints about the political process often are focused on how the incessant use of public opinion polls distorts our conception of what political thinking is and diverts our attention from substantive problems. Arendt's understanding of opinion could be a source for theoretical intervention in political discourse, a way to reconceptualize the public meaning of "opinion" by questioning what opinions are, how they are arrived at, and what's necessary for something to count as an opinion. Opinions in the Arendtian sense require the presence of diverse perspectives actively oriented toward some common worldly object. A genuinely public opinion, as opposed to the simple aggregation of attitudes, requires us "to look upon the same world from one another's standpoint, to see the same in very different and frequently opposing aspects."[2]

In McClure's discussion of Arendtian opinion formation, or judgment, the focus is on the clash between different ways of making judgments, which for McClure illuminates the role of "propriety" or "decorum" in political communication. She invokes Cicero: to be heard, we have to think about how to speak in a particular context, and to figure out what conventions of judgment we need to show we've observed. We have to appeal to "tacit understandings of appropriateness" and engage ordinary understandings of propriety. Without this attention "to the customs and conventions that undergird ways of thinking," opinions become incommunicable—as, McClure points out, Arendt's on Little Rock were. Her words were regarded by her critics as simply nonsensical, unintelligible. Still, Arendt's words may have been "the right words" from our perspective, because as worldly artifacts they throw into relief the different proprieties of judgment—for us to judge.

In judging, as Arendt so strikingly says, "one tells one's choices and chooses one's company."[3] I've always thought this quotation precisely describes Arendt's own sense of "independent" thinking. Given this committed independence, to use "propriety" or "decorum" to describe anything to do with Arendt seems to me so odd that it can only be deliberate. What can McClure mean by it? Part of the point must be to underscore the consequences of the specifically public character of judgment. We can think and judge only "in company," in the presence of others, and thus we must always be aware of what "modalities of judgment" are appropriate in that company, to those particular others. By highlighting the clash between these ways of judging, McClure is perhaps also trying to give us a tool for understanding certain kinds of political conflict.

But I confess I'm unconvinced that talking in terms of decorum, or "proprieties of judgment," helps; I'm wondering, in fact, if it might be something we want to avoid. Because we might also think of the Little Rock controversy as illuminating the tension *between* propriety and judgment—that is, between following norms of appropriateness that would make our opinions communicable, or judging in a different mode and risking incommunicability. I want to argue that most political action involves being between these two options somehow, or figuring out how not to get trapped in that either/or. And that "figuring out" has to do in part with how we think about those others to whom we are communicating.

Let me say more about this by calling up one of my own exemplars, from Thucydides. I've been absorbed lately by the figure of Nicias, particularly as he addresses the Athenian assembly as they debate whether to proceed with the Sicilian invasion (which invasion will turn out to be the downfall of Athens). Thucydides portrays Athenian public discourse as already pretty corrupt (this is after the Mitylene debate, after the Melian conference). Nicias is trying to figure how, in these circumstances, to persuade the assembly not to embark on the invasion. He knows he can't speak in a way they want to hear, or say what they want to hear; he and they think and judge too differently: "against you any words of mine would be weak enough."[4] Yet he doesn't give up, go home, turn away disgusted, refuse to engage in a corrupt public discourse. Nor does he insist on speaking in an abstractly principled way that does not attend to the perspectives of the assembly. Rather, he tries to convince the assembly to give up the invasion by arguing in terms he thinks they will find compelling. When that fails, he tries to dissuade the assembly (or at least mitigate the danger the Athenians would face) by arguing for an enormous and heavily armed force. And then, of course, he ends up leading an expedition to which he is opposed.

What I find so moving about Nicias is that he's no hero. He's no Pericles, who could anger the many, scold them, and still persuade them to act as he advises. And in some ways, Thucydides tells us, it's

Nicias's own overly cautious character that exacerbates the difficulties the Athenian forces later find themselves in. But there Nicias is, knowing that his real judgment won't be heard yet trying to figure out what to say that *could* be heard, what would be the best advice under the circumstances, and how to convey it. Josiah Ober tells us that the ritual question with which the Athenian assembly was opened was "Who of the Athenians has advice to give?"[5] Imagine how troubled Nicias must have been as he rose to answer.

McClure might contend that this situation is one not of different *modalities* of judgment but of disparate substantive opinions. But surely the mode influences and restricts the content in consequential ways; I think this is clear in McClure's own analysis of the exchange regarding Little Rock. What counts as a valid consideration in the practice of judgment is inextricably bound up with what counts as a valid judgment. This may not be so much a criticism of McClure as it is a claim that her argument presents us with further complexities of political judgment. Nicias's position, I would argue, is precisely the position that is characteristic of being in public, not (or at least not only) because the polity is corrupt but because we live in a diverse society with multiple speech communities, multiple conventions of communication and judgment. And public argument is likely, almost inevitably, to bring together those with different conventions. In such conditions, the opinion that we've come to and now want to test by free and open examination may be booed off the stage as an inappropriate performance of an unacceptable opinion. We may choose our company by telling our choices, but we are quite likely to be telling them to a company whose company we didn't choose and whose proprieties we do not believe in.

Nicias was trying to figure out what to do in precisely these kinds of conditions. How to tell his choices to a company whose character had changed, a company with whom he couldn't identify and yet with whom he was bound up? A difficult situation, certainly; but remember that although Nicias may have been troubled, he was not hopeless or defeated. He did not refuse public debate under these circumstances, he did not retreat into silence or try to maintain a self-absorbed kind of purity. He made the effort of offering the best advice he could. I think Nicias made that effort not just because he thought he was capable of talking in terms that the Athenians would take seriously, but also because he thought the citizens themselves were capable of a certain effort of attention. In other words, the perspectives of the Athenians (in terms of substance *or* standards of judgment) were not fixed and immutable. It was not a choice between adhering to the right proprieties or speaking unintelligibly, and Nicias was not trapped in this either/or precisely because he regarded the Athenians as active listeners who themselves were in the process of forming their opinions. This is, as McClure has argued, an Arendtian understanding of public debate; but it's an *Aristotelian* conception of rhetoric. Aristotle says that of course we have to pay attention to the conventions (and constitutions) of those with whom we are arguing. We need to take into account all kinds of things about our listeners and about the context in which we're speaking. But an orator is speaking to creatures who themselves possess some degree of practical reason, who are active in this sense. So Aristotle argues for the persuasiveness of devices that challenge an audience. (One strategy he recommends is to contradict common opinion but in a way that shows one's own moral qualities.) He also suggests using language in strange and surprising ways, because it's pleasing to the listener to learn to see something in a different way. Finally, he asserts that speakers must be sure to exhibit fair-mindedness; even if it means disagreeing with one's audience, it will be more persuasive in the long run.[6]

What I think we learn from this pursuit of McClure's themes is that judgment is subject to specific conditions once it is in the public realm, and that what speakers and listeners expect of each other matters. (Otherwise, Nicias might well have given up and gone home or been booed off the stage.) These expectations are never neatly fulfilled or utterly harmonious, precisely because of the diversity of opinions, multiple conventions of judgment and communication, and the general unpredictability of action. A central source of conflict in politics is thus what we might describe in Arendtian terms as the clash between appearance and reception: we want to appear in a particular way to particular others, but those others will judge for themselves in unpredictable ways. What we want to communicate may not be possible through the modes of performance available; and what we thought we wanted to say may not be what we are perceived to have said. Performance and communication are thus intertwined in unavoidable and discordant ways in the practice of making political judgments in the presence of actual others.

It is precisely this central paradoxical quality of the public interaction of plural others that is obscured by insisting on an opposition between performative action and persuasive communication. Those who defend one side of the dichotomy against the other seem to agree on the opposition itself—which is to say, in the context of this volume, that it is evident in Dana Villa's essay no less than it is in Martin Jay's. By treating appearance and resistance as phenomena antithetical to intersubjectivity and dialogue, Villa undercuts his own insight that the "boundary between performance and persuasion" is not a necessary one but rather results from certain theoretical enforcements. Jay in his turn gives no reasons for why this boundary is necessary or why it needs to be so enforced (his wonderful example of the performative Rush Limbaugh notwithstanding).

It is Kim Curtis who makes the connection between performance and communication explicitly, with respect to political action, in her analysis of the way in which the aesthetic foundations of Arendt's work point to a radical democratic politics. Curtis's essay begins with the question of meaning that is the theme of this book, and she contextualizes and specifies that question by asking, why does Arendt seem to have such meaning *for us?* If, as Curtis says, Arendt is our "poet of political life," then Curtis is our poet of Arendtian politics. She gives us an analysis of Arendt's aestheticism that traces its deeply ethical character and its political implications. Her argument challenges those critics of Arendt's aestheticism who stress its immorality, amorality, or political irrelevance. And as Curtis argues for the ethical import of Arendt's aesthetics, she also points to the way in which separating the performative agonistic moments from the communicative or consensual moments ignores the complicated character of political life.

Curtis situates her argument in terms of Arendt's claim that the existence of a common world is in danger because we have lost the pillars of truth that give the world stability. Standing amid the rubble, we risk losing our "sense of reality." Our primary ethical dilemma, Curtis says, is "how to take in and remain provoked by the real." Arendt's aestheticism is a response to that dilemma, and it points not away from politics but precisely toward our need for a vigorous democratic public. We need the presence of other unique and uniquely situated beings—of "strong particular others"—to sustain our sense of and commitment to reality, which commitment is itself necessary for living in and caring for the world.

Worldly reality is intimately connected to human plurality; our sense of the real can be sustained only through the presence of others. Plurality is a central condition of human existence—it's so crucial yet so circumstantial. It can disappear under conditions of tyranny or mass society, or anytime the public realm is supplanted or destroyed. But, Curtis points out, Arendt gives some ontological stability to this plurality and, hence, an existential ground to the "passion for reality" that is central to living in the world together. As we stumble through the rubble, we have no guarantees; but, as Curtis puts it, Arendt "is suggesting that, far from being groundless, what we have is indeed the ground." We just have no bannisters to keep us from falling down. Arendt does not try to provide ontological certainty; but she does provide "ontological reassurance" rooted in an "ontology of display."

Humans share with other earthly creatures the urge to self-display, the result of appearing in a world in which others also appear, a world in which we are perceiving and perceived at the same time. Perceiving the presence of others calls forth the urge to display; thus, both reception and appearance are the phenomenal result of a world characterized by plurality, by more-than-one. In Arendt's striking phrase, which Curtis cites, "*[W]hatever can see wants to be seen, whatever can hear calls out to be heard, whatever can touch presents itself to be touched.*"[7] Reception and appearance are bound up together, or as Curtis says, they *provoke* one another: "reality in an appearing world such as ours is something born out of a highly charged mutual sensuous provocation between actors and spectators that is essentially aesthetic in nature." This aesthetic provocation animates "the potent triangle of relationships between human particularity, beauty, and permanence."

For humans, the mutual urge to self-display takes the form of self-presentation; humans do not just display, they "indicate how they *wish* to appear, what in their opinion is fit to be seen and what is not."[8] They do so primarily through speech and through perceiving the perspectives of others. The reality of the appearing world can take shape and gain solidity only through awareness of the "perceptual acts of distinct others," through knowledge of the presence and content of other perspectives. Such perception and communication establish and undergird our sense of a common world. It's important to note that this sense of a "common" world is not a result of people seeing identically; their perspectives maintain their distinctiveness rather than merging into one. I think no one has helped us understand this crucial and complicated point better than Lisa Disch, in her inspired discussion of the "cubist" character of Arendtian public space (this volume). The possibility of a common world as cubist creation is itself rooted in the urge of distinct others to self-display; in Curtis's words, "Both our ability to engender or actualize the plurality of the human condition and our ability to give human experience some degree of permanence by establishing a minimal sense of a common world depend upon the vitality of this mutual aesthetic provocation."

This conception of appearance as provoked and provocative—an "eliciting display" on which reality depends—is, I think, quite suggestive, as is Curtis's illumination of the ethical and political import of theatricality. *Provoke* has two connotations: the first indicates a kind of prodding or eliciting of some feeling or action, and the second is more specifically about the feeling of anger or aggravation. Together these two meanings of *provoke* represent the distinctive experience of democratic political life, which is characterized by both exhilaration— the pleasure of particular others and the joy of acting in company with one's peers—and exasperation. (Curtis reminds us of the choral ode in *Antigone*, which offers the "ambiguous praise" of humans as *deinon*— wonder-inspiring, unpredictable, fearfully strange.)

We can underscore this quality of human political life by working with a theatrical metaphor that Arendt doesn't use but that might be more suited to her conceptualization and to Curtis's analysis. I think the human experience of reality and relatedness, particularly in its political form, is not best characterized by referring to the relationship of actor/spectator, even if we stress that all are actors/spectators at the same time. The relationship that seems more apropos is the one *between* actors—between actor and fellow actors. This is a relationship that involves a kind of working together, one that is performative and communicative, agonistic and purposeful and not predictable. We perform together—we have to attend to each other's lines and play off each other—yet we might also be trying to upstage each other. We might be provoked by a fellow actor's insistence on what we regard as histrionic misinterpretation, or we might be provoked in a quite different sense, moved to our own best performance by the compelling performance of another. Moreover, we may be proceeding from very different understandings of what the play is about and have very different takes on what we're playing at and how it should be played. So maybe the precise metaphor for politics is the relationship between fellow actors in the absence of a strong director—a strong director such as rationality, fate, friendship, or shared proprieties of judgment.[9]

To extend the metaphor still further, we don't necessarily choose who to act with; we may not have wanted so-and-so to be the lead, we may think the Chorus has it all wrong, we may desperately want a particular role for economic, ethical, or egotistic reasons. (This is unlike a situation of spectatorship, where we've made a choice of company at least to the extent that we've bought a ticket.) And perhaps one of the most terrible dangers that we face, whose consequences Arendt has continually shown us, is the emergence of the desire to wholly control the company in which we act, to determine who appears in the world and who doesn't. This is a profoundly antipolitical desire, and a very real danger, in a world where there continue to be so many attempts to determine through violence who will live in the world and who will not, and where what we feel pleasured and pained by is disturbingly malleable. That dire possibility gives rise to what Curtis has identified as our need, the need to cultivate "our pleasure in the feeling of reality intensified through the presence of particular others and through the recalcitrant and plural quality of the world thus engendered." We need to call up and nurture a particular kind of desire, "a real gladness in the recalcitrant and plural quality of the world," a gladness that incites us to a democratic political life and a public realm full of "strong particular others."

Such gladness doesn't exactly require unmitigated joy; this recalcitrance, and the strong particular others it comes from, can often be just plain exasperating, as I have noted. But even exasperation is a result of being open to provocation, of passionately responding to another's "eliciting display." And it is this kind of passion that can serve as the ground—however bumpy and bannisterless—of a radical democratic public realm.

From a perhaps unexpected source, Arendt's aestheticism, both Curtis and McClure have discerned crucial teachings *for us* about the political and ethical substance given to the human condition by the presence of plural others. Both essays entice us to an appreciation of that plurality and to the cultivation of a taste that Arendt herself, in all her sometimes exasperating independence, had: a sensitivity to and a desire for the provocation to public action and judgment.

Notes

1. Hannah Arendt, *Lectures on Kant's Political Philosophy*, ed. Ronald Beiner (Chicago: University of Chicago Press, 1982), 40–41.

2. Hannah Arendt, *Between Past and Future*, enl. ed. (New York: Penguin Books, 1968), 51.

3. Arendt, *Lectures on Kant's Political Philosophy*, 74.

4. Thucydides, *The Peloponnesian War*, trans. Richard Crawley (New York: Random House, Modern Library, 1982), 364.

5. Josiah Ober, *Mass and Elite in Democratic Athens* (Princeton: Princeton University Press, 1989), 296.

6. Aristotle, *On Rhetoric*, trans. Geroge A. Kennedy (Oxford: Oxford University Press, 1991), 2.21.13–14; 3.2, 11; 1.2.4.

7. Hannah Arendt, *The Life of the Mind* (New York: Harcourt Brace Jovanovich, 1981), 29; Arendt's emphasis.

8. Ibid., 34.

9. Relations between actors may not be organized by a strong director, but it's worth noting that these relations require the existence of the theater itself. As John McGowan quite rightly emphasizes, worldly relatedness rests on "the embodiment of plurality in as many political, institutional settings as possible" (this volume).

Part II

Four

Communication and Transformation: Aesthetics and Politics in Kant and Arendt

Anthony J. Cascardi

The whole factual world of human affairs depends for its reality and its continued existence, first, upon the presence of others who have seen and heard and will remember, and, second, on the transformation of the intangible into the tangibility of things.
Hannah Arendt, *The Human Condition*

In a late essay first published along with *The Contest of the Faculties* in 1798, Immanuel Kant took up an "old question" that has subsequently been identified as central to the historical self-understanding of the Enlightenment: Is the human race constantly progressing?[1] Kant's affirmative response to this question, and the subsequent engagement of that response (whether explicit or implicit) by a range of thinkers reaching from Hegel and Habermas to Adorno and Arendt, is crucial for understanding the relationship between the political ambitions of contemporary critical theory and the Enlightenment. Kant's essay is crucial, first, because it offers a complex and decisive stance on questions that are central to the Enlightenment's vision of morality as the existence of humanity in a true "kingdom of ends"; and second, because it trades the stringent requirement of obedience to the moral law as the price of entry into that kingdom for what would seem to be the more malleable demands of reflective judgment, by asking not how we must *act* in order to behave in accordance with the moral law but where (and with whom) we should *stand* in order to move from our engagement in particular actions and events to a comprehension of the shape of history as a whole. When faced with the events of history, which do not in and of themselves demonstrate any apparent order,[2] Kant was led to ground the progressive moral vision of the Enlightenment on principles that could most accurately be called "aesthetic." Specifically, Kant was impelled to stake his conviction in progress on our ability to recognize and judge the meaning of the historical *signs* or *symbols* of that progress. Although history may be available to us only in fragments, our task is to see in those fragments the shape of history as a whole. In short, Kant's answer to the "old question" about progress hinges on the way in which history in its final form is represented to us.

Not surprisingly, what is ultimately a matter of representation in Kant is initially formulated as a question about cognition.[3] What kind of knowledge about history in its totality might be consistent with the principles of Enlightenment and, specifically, with the Enlightenment's suspicion of false signs, superstitious beliefs, and potential mystifications? Kant is not just interested in asserting dogmatically that the human race is progressing morally or, contrastively, in sustaining the hope that humanity is bound toward moral perfection, but in validating that claim and in establishing the stance from which it could be known as true.[4] The demand to know history as a whole poses special problems precisely because we must learn to read signs as exemplary of a totality we cannot possibly see and can represent only with difficulty. Indeed, Kant freely admits that the problem posed by the question of progress in history is that the much vaunted Copernican turn in knowledge does not seem to apply to it, for at stake in the question of progress is not just a way of seeing but something closer to foreseeing. Moreover, seeing and foreseeing are not easily reconciled, just as the coherence of natural laws (the world accessible by "seeing") is not in any obvious way amenable to the exercise of pure freedom (which leads us to the kingdom of ends by means of foreseeing). We are not capable of executing a "Copernican turn" with respect to our knowledge of future time, for that would require "the standpoint of Providence which is situated beyond all human wisdom, and which likewise extends to the free actions of man"; as Kant goes on to say, "these actions, of course man can *see*, but not *foresee* with certitude (for the divine eye there is no distinction in this matter); because, in the final analysis, man requires coherency according to natural laws, but with respect to his future free actions he must dispense with this guidance or direction" (*P*, p. 142). If we are unable to see what Kant in another essay calls the "end of all things" (*OH*, pp. 69–84), and if we must therefore judge the shape of history by fragments, then it would seem that we would require a fragment of human history "drawn not from past but from future time, therefore a predictive history" (*P*, p. 137). To know the future from a fragment, we would seem forced to claim truly "divinatory" or "premonitory" powers. Kant calls the power of prediction in history "divinatory" if it is not based on any known laws; if it can be acquired only through supernatural channels, it is called "premonitory."

On one level Kant's analysis of "divination" and "premonition" reflects the logic of an Enlightenment that seeks to root out all forms of false prophecy. But against that disbelief is staked the Enlightenment faith in moral progress, which Kant says requires a knowledge of future time. When faced with this tension, Kant reasons that the question of a priori knowledge in history is satisfiable only "if the diviner himself creates and contrives the events which he announced in advance" (*P*, p. 137). Freedom is clearly a precondition of progress, which suggests on one level that progress in history can indeed be caused; but in this instance what seems to require a privileged, premonitory form of knowledge is demoted to the status of an event that is *merely* caused. Kant provides two examples of such self-fulfilling prophecies, both of which have a direct bearing on issues relevant to a discussion of Hannah Arendt, for they raise fundamental questions about the task of politics in relation to the Enlightenment's faith in the moral progress of humankind. In each of these instances, Kant suggests that the modern political state is not so much the future "kingdom of ends" brought into history, as the secularization of a prior unity that was founded upon beliefs that stand beyond all knowledge. The first example concerns the role of the Jewish prophets in predicting the decline of the state founded on the basis of their own directives. If any political state, religious or otherwise, is the materialization of beliefs held in common, then the decline of this particular state is, oddly enough, a confirmation of the prophets' own predictive powers:

It was all very well for the Jewish prophets to prophesy that sooner or later not simply decadence but complete dissolution awaited their state, for they themselves were the authors of this fate. As national leaders they had loaded their constitution with so much ecclesiastical freight, and civil freight tied to it, that their state became utterly unfit to subsist of itself, and especially unfit to subsist together with neighboring nations. Hence the jeremiads of their priests were naturally bound to be lost upon the winds, because the priests obstinately persisted in their design for an untenable constitution created by themselves; and thus they could infallibly foresee the issue. (*P*, pp. 137–38)

In Kant's estimation, those in charge of governing the modern state (the "politicians") are all too much like these false prophets, secretly creating the false needs whose solutions they alone seem able to satisfy:

[O]ur politicians do precisely the same thing and are just as lucky in their prophecies. We must, they say, take men as they are, not as pedants ignorant of the world or good-natured visionaries fancy they ought to be. But in place of that "as they are" it would be better to say what they "have made" them—stubborn and inclined to revolt—through unjust constraint, through perfidious plots placed in the hands of the government; obviously then, if the government allows the reins to relax a little, sad consequences ensue which verify the prophecy of those supposedly sagacious statesmen. (*P*, p. 138)[5]

Kant's second example concerns priests who foretell the progressive decline and destruction of religion, leading ultimately to the apocalyptic coming of the Antichrist. In this case it is their own predictions that are the cause of the "mechanical unanimity" that marks the transition from the spiritual unity of a religious body to a merely civil state. Kant's opinion is that the "mechanical unanimity" that can be achieved through a civil constitution can never ensure the "moral disposition" available in a genuine community of sense:

Ecclesiastics, too, occasionally prophesy the complete destruction of religion and the immanent appearance of Antichrist; and in doing so they are performing precisely what is requisite to call him up. This happens because they have not seen to impressing on their parishes moral principles which lead directly to the better, but rather fabricate into essential duty observances and historical beliefs which are supposed to effect it indirectly; from this, of course, can grow the mechanical unanimity as in a civil constitution, but none in moral disposition. But then they complain about irreligion, which they themselves have caused and thus could predict even without any special talent. (*P*, p. 138)

Kant's description in this passage of the "mechanical unanimity" of a civil state may be taken as indicative of the process that Max Weber called the "rationalization" of culture. The rationalization thesis that was central to Weber's critique of Western modernity has in part been rehabilitated by Habermas, who sees it as providing the basis for norms of human interaction. As Habermas sees it, the process of rationalization wrests an objective world from mythical thinking, and this in turn allows us to make validity claims that would otherwise be groundless: "Only against the background of a normative reality that has become autonomous, and measured against the criticizable claim to normative rightness, can intentions, wishes, attitudes, feelings appear as illegitimate or merely idiosyncratic, as nongeneralizable and merely subjective."[6] As Habermas is aware, and as Weber before him pointed out, the very process that makes such validity claims possible lays bare the risk that the social order based upon them may be merely "mechanical" in nature. In Arendt's perspicuous analysis, this brings about the "substitution of behavior for action and its eventual substitution of bureaucracy, the rule of nobody, for personal rulership." These are the features she characterizes as typical of politics and society in the modern age.[7]

The modern democratic state is thus the point at which seemingly irreducible tensions converge. On the one hand, rationalization is the process by means of which beliefs are made representable, negotiable (some would say "communicable"), and open to competing validity claims. But, on the other hand, the genealogy of the modern state also lies in the materialization of what were once wholly immaterial beliefs and yields the "mechanization" of a "living community." And precisely because rationalization, so understood, is open to the threat of reification, it is not surprising to find that thinkers such as Habermas, and to some extent Arendt as well, have suggested that it is the business of enlightened politics to secure the free and open space in which the communication necessary for the testing of beliefs can occur.[8] How can this be done? Arendt's account of the public sphere draws heavily on the Kantian notion of "publicity" as the bridge between morality and politics. In the essay "What Is Enlightenment?" for instance, Kant says that freedom of public expression is a necessary precondition of the exercise of reason: "The public use of one's reason must always be free, and it alone can bring about enlightenment among men. . . . By the public use of one's reason I understand the use which a scholar makes of it before the reading public."⁹ As far as politics is concerned, the fact that it is public, that is, conducted in the public sphere, also enables it to be moral. For both Habermas and Arendt, the public political sphere is the space in which judgments can be fashioned around the regulative ideal of a common (community) sense, and this in turn allows the participants in the political conversation to secure a stable identity for themselves.¹⁰ As a communicative space, the polis is the place where identification can freely be attained and recognition won. This is no small accomplishment, but the question that remains is whether the polis, so conceived, is also a space in which transformation can be achieved. Can such a polis allow for the radical transformation necessary for passage into the "kingdom of ends"?

Given this question, it is not surprising to find that Kant himself invested substantial faith in our ability to know the signs of a future history and to recognize in them evidence of the progress of the human race. Yet it remains clear that such a tack does not avoid the problem of representation previously mentioned. How can one adequately represent the ultimate convergence of the opinions of all, which presumably can occur only in the fullness of time? Lacking the ability to know (i.e., to see or to foresee) the future of the human race, Kant looks instead in history; there he hopes to find a fragment that would point to

> the disposition and capacity of the human race to be the cause of its own advance toward the better (since this should be the act of a being endowed with freedom), toward the human race as being the author of this advance. An event must be sought which points to the existence of such a cause and to its effectiveness in the human race, undetermined with regard to time, and which would allow progress toward the better to be concluded as an inevitable consequence. This conclusion then could also be extended to the history of the past (that it has always been in progress) in such a way that that event would have to be considered not itself as the cause of history, but only as an intimation, an historical sign (*signum rememorativum, demonstrativum, prognostikon*) demonstrating the tendency of the human race viewed in its entirety. (*P*, p. 143)

As is well known, Kant located what he thought was a true sign of the progress of the human race in the French Revolution.¹¹ In a passage that Arendt was fond of citing, Kant argued that what is important about the Revolution is not the overthrow of political institutions and individuals once thought great, but rather "the mode of thinking of the spectators which . . . manifests such a universal yet disinterested sympathy for the players on one side against those on the other, even at the risk that this partiality could become very disadvantageous for them if discovered" (*P*, p. 143). In "The End of All Things," Kant says that only those actions arising from disinterested motives can inspire human respect and that without respect there is no true love (*OH*, p. 84).

In recognizing the actions and events of history as signs and in judging their meaning, Kant proposes that we occupy the position of the spectators at events played on the world-historical stage. It is "in the spectators (who are not engaged in this game themselves)" that Kant finds "a wishful participation that borders closely on enthusiasm, the very expression of which is fraught with danger; the sympathy, therefore, can have no other cause than a moral disposition in the human race" (*P*, p. 144). As spectators, we maintain a sympathy for the players on the stage, but we also sustain a detached and disinterested stance, participating in the action only from a distance, or, as Kant says in the preceding passage, "wishfully."[12] In Kant's estimation, our sympathy for the players on the stage demonstrates our ability to take the position of others and in the process confirms the moral predisposition of the human race. Our disinterestedness in turn guarantees the validity of judgments that could not possibly be confirmed by any individual in time. (Kant writes that "owing to its universality, this mode of thinking demonstrates a character of the human race at large and all at once; owing to its disinterestedness, a moral character of humanity, at least in its predisposition, a character which not only permits people to hope for progress toward the better, but *is already itself progress* insofar as its capacity is sufficient for the present" [*P*, pp. 143–44; emphasis added].) By occupying the position of the spectator, Kant proposes that we are able to move from the specific and immediate events of history (the glories and atrocities of the French Revolution) to a conclusion regarding the shape of history as a whole for the human species.[13]

Kant's notion of the spectator's position, roundly embraced by Arendt, demonstrates the clear influence of Rousseau's thinking on the issue of theatricality. In the "Letter to M. d'Alembert on the Theatre," Rousseau recognized that theatrical actors could be seen as "alienated" from themselves insofar as they gave their authentic being to that of the characters they represented: "An actor on the stage, displaying other sentiments than his own, saying only what he is made to say, often representing a chimerical being, annihilates himself, as it were, and is lost in his hero. And, in this forgetting of the man, if something remains of him, it is used as the plaything of the spectators."[14] But Rousseau goes on to resolve this issue by transforming the spectators themselves into actors, thereby joining all concerned in a new community: "Let the spectators become an entertainment to themselves; make them actors themselves; do it so that each sees and loves himself in the others so that all will be better united."[15]

For Kant the notion of the spectator's position provides an opportunity to map the issue of community along temporal and historical lines. It is one way in which the problem of representation posed by the question of progress in history can be resolved. The notion of great events seen as exemplary signs and witnessed from the spectator's point of view allows Kant to reduce the disparity between the unanimity that resists all efforts at representation, on the one hand, and the merely historical and therefore partial evidence of that unanimity, on the other. For Kant, we are *of* history, actors on the world stage, or at least able to place ourselves vicariously in the position of those who act (which is to say that we inhabit a causal world); but we are also *beyond* the historical world, acting as noumenal subjects toward the moral perfection embodied in reason or toward what Kant elsewhere calls the true universality of the "final judgment," the gateway through which we pass into the kingdom of ends.[16] The theory of signs as witnessed by spectators allows Kant to imagine a movement from the specific events of history (which by definition are part of a network of relations that on one level can be seen as the "causes" of progress) to the "beyond" that by definition resists all representation. In Kantian or Arendtian terms, the French Revolution is not—or not only—the "cause" of progress; as a sign, it transcends what can be said about it as a mere phenomenon.[17] But neither is it in and of itself a moment of pure, noumenal freedom or the passageway through which we enter the kingdom of ends.[18] Rather, as a fragment in which we perceive the whole, it is the solution to the problem of the unpresentability of the end-state of progress.[19] (True "progress" for Kant stands for a radical form of agreement, a convergence upon true unanimity.[20]) For Arendt, the "completion" of the work of the actor by the spectator is also a solution to the problematic separation of theory and practice:

[I]n Kant the common distinction or antagonism between theory and practice in political matters is the distinction between the spectator and the actor, and to our surprise we saw that the spectator had precedence; what counted in the French Revolution, what made it a world-historical event, a phenomenon not to be forgotten, were not the deeds and misdeeds of the actors but the opinions, the enthusiastic approbation, of spectators, of persons who themselves were not involved. We also saw that these uninvolved and nonparticipating spectators . . . *were* involved with one another. (*L*, p. 65)

By occupying the spectator's stance with respect to history, we identify ourselves not with any individual but with the species. As Kant said in his third review of Herder's *Ideas for a Philosophy of the History of Mankind*, it is the species, not the individual (not even the sum of all individuals), that constitutes the subject of history as such. The "species" is conceptually equivalent to a symbol that stands for an infinity that in its interminability resists representation. Specifically, Kant says that "species" means "the totality of a series of generations proceeding to infinity (the indeterminable). . . . [This] line of descent ceaselessly approaches its concurrent destination. . . . [It] is asymptotic in all its parts to this line of destiny, and on the whole coincides with it. In other words, no single member in all of these generations of the human race, but only the species, fully achieves its destination. . . . The philosopher would say that the destination of the human race in general is perpetual progress."[21] The notion of the "species" as the subject of history thus serves further to resolve the difficulty in representing the agreement of all implicit in the Kantian notion of progress.

The problems posed by the need to render representable and legible that which stands beyond all representation—in this instance, the radical agreement of all in the "kingdom of ends"—echo with the efforts of the third *Critique* to negotiate a passageway between the noumenal and phenomenal realms, and so anticipate the questions Arendt addressed in terms of politics. The difficulty raised by the third *Critique* stems from the fact that, on the one hand, Kant wishes the split between the phenomenal and the noumenal worlds to be categorical and complete, whereas on the other hand, he wishes to recognize the possibility of passing from one realm to the other as a way of realizing freedom. In Kant's terms, the purpose of the third *Critique* is to show that "the concept of freedom is meant to *actualize* in the sensible world the end proposed by its laws" *and* that "nature must consequently also be capable of being regarded in such a way that in the conformity to law of its form it at least harmonizes with the possibility of the ends to be effectuated in it according to the laws of freedom."[22]

In the third *Critique*, it turns out that the idea of an aesthetic "bridge" over the gap between these worlds is impossible to build; more accurately, to find a way of representing (in Kant's terms, "actualizing") noumenal freedom in the fact-world of cognition and causality involves a building process that is impossible to complete because the "unity of experience," or the "world as a whole," can only be reconstructed, remembered, or presupposed, and can never be attested as true. It is impossible to travel the route from the common sense that we remember in aesthetic judgments to the "as if" posture we must adopt to carry out such judgments in anything but a fictional or mythic sense, which is to say that the position in which we stand is indeterminate and undeterminable in much the same way that the peculiar (dis)interest we take in beauty is indeterminate with respect to the particular interests that govern theory and practice. Indeed, Kant himself indicates that the best that can be hoped for in respect to a conclusive derivation of the transcendental principle of aesthetic judgment is a clear statement of what amounts to an antinomy—that the principle of the universal validity of claims of taste must indeed exist, but that the principle cannot be shown to exist—rather than a final resolution of it. This antinomy accounts for the "difficulty" of aesthetic judgment and, more specifically, for the structure of reflective judgment with respect to our concept of experience as a whole. Thus, Kant concludes the preface to the third *Critique* with an avowal of "the difficulty of unravelling a problem so involved" as the principle of aesthetic judgment. He can hope only that this difficulty may serve to excuse "a certain amount of hardly avoidable obscurity in its solution, provided that the accuracy of our statement of the principle is proved with all requisite clearness" (*CJ*, pp. 6–7).[23] Although the third *Critique* was meant to bring the project of critical philosophy to a close, it would be more accurate to say that the third *Critique* uncovers a much larger gap in the discourse of Enlightenment and attests to the nonclosure of the Kantian project itself.

Arendt's interest in Kant in the 1970 *Lectures on Kant's Political Philosophy* represents an attempt to derive a political theory from Kant's aesthetics and, I would argue, thereby to bring closure to the project of critical philosophy. Specifically, Arendt asks us to imagine that what Kant means by "reflective judgment" in the third *Critique* must take a political form. For Arendt, judgment complements and completes the activities of knowing (cognition) and willing (action) taken up in Kant's first two *Critiques* and in the two volumes of *The Life of the Mind*. Arendt follows Kant in identifying the capacity for judgment with the position of the spectator and in treating the position of the spectator as both sympathetic and disinterested in the ways described by Kant in the essay on the "old question" of progress. In spite of Arendt's many criticisms of the modern world elaborated in *The Human Condition*, she remained determined to show that an Enlightenment stance that prizes thinking, willing, and above all judging, and that aims at a politics of community, is what underwrites the notion of moral progress dear to Enlightenment thinkers such as Kant. Arendt's notion of democratic community represents an attempt to salvage the commitment to progress that Kant sustains on moral and historical grounds. In Arendt a democratic politics is dependent upon an account of reflective judgment as the process through which a "community sense" can be built. By politicizing aesthetic reflective judgment, she aims to rescue the possibility of moral progress from the radical discontinuity imposed upon it by the apocalyptic image of a "final judgment." Implicitly, she takes as the task of politics to reduce the radical discontinuity between the events of history and the "final judgment" or "end of all things" in which history comes to an end. For her it is the task of politics to make legible what is unpresentable, to transform the "radical agreement" of the kingdom of ends into the process and the space in which we solicit the agreement of others. In the process, however, Arendt reduces the tension in Kant's late writings between the need to represent that which stands beyond all knowledge and the resistance to representation offered by the totality of a true kingdom of ends.

In ascribing a political content to what in Kant is radically indeterminate with respect to any particular sphere of social life, Arendt provides a closure for the Enlightenment project that Kant himself could not secure, finding what some have described as a "fourth critique" buried in the third by turning from the indeterminate concept of reflective aesthetic judgment to a politics of community.[24] The politics that Arendt derives from Kant's aesthetics is a democratic politics of common sense, of the *sensus communis*, of (good) taste. It represents a way in which the temporal open-endedness of an indefinite future and the radical convergence of opinions in the kingdom of ends can be mapped onto a determinate social space. If, as Arendt quotes Kant, in making claims of taste we are indeed "suitors for the agreement of everyone else," and if it is this process of "wooing consent" that is a necessary condition for the moral progress of humankind (*CJ*, p. 82), then the task of politics for Arendt is to create a space in which the discourse necessary for that process can occur.

The Arendtian interpretation of the problem of reflective judgment represents one of the most important attempts to transpose the Kantian conception of aesthetic judgment into a democratic politics, by focusing on the polis as the space in which the common sense that is required in judgments of taste can appear. And yet, for reasons I will outline shortly, Arendt's account of reflective judgment as political rather than aesthetic raises a number of questions that her interpretation of Kant seems unable to resolve, and these in turn are important for assessing the efforts of more recent political thinkers (among whom I would include Ernesto Laclau and Roberto Unger) to base a democratic politics on principles that might also be described as "aesthetic." If politics calls for the exercise of reflective judgment, and if such judgments are provoked by instances of the beautiful and the sublime, then what is the role of beauty and sublimity in democratic political life? Why do beauty and sublimity solicit the type of reflective judgment that searches for a common (community) sense? If judgments of taste in Kant are provoked by the sensuous subjective experiences of pleasure and pain, then what is the source of this pleasure and this pain, and what trace, if any, do they leave in democratic politics? If politics represents a way to bridge the gap between the phenomenal and the noumenal worlds, then what are the consequences of the claim to have arrived at an adequate representation of something that stands beyond all knowledge?

Arendt's account of judgment represents one among several recent attempts to make rational and regular the passage between the noumenal and phenomenal worlds, hence to render legible what in Kant is strictly unpresentable or is presentable only by analogy or metaphor—namely, the encompassing totality or convergence of opinions implicit in the notion of a "kingdom of ends." In Arendt the attempt to regularize this passage becomes evident in, among other places, her emphasis on the Kantian notion of the beautiful, which she pursues in favor of much of what Kant has to say about genius and the sublime.

Yet it is the Kantian account of the sublime that best registers the pressure of truly unpresentable ideas—including the idea of the opinion of "everyone else" and the notion of an "enlarged mentality"—upon our existing routines and states of affairs. The transposition of infinite, future time into the discursive or "communicative" space of the polis, by contrast, reduces the disparity between the ongoing process of challenging opinions and testing claims, on the one hand, and the categorical inclusiveness of a "final judgment," on the other. (What Kant imagines as the "final judgment" is potentially sublime insofar as any spatially imagined or materially constituted "thing" that contains an infinity will defeat the powers of reason devoted to representing it.)

In imagining the polis as a discursive space and in associating politics with the "public sphere," the tendency is to refuse the power of the sublime to hold in check the impulse to ascribe an object to an unpresentable idea. As Kant insists, "true sublimity must be sought only in the mind of the judging Subject, and not in the Object of nature that occasions this attitude by the estimate formed of it."[25] The Arendtian understanding of reflective judgment recoils from the sublime (subjective) moment and gives us instead an interpretation of the beautiful in which the object of beauty itself is the moral quality of the "enlarged mentality," seeing from the perspective of everyone else. In so doing, the difficulties posed by the need to represent "everyone else" are elided, and Arendt diminishes what I take to be the animating tension of the third *Critique*: that although the realms of cognition and morality must be held apart, we must also be able to imagine a transition between the two. As I hope to suggest, we need to preserve something of this aporia if we are not to rob democratic politics, on the one side, of its transformative possibilities and, on the other, of the possibility of its becoming regular and legitimate, thereby founding a state in which the project of identity formation can be pursued. In deriving a theory of (political) judgment from the aesthetics of the beautiful, Arendt's reinterpretation of Kant represents a consequence and a continuation of the Enlightenment project to diminish fear and perpetuate the everlasting peace brought by the arbitration of reason.

In what follows here, I want to juxtapose Arendt's interpretation of Kant with certain passages from the third *Critique* to suggest that this resolution of the aporia of reflective judgment is false, that it avoids the thorniest problems of representation apparent in Kant's essays on history and progress from which Arendt derives her notion of the "spectator's judgment," and, finally, that she is driven to see the polis as an objectification of the *sensus communis* as the best way in which to assure its rationality.[26] To be sure, Arendt herself was a staunch critic of the processes of rationalization and reification, and it is in this capacity that she remains well known. But I hasten to add that objectification—if not exactly reification—is, by her own account, the necessary price that must be paid to ensure that subjective elements of consciousness (among which would be included not just reflective judgments but our memory of the past as well) will in fact endure beyond their own moment. This is simply a consequence of any effort at world building: "Without the reification which remembrance needs for its own fulfillment . . . the living activities of action, speech, and thought would lose their reality at the end of each process and disappear as though they had never been. The materialization they have to undergo in order to remain in the world at all is paid for in that always the 'dead letter' replaces something which grew out of and for a fleeting moment indeed existed as the 'living spirit'" (*HC*, p. 95).

In response, one is immediately reminded of Kant's remark in the "Analytic of the Sublime" that "the fear that if we divest this [sublime] representation of everything that can commend it to the senses, it will thereupon be attended only with a cold and lifeless approbation and not with any moving force or emotion, is wholly unwarranted. For when nothing any longer meets the eye of sense, and the unmistakable and ineffaceable idea of morality is left in possession of the field, there would be need rather of tempering the ardour of an unbounded imagination to prevent it from rising to enthusiasm." Recall that the sublime in Kant is described as "altogether negative as to what is sensuous." As Kant goes on to say, "there is no more sublime passage in the Jewish law than the commandment: Thou shalt not make unto thee any graven image, or any likeness of any thing that is in heaven or earth, or under the earth, &c." (*CJ*, p. 127). Arendt's political theory, which, by contrast with Kant's aesthetics, is deeply rooted in the processes of world building, is thus by her own account a necessary moment in the "reification" of the soul (I place "reification" in quotation marks so as to indicate its incomplete and problematic association with the process by means of which the relations among persons come to assume a thinglike quality): "Human life, in so far as it is world-building, is engaged in a constant process of reification, and the degree of worldliness of produced things, which all together form the human artifice, depends upon their greater or lesser permanence in the world itself" (*HC*, p. 96).

At various points in the 1970 lectures, Arendt speaks of the principle of common sense or "community sense" (*sensus communis*) as that to which we make implicit reference in aesthetic or reflective judgments. First, Arendt distinguishes "common sense" from the "private senses," such as taste and smell. These are radically subjective and inward, Arendt says, because "the very objectivity of the seen or heard or touched thing is annihilated in them or at least is not present; they are *inner* senses because the food we taste is inside ourselves, and so, in a way, is the smell of the rose" (*L*, p. 66).[27] On her account these sensations are "not object-bound and cannot be recollected." Second, she argues that "common sense" refers in Kant both to a norm of reasonableness and to a form of cognition that is open and accessible to all. More precisely, it is the openness and "publicity" of the *sensus communis* that is the guarantee of its reasonableness; likewise, the reasonableness of common sense can claim normative validity because its items can be scrutinized publicly. In contrast to "private sense," the validity of the *sensus communis* depends upon the fact that it represents and makes reference to objects that are open for all to view. As she says in *The Human Condition*, there are some things that need to be displayed publicly if they are to exist at all (*HC*, p. 73).

As we have already seen, these views are supported by what Kant himself has to say about the relationship between the claims of Enlightenment and the emergence of the public sphere. Arendt limits the interest of politics to what can be represented to and by this "public reason," and in the process she makes representability a precondition for rationality. The consequences for her own political vision are clear enough: Arendt favors a politics of rational communication over a politics of radical transformation, even if her own interest in the phenomenon of revolution would seem to require her to reckon with the force of ideas that are beyond all representation. Reading her work in light of Kant's late writings nonetheless forces us to grapple with the tension between rationality as communication grounded in common sense, and a transformative vision that relies on the feelings generated by those things that stand beyond the available limits of representation.

In Kant claims of taste begin from purely subjective experiences yet claim universal validity; this suggests that there must be a linkage between the "private" and "public" (common) senses. For Kant the problem of this linkage constitutes the antinomy of taste. It is expressed in the tension between the following commonplace propositions: on the one hand, that "everyone has his own taste" (or, in another formulation, that "there is no disputing about taste") and, on the other hand, that there could be no such thing as contention about taste were there not also a hope of coming to agreement. The tension between these propositions means that "one must be able to reckon on grounds of judgment that possess *more than private validity* and are thus not merely subjective" (*CJ*, p. 205); it does not, however, mean reflective judgments negate everything that is truly private and subjective about claims of taste—namely, the experiences of pleasure and pain in which they originate. For Arendt, by contrast, the antinomy of taste is resolved by *rooting* private sense in community sense. In the process, what begins as something so "private" that it annihilates its objects is transformed into something publicly communicable. Arendt calls the process of this transformation "reflection":

> [C]ommon sense is community sense, *sensus communis*, as distinguished from *sensus privatus*. This *sensus communis* is what judgment appeals to in everyone, and it is this possible appeal that gives judgments their special validity. The it-pleases-or-displeases-me, which as a feeling seems so utterly private and noncommunicative, is actually rooted in this community sense and is therefore open to communication once it has been transformed by reflection, which takes all others and their feelings into account. . . . When one judges, one judges as a member of a community. (*L*, p. 72)

Yet Arendt's reliance on the notion of reflection in this passage and others like it raises at least as many problems as it solves, for the mechanism of reflection she describes in fact *presupposes* the totality of sense that it is the task of judgment to create. How can one put oneself in the place of *everyone else*, if that all-inclusive community is yet to be formed? Conversely, in taking the feelings of all others into account, what becomes of the "private sense" that served as the provocation for reflective aesthetic judgment in the first place?

These questions cannot easily be escaped, because Arendt relies on the idea that reflection on "all others and their feelings" is the way in which taste can make its claims moral. (Arendt quotes Kant as saying that taste represents "egoism overcome" [*L*, p. 67].) In this context Arendt embraces the Kantian principle of the "enlarged mentality" developed in section 41 of the *Critique of Judgment*, interpreting it as one of the three "maxims" of the Enlightenment ("[P]ut oneself in thought in the place of everyone else" [*L*, p. 71]). Communicability is, for Arendt, the test of one's ability to adopt an "enlarged mentality," to stand in the position of all others. But what does it mean for Arendt to presuppose the existence of a "community sense" and to treat it as a faculty that *enables* one to adopt the stance of everyone else (e.g., "[O]ne's community sense makes it possible to enlarge one's mentality" [*L*, p. 73])?

For Arendt the importance of communicability lies in the fact that it ensures representability, and representability is crucial for maintaining politics in the public sphere. But as Kant clearly saw, the communicability of claims of taste potentially eclipses and threatens to destroy the pleasures taken in beautiful objects, thereby weakening and eventually undermining the motives that first incited us to make reflective judgments. In a memorable passage that is important for a discussion of Arendt insofar as it confirms the social basis of taste, Kant speculated that a person abandoned on a desert island would neither adorn himself nor find himself inclined to look for flowers for decoration: "Only in society does it occur to him to be not merely a man, but a man refined under the manner of his kind (the beginning of civilization)—for that is the estimate formed of one who has the bent and turn for communicating his pleasure to others, and who is not quite satisfied with an Object unless his feeling of delight in it can be shared in communion with others" (*CJ*, p. 155). Kant explains how an interest in colorful adornments eventually yields to beautiful forms that convey no gratification at all and that only confirm the principle of universal communication: "[E]ventually, when civilization has reached its height it makes this work of communication almost the main business of refined inclination, and the entire value of sensations is placed in the degree to which they permit of universal communication. At this stage . . . even where the pleasure which each one has in an object is but insignificant and possesses of itself no conspicuous interest, still the idea of its universal communicability almost indefinitely augments its value" (*CJ*, p. 156). In so saying, Kant suggests not just that claims of taste (which Arendt epitomizes as communicable) threaten to eclipse the experience of pleasure in the beautiful, but also that pleasure in the beautiful should in principle be recoverable from claims of taste. The ideal of universal communicability is not just a substitute for, but should also be an "augmentation" of, the pleasures of the beautiful.

In Arendt's account, claims of taste depend upon the publicity and objectivity of the "community sense," both of which require representability. At a certain level they also presuppose the existence of the community which it is their task to create. Arendt's commitment to the representability of the *sensus communis* in the polis and in the objectivity of reflective judgment can be set in contrast with Kant's account of the indeterminacy of reflective judgments and the fragility of claims of taste. In making claims of taste, Kant says, we invoke concepts "from which nothing can be cognized in respect of the Object, and nothing proved, because it is in itself indeterminable and useless for knowledge" (*CJ*, p. 208). Similarly, Kant insists that although the principle of reflective judgment rests on an underlying a priori concept, this is a concept "from which, properly speaking, we get *no cognition of a thing*" (*CJ*, p. 5; emphasis added). So too Kant claims in section 2 of the "Analytic of the Beautiful" that aesthetic pleasure concerns itself not at all with the "real existence of the thing, but rather [with] what estimate we form of it on mere contemplation" (*CJ*, p. 43).[28] Yet Kant goes on to suggest that there may indeed be something valid in regard to knowledge that we communicate in making aesthetic judgments, thus holding out the possibility that the power of beauty is to show that cognition may not be all of knowledge. As Kant says, although claims of taste "do not of themselves contribute a whit to the knowledge of things, *they still belong wholly to the faculty of knowledge*" (*CJ*, pp. 5–6; emphasis added).

What is it that we claim to know in aesthetic judgments that is not the knowledge of any "thing"? What is it in Kant that Arendt reads as politics? In section 8 of the "Analytic of the Beautiful," Kant specifies that the universality of the pleasure informing judgments of taste is a "*subjective universal validity*" (*CJ*, p. 55; emphasis added). But this still leaves open the question how something that is "subjective" can also be categorically and universally true. Kant reasons that if claims of taste represent any kind of knowledge at all, this must be a knowledge that does not subsume the particularities of sensuous experience under the laws associated with categories and concepts, if only because the particularities in question—the feelings of pleasure or pain that arise in response to instances of the beautiful and the sublime—cannot be associated with any objects.[29] Only by means of a fallacy of the pathetic or projective imagination would anyone ascribe subjective feelings to artifactual creations or to the things of the natural world.[30] (Arendt runs this risk in associating the *sensus communis* with an artifactual creation, the polis or the public sphere.)

The point most directly at issue is that claims of taste are grounded in subjective feelings of pleasure and pain and constitute what Kant calls "reflective" as opposed to "determinant" judgments. Kant's account of reflective judgment is substantially different from Arendt's. Kant's account is as follows: "If the universal (the rule, principle, or law) is given, then the judgment which subsumes the particular under it is *determinant*. This is so even where such a judgment is transcendental and, as such, provides the conditions *a priori* in conformity with which alone subsumption under that universal can be effected. If, however, only the particular is given and the universal has to be found for it, then the judgment is simply *reflective*. . . . The reflective judgment which is compelled to ascend from the particular in nature to the universal, stands, therefore, in need of a principle" (*CJ*, p. 18). Whereas determinant judgments in Kant *subsume* or *subordinate* particulars to some universal law that is given in advance, in reflective judgments only the particular is given. Insofar as claims of taste are indeed valid judgments and not merely statements of preferences or pronouncements about what one happens to find agreeable, a universal must somehow be found to govern them. Lyotard notes that this process is what in Kant's *Anthropology* is called *Witz* or *ingenium*.[31] Arendt says at one point that in reflective judgments we "derive" the rule from the particular.[32]

Insofar as Arendt finds it necessary to explain in any further detail how it is we can move from the particular to the universal, it is by recourse to the theory of the imagination. If the imagination has a privileged role in Arendt's account of judgments of taste, this is because it allows us to judge objects that are not directly present to the senses. Specifically, the imagination is the faculty that renders representable that which is not present before us: "There is the operation of the imagination, in which one judges objects that are no longer present, that are removed from immediate sense perception and therefore no longer affect one directly, and yet, though the object is removed from one's outward senses, it now becomes an object for one's inward senses. When one represents something to oneself that is absent, one closes, as it were, those senses by which objects in their objectivity are given to one" (*L*, p. 68). The imagination is the mechanism of "reflection" that transforms private sense into the *sensus communis*. As with Kant's notion of the historical sign, the imagination provides the "foresight" required to calculate the point at which all possible lines of argument will converge upon the final and complete agreement of all. Arendt insists that in no case is the imagination radically creative. Not even the genius can create that which does not exist; in her example, the genius produces the centaur out of the given—the horse and the man (*L*, p. 79).

If claims of taste do not (indeed, cannot) represent the form of the final agreement that would be necessary to validate them on a priori grounds, this leaves open the possibility that the form of that agreement might nonetheless be *remembered*. What is it that claims of taste might remember? In Kant's analysis, the moment of the beautiful makes reference to and in this sense "recalls" an original moment of knowledge that itself was pleasurable. As Kant describes it, this moment was filled with wonder and awe; these are the wonder and the awe associated with finding that the particular facts of experience can be subsumed under universal laws. Wonder and awe are a first, affective response to the discovery that there is a purposiveness in nature, however hidden, and that although it may be impossible to perceive the whole of nature, nature can nonetheless be conceived *as* a whole. Whereas this process remains largely hidden from view in Arendt, Kant argues that every subsequent act of cognition replicates (albeit in an extremely diminished mode) the moment of this first excitement, this wonder or awe produced at our original awareness of the purposiveness of nature: "[J]ust as if it were a lucky chance that favoured us, we are rejoiced (properly speaking relieved of a want) where we meet with such systematic unity under empirical laws" (*CJ*, pp. 23–24). We glimpse this purposiveness momentarily when we discover a unity in the empirical laws of nature, as happens fleetingly in ordinary acts of cognition:

> We do not, and cannot, find in ourselves the slightest effect on the feeling of pleasure from the coincidence of perceptions with the laws in accordance with the universal concepts of nature (the Categories), since in their case understanding necessarily follows the bent of its own nature without ulterior aim. But, while this is so, the discovery, on the other hand, that two or more empirical heterogeneous laws of nature are allied under one principle that embraces them both, is the ground of a very appreciable pleasure, often even of admiration, and

such, too, as does not wear off even though we are already familiar enough with its object. It is true that we no longer notice any decided pleasure in the comprehensibility of nature, or in the unity of its divisions into genera and species, without which the empirical concepts, that afford us our knowledge of nature in its particular laws, would not be possible. Still it is certain that the pleasure appeared in due course, and only by reason of the most ordinary experience being impossible without it, has it become gradually fused with simple cognition, and no longer arrests particular attention. Something, then, that makes us attentive in our estimate of nature to its finality for our understanding . . . is required, in order that, on meeting with success, pleasure may be felt in this their accord with our cognitive faculty. (*CJ*, pp. 27–28)

The pleasure we take in the beautiful is rooted in the original pleasure Kant describes in this passage. (Even in Arendt the reflective powers of the imagination depend not simply upon one's ability to represent something that does not exist, but also on one's ability to remember something that is no longer present.) If that pleasure contains a memory trace of what it was like to perceive the purposiveness of nature in a single act of cognition, then the question raised by the famous section 59 of the third *Critique* is whether the appearance of beauty is *itself* a representation (specifically, a "symbol") of the convergence of facts and values or merely a reminder on the basis of which we remember the possibility of universal agreement. On the basis of a literal reading of Kant, it would be tempting to say that beauty itself figures or represents a form of freedom that does not yet exist and to think that beauty, like the religious states Kant describes in the essay on progress or the "community" that Arendt grounds in the *sensus communis*, is the materialization of things that are essentially immaterial and unrepresentable. In the case of beauty, these would be the ideas and concepts of morality; in the case of politics, this would be the "agreement of all" that is presupposed in free and open conversation. But this portrays the beautiful as something objective and material, whereas Kant specifically says that it is subjective. In other words, it takes beauty as itself the representation of what is unpresentable— whether this begins in the purely private experiences of pleasure and pain or, in judgments (claims) of taste, attempts to reflect upon the opinions and feelings of "everyone else." (In fact, this reading elides the appearance of beauty as the "symbol of morality" with the exercise of reflective judgment in claims of taste.) Moreover, it overlooks the fact that were we indeed faced with the advent of the kingdom of ends in the form of the beautiful, judgments of taste would be unnecessary. Similarly, one could reason that if the experiences of "private sense" are indeed rooted in the community sense, claims of taste would be superfluous. As Jay M. Bernstein has argued, in a completely rational universe judgments of taste would be unnecessary; likewise, judgments of taste would be impossible in a strictly causal universe.[33]

As Arendt duly notes in her contrast of *sensus privatus* and "common sense," reflective judgments hope to accomplish something more than the validation of the particularity of the free, sensuous particulars associated with pure subjective experience (*this* pleasure, *this* pain) in their freedom or their particularity. As she is quick to recognize, "free particulars" are of little use to the project of politics, which aims at founding, and constituting, a state. By the same token, a Kantian account of the critical potential of aesthetic judgment must be imagined as involving something more than a revolt by particulars against the tyranny of those preexisting concepts that would prohibit all possible transformation, if only because the aesthetic judgments lodged in claims about beauty and sublimity are communicable and so seem to commit us to the task of finding universal laws. What is articulated in the third *Critique* is something rather like the process in which the "free particulars" of subjective experience challenge or escape the governing powers of those universals that stand waiting for them in advance, calling for the creation of new communities of sense by reference to the experience of pleasure in which we remember the awe first felt upon recognizing the purposiveness and unity of nature. The memory of that recognition leaves affective traces recoverable in the experience of the beautiful, and it is these that provide the impetus for the transformation of society as it stands. For Kant the "free particulars" that incite aesthetic reflective judgment stand outside the system of thought that operates on the basis of the separation of the empirical and the transcendental realms. For Arendt, as for Kant, these free particulars call for judgment, which in accordance with the notion of taste implies regularity and rule; they are the source from which we "derive" universals, and so they stand at the origin of everything that is potentially rational about the political communities we create.

In Kant, the origins of Enlightenment in peaceful conversation among members of the polis stand in clear and yet unresolved tension with the radical transformation required to bring us into the kingdom of ends. Even within the sphere of what Kant means by conversation there is a tension between the rational (commonsense) element in communication and the force of the (unpresentable) agreement of all, and this tension is preserved in the third *Critique*. An account of reflective judgment that would reflect the transformative power of the aesthetic would be one in which beauty would be seen either as a memory of our first excitement upon finding the unity of nature as a whole compressed into a single act of cognition, or as the projection of a truly universal agreement that cannot be represented. It would likewise be an account in which both the pleasures remembered in the beautiful and the common sense presupposed by judgments of taste were paired with the pain felt at the inability to represent our convergence upon a true unanimity or to represent what is beyond all knowledge (in Arendt's terms, the opinions and feelings of "everyone else"). In short, such an account would be one in which the pleasure associated with the beautiful would be coupled with the pain characteristic of the sublime, where the pain of the sublime derives specifically from our feeling overwhelmed by the presentation of the unpresentable—in Kant's words, the "absolutely great" (*CJ*, p. 94). (Recall that in characterizing the spectators of world history, Kant echoes the language of the sublime in saying that their experience "borders closely on enthusiasm, the very expression of which is *fraught with danger*" [*P*, p. 144].) Unlike more recent critical theory, however, which has focused on the sublime almost to the exclusion of the beautiful in discussing the *Critique of Judgment*, Arendt was drawn to those moments when Kant himself seemed to recoil from its pain and power, as in all those instances where he emphasizes that the fear raised in us is a faux fear or where he turns from representations of the violence of war to the far more comforting image of bourgeois peace, as in the remarks on war in *Perpetual Peace* (see *OH*, pp. 88–135) and in section 28 of the *Critique of Judgment* (e.g., "War itself, provided it is conducted with order and a sacred respect for the rights of citizens, has something sublime about it. . . . On the other hand, a long peace favors the predominance of a mere commercial spirit, and with it a debasing self-interest, cowardice, and effeminacy, and tends to degrade the character of the nation" [*CJ*, pp. 112–13]).

Arendt's tendency to privilege the beautiful over the sublime must be seen as part of her larger passion to save politics from irrationalism.

For this effort she takes her bearings relative to Kant's claim that taste represents a way of bringing the potentially fearsome and arbitrary power of the legislator-genius under the control of something like the "rule of law." Taste is, according to Kant, "the discipline (or corrective [training]) of genius": "it severely clips its wings, and makes it orderly . . . it gives it guidance, directing and controling its flight. . . . It introduces a clearness and order into the plenitude of thought, and in so doing gives stability to the ideas, and qualifies them at once for permanent and universal approval, for being followed by others. . . . Where the interests of both these clash in a product, and there has to be a sacrifice of something, then it should rather be on the side of genius" (*CJ*, p. 183; see *L*, p. 62). Moreover, Arendt emphasizes those elements in Kant's theory of taste that locate the very possibility of aesthetic reflective judgment in humankind's "sociability," which for Kant is both a point of departure (as in the "original compact" referred to in section 41 of the *Critique of Judgment*) and the "highest end" intended for humanity (as in the "Conjectural Beginning of Human History"[34]). Referencing section 41 of the third *Critique*, Arendt draws on Kant to explain how the possibility for aesthetic reflective judgments must be grounded in "sociability," which is in turn constitutive of human nature:

> If we admit that the impulse to society is natural to mankind, and that the suitability for and the propensity towards it, i.e. *sociability*, is a property essential to the requirements of man as a creature intended for society, and one, therefore, that belongs to *humanity*, it is inevitable that we should also look upon taste in the light of a faculty for estimating whatever enables us to communicate even our feeling to every one else, and hence as a means of promoting that upon which the natural inclination of every one is set. (*CJ*, p. 155)

That this sociability is "constitutive" in Kant's view is apparent from the fact that from the communicability of judgments of taste one can infer an "original compact" among members of the human species (Kant: "[A] regard to universal communicability is a thing which every one expects and requires from every one else, just as if it were part of an original compact dictated by humanity itself" [*CJ*, p. 155]). Quite understandably, however, Arendt wishes to historicize this archaeology of the communicable. The context for her discussion of judgment is not nature but the polis, which itself is historical. More specifically, her analysis of the role of judgments of taste in the making of a rational (i.e., peacefully communicative) community represents a way of re-membering and thereby carrying forward the discursive ideals embod-ied in the Greek polis. The prevailing model of judgment in modernity (which she links to the writings of Gracián and Cicero) is one that privileges the testing and negotiating of claims as a way to form the "community sense" that would otherwise be available only in mem-ory. Because it is representable and, in principle, open to all, the "com-munity sense" ensures the rationality and objectivity of the discourse of the polis.

But even Arendt's own writings would suggest that rationality and shareability are not sufficient criteria for the judgments made in the public-political sphere. Indeed, Arendt's understanding of the dynam-ics of politics would suggest that she recognized a tension between the framework of rationality established by communication and the trans-formative ideals that transcend existing representations and that help account for the acts of founding or constituting a state. In the 1970 *Lectures*, this tension shows up in the way she treats the categories of exemplary validity and genius. (For all the effort to "discipline" or "train" genius, the undisciplined, exemplary genius plays a crucial role in the concluding pages of Arendt's *Lectures*.) As in Kant, Arendt takes the genius as the one who is capable of a radical act of founding, though presumably not ex nihilo. The genius establishes the rule and makes an example of his or her unprecedented practice. For Arendt, the exemplar "is and remains a particular that in its very particularity reveals the generality that otherwise could not be defined" (*L*, p. 77): "If we say of somebody that he is good, we have in the back of our minds the example of Saint Francis or Jesus of Nazareth. The judg-ment has exemplary validity to the extent that the example is rightly chosen. Or to take another instance: in the context of French history I can talk about Napoleon Bonaparte as a particular man; but the mo-ment I speak about Bonapartism I have made an example of him" (*L*, p. 84). Arendt's "exemplar" and "genius" establish not just a new law or a new paradigm of lawfulness, they regularize or objectify creativity itself, which is also to say that the "exemplary" work of the genius proves valid insofar as it establishes a succession of followers. But in the objectification of the genius's example also lies the betrayal of the genius's creativity. Indeed, it is clear that for Arendt everything the ge-nius creates in new rules and in unprecedented examples seeks a more tangible, material, objective, and stable form in the public discourse of the polis.

Not surprisingly, in view of her interest in the *vita activa*, Arendt is drawn to the acts of founding and constituting a state, especially insofar as these "poetic" political acts make substantive and representable (and, therefore, rational and regular) that which might otherwise stand beyond all powers of representation. Hence her clear admiration in *On Revolution* for the Constitution of the United States as the materialization of the power of law vested in a people.[35] Only in America, she notes, did a revolution issue in the act of "constituting" a republic (*OR*, p. 157). She views the Constitution as the making of an enduring object that serves to materialize a series of otherwise unpresentable beliefs held in principle by all. Similarly, she is drawn to the ways in which a documentary record makes that act rational precisely because it is the *materialization* of a set of principles or beliefs. To the founding fathers, she notes, "the seat of power . . . was the people, but the source of the law was to become the Constitution, a written document, an endurable objective thing, which, to be sure, one could approach from many different angles and upon which one could impose many different interpretations, which one could change and amend in accordance with circumstances, but which nevertheless was never a subjective state of mind, like the will" (*OR*, p. 156). In the context of politics, the reflective judgments incited by "free particulars" shape the state as an object open for all to view, where rationality can be guaranteed. In Arendt's own analysis, the problem with "discourse," "speech," and "action" is that they are not in themselves productive of any object. As she says in *The Human Condition*, "they do not themselves 'produce,' bring forth anything, they are as futile as life itself. In order to become worldly things, that is, deeds and facts and events and patterns of thoughts or ideas, they must first be seen, heard, and remembered and then transformed, reified as it were, into things—into sayings of poetry, the written page or the printed book, into paintings or sculpture, into all sorts of records, documents, and monuments" (p. 95). Arendtian "action" needs a world, which incorporates labor and fabrication; likewise, judgment needs to be exercised within a determinate object-sphere: a polis or a state.

Arendt's analysis of the political act of "constitution" as a form of material making helps bring to light the Heideggerian (as opposed to the Kantian or Marxist) strain in her writing and becomes evident in her comment that the products of work are what go to make up a world ("Viewed as part of the world, the products of work—and not the products of labor—guarantee the permanence and durability without which a world would not be possible at all" [*HC*, p. 94]). Action needs a world if it is to have any endurance at all. At the same time, her analysis of "constitution" reveals the fact that, in politics at least, the "made thing" is fraught with tension. This is the tension between the creativity involved in founding or constituting a *political* world, which is meant to be a realm of free action but which relies on acts of making, and the expectation that any polis should conform to and ensure the standards of rationality embodied in "common sense." We might describe the twin poles of this tension as "genesis" and "normativity." As Arendt recognizes, every act of founding, of inauguration, or of radical beginning runs the risk of arbitrariness. What begins in an arbitrary way must be transformed into principle or rule if it is to be held in common by all. Indeed, she remains committed to a politics grounded in the objectification of the *sensus communis* even if it requires her to take the risk of false prophecy described in Kant's essay on progress. For her, however, the problem is not so much how to avoid the false or self-fulfilling prophecy as how to preserve the creativity of the new beginning as it is transformed into the lawful rule that a democratic polis needs to presuppose. Her answer, given in *On Revolution*, is to treat as a potentially productive paradox what elsewhere is resolved or reduced in favor of "principle" or "rule":

> What saves the act of beginning from its own arbitrariness is that it carries its own principle within itself, or, to be more precise, that beginning and principle, *principium* and principle, are not only related to each other, but are coeval. The absolute from which the beginning is to derive its own validity and which must save it, as it were, from its inherent arbitrariness is the principle which, together with it, makes its appearance in the world. The way the beginner starts whatever he intends to do lays down the law of action for those who have joined him in order to partake in the enterprise and to bring about its accomplishment. As such, the principle inspires the deeds that are to follow and remains apparent as long as the action lasts. (*OR*, p. 214)

In *On Revolution*, it is the materiality of the Constitution that provides both the new beginning and the rule. In the *Lectures* of 1970, the *sensus communis* itself becomes the rule. Despite the differences between them, both works reveal Arendt's will to defend the rationality of political judgment by grounding the state in the processes of representation and materialization, which the power of judgment divorced from world-making work cannot accomplish. As the guarantor of rationality, representation is the way in which Arendt resolves the tension in Kant between genesis and normativity, which we might also phrase as the tension between the creativity of the genius and claims of taste, or between the transformative (and potentially sublime) energies of revolution and the normativity of political life. To understand the task of politics as ensuring normativity through representability is admittedly to weaken its transformative potential and to risk rendering unintelligible the question of founding. By contrast, to view politics as "aesthetic" only insofar as it depends upon the representation of ideals that are available only to the creative genius is to risk the legislative arbitrariness that Arendt so deeply feared.[36] (Glossing Kant's moral philosophy, she reminds us that "man, insofar as he does anything at all, lays down the law; he is the legislator" [L, p. 50].) In light of the tensions between the legislative "genius" and the regularity of taste that makes reference to our "common sense"—tensions that are brought to light by Arendt's reading of Kant—it seems that the task ahead is to see the ways in which we can resist the temptation to reduce the complexity of the aporia of reflective judgment. We can, moreover, continue to probe the ways in which the terms of aesthetics can provide the basis for a nonreductive critique of politics, in the hope of seeing the polis as the space in which the interests of communication and transformation converge.

Notes

1. Immanuel Kant, "An Old Question Raised Again: Is the Human Race Constantly Progressing?" in Kant on History, ed. Lewis White Beck (Indianapolis: Bobbs-Merrill, 1963), pp. 137–54; hereafter referred to as P and OH, respectively.

2. Kant outlines three models of history, determined according to the play of good and evil in each. The first is "terroristic" and indicates decline and disintegration. The second is "eudemonistic" and proceeds according to the free will of the subject-agent. The third is "abderitic" and is exemplified by those who "reverse the plan of progress, build in order to demolish, and impose upon themselves the hopeless effort of rolling the stone of Sisyphus uphill in order to let it roll back down again" (P, p. 140).

3. Jean-François Lyotard makes this the subject of his discussion of the differend in Kant in The Differend: Phrases in Dispute, trans. Georges Van Den Abbeele (Minneapolis: University of Minnesota Press, 1988), pp. 161–71.

4. In the first Critique, Kant writes that "The touchstone whereby we decide whether our holding a thing to be true is conviction or mere persuasion is . . . the possibility of communicating it and of finding it to be valid for all human reason. For there is

then at least a presumption that the ground of the agreement of all judgments with each other, notwithstanding the differing characters of individuals, rests upon the common ground, namely, upon the object." Immanuel Kant, *Critique of Pure Reason*, trans. Norman Kemp Smith (New York: St. Martin's Press, 1965), p. 645, A820, B848. This means that establishing the validity of these signs is dependent upon creating a space for communication about them. The only "present" space in which the validity of these signs can be established is that of a communicative community, or what Arendt calls the "public sphere."

5. Little wonder, then, that recent political theorists such as Roberto Unger have argued that no true revolution will be possible if we do not first identify and clear ourselves free of false necessity. See especially volume 1 of Unger's *Politics*, entitled *False Necessity* (Cambridge: Cambridge University Press, 1987).

6. Jürgen Habermas, *The Theory of Communicative Action*, trans. Thomas McCarthy (Boston: Beacon Press, 1984), vol. 1, p. 51.

7. Hannah Arendt, *The Human Condition* (Chicago: University of Chicago Press, 1958), p. 45; hereafter referred to as *HC*.

8. Habermas writes that the "world" of the public sphere "was not world in the transcendental sense, as the quintessential concept of all phenomena, as the totality of their synthesis and to that extent identical with 'nature.' Rather, 'world' here pointed to humanity as a species, but in that guise in which its unity presented itself in appearance: the world of a critically debating reading public that at the time was just evolving within the broader bourgeois strata." Jürgen Habermas, *The Structural Transformation of the Public Sphere: An Inquiry into a Category of Bourgeois Society*, trans. Thomas Burger with Frederick Lawrence (Cambridge: MIT Press, 1993), p. 106; henceforth *ST*.

9. Immanuel Kant, "Answer to the Question: What Is Enlightenment?" in *OH*, p. 5.

10. This is emphasized in Arendt's *Lectures on Kant's Political Philosophy*, ed. Ronald Beiner (Chicago: University of Chicago Press, 1982); henceforth referred to as *L*. In historical terms, Arendt says elsewhere that the private sphere of society becomes public as a function of the rise of the social: "Society is the form in which the fact of mutual dependence for the sake of life and nothing else assumes public significance, and where the activities connected with sheer survival are permitted to appear in public" (*HC*, p. 48).

11. Lyotard emphasizes the role of hypotyposis (and, in the case of the Revolution as a sign of progress, of "extreme hypotyposis") in Kant's thinking: "The historical-political makes itself present to the assertion ['there is progress'] only through cases, which operate not as exempla and still less as schemata, but as complex hypotyposes, the more complex ones being the surer. The popular enthusiasm for the Revolution is a very validating case for the historical-political phrase, and thus allows for a very sure hypotyposis. This is for the simple reason that it is itself a very improbable hypotyposis (the recognition of the Idea of the republic in a 'formless,' empirical given)." Lyotard calculates the larger implications of this in Kant as follows: "As for the philosophy of history, about which there can be no question in a critical thought, it is an illusion born from the appearance that signs are exempla or schemata" (*The Differend*, p. 171).

12. Lyotard reads the enthusiasm of the spectators as an aesthetic analogue of the republican fervor of the actors in the Revolution, thus raising the question whether we are to regard aesthetic judgment as itself analogous to action or as the site in and through which analogies can be established. The latter is Lyotard's general position, but in this instance he does not clearly explain how it can be derived from Kant, whom he suggests sustains the former:

On stage, among the actors themselves, interests, ordinary passions, and the whole pathos of empirical (psychical, sociological)
causality are forever inextricably bound up with the interests of
pure moral reason and with the call of the Idea of republican law.
The spectators, placed on other national stages, which make up
the theatre hall for the spectacle and where absolutism generally
reigns, cannot on the contrary be suspected of having empirical
interests in making their sympathies public (*öffentlich*), they
even run the risk of suffering repression at the hands of their governments. That itself guarantees the–at least aesthetic–value of
their feelings. *It must be said of their enthusiasm that it is an aesthetic analogue of pure, republican fervor.* (Ibid., p. 167; emphasis
added)

13. Lyotard emphasizes the potential universality of the spectacle when he writes
that "the *Teilnehmung* through desire is not a participation in the act. But it is worth
more, because the feeling of the sublime, for its sake, is in fact spread out onto all the
national stages. Potentially, at least, it is universal. It is not universal in the way a well-
formed and validated cognitive phrase may be. . . . Like the feeling of the beautiful,
though, it does have an *a priori* which is not a rule that is universally recognized but a
rule awaiting its universality. It is this universality in abeyance or in suspense that is invoked in the aesthetic judgment" (Ibid., pp. 167–68).

14. Jean-Jacques Rousseau, "Letter to M. d'Alembert on the Theatre," in *Jean-
Jacques Rousseau: Politics and the Arts*, trans. Allan Bloom (Ithaca: Cornell University
Press, 1968), p. 81. Among Kant's other influences on the subject of the "disinterested
sympathy" of the spectator was David Hume. In his *Treatise* (Book 2, section 11),
Hume wrote that "no quality of human nature is more remarkable, both in itself and in
its consequences, than that propensity to sympathize with others, and to receive by communication their inclinations and sentiments, however different from, or even contrary
to our own." David Hume, *A Treatise of Human Nature*, ed. L.A. Selby-Bigge (Oxford:
Clarendon Press, 1978), p. 316.

15. Rousseau, "Letter to M. d'Alembert," p. 126.

16. See the essay "The End of All Things," in *OH*, pp. 69–84.

17. Lyotard's concern in addressing this issue is to guard against the "transcendental
illusion" of revolutionary politics invited by the French Revolution, to "confuse what is
presentable as an object for a cognitive phrase with what is presentable as an object for
a speculative and/or ethical phrase, that is, schemas and examples with *analoga*" (*The
Differend*, p. 162). David Carroll says in his commentary on Lyotard that

in the ethical–political realm, no example can be given of the law,
no direct presentation can be made of what constitutes justice. But
this does not mean that one is totally "abandoned" by the law and
placed in an ethical abyss, left with only subjective whim or the un-
controllable flux of libidinal drives that act in the absence of knowable laws (as, for example, Lyotard had argued in *Economie libid-
inale*). One is, rather, left with feelings, signs, and *analoga*, and in
Levinas's terms, "hostage" to an obligation that cannot be defined
in terms of a knowable law or moral code. What cannot be presented directly is evoked indirectly, presented in terms of its unpresentability, as unpresentable except by means of analogies.
(David Carroll, *Paraesthetics: Foucault, Lyotard, Derrida* [New
York: Methuen, 1987], p. 174)

18. In his edition of *L* (pp. 144–56), Ronald Beiner discusses the relevance to Arendt of Nietzsche's notion of the "gateway" in *Thus Spoke Zarathustra*.

19. Cf. Lyotard's emphasis on the role of the sublimity of the Revolution, as evidenced by the enthusiasm of the spectators, in his discussion of Kant: "Enthusiasm as an 'event of our time' . . . obeys the rule of the aesthetic antinomy. And it is the most contradictory of aesthetics, that of the most extreme sublime. First of all, because the sublime is not only a disinterested pleasure and a universal without a concept, such as taste, but also because it entails a finality of antifinality and a pleasure of pain, as opposed to the feeling of the beautiful whose finality is merely without an end and whose pleasure is due to the free agreement of the faculties with each other" (*The Differend*, p. 169).

20. In animals, "species" means "the characteristic in virtue of which all individuals must *directly* agree with one another" (Kant, third review of Herder's *Ideas for a Philosophy of the History of Mankind*, in *OH*, p. 51; emphasis added).

21. Ibid. Arendt cites this passage in *L*, p. 58.

22. Immanuel Kant, *Critique of Judgment*, trans. James Creed Meredith (Oxford: Clarendon Press, 1957), p. 14; emphasis added. This work is hereafter referred to as *CJ*.

23. Kant returns to the issue in section 57, "Solution of the Antinomy of Taste," where he nonetheless pursues the issue to the point where he believes it orients us undeniably toward the "supersensible" realm:

> If, however, our deduction [of the principle of reflective judgment] is at least credited with having been worked out on correct lines, even though it may not have been sufficiently clear in all its details, three ideas stand out in evidence. *Firstly*, there is the supersensible in general, without further determination, as substrate of nature; *secondly*, this same supersensible as principle of the subjective finality of nature for our cognitive faculties; *thirdly*, the same supersensible again, as principle of the ends of freedom, and principle of the common accord of these ends with freedom in the moral sphere. (*CJ*, p. 215)

The principal problem with this statement is that now we do not know whether the "supersensible substrate" is part of the problem or part of the solution to it. On the "difficulty" of judgment and the finally aporetic status of the problem in Kant, see Howard Caygill, *Art of Judgement* (Oxford: Blackwell, 1989).

24. Arendt clarifies that "I do not mean to say that Kant, because of the shortness of his life, failed to write the 'fourth Critique' but rather that the third Critique, the *Critique of Judgment*—which in distinction from the *Critique of Practical Reason* was written spontaneously and not, like the *Critique of Practical Reason*, in answer to critical observations, questions, and provocations—actually should become the book that otherwise is missing in Kant's great work" (*L*, p. 9). The notion that Kant's historical writings comprise a "fourth critique" was first put forward by Renato Composto in *La quarta critica kantiana* (Palermo: Palumbo, 1954).

25. Kant, *CJ*, p. 104.

26. Cf. Lyotard:

> The *sensus communis* is thus in aesthetics what the role of practical, reasonable beings is in ethics. It is an appeal to community carried out *a priori* and judged without a rule of direct presentation. However, in the case of moral obligation, the community is required by the mediation of a concept of reason, the Idea of Freedom, while in the phrase of the beautiful, the community of addressors and addressees is called forth immediately, without the

mediation of any concept, by feeling alone, inasmuch as this feeling
can be shared *a priori*. The community is already there as taste, but
it is not yet there as rational consensus." (*The Differend*, p. 169)

For Arendt, the task of politics is to provide a "rule of direct presentation" in order to move from the community as taste to the community as rational consensus. In the process, she relies on a series of analogies that are never quite recognized as such: taste is read as moral (through the principle of the "enlarged mentality"), and this morality is in turn read into the politics.

27. Arendt's formulation raises interesting questions not addressed by her: Is the taste of the food in the food or in us? Likewise with the smell of the rose: is the smell in the rose or in us? Nonetheless, the thrust of Arendt's argument is clear enough. In arguing that private sense is "rooted" in public sense, we are forced to do precisely what Kant said we must not in matters of claims of taste, namely, ascribe an object to them.

28. Section 9 provides a somewhat more intricate formulation of this claim. There Kant argues that when we call something beautiful, beauty is to be regarded as "a quality of the object forming part of its inherent determination according to concepts; although beauty is for itself, apart from any reference to the feeling of the Subject, nothing" (*CJ*, p. 59).

29. I note here that the first problem is not, as Eagleton has suggested, that these particulars cannot be subsumed under laws, nor that the act of subsumption serves the interests of the state, but rather that they are not readily associable with objects. See Terry Eagleton, *The Ideology of the Aesthetics* (Oxford: Blackwell, 1990). Given sufficient space to argue the point, it could be shown that the problem of objectification (qua reification) stems from this fact.

30. Which is not to say that we do not wish to make such ascriptions. The history of our critical engagement with romanticism could be understood as the ongoing negotiation of this wish; Kant himself refers to something like it in his account of the sublime, which is said to involve "a certain . . . substitution of a respect for the Object in place of one for the idea of humanity in our own self—the Subject" (*CJ*, p. 106).

31. Immanuel Kant, *Anthropology from a Pragmatic Point of View*, ed. and trans. Mary J. Gregor (The Hague: Martinus Nijhoff, 1974), sec. 44.

32. Arendt, "Imagination" (seminar on Kant's *Critique of Judgment* given at the New School for Social Research, fall 1970), in *L*, p. 83.

33. Jay M. Bernstein, *The Fate of Art* (University Park: Pennsylvania State University Press, 1992), pp. 37–38.

34. Arendt, *L*, p. 73, citing Kant, "Conjectural Beginning of Human History," in *OH*, p. 54.

35. Hannah Arendt, *On Revolution* (New York: Viking, 1965), p. 156; hereafter referred to as *OR*.

36. David Ingram has an insightful discussion of these and related issues in his recent *Reason, History, and Politics: The Communitarian Grounds of Legitimation in the Modern Age* (Albany: State University of New York Press, 1995), especially pp. 361–62. For Ingram, it is Derrida (against whom he poses Arendt) who most forcefully articulates the problem with any notion of politics or ethics founded on "indeterminacy." "Indeterminacy" is here aligned to radical transformation, which Ingram rightly recognizes as dangerous:

> [I]n Derrida's anarchistic universe, the rebellious reinvention of the
> constitution in every legislative and adjudicative act ensures the
> freedom of future generations. However, its fleeting legitimacy will
> be purchased at the expense of liberties that might otherwise have

had the protection of standing law. . . . Needless to say, the antipodes of permanent (legal) repetition and permanent (ethical) revolution do not leave much room for that historical progress so sought after by Derrida. Indeed, if Blumenberg is right, they do not leave much room for historical change as distinct from mere succession. In this dichotomous universe, progression of the past that progresses beyond the past remains essentially enigmatic." (p. 362)

Five

"Please Sit Down, but Don't Make Yourself at Home": Arendtian "Visiting" and the Prefigurative Politics of Consciousness-Raising

Lisa Disch

Consciousness-raising can be justifiably singled out as the most distinctive political practice of women's liberation in the United States. A grassroots movement that emerged in 1967, consciousness-raising radicalized the struggle for women's rights, the century-old effort to win legal and legislative reform of sex discrimination.[1] Practiced by small groups of women who gathered in living rooms and dorm rooms, consciousness-raising turned those domestic places into "free space" where women could find support and understanding and could experience the power of sisterhood.[2] More important, consciousness-raising engaged women in "theory-production"[3] that was revolutionary for being oral, collective, and—in Sara Evans's words—"phenomenological" because of its use of experience as the starting point for theory. Evans also praises consciousness-raising for its democratic innovations, calling the small groups a "brilliant tool" that enabled grassroots organizing on a national scale and infused the women's movement with "the anarchist democracy and spirit of radical egalitarianism characteristic of the early new left."[4] With more than 100,000 women participating in groups across the nation in 1973 alone, consciousness-raising was "one of the largest ever education and support movements of its kind for women in the history of this country."[5] But besides being a democratic breakthrough orchestrated by women and for women, consciousness-raising originated what turns out to be radical feminism's most genuinely baffling bequest to contemporary feminist theory: the "commonplace" that "every woman has wisdom and knowledge through her own life experiences that will lead to working for revolutionary changes in her position."[6]

Among academic feminists in the United States, it has become almost obligatory to deny this axiom or at least to qualify it to the point of once again divorcing theory from experience. Various academic feminists acknowledge that connecting the two was "the most vital and imaginative force within the women's liberation movement."[7] The theory-experience nexus authorized ordinary women to contest the various interpretive frameworks—whether mainstream liberal or radical New Left—that denied the political validity of critiques of sexual inequality. At the same time, however, this focus on experience is charged with anti-intellectualism, with precipitating the degeneration of critical social analysis into personal therapy, and with fostering the emergence of a "cultural feminism" that abandoned the critique of women's oppression to indulge the "fantasy of a morally pure sisterhood" among educated, middle-class white women.[8] Ironically, then, the same radical feminism that rhetoricians of the grassroots right execrate for assaulting public morality and precipitating the breakdown of the American family is criticized by feminists themselves as, in Donna Haraway's words, "the moral majority within."[9]

In this essay I take issue with the trend to repudiate consciousness-raising as the dogmatic practice of a self-righteous sisterhood. My stake in these debates about the political and intellectual legacy of the women's movement is that the stories told about it—in histories, theories, and popular culture—are my principal means of access to its period of greatest activism.[10] I object to narratives that hold consciousness-raising responsible for the moralization of sisterhood, because they effectively rule out that movement as a model for participatory theory building and democratic politics. And because I am a feminist academic in the discipline of political theory—a field in which it is not uncommon for scholars to invoke fifth-century Athens or eighteenth-century republicanism as exemplars of democratic promise incompletely realized—this feminist "trashing" of consciousness-raising strikes me as ironic.[11] It seems to me that if there is democratic promise to be found in those more remote examples, then radical feminism must also harbor something worth reclaiming.

I look to the work of Hannah Arendt to assist me in this project because she takes up this same question of the relationships among life experiences, theory, and action, albeit under different historical circumstances. Her context was Nazism, which she, like many other contemporary Continental thinkers, understood to challenge Enlightenment fundamentals such as autonomy and critical reflection. Could such foundations be trusted to hold up against inhumanity in an age marked by the "banality of evil"?[12] Arendt's exemplar for this evil was Adolf Eichmann, who struck her with what she called his "horrible gift for consoling himself with clichés." The horror of banality is that it is a moral failure utterly devoid of genius. It is not rooted in a tragic flaw of character or a magnificent obsession with greatness, but in an "inability to *think*, namely, to think from the standpoint of somebody else." Her point was not to suggest that Eichmann's actions were commonplace but to destabilize the legal distinction between deviancy and normalcy that more dramatic images of evil serve to anchor. This in turn should call attention to the conundrum of prosecuting crimes committed without criminal intent, "under a criminal *law* and by a criminal *state*." The banality, Arendt claimed, was that the legalization of criminality made it possible for someone as "terrifyingly normal" as Eichmann to commit crimes but not "to know or feel that he is doing wrong."[13] Despite her insistence that this was no ordinary occurrence but an unprecedented evil uncomprehended by Western law, many of her readers mistook "banality" for a perverse understatement that trivialized the crime and apologized for the criminal.

Despite the anger it provoked, "banality" was not an ill-chosen term on Arendt's part but the driving concern behind this central question of her work: How can critical thinking proceed when the religious and secular systems of thought that once provided a living (although not necessarily common) vocabulary of critique and aspiration have ossified into ideological formulas? Arendt's answer to that question is widely acknowledged to anticipate contemporary debates about the place of antifoundationalism in late modern humanism. She asserted that criticism must proceed "without bannisters," by relinquishing the habits of mind that simplify the task of making sense out of experience and acknowledging that "thought itself arises out of incidents of living experience and must remain bound to them as the only guideposts by which to take its bearings."[14]

Banality was a clarion call of second-wave feminism as well, although not in so many words. Whereas liberal feminists such as Betty Friedan appealed to the everyday disaffection of the bourgeois housewife, radical feminists called attention to the dissonance between the "incidents of living experience" and the habits of mind learned in the (principally bourgeois) family. Mary Daly writes, "In the beginning is the awakening awareness, which is spindled, spent, mutilated by false words. Our call of the wild is a call to dis-possess our Selves of the shrouds, the winding sheets of words. We eject, banish, depose the possessing language—spoken and written words, body language, architectural language, technological language, the language of symbols and of institutional structures—by inspiriting our Selves."[15] Exhortations such as this one make visible both the connections and the tensions between Arendt's work and the problems of contemporary feminism. Consciousness-raising began as a resistance against the stultifying normalcy of the household, which feminists characterized as an obstacle not simply to women's career ambitions but also to their abilities to think, imagine, and analyze. In this sense, then, consciousness-raising began from the dilemma of banality that Arendt took to characterize late modernity. In turn, with its commitment to "spin" new terms of understanding from women's experience, radical feminism arrived at an appeal to Arendt's thinking "without bannisters." In significant contrast to Arendt, however, Daly frames both dilemma and answer in gender-specific terms that Arendt would not have credited. Daly denounces received vocabularies not simply because they are banal but also because they are "contaminated" by patriarchy and betray women's efforts to make sense of their lives on their own terms.[16]

Given her antipathy to social categories such as gender, what justifies bringing Arendt's work to bear on consciousness-raising? Simply, Arendt's antipathy is shared even by some feminist critics of the early second wave who take to task its gender-specificity for failing to "combat the manifold and simultaneous oppressions that all women of color face."[17] In Arendt's terms, radical feminists fixed gender as the "bannister" of their movement, thereby reassembling the patriarchal structuring of women's experience that they set out to dismantle.[18] It is noteworthy that "experience" holds a place in the writings of women of color even as gender does not. This brings me to the question that I enlist Arendt in puzzling out: Does an experience-based critical practice necessarily tend toward foundationalism in theory and fundamentalism in politics?

I am not arguing for a literal revival of consciousness-raising but for a rereading of the promise that this practice might hold for contemporary democratic theory and feminist politics. Without denying that the fantasy of sisterhood as a moral home for all women did fund consciousness-raising, I contend that working alongside that ideal and, in fact, checking its impetus toward unanimity was the practice Hannah Arendt calls "visiting." By visiting, Arendt meant engaging in "representative thinking," a "process . . . [that] does not blindly adopt the actual views of those who stand somewhere else, and hence look upon the world from a different perspective . . . [but involves] being and thinking in my own identity where actually I am not" (*BPF*, 241). This practice is neither insistently egocentric nor self-effacingly empathic, although it might be easily confused with both of these. Instead it involves retelling the story of an event from a plurality of unfamiliar standpoints, thereby making a shift from thinking from a private perspective to thinking from a public vantage point. Arendt appropriates it to account for the possibility of moving from description to criticism without leaving experience behind; it meets the criterion of being *in* experience but not *of* it.

The uniqueness of this conception of judgment, which Arendt draws out of Kant's third *Critique*, is its departure both from typically rationalist epistemologies, where critical insight depends on assuming a vantage point of spectatorial disinterest, and from communitarian models, where right action is reducible to a unanimous general will that is rooted in shared history, beliefs, and identity. Critical insight in Arendt's visiting model depends on an impartiality that is earned by what Immanuel Kant called "enlarged thought." Although this model of impartiality does involve taking the standpoints of others, enlarged thought is not empathy. It does not indulge the fiction that "one can know what actually goes on in [another's] mind," an assimilationist fantasy by which I make myself so at home in your position that I erase the differences between us.[19] As a visitor, I think my own thoughts but from the place of somebody else, permitting myself to experience the disorientation necessary for understanding how the world looks different to that person. Visiting, then, is contrary to parochialism, which means staying home; contrary to tourism, which means providing myself with all the comforts of home even as I travel; and contrary to assimilationism, which means forcibly making myself at home in a new place by appropriating its customs.

In this essay I reconsider consciousness-raising through the lens of visiting. By foregrounding mobility, translation, and perspectivity, this concept complicates the opposition between experience and theory. Taking up Arendt's assumption that "experience" is always narrated and hence imbued already with theory enables me to separate the critical promise of consciousness-raising both from the effects it produced in particular contexts and from those that are attributed to it in some retrospective accounts.

My confidence that Arendt's work will assist me in this critical reconstruction of consciousness-raising will strike some readers as misplaced. Jürgen Habermas, for example, has argued that Arendt's allegiance to an outmoded epistemology rules out the possibility of experience-based critical understanding altogether. Habermas argues that Arendt carries too far her concern to protect the free play of public opinion. Discrediting objectivity to arrest the violence of dogmatism, Arendt leaves no grounds for differentiating between warranted public opinion and strategically manipulated ideology. I contend that this charge has established Habermasian rational discourse as the template for subsequent scholars' readings of Arendt's conception of judgment.[20] In this essay I answer Habermas both conceptually and historically. I explicate Arendt's terms "visiting" and "exemplary validity" and then use them as a template for reconstructing the theory-experience nexus in the practice of radical feminism. Arendt's judgment writings afford me the vocabulary to articulate how consciousness-raising was no simpleminded positivism or essentialism but a model of critical engagement to rival that which Habermas has reconstructed from the eighteenth-century bourgeois public sphere.[21]

The Feminist Impasse regarding Experience

"Sisterhood" was undeniably an explicitly moral ideal. It was the "prefigurative" dimension of women's liberation, the utopian aspiration of radical feminists who wanted more than an equal right to the rewards of a competitive, individualist society; they wanted to transform that society in accordance with an egalitarian, cooperative democratic ethos.[22] But although sisterhood always carried a moral charge, there is a significant, if subtle, distinction between a prefigurative aspiration and a moral touchstone. Whereas a prefiguration is an explicitly imaginary ideal that regulates action but cannot determine it, a moral touchstone pretends certitude. It becomes all too easily an absolute standard that its self-appointed guardians impose on actions and ideas as a test of political purity.

No doubt, wherever sisterhood was treated not as a utopian aspiration but as a test of correctness, the small groups that had powered the radical women's movement turned from free spaces into enclaves of correctness. As Sara Evans observes, "keen insights into the way in which women had been repressed by hierarchical structures . . . developed into moral imperatives that were out of touch with the *necessary tension between means and ends.*"[23] This tension between means and ends facilitates the work of building common cause across lines of privilege, because it opens space for people who share a common goal to disagree about how to frame that goal and how to achieve it. The space of disagreement is especially important to the work of politics among strangers, a work that involves compromises and connections that defy the test of purity.

When sisterhood is claimed as the moral basis of feminism, this tension between means and ends, with all its discomfort and impurities, is suppressed. The moralization of sisterhood forecloses analysis of domination so that "women's experience" is mistaken for a universal standpoint uncontaminated by power and absolved of all complicity with class or race privilege.[24] Political rhetoric suffers, in turn, as "moral reproach" takes the place of political critique and the fantasy of unity stands in for "an alternative vision of collective life."[25] Drawing an apt but surprising parallel between the radical women's movement and the eighteenth-century civic public, Carmen Sirianni sums up these criticisms, arguing that consciousness-raising groups that established sexual orientation, "intense emotional risk taking," nurturance, and openness as conditions for trust and inclusion enforced a "sisterly version of Rousseauian virtue."[26] Insofar as the imperative for women to give voice to a common experience *as women* took precedence over attending to social relations of domination *among* them, feminists transfigured sisterhood into their own "ideal of impartiality," taking up a model of republican virtue that would foreclose efforts to make common cause across lines of privilege.[27]

Could it be that the commitment to produce theory out of women's experience—feminists' most radical resistance against moral universalism and abstract impartiality—actually reproduced a version of both of these in the politics of sisterly virtue? Feminist scholars in various disciplines have suggested that there is a significant, if not necessary, connection between experientialism and this repressive body politic. Joan Scott cautions that insofar as feminism "attribute[s] an indisputable authenticity to women's experience . . . it literally equates the personal with the political, for the lived experience of women is seen as leading directly to resistance to oppression, that is, to feminism." Although she does not simply equate consciousness-raising with virtue politics, Scott casts suspicion on any claim to the "authority of experience," because it shuts down inquiry into the "ways in which politics organize and interpret experience," into the contexts that determine what counts as women's oppression and who is authorized to speak about it.[28] Alice Echols regards consciousness-raising as moralistic to the core, defining as its underlying premise the belief that "women's experience was in some sense universal, and that gender, not race or class, was the primary and defining contradiction."[29] Similarly, Judith Grant argues that the focus on experience disposed radical feminism toward foundationalism and ethnocentrism, asserting that the "idea behind experience was that it would unite women through what it was assumed would be their common feelings about oppression."[30] Finally, taking what appears to be a pragmatic stand on "women's experience," Denise Riley writes: "Because of its drive toward a political massing together of women, feminism can never wholeheartedly dismantle 'women's experience,' however much this category conflates the attributed, the imposed, and the lived, and then sanctifies the resulting mélange."[31] In short, Riley deems "women's experience" to be a conceptually hopeless but politically necessary evil.

My objection to these retrospective accounts is that they sell out radical movement insights in a typically "academic" fashion.[32] Furthermore, these critics are implicitly working from a particular account of consciousness-raising—that offered by standpoint epistemology, which despite being the earliest and most influential academic reformulation of that practice, is in no way definitive. Early formulations of feminist standpoint epistemology tended to evade the problem of accounting for the relationship between experience and critical understanding by positing experience as a fixed point of departure that is critical by definition at particular social locations. With this foundationalist move, standpoint theorists rendered feminist consciousness, in Terry Winant's terms, an "epistemic consolation prize" of women's oppression.[33] These versions of standpoint epistemology leave both too much and too little for the theorist to do. By stipulating women's experience of oppression as the ground of feminist subjectivity, these theories leave no need to account for the relationship between oppression and critical agency. Instead, it is the task of the theorist, as Sandra Harding has recently put it, to engage in "a critical evaluation to determine which social situations tend to generate the most objective knowledge claims." Although Harding simplifies the problem of feminist theory, she greatly augments the authority of the theorist, who is now charged with identifying, in her words, "the social causes of good beliefs."[34] Helen Longino has argued that theories such as these reaffirm the principled outside that they set out to refute in the first place. By establishing feminist theory at a position of ultimate privilege over the many "multiple and incompatible knowledge positions" of women, they paradoxically authorize it to identify the standpoints of "genuine or better knowledge" among them.[35] Besides defining feminist consciousness as a consolation prize, standpoint epistemologies position the feminist theorist as the game-show host who decides which contestant should get it.

Experience, as it is constructed in these versions of standpoint theory, reproduces the problem of labor as it is constructed in the particular version of Marxism from which standpoint feminism draws its theoretical energy: it functions as an ontological ground of resistance that cannot account for its own critical purchase except by making a knowledge claim that privileges the perspective of the oppressed rather than that of the powerful.[36] Wendy Brown has put this point particularly forcefully, arguing that "within feminist standpoint theory as well as much other modernist feminist theory, . . . consciousness raising operates as feminism's epistemologically positivist moment. The material excavated there, like the material uncovered in psychoanalysis or delivered in confession, is valued as the hidden truth of women's existence—true because it is hidden, and hidden because women are oppressed, silenced, and privatized."[37] As Judith Grant has observed, it answers a paradox with a tautology by grounding feminism, which is "the lens through which experiences are interpreted," in the very experiences it is said to interpret.[38] Although it is termed an epistemology, standpoint theory evades the challenge to provide a critical theory of the position of experience within feminist practice and instead falls into the cliché of romanticizing the insights of the oppressed.

Standpoint epistemology is not the only effort to reformulate theoretically the "commonplace" that every woman's life experience is a resource for radical feminist theory. Both Donna Haraway and Teresa de Lauretis have made efforts to conceive the role of experience in feminist practice without positing it as the foundation of sisterhood. Haraway argues that " 'women's experience' [is] . . . a fiction and fact of the most crucial, political kind," especially for a "cyborg politics" in which solidarity is premised on "affinity, not identity."[39] In turn, de Lauretis chooses to read as paradox what others might dismiss as contradiction, namely, that consciousness-raising engaged women in taking possession of their experience by a means—storytelling—whose very practice discredits experience as a secure ground of identity. Moreover, she asserts that working out the theoretical contributions of this paradox is "the real difficulty, but also the most exciting, original project of feminist theory."[40]

I take this difficulty to be, in part, a consequence of the deceptive simplicity of what I understand to be the central insight of consciousness-raising: that gender is the *condition* of women's experience. Understood in the many senses of the term "condition," this insight suggests that gender *stipulates the terms* of women's oppression; it is a *restrictive clause* that hampers and enables women's self-expression; finally, it is both the *articulating principle* of identity in gender-structured societies and women's peculiar *affliction*. Because of all that "condition" signifies, the status of "gender" is uncertain. It is not an ontological ground or an empirically verifiable fact but an effect of social and legal contingencies. If gender is indeterminate, then "women's experience" must be more so. De Lauretis names this indeterminacy when she writes that experience figures in consciousness-raising "not [as] a fixed point of departure or arrival from which one then interacts with the world," but as the effect of an ongoing "*process*" of interaction.[41] Consequently, the "problem and struggle" for feminist theory is to explain how feminist critical agency can be *in* experience without being *of* experience, that is, to explain "its being at once inside its own social and discursive determinations and yet also outside and excessive to them."[42]

These various writings work both to set up an impasse on this question of experience and to point the way out of it. On the one hand, there is the certainty about the truth of women's experience that produced the doctrinaire self-righteousness of some parts of the radical women's movement; on the other hand, there is the radical skepticism toward experience, truth, and sisterhood that unsettles any confidence that feminism could be a movement to liberate women. I contend that one way to lever feminist theory out of this impasse is to complicate these retrospective accounts of the place of experience within radical feminist practices and, by extension, to appreciate just how complex an understanding of feminist agency was prefigured by movement practices. I suggest that Arendt's "visiting" names a mode of critique that treats experience as an interactive process rather than a fixed point of departure. It begins, thereby, to account for the position of experience in radical feminist practice without reducing it to the unitary foundation of feminist identity.

Moving from Identity to *Inter-est*

What if experience were understood not as the foundation of feminist identity but as the "*inter-est*" that sustains public conversation among feminists? *Inter-est*—literally "between them" or "in-between"—is the term Hannah Arendt uses to account for the possibility of political solidarity among people who must make common cause in the absence of a common origin or a shared identity. Arendt uses this term with characteristic perversity, departing in important ways from both liberal and communitarian understandings of interest without calling attention to the differences. In contrast to the rational individualism of interest-group pluralism, Arendt's *inter-est* is not a bargaining position to be deduced from private goals and traded competitively on the political market. Instead, it is an "agreed purpose" that she calls an "in-between, which varies with each group of people and serves to relate and bind them together."[43] Although "this 'between' can be a common ground and it can be a common purpose," it is not a communitarian common good that in some way expresses the authentic needs or beliefs of its disparate participants and harmonizes their wills. Rather, she writes, "it always fulfills the double function of binding men together *and* separating them in an articulate way" (*HC*, 81). In turn, this common ground is not discovered but constructed, determined by a process of disputation that "links and separates" people, thus accomplishing the "double function" of uniting individuals and separating them in an "articulate way." Paradoxically, then, the commonality that sustains this version of political solidarity is not shared identity or truth. As Margaret Canovan has put it, "it is the space between them that unites them, rather than some quality inside each of them."[44]

Arendt introduces the term *inter-est* to mediate between the extremes of pluralist fragmentation and communitarian fusion. It gives her a way to shift the locus of solidarity from the interiorities of political actors to the public realm, a uniquely perspectival "reality" that "relies on the simultaneous presence of innumerable perspectives and aspects in which the common world presents itself and for which no common measurement or denominator can ever be devised. . . . Under the conditions of a common world, reality is not guaranteed primarily by the 'common nature' of all men who constitute it, but rather by the fact that, differences of position and the resulting variety of perspectives notwithstanding, everybody is always concerned with the same object" (*HC*, 57–58). Arendt's conception of public *inter-est* is striking for the fact that she insists on the irreducibility of these perspectives to an identical measure while at the same time maintaining that there is a "sameness in utter diversity" of public objects (*HC*, 57). This abstract and paradoxical quality brings to my mind cubist paintings of ordinary things that are nearly unrecognizable by virtue of being represented, in a single composition, from a multiplicity of discontinuous perspectives. Cubism achieves visually what Arendt is trying to do conceptually: to challenge the unitary assumption that sameness is necessarily coterminous with identity. *Inter-est* is the same but nonidentical object of public concern. By proposing the concept *inter-est*, Arendt attempts to afford a conception of political solidarity or sameness that is not founded on a moral touchstone or an identical nature.[45]

Contrary to the academic reconstruction of radical feminism as a politics of sisterly virtue, various radical feminist pamphlets and talking pieces suggest that many activists appreciated the difference between basing a movement on the construction of a common *inter-est* and grounding it in a unitarian identity. For example, radical feminists early on attempted to specify how the sisterhood prefigured by consciousness-raising differed in kind from that fostered by either "study groups" that put theory ahead of action, or "rap" groups that put therapy ahead of social change. This determination often turned on how "experience" figured into a group's practice. One Redstockings pamphlet characterized study groups as dogmatic for imposing "preordained" conclusions and making "generalizations divorced from personal experience" and characterized rap groups as empiricist for indulging in testimony without pressing forward to generalizations.[46] By contrast, Kathie Sarachild asserts that in consciousness-raising "the decision to emphasize our own feelings and experiences as women and to test all generalizations and reading we did by our own experience was actually the scientific method of research."[47] The problem with Sarachild's conception of scientific method, however, is that it is barely distinguishable from empiricism and, consequently, as Cellestine Ware argues, is inadequate to differentiate between consciousness-raising and rapping. Ware notes that Redstockings meetings tended toward an "anti-intellectualism" so that "members [were] unwilling, fearful and sometimes unable to move from an intuitive assessment of their experience to sociological understanding of what happened to them and why it . . . happened."[48]

Ware counters Sarachild with an (implicitly postempiricist) account of consciousness-raising as a constructivist practice that does not simply take its bearings from experience but also constitutes experience. On Ware's account, testifying to one's experiences is only the first step in consciousness-raising. The moment of science comes in generalizing from that testimony "to perceive how certain patterns of behavior, and occurrences formerly thought individual problems, are actually socially determined and politically contested."[49] Experience is the *interest* or public object of consciousness-raising as Ware describes it, not the ground.

This was no simple politics of authenticity but, as Liz Bondi puts it, an "essentially inauthentic identity politics" in which women struggled to maintain that "feminist identity was necessarily constructed rather than uncovered" while also sustaining "a sense of purpose and authorship, essential for political action."[50] This need to politicize identity but at the same time to authorize women to define themselves on their own terms meant learning how to take experience seriously without regarding it as definitive and uncontestable. In Bondi's terms, it required an "insistence on the *validity*, rather than the transparency, of collectively articulated experiences."[51] This distinction that Bondi draws between according to experience validity or transparency suggests another way to differentiate between practicing consciousness-raising as theory building and as rapping. Ware underscores this distinction, explaining that to build theory by consciousness-raising was "to relate fragmented and seemingly unrelated lives of individual women and to construct a politic [*sic*] from the issues discovered in the process."[52] Theory building is not an intuitive process of mutual identification but a comparative process of constructing Arendt's cubist public object, an *inter-est*.

Donna Haraway has argued that articulating such a common but nonidentical public object would call for a specifically "feminist objectivity" that she terms "situated knowledges."[53] In contrast to standpoint theory, Haraway's objectivity refuses the subject/object binary from both sides. It claims neither to be a disembodied and therefore all-seeing sovereign nor to be the consolation standpoint of a "subjugated" other.[54] Instead, it is an objectivity premised on "partial perspective," which is not parochialism but a critical perspective on partiality that "allows us to become answerable for what we learn to see."[55] Achieving feminist objectivity requires engaging in what Haraway calls "non-innocent conversations" about the "redrawing of boundaries" to "nam[e] things to be stable and to be like each other."[56] Haraway politicizes objectivity as an epistemic reward of a kind of solidarity that, in Arendt's terms, comes from discerning a "sameness in utter diversity" that cannot be reduced to singular identity (*HC*, 57). Feminist objectivity, like Arendt's public *inter-est*, depends on putting different views in perspective in relation to each other without reducing them to a common denominator.

Haraway's concept of "situated knowledges" affords an opening into Arendt's unfinished writings on judgment. Whereas Haraway redefines objectivity as "mobile positioning and . . . passionate detachment," Arendt redefines impartiality, through a creative appropriation of Kant's "enlarged thinking," as "visiting."[57] Reading Arendt's judgment writings in relation to Haraway's politicized conception of objectivity brings to light how Arendt's "visiting" rivals Habermas's rational argumentation as a model of discourse for a democratic public.

From Essential Truth to Exemplary Validity

In her unfinished writings on political judgment, Arendt entertains the question how validity can be premised on a generalization from experience without dogmatically affirming its truth. The answer turns on what she calls "*exemplary* validity," a political and positional standard of judgment that serves not to certify a principle or decision but rather to survey the *inter-est*, that disaggregated common object of the public space (*LKPP*, 76; Arendt's emphasis). In this model of public rationality, establishing the validity of an opinion is not principally a matter of advancing reasons but of offering exemplars. In contrast to reasons, which fuel argumentation, exemplars spark visiting, a kind of cubist imagining by which one rewrites the story of an event from the plurality of perspectives it would engender in a particular context. The exemplar serves not to certify that any single decision is right but to map the terrain of a dispute to ascertain where I or we stand in relation to you.

I contend that Arendt's visiting anticipates the work of contemporary feminist political theorists who dispute the narrowness of democratic theories that equate public rationality with legalistic reasoning. For Arendt, as for Jane Mansbridge, "normative arguments do not consist solely, or even primarily, of deduction from agreed or self-evident principles . . . [but] involve telling stories, making analogies, and asking readers to imagine themselves in situations they have never experienced."[58] Through the argument she makes to link visiting to exemplary validity, Arendt enables me to carry this feminist critique forward. She defends exemplary validity as a means to bridge the gap between judgment and unreflective preference without collapsing the space of disagreement that is so necessary to the practice of politics among strangers.

It will seem odd to credit Hannah Arendt with proposing a radical conception of validity when so many readers have argued that she offers little basis for her own dogmatic pronouncements, let alone a framework for public rationality. Jürgen Habermas leaves little doubt as to the implausibility of the claim that Arendt's work might yield a conception of validity that could bridge theory and experience, writing that she opens a "yawning abyss between knowledge and opinion that cannot be closed with arguments."[59] Before explicating Arendt's "visiting," I must address Habermas's claim, which has set the terms of a one-sided dialogue with Arendt's judgment writings.[60] Even scholars who take Arendt's part against Habermas have not succeeded in absolving her, on her own terms, of the charge that she deprives judgment of any ground in validity and thus leaves public matters to be settled arbitrarily.[61] Ronald Beiner, for example, refutes Habermas's charge by disarming it, arguing that Arendt makes no pretense to close the abyss between knowledge and opinion because, over the course of her career, she relinquished her concern with the relationship between judging and acting. Her last writings, according to Beiner, aspire only to extend Kant's conception of aesthetic judgment to politics, describing political judgment as a "prerogative of the solitary (though public-spirited) contemplator as opposed to the actor."[62]

Although Beiner means to take Arendt's side, I think his defense actually diminishes Arendt's work by assimilating her thinking to that of Kant. In contrast, Habermas—whose criticism seems more devastating—actually praises Arendt as a profoundly original thinker who taught him "to approach a theory of communicative action," and thereby leaves open the possibility that Arendt might have something to say about the problem of political judgment and about democratic theory more generally.[63] Like Habermas, I contend that Arendt makes a potentially distinctive and important contribution to efforts to analyze solidarity in democratic publics, especially grassroots publics such as consciousness-raising groups or neighborhood organizations. But by judging her work according to his own conception of democratic public rationality—namely, cooperative action oriented by morally valid norms—Habermas obscures the unique conception of common sense that Arendt takes from Kant's third *Critique* and, with it, the connection between Arendt's work and consciousness-raising.

Ironically, Habermas claims to learn from Arendt's work the very ideal of public rationality that is the centerpiece of his dispute with her. In what he calls her distinctive credo concerning the "impotence of the powerful," Habermas finds a conception of power that is uniquely democratic because it is intersubjective, deriving from solidarity rather than force.[64] The thesis to which he refers is Arendt's claim that political power cannot be "possessed like strength or applied like force," because it is not a singular attribute or property but a possibility contingent on plurality. It "springs up between men when they act together and vanishes the moment they disperse" (*HC*, 200–1). Habermas sees in this credo a promise, unrecognized by Arendt, for a "communications conception of power"[65] whereby "the validity rather than the social currency of a norm [would be] the determining ground of . . . action."[66] Validity, for Habermas, turns on whether or not an action is rationally motivated; that is, whether it conforms to a norm that could, in principle, secure from each person who would be affected by its "consequences and . . . side effects" assent to the claim that it "is equally good for all."[67] For Habermas, no political action can be genuinely public unless it is impartial. Impartiality, in turn, rests on the twofold conviction that the proposed action rests on a norm that everyone could, in principle, agree was morally right and could recognize as appropriate to the situation at hand.[68]

The principal distinction between their conceptions of public rationality is that Arendt does not believe that political actions can or should be grounded in justified moral convictions. Although she maintains a conception of public rationality, she disconnects it from moral validity. For his part, Habermas is well aware of this difference; this is exactly what he takes to be incoherent in Arendt's work.[69] For her part, Arendt puts forth what she takes to be good reasons for protecting what she calls "political maxims" against the authoritative force of moral dictates.

Advancing what Habermas quite correctly terms an "antiquated" epistemology,[70] Arendt asserts that moral norms have no place in politics because they are not matters for judgment but "matters of cognition" that are "compelled" by foundational truths and, consequently, invite no disagreement. Political maxims do call for judgment, however, because they cannot be resolved by truth claims and, consequently, do not admit of consensus. Habermas seizes on this distinction as evidence of Arendt's allegiance to a foundationalist conception of "theoretical knowledge that is based on ultimate insights and certainties."[71] He argues that it is this dogmatic and traditionalist understanding of theory that requires her to open the "yawning abyss between knowledge and opinion" whereby the validity of opinions cannot be redeemed by argumentation. For his own conception of public rationality, Habermas departs from Arendt (and Kant) to bridge the gap between knowledge and opinion by arguing that norms and theories alike depend on critical argumentation for their validation. Because he rejects the empiricist claim that theoretical knowledge is validated decisively by its correspondence to reality, Habermas can affirm that "normative claims to validity have cognitive meaning and can be treated *like* claims to truth" without imputing to norms an a priori claim to validity that forecloses disputation.[72] Having established that moral truths, like empirical claims, are discursively redeemed, Habermas has, in effect, recalibrated Kantian practical reason from a solitary monologue to an intersubjective dialogue.[73]

Habermas suggests that if not for her "antiquated" epistemology, Arendt might also have recognized that in the case of claims to both scientific truth and moral rightness, validity is not dictated (by fact or by reason) but is discursively achieved through fair and persuasive argumentation. Had she made this leap, she too could have seen how public principles could be justified without compromising their status as debatable claims and could have seen how to close the abyss between knowledge and opinion without jeopardizing politics.[74] Instead, according to Habermas, Arendt "retreats" from this radical position to defer to the "venerable figure of the contract," which posits an arbitrary and incontestable act of will as the ground of political validity.[75] In sum, Habermas imputes to Arendt a reaffirmation of social contract theory and then concludes that it is by her return to the myth of the originary moment that she subverts the democratic possibilities of her work.[76]

I cannot help noticing the story that Habermas tells through the rhetoric he uses to position his own work in relation to Arendt's. He casts her as a grandmother who is too timid to appreciate the originality of the legacy she hands down to him and who retreats instead behind the "venerable figure" of Enlightenment contract theory. Habermas, the rebellious custodian of the family treasure, will spend it on radically redesigning the Enlightenment project to conceive a rational foundation for political authority. Executing that design by means of communicative praxis rather than consciousness, Habermas puts his ancestral house—disarrayed by the phenomenon of totalitarianism—back in order. My objection is not that Habermas misinterprets Arendt but that this influential interpretation set the terms of a dialogue that figures her as an Enlightenment antique and him as the rebel grandson. I propose to explore what might be gained by turning the tables to position her as the rebel and him as the relic.

Turning the Tables

> *Power is actualized only where word and deed have not parted company, where words are not empty and deeds not brutal, where words are not used to veil intentions but to disclose realities, and deeds are not used to violate and destroy but to establish relations and create new realities.*
> —Hannah Arendt, *The Human Condition*

> *I call interactions communicative when the participants coordinate their plans of action consensually, with the agreement reached at any point being evaluated in terms of the intersubjective recognition of validity claims.*   —Jürgen Habermas, "Discourse Ethics"

Aside from the obvious differences in their ways of writing, it would seem that Habermas has good reason to claim that his conception of communicative interaction brings to fruition the radical democratic possibilities of Arendt's conception of public power. For both Habermas and Arendt, democratic public rationality depends on the capacity of words to create intersubjective relationships. But I suggest that there are subtle but important differences between the ways that Habermas and Arendt conceive of intersubjectivity and that something is lost by assimilating her ideal of public rationality to his. Despite his appreciation for the democratic promise in Arendt's effort to define power as acting in concert, I contend that Habermas depoliticizes her conception of intersubjectivity when he assimilates it to his own, imputing to Arendt the view that "*language* [is] the mechanism for coordinating the concert of different actions."[77] From an Arendtian perspective, to conceive of language in such instrumental terms is to contain the very thing she most admires about it: the power of words to bring new relations into being.

To discern the differences between Arendt's and Habermas's conceptions of language and appreciate the import of those differences for their conceptions of public rationality, it is important to take up the differences in their ways of writing as something more than a difference of style. Habermas holds a justificatory model of public rationality that depends on exactly the kind of formalistic precision with language that is evidenced in the preceding passage. For Habermas, no norm of political action can be genuinely public unless it is also morally valid, which means that it would meet with the free and consensual "approval of all affected *in their capacity as participants in practical discourse.*"[78] To ensure that approval is freely given, Habermas has to set parameters for the legitimate "use" of language—the "mechanism" whereby approval is consolidated. He does this by elaborating the requisite conditions of practical discourse, the regulatory ideal that Habermas claims is necessarily presupposed by anyone who participates in argumentation. Note that practical discourse is not a procedure for determining political ends; to the contrary, one cannot act in one's capacity as a participant in practical discourse without adopting, for the purpose of argument, a "hypothetical attitude" toward an existing state of affairs and prevailing norms. By suspending the context of decision making, actors make it possible to engage in an especially rigorous kind of argumentation that is *not* strategic (oriented toward promoting self-interest) but is, rather, "a reflective form of action oriented toward reaching an understanding."[79] It is only through this kind of argumentation that actors can test whether a proposed course of action is triggered by popular prejudice or oriented by publicly held convictions.

On the surface, Arendt holds a similar conception of public rationality. She insists that norms of action submit to "reflective judgment," the faculty that Kant (idiosyncratically) called "common sense." Kantian common sense is not a fixed body of doctrine held unreflectively by a particular people but a practice of thinking "with an enlarged mentality." This practice—which Arendt characterizes with the vivid metaphor of training "one's imagination to go visiting"—involves testing my conclusions against "other people's thinking" to "fit" my views into the particular community to which I belong as I judge (*LKPP*, 72–73, 43). Although visiting does not involve validating one's conclusions by convincing others to approve them, neither is it simply a matter of conforming one's own views to a prevailing common sense. Visiting affords an impartiality that "is obtained by taking the viewpoints of others into account" (*LKPP*, 42). Its practice of positioning is the means whereby I map the terrain of a dispute to figure out how to "meet" others. By visiting, I endow my views with "communicability" by figuring out how to frame and word them "in such a way that [others] understand," regardless whether they concede validity to them (*LKPP*, 42, 69, 74). In contrast to Habermas, then, Arendt argues that norms of action need be only communicable, not justifiable, to be public.

This distinction between communicability and justification is manifest in the different ways that Arendt and Habermas construct the relationship of principles to public action. Habermas's justificatory model of public rationality presupposes that principles can be conceptually specified and agreed upon. Principles prescribe limits to action, marking the boundary, even if only hypothetically, between what is morally justifiable and what is merely strategic. By contrast, Arendt regards principles as forces that are disclosed in action, not as its limiting conditions. They are infectious, "communicable" in a way that defies containment. From Arendt's perspective, to assume that principles can be conceptually specified and warranted in argumentation, albeit hypothetically, is to reduce action to behavior by making principles analogous to motives and goals, "determining factors" that are external to agency and command it in the way that a cause commands an effect. In contrast to causes, Arendt insists that principles are at once "in" action but not comprehended by it and "without" action but not external to it. She writes that they "inspire, *as it were*, from without," which is to say that their relationship to action unsettles typical metaphysical oppositions such as cause versus effect or outside versus inside (*BPF*, 151, 152; emphasis added).

I suggested that the difference between these two models of public rationality—Habermas's justificatory model and the "communicability" model that Arendt claims to take from Kant—is driven by a basic disagreement about language. Just what does this disagreement consist in? Certainly neither Arendt nor Habermas holds language to be a pure medium of interaction, a system of representations that mirrors the world, or a straightforward medium of self-expression. Habermasian practical discourse does depend, however, on the assumption that the orientation of argumentation toward reflective critical agreement is not merely a normative ideal imposed on language from outside but one of the "constitutive *presuppositions*" to which anyone who speaks publicly necessarily conforms.[80] In Habermas's terms, "reaching understanding is the inherent telos of human speech."[81] If speech is to realize this telos, consolidating agreement in particular conflicts, Habermas must require that participants in justificatory discourse be exacting in its use.

For Arendt, in contrast, who follows Heidegger on this point, language is not primarily a means to consolidate relationships, specify meanings, and " 'name' things which we already perceive as distinct."[82] As Arendt puts it, "a word has a much stronger relation to what it denotes or what it is than just the way it is *being used* between you and me." In addition to its use in communication, or "communicative value," language has a "disclosing quality."[83] Not just a means of self-expression but also "the repository of a particular way of apprehending the world that grows out of collective symbols and memories," language constitutes identities as well as relationships.[84] This disclosing quality of language is an effect of plurality, the "condition" of public life that makes certain that whenever we speak, our words "always fall into an already existing web . . . of human relationships, with its innumerable, conflicting wills and intentions" (*HC,* 184).

However much this web thwarts purpose and frustrates intent, it is not the enemy of agency. Rather, Arendt writes that it is the "medium, in which action alone is real," and asserts "that it 'produces' stories with or without intention as naturally as fabrication produces tangible things" (*HC,* 184). Arendt suggests that agency inheres in the initiatory capacity of words. Invoking pre-Socratic Athens to exemplify this quality, Arendt writes: "[In pre-Socratic Athens,] speech and action were considered to be coeval and coequal . . . and this originally meant not only that most political action, in so far as it remains outside the sphere of violence, is indeed transacted in words, but more fundamentally that finding the right words at the right moment, *quite apart from the information or communication they may convey*, is action" (*HC*, 26; emphasis added). Although we certainly do put words to use in communicative transactions, it is because of the unanticipated effect (peculiar to words) of saying the right word at the right moment that language precipitates new beginnings beyond the bounds of prior agreement.

Habermasian discourse calls for an almost technical precision with language. As is evidenced by the earlier passage, Habermas models that precision in his own writing. He employs language to establish definitions, clarify distinctions, and make it possible to consolidate agreements based on no more than the intersubjective power of discursive logic. For a theorist such as Hannah Arendt, who appreciates the disclosive quality of language, it is impossible to say for certain where words stop and action begins. Consequently, mutual agreement may be, for her, not a guarantee that a public norm is valid but rather a constraint on the spontaneity of action and its proliferation of effects. Even so, Arendt does not eschew precision but practices a precision of a different kind, one tuned to meet the resistance of what M. M. Bakhtin describes as "a dialogically agitated and tension-filled environment of alien words, value judgments and accents." Every "living utterance," Bakhtin contends, "weaves in and out of complex interrelationships, merges with some, recoils from others, intersects with yet a third group: and all this may crucially shape discourse, may leave a trace in all its semantic layers, may complicate its expression and influence its entire stylistic profile." Under these conditions, communication is necessarily and ineluctably strategic such that "the word in living conversation is directly, blatantly, oriented toward a future answer-word: it provokes an answer, anticipates it and structures itself in the answer's direction."[85] Arendt's visiting is one means of anticipating that future word. It enables a precision that consists in carefully crafting one's words to take aim at one's listeners in such a way as to limit the positions from which they can take them up and answer back.

All this is to say that Arendt does not conceive of principles as entities to be "distilled into concepts."[86] In turn, the task of judgment as Arendt conceives it is neither to justify an action nor to explain it. Rather, it is to render its "inspiring principle" tangible in the form of a story so that it can be remembered and even contested (*BPF*, 152).[87]

On its face, this contention poses a problem in that this link between stories and principles seems to contradict Arendt's insistence about the indeterminacy of principles. Certainly narration can be said to transmit principles even more definitively than argumentation does, by virtue of its capacity to seem true to experience in ways that argumentation obviously is not.[88] But stories engage Arendt not for being "closer" to experience and "truer" to its principles but for the way they proliferate meanings. She explains that stories, the "products" of action, do not determine its principles once and for all but disclose them "through a kind of repetition" that precipitates further repetitions (*HC*, 187).

No story can express the principle of an action in any simple way; rather, the meaning of any story is dispersed by the "web of relations" that produced it. In Arendt's public, language—to borrow again from Bakhtin—effects a "spectral dispersion" of public principles. Like a ray of light illuminating an image, a story must pass through "an atmosphere filled with alien words, value judgments and accents" on its way to an audience. And it is by virtue of this atmosphere—not in spite of it—that a story illuminates, not by simply reproducing an action but by making "the facets of the image sparkle."[89] Habermas proposes the "communications concept of power" to contain the effects of the "disclosing quality" of language and to defend a justificatory model of public rationality in which principles are sites where agreement can hypothetically be consolidated. For Arendt, principles are the common but—as in the cubist painting—dispersed objects of the public space.

It might be objected that I have made too much of this disagreement about language. The difference between Habermas and Arendt is that they address different problems and they do so at distinctly different levels. In Habermas's terms, Arendt's work takes up the question of judgment at the level of "ethics," where argumentation is so permeated by values that people cannot take the hypothetical attitude required for the more "exacting" communication of discourse oriented toward moral justification. Because of this, Arendt cannot speak to the question how principles can be valid absent the fictions of a universal community or faculty, but only to the "application" of principles to public problems "*within* the horizon of a concrete historical form of life."[90] Because she works at this level of application, Arendt simply takes for granted the hypothetical conditions of validity that Habermas so painstakingly attempts to justify.

One problem with assigning Arendt's work to the level of ethics is that by doing so, Habermas directly contradicts Arendt's own understanding of her *Lectures on Kant's Political Philosophy*. Her project, as she describes it, is to find in Kant's third *Critique* a model of political judgment whose condition of validity is neither truth nor consensus but rather common sense, as Kant redefines that term. Furthermore, Habermas's insistence that Arendt cannot speak to the question of validity depends on his asserting a categorical distinction between ethical-political and moral-political disputes that itself, as Thomas McCarthy has pointed out, is open to disputation.[91] Finally, McCarthy has also observed that by making this distinction, Habermas opens a "yawning abyss" of his own. He admits only two alternatives to coercion as a means of social coordination: a democratic, public-interest-based compromise or a rationally motivated consensus. Given a heterogeneous and stratified society, McCarthy argues that even reasonable people who are willing to engage in reflective argumentation may find that they disagree about the public interest. To provide a basis for social cooperation, they need something more compelling than strategic compromise but less exacting than rationally motivated consensus. The alternatives of compromise or consensus are "too restrictive" to permit them a resolution of their differences that is both rational and compelling.[92]

I do not suggest that McCarthy would accept Arendt's account of judgment as an improvement on Habermasian critical discourse. But I do contend that for readers who refuse to interpret Arendt's work through the restrictive lens of Habermas's model of public rationality, it may be possible to illuminate a different facet of the relationship between these two thinkers. Perhaps Habermas is too hasty in his claim to realize the unfulfilled promise of her work. Perhaps Arendt herself, when she is permitted to address the question of validity on her own terms, offers an account of judgment that is better suited than Habermasian justification to serve as a model of public rationality in a heterogeneous and stratified democracy.

Conclusion

In a sense, then, Habermas is justified in claiming that Arendt sees an "abyss" between knowledge and opinion that cannot "be closed with *arguments*." He fails her as a reader, however, when he assumes that this means she has no way to cross that abyss at all and, consequently, nothing to say about the question of validity. Arendt models her conception of judgment after Kant's third *Critique* not because she believed that greatness should take precedence over questions of right but because she believed that one forms judgments about political events as one forms judgments of taste, by "reflect[ing] upon others and their taste, tak[ing] their possible judgments into account" (*LKPP*, 67).[93] Furthermore, in politics as in aesthetics, when I say "this is right (or beautiful)" I neither expect that my assessment will be universally binding, as I might when I say "this is obligatory," nor that it will be convincing, as I might when I say "this is true," but I do regard that assessment to be public. For Arendt, as I have noted, "visiting" accounts for this expectation of publicity.

How does visiting—mapping a dispute by thinking my thoughts from the place of somebody else—account for the difference between subjective preference and reflective judgment? I suggest two possible answers. First, visiting ensures that when I judge, I know where I stand—not in the abstract, in relation to general principle, but in the relations that a particular conflict engenders among its various parties. Second, by visiting I ensure that my judgment will be communicable to others, regardless whether it convinces them. The peculiarity of visiting, however, is that it produces no results. That is to say, it "does not tell one how *to act*" or even, ultimately, what to make of the situation at hand (*LKPP*, 44). As Susan Bickford has put it, "there is no automatic answer that comes from this process; the tension between thinking in my own place and thinking with an enlarged mentality is never simply or neatly resolved. At the end of my travels, I still have to judge."[94]

It seems that Arendt's account of visiting does not answer the problem of validity but evades it. How can a faculty that reflects on particular events without seeking to justify or explain them claim to be critical? Is it not purely descriptive? How can validity be premised on such a faculty? Arendt refers to these questions as the problem of the "*tertium quid*" or "*tertium comparationis*," which is the problem of finding a third term or a term of comparison that enables one to move beyond merely juxtaposing one position against another, to a reflective assessment of their relative worth. Arendt claims that Kant offers a unique solution to this problem in the third *Critique* where he introduces what she terms "*exemplary* validity," a term of comparison that renders judgment by example (*LKPP*, 76; Arendt's emphasis). An example turns a particular—on its own terms—into an evaluative standard that has communicability among people who share a "particular historical tradition." It is a term of comparison that "has its origin in some particular historical incident" but "is valid for more than one case" *without* being valid for all cases at all times (*LKPP*, 85).

What accounts for the validity of a judgment that is communicated by example? Arendt offers a deceptively simple answer to this question: "The judgment has exemplary validity to the extent that the example is rightly chosen." True to form, Arendt does not suggest precise, technical criteria for determining when an example is rightly chosen but instead illustrates her own maxim by example. She writes: "[I]n the context of French history I can talk about Napoleon Bonaparte as a particular man; but the moment I speak about Bonapartism I have made an example of him" (*LKPP*, 84). The difference here between the man and the exemplar, although Arendt does not elaborate it, is between referring literally to Bonaparte and citing him as a figure for a more general political phenomenon. By citing Bonaparte to illuminate the Ross Perot phenomenon, I put the present into historical perspective; although Perot is present, to align him with Bonaparte is to view him *as if* with historical distance. In contrast to a spectatorship that purports to be above time, historical distance does not pretend to be a disinterested or value-neutral standpoint of judgment; on the contrary, to invoke "Bonapartism" as an evaluation of a present event is to take up an explicitly partisan position.

Determining whether or not an example is rightly chosen would involve asking two questions. First, did the audience recognize the example? And second, what did they make of it? That is, did the example illuminate a new facet of a current event or situation? Did it stimulate its audience to a critical response? It is important to note that these questions afford no definitive answers, because the validity of an exemplar turns neither on its correspondence to an empirical referent nor on its auditors reaching consensus as to its appropriateness. As in matters of taste, where "one can never compel anyone to agree with one's judgments [but] . . . can only 'woo' or 'court' the agreement of everyone else," I do not defend my choice of example by trying to convince you that I am right (*LKPP*, 72). Rather, I appeal to you to retell the story from my perspective, to imagine what about the Perot phenomenon induces me to characterize it using an exemplar such as Bonapartism. This process of appeal may partly entail our reaching agreement on what we mean by the term "Bonapartism," although we cannot settle the question by definition. Even if we come to agree on our terms, we may still disagree on the question whether Perot is a Bonapartist figure.

What is unique and, to some readers, disturbing about Arendt's reconceptualization of public rationality is that she detaches validity from rightness. One implication of this is that a judgment can have exemplary validity without being regarded by its proponent as right.[95] The separation of validity from rightness would have a somewhat different implication in an instance when I advance a judgment that I believe to be right but that provokes my audience to disagreement and outrage. Despite my failure to convince them, their anger might confirm that I chose a valid example to communicate my position, precisely because it fails to convince them that I am right. The deployment of an exemplar, as Arendt describes it, works to sound out a conflict, not to consolidate a standpoint.

The beauty of exemplarity is that it figures experience into the process of judging in a way that, to recall Bondi, implies neither its authenticity nor its transparency. Think of the different conventions of validation that are activated by citing an example to illuminate an event and bearing witness or testifying to that event. Testimony necessarily engages questions about the reliability of a witness and about the extent to which the accounts of different witnesses corroborate and contradict each other. In effect, the process of validating testimony works to consolidate the cubist object of the public space onto a unitary plane. In contrast, the claim "Ross Perot is a Bonapartist figure" is manifestly an interpretive claim that cannot be taken literally and so need not be corroborated to be valid. It is not altogether indifferent to the problem of truth, however, in that it asserts a comparison and invokes a principle by means of that comparison. As Arendt suggests, it is like an expression of taste in that it is not a purely subjective assertion of idiosyncratic preference or perception but a statement that calls for assent from others.

I see exemplary validity as one way to lever consciousness-raising out of the impasse between radical skepticism and dogmatic moralism because it permits me to complicate various retrospective accounts of the relationship of experience to radical feminist practice. Arendtian visiting and its attendant use of exemplars gives us a way to understand feminist thinking and practice as *in* experience but not *of* it. Experience is *inter-est*, between us, and visiting lets us render it comparable as a public object. In contrast to theories that treat a story as testimony to what I believe to be true, from my standpoint, Arendtian visiting suggests that experience might play into critical understanding figuratively rather than literally. Storytelling cites experience, it does not relay it. It does not call for empathy or recognition but may aim even to provoke discomfort by figuring differences rather than commonalities. Among strangers who must make common cause in the absence of a common origin, storytelling is an invitation to sit down but not to make yourself at "home."[96]

Reconstructed by means of visiting, a practice such as consciousness-raising need not be seen to effect a sisterly reversal of the public sphere, creating a domain of mutual understanding by means of empathy rather than argumentation. Instead, it can be a practice that, to borrow another phrase from Bakhtin, "pushes to the limit the mutual nonunderstanding represented by people who speak in different languages."[97] Mutual nonunderstanding is the "common sense" of Arendt's cubist public space. In contrast to the Habermasian model, where public rationality depends on showing that actions can be supported by convictions, Arendt holds that principles are disclosed in action; they do not precede or justify it. Visiting involves imagining the plurality of stories that any action might disclose on the assumption that they cannot be reduced to a common measure. Its purpose is not to justify an action but to treat it as a legend that explains the differences within the public that initiated it.

Notes

This essay has incurred more than its share of debts to the generosity of colleagues. At Northwestern University in fall 1994, Sara Monoson, Jenny Mansbridge, and the Critical Theory Workshop offered insights into the section on consciousness-raising. At the University of North Carolina in early 1995, Richard Bernstein, Craig Calhoun, Nancy Fraser, John McGowan, and Mark Yellin gave advice and support to an early, sketchy draft. For their comments at the 1995 meetings of the American Political Science Association, I thank Joanna Scott and Suzanne Jacobitti. I thank Jeffrey Isaac for posing a question to me several years ago that sparked this engagement with Habermas. At the University of Minnesota, I thank Samuel Chambers, for getting me to think about language. I also thank Anne Enke, Ryan Fortson, and the Critical Theory Summer Reading Project. I am grateful to Lisa Bower, Jeani O'Brien, and Jennifer Pierce—the invincible women's writing group—who will see their collaboration between the lines. And finally, I acknowledge a debt to Susan Bickford for her inspiration, our friendship, and our "visiting": she lent the words that helped me bring this chapter to a close.

    1. That is not to say that consciousness-raising was unique to feminism. It has its

roots in the "speak bitterness" movement during the cultural revolution in China, in revolutionary struggles in Guatemala, and in the Civil Rights movement in the southern United States. See Alice Echols, *Daring to Be Bad: Radical Feminism in America, 1967–1975* (Minneapolis: University of Minnesota Press, 1989), 84. What was distinctive about its practice by women's liberationists, however, was its centrality to theory production and to the creation of alternative political structures by movement women who rejected the reformist politics of liberal feminists. See Sara Evans, *Personal Politics: The Roots of Women's Liberation in the Civil Rights Movement and the New Left* (New York: Knopf, 1979), 215; and Jo Freeman, "The Tyranny of Structurelessness," *Berkeley Journal of Sociology* 17 (1972): 151–64.

2. Evans, *Personal Politics*, 215.

3. Katie King, *Theory in Its Feminist Travels* (Bloomington: Indiana University Press, 1994), 20.

4. Evans, *Personal Politics*, 214–15, 222.

5. Anita Shreve, *Women Together, Women Alone* (New York: Viking, 1989), 6.

6. Cellestine Ware, *Woman Power: The Movement for Women's Liberation* (New York: Tower Publications, 1970), 44.

7. Echols, *Daring to Be Bad*, 3. See also Judith Grant, *Fundamental Feminisms* (New York: Routledge, 1993).

8. Echols, *Daring to Be Bad*, 455. See also Chris Weedon, *Feminist Practice and Poststructuralist Theory* (Oxford, England, and Cambridge, Mass.: Blackwell, 1987); Wendy Brown, "Feminist Hesitations, Postmodern Exposures," *differences: A Journal of Feminist Cultural Studies* 3, no. 1 (1991): 63–84; and Joan Scott, "The Evidence of Experience," *Critical Inquiry* 17 (1991): 773–97.

9. Donna Haraway, "A Manifesto for Cyborgs: Science, Technology, and Socialist Feminism in the 1980's," *Socialist Review* 80 (1985): 65.

10. In the summer of 1967, when radical women in Chicago initiated their first sustained resistance against the New Left, I was not quite six years old. That fall, as women's groups began to form around the country, I entered first grade at Foster Elementary School, an experimental school in Evanston, Illinois, which was among the first public schools in the nation to take up the Supreme Court's mandate for racial integration.

11. See Jane Gallop, Marianne Hirsch, and Nancy K. Miller, "Criticizing Feminist Criticism," in *Conflicts in Feminism*, ed. Marianne Hirsch and Evelyn Fox Keller (New York: Routledge, 1990).

12. This phrase, the infamous subtitle of Arendt's *New Yorker* installments on the trial of Adolf Eichmann, appears to have been coined by her from an observation that Karl Jaspers made to her in 1946. See Hannah Arendt and Karl Jaspers, *Correspondence: 1926–1969*, trans. Robert Kimber and Rita Kimber, ed. Lotte Kohler and Hans Saner (New York: Harcourt Brace Jovanovich, 1992), 62.

13. Hannah Arendt, *Eichmann in Jerusalem: A Report on the Banality of Evil* (New York: Penguin, 1983), 55, 49, 262, 276. For an illuminating exploration of the meaning of the term "banality" and its relationship to what Arendt had earlier termed "radical evil," see Richard J. Bernstein, "Did Hannah Arendt Change Her Mind? From Radical Evil to the Banality of Evil," in *Hannah Arendt: Twenty Years Later*, ed. Larry May and Jerome Kohn (Cambridge: MIT Press, 1996), 127–46.

14. Hannah Arendt, *Between Past and Future* (New York: Penguin, 1983), 14; hereafter cited in text as *BPF*.

15. Mary Daly, *Gyn/Ecology: The Metaethics of Radical Feminism* (Boston: Beacon Press, 1990), 345.

16. Ibid., 368.

17. Combahee River Collective, "The Combahee River Collective Statement," in *Home Girls: A Black Feminist Anthology*, ed. Barbara Smith (Latham, N.Y.: Kitchen Table: Women of Color Press, 1983), 272.

18. Of the various scholars who remark on the connection between Arendt's work and the political theory of women of color, Susan Bickford is the only one to attend to it in detail. Against critics who reduce this work to a politics of victimhood inimical to Arendt's politics of action, Bickford argues that many of these theorists demand a political identity that is not social but public as Arendt understands it: "something created, constructed in the presence of others, and largely through words (speech and writing)." Susan Bickford, "In the Presence of Others: Arendt and Anzaldúa on the Paradox of Public Appearance," in *Feminist Interpretations of Hannah Arendt*, ed. Bonnie Honig (Philadelphia: Pennsylvania State University Press, 1995), 325.

19. Hannah Arendt, *Lectures on Kant's Political Philosophy*, ed. Ronald Beiner (Chicago: University of Chicago Press, 1982), 43; hereafter cited in text as *LKPP*.

20. See Seyla Benhabib, "Judgment and the Moral Foundations of Politics in Hannah Arendt's Thought," in *Situating the Self* (New York: Routledge, 1992); Patrick Riley, "Hannah Arendt on Kant, Truth, and Politics," *Political Studies* 35 (1987): 379–92; and Peter J. Steinberger, "Hannah Arendt on Judgment," *American Journal of Political Science* 34, no. 3 (1990): 803–21.

21. Jürgen Habermas, *The Structural Transformation of the Public Sphere: An Inquiry into a Category of Bourgeois Society*, trans. Thomas Burger with Frederick Lawrence (Cambridge: MIT Press, 1989).

22. Wini Breines, *Community and Organization in the New Left, 1962–1968*, rev. ed. (New Brunswick: Rutgers University Press, 1989).

23. Evans, *Personal Politics*, 223; emphasis added.

24. See Haraway, "Manifesto for Cyborgs."

25. Brown, "Feminist Hesitations, Postmodern Exposures," 77.

26. Carmen Sirianni, "Learning Pluralism: Democracy and Diversity in Feminist Organizations," in *Democratic Community*, ed. NOMOS XXXV (New York: New York University Press), 291.

27. See Iris Marion Young, *Justice and the Politics of Difference* (Princeton: Princeton University Press, 1990), ch. 4; Haraway, "Manifesto for Cyborgs"; and Brown, "Feminist Hesitations, Postmodern Exposures."

28. Scott, "Evidence of Experience," 787.

29. Echols, *Daring to Be Bad*, 90.

30. Grant, *Fundamental Feminisms*, 31.

31. Denise Riley, *"Am I That Name?": Feminism and the Category of "Women" in History* (Minneapolis: University of Minnesota Press, 1988), 100.

32. Ann Leffler, Dair Gillespie, and Elinor Lerner, *Academic Feminists and the Women's Movement*, women's liberation pamphlet (Iowa City: Iowa City Women's Press, 1973).

33. Terry Winant, "The Feminist Standpoint: A Matter of Language," *Hypatia* 2, no. 1 (1987): 133.

34. Sandra Harding, *Whose Science? Whose Knowledge?* (Ithaca: Cornell University Press, 1991), 142, 149.

35. Helen Longino, "Subjects, Power, and Knowledge: Description and Prescription in Feminist Philosophies of Science," in *Feminist Epistemologies*, ed. Linda Alcoff and Elizabeth Potter (New York: Routledge, 1993), 107.

36. In *Time, Labor, and Social Domination* (New York: Cambridge University Press, 1993), Moishe Postone proposes an important distinction between a critical theory

from the standpoint of labor, and a *critical theory of labor in capitalist society*. Meticulously differentiating between Marx and Lukács, Postone maintains that to argue from the standpoint of labor is only to reproduce the subject/object split that is characteristic of social relations determined by the commodity form and, therefore, to be incapable of transforming them. In contrast, a critical theory of labor under capitalism both names such fundamental assumptions as that labor is the subject (i.e., agent and oppressed producer) of value, and calls those assumptions into question (chaps. 1–2). Similarly, as I will discuss, feminist theorists have begun to abandon arguments based on privileging the standpoint of oppression and have moved instead to question subject/object formulations of agency altogether.

37. Brown, "Feminist Hesitations, Postmodern Exposures," 72.

38. Grant, *Fundamental Feminisms*, 101.

39. Haraway, "Manifesto for Cyborgs," 65, 73.

40. Teresa de Lauretis, *Alice Doesn't* (Bloomington: Indiana University Press, 1984), 166.

41. Ibid., 159.

42. Teresa de Lauretis, "Eccentric Subjects: Feminist Theory and Historical Consciousness," *Feminist Studies* 16, no. 1 (1990): 116.

43. Hannah Arendt, *The Human Condition* (Chicago: University of Chicago Press, 1958), 245, 182; hereafter cited in text as *HC*.

44. Margaret Canovan, "Politics as Culture: Hannah Arendt and the Public Realm," *History of Political Thought* 6, no. 3 (1985): 634.

45. The conception of political membership that Arendt introduces with this concept *inter-est* is evocative of the "radical democratic" politics of Ernesto Laclau and Chantal Mouffe. *Inter-est* would be, in Mouffe's terms, an "articulating principle" that allows for the "common recognition" of ideals such as liberty and equality by persons who interpret those ideals differently because they are "engaged in many different purposive enterprises and [hold] different conceptions of the good." Chantal Mouffe, "Democratic Citizenship and the Political Community," in *Community at Loose Ends*, ed. Miami Theory Collective (Minneapolis: University of Minnesota Press, 1991), 79. There is an important difference between Arendtian and radical democratic understandings of politics, however. Mouffe contends that the articulation of a common interest in a shared ideal is not only conflictual but also *divisive* and *antagonistic*: "to construct a 'we,' it must be distinguished from the 'they' and that means establishing a frontier, defining an 'enemy'" (78). Although Arendt acknowledges the irreducibility of political difference and, hence, the inevitability of public conflict and contestation, she nonetheless maintains an inclusive concept of political solidarity where excluding "them" is not necessary for recognizing "us."

46. Redstockings, ed., *Feminist Revolution*, abr. ed. (New York: Random House, 1978), 150.

47. Kathie Sarachild, "Consciousness-Raising: A Radical Weapon," in ibid., 145; first published 1968.

48. Ware, *Woman Power*, 40.

49. Ibid., 44.

50. Liz Bondi, "Locating Identity Politics," in *Place and the Politics of Identity*, ed. Michael Keith and Stephen Pile (New York: Routledge, 1993), 95.

51. Ibid., 92; Bondi's emphasis.

52. Ware, *Woman Power*, 100. I am grateful to Katie King for directing me to Ware's text by crediting to Ware the position that the purpose of consciousness-raising "is not to exchange or relive experience, nor is it cathartic; rather, its purpose is to teach women

to think abstractly in order to make theory, and the purpose of theory is to clarify and to clear a ground for action." See King, *Theory in Its Feminist Travels,* 127.

53. Donna Haraway, "Situated Knowledges: The Science Question in Feminism and the Privilege of Partial Perspective," *Feminist Studies* 14, no. 3 (1988): 581.

54. Ibid., 584.

55. Ibid., 583.

56. Ibid., 597 n. 5. Note the care Haraway takes to emphasize that this is a task not of recognition but of construction. As such, it could not be achieved by empathy and would not reveal itself in a "click"—the moment of clarity that media accounts attributed to consciousness-raising. Jane Mansbridge observed to me in October 1994 that this popular image leaves out the theory-building aspect of consciousness-raising, depicting it instead as a kind of indoctrination from which women emerge fully outfitted with a "full-blown ideology."

57. Haraway, "Situated Knowledges," 585.

58. Jane Mansbridge, "Feminism and Democratic Community," in NOMOS XXXV, *Democratic Community,* 372.

59. Jürgen Habermas, "Hannah Arendt's Communications Concept of Power," *Social Research* 44 (1977): 23.

60. Even Seyla Benhabib, who draws upon Arendt's work to remind Habermas of the fine but crucial distinction between "reaching agreement" (Arendt) and "achieving consensus" (Habermas), argues that Arendt's "problematic separation of morality from politics" short-circuits her potential contribution to a theory of democratic public dialogue (*Situating the Self,* xx, 124).

61. In "A Case of Distorted Communication," *Political Theory* 11, no. 1 (1983), Margaret Canovan makes a particularly incisive response to Habermas, charging that his "excessively intellectualist" preoccupations cause him to overlook "Arendt's concern with *action*" (109; Canovan's emphasis). Yet although Canovan insists that Arendt did not subscribe to "the purely subjectivist view that opinions on matters of politics and morals are simply private and incorrigible" (108), she does not specify just how Arendt accounts for the possibility of correcting them.

62. Ronald Beiner, "Interpretive Essay," in *LKPP,* 138, 92. See also Benjamin R. Barber, *The Conquest of Politics* (Princeton: Princeton University Press, 1988).

63. Habermas, "Communications Concept," 20.

64. Ibid., 21.

65. Habermas, "Communications Concept."

66. Jürgen Habermas, *Moral Consciousness and Communicative Action,* trans. Christian Lenhardt and Shierry Weber Nicholsen (Cambridge: MIT Press, 1990), 162.

67. Ibid., 93, 71.

68. See Jürgen Habermas, *Justification and Application,* trans. Ciaran B. Cronin (Cambridge: MIT Press, 1993), 36–37.

69. In "Communications Concept," Habermas acknowledges that Arendt denies both that a "cognitive foundation can . . . be claimed for the power of common convictions" and that power can be "anchored in the de facto recognition of validity claims that can be discursively redeemed and fundamentally criticized" (23).

70. There are many points in the Kant lectures where Arendt lends credence to this criticism. For example, when Arendt writes that morality is grounded in truths that are "necessary because they are dictated by practical reason," she constructs ultimate certainty as the ground of morality (*LKPP,* 70). Even more striking is the following passage, where Arendt categorically separates judging from willing and then assigns morality to the will: "Judgment is not practical reason; practical reason 'reasons' and tells me

what to do and what not to do; it lays down the law and is identical with the will, and the will utters commands; it speaks in imperatives" (15). Finally, there is Arendt's assertion that "truth in the sciences is dependent on the experiment that can be repeated by others," a statement that betrays an empiricist conception of science (40).

71. Habermas, "Communications Concept," 22.

72. Habermas, *Moral Consciousness and Communicative Action*, 168; Habermas's emphasis.

73. Ibid., 67.

74. In *Arendt, Camus, and Modern Rebellion* (New Haven: Yale University Press, 1992), Jeffrey C. Issac explicates this claim more thoroughly with his discussion of the ways that the perspective of critical social science might have challenged Arendt's criticisms of behaviorism (235–42).

75. Habermas, "Communications Concept," 24.

76. In "Hannah Arendt and the Problem of Critical Theory," *Journal of Politics* 41 (1979), Gerard P. Heather and Matthew Stolz characterize this claim about a retreat to social contract theory as an "almost fantastic conclusion" that utterly disregards Arendt's "persistent" criticism of the Western political tradition (5, 7).

77. Jürgen Habermas, "On the German-Jewish Heritage," *Telos* 44 (1980):128; Habermas's emphasis. Margaret Canovan, in "A Case of Distorted Communication," and Gerard P. Heather and Matthew Stolz, in "Hannah Arendt and the Problem of Critical Theory," have also argued that Habermas depoliticizes Arendt's work. In contrast to the argument I develop here, however, they contend that this depoliticization consists in supplanting Arendt's appreciation for political disputation, her commitment to plurality, and her concern with action, with a philosophic ideal of rational conviction. This line of argument assumes that the principal point of disagreement between the two is, as Canovan puts it, that Arendt "saw no reason to suppose that we *can* settle practical political disputes by purely rational means" (109). I think this objection does not get at the heart of the dispute because it takes Habermasian discourse literally, as a means to produce solutions to concrete problems and, thereby, imputes to Habermas a kind of dogmatism that he—like Arendt—rejects. See Habermas, *Moral Consciousness and Communicative Action*, 122.

78. Habermas, *Moral Consciousness and Communicative Action*, 66; Habermas's emphasis.

79. Ibid., 158, 100.

80. Thomas McCarthy, "Practical Discourse: On the Relation of Morality to Politics," in *Habermas and the Public Sphere*, ed. Craig Calhoun (Cambridge: MIT Press, 1992), 65 (McCarthy's emphasis).

81. Jürgen Habermas, *The Theory of Communicative Action*, trans. Thomas McCarthy (Boston: Beacon Press, 1981), 1:287.

82. Lewis P. and Sandra K. Hinchman, "In Heidegger's Shadow: Hannah Arendt's Phenomenological Humanism," *Review of Politics* 46 (1984): 200.

83. Hannah Arendt, "On Hannah Arendt," in *Hannah Arendt: The Recovery of the Public World*, ed. Melvyn A. Hill (New York: St. Martin's, 1979), 323; emphasis added.

84. Sandra K. Hinchman, "Common Sense and Political Barbarism in the Theory of Hannah Arendt," *Polity* 17, no. 2 (1984). Hinchman argues that by virtue of her appreciation for the world-constitutive feature of language, Arendt shares the Habermasian concern for undistorted speech more than Habermas himself recognizes. For Arendt, she writes, "Where language is truncated or restricted, as it is in some communities, the constitution of one's self-identity and that of the external world are impaired, since both depend on common sense" (324–25). The question Hinchman does not raise is whether

Arendt would regard Habermasian critical discourse as an answer to the problem of distorted speech or as one of its causes.

85. Mikhail M. Bakhtin, *The Dialogical Imagination*, trans. Caryl Emerson and Michael Holquist, ed. Michael Holquist (Austin: University of Texas Press, 1981), 276, 280.

86. I owe this turn of phrase to Stephen Salkever who used it in conversation (September 1995, Chicago, Ill.) to characterize what it is about Arendt's writing that makes her work difficult to teach to students who expect theories of politics to yield labels and definitions that can readily be applied to worldly disputes.

87. See also Beiner, "Interpretive Essay," 118.

88. See Hayden White, *The Content of the Form* (Baltimore: Johns Hopkins Press, 1987).

89. Bakhtin, *The Dialogical Imagination*, 277.

90. Habermas, *Moral Consciousness and Communicative Action*, 178.

91. McCarthy, "Practical Discourse," 67.

92. Ibid., 66–68.

93. In his *Critique of Judgment*, trans. J. H. Bernard (New York: Hafner, 1951), Kant makes a distinction between taste, which is a matter of reflective judgment, and moral propositions, which are matters for "determinant" judgment because they involve subsuming a particular instance under a rule or concept that is universally binding. Assessing the validity of such a judgment is a matter of proving it to be true or false in terms of the prior standard. In contrast, reflective judgment is not deducible from concepts, and it is exercised in matters of relative worth or merit that are not reducible to a true/false distinction.

94. Bickford, "In the Presence of Others," 322.

95. This is evident in Arendt's praise for Gotthold Lessing, whom she regarded as an exemplar of political judgment for what she called his "partisanship for the world." What she admired in Lessing was that he staked out his position on a question "quite independently of whether it was true or false," putting the force of his rhetoric behind whatever position looked as if it were in danger of disappearing from the debate. See Hannah Arendt, *Men in Dark Times* (New York: Harcourt Brace Jovanovich, 1968), 7.

96. Bernice Johnson Reagon, "Coalition Politics: Turning the Century," in Smith, *Home Girls*.

97. Bakhtin, *The Dialogical Imagination*, 356.

Six

Communication, Transformation, and Consciousness-Raising

Nancy Fraser

Both Anthony Cascardi and Lisa Disch focus on Hannah Arendt's conception of political judgment. But they offer radically different interpretations of her view and sharply divergent assessments of its merits. The contrast between their essays presents an opportunity for reflecting not only on the issues they raise explicitly but also on the larger question of the meaning of the current Arendt revival.

For Cascardi, Arendt's work on judgment is a botched attempt to mediate some tensions arising from the Kantian philosophical problematic. As he reads her, Arendt tried to provide "a closure for the Enlightenment project" by transforming Kant's account of reflective judgment into a "rationalized" politics, a "democratic politics of common sense, of the *sensus communis*, of (good) taste." Construing the task of politics as "to make legible what is unpresentable," Arendt is supposed to have translated Kant's sublimely unpresentable idea of a final convergence of opinion in a kingdom of ends at the end of history into the mundane, uninspiring, and all too presentable notion of an overregulated, norm-governed public space in the here and now. The result, according to Cascardi, is a mere "politics of rational communication," as opposed to a "politics of radical transformation." Thus, Arendt is said to lose the fruitful tension, kept open by Kant, between genesis and normativity. She denies the radical creativity of the imagination and robs democratic politics of its transformative possibilities.

This, of course, is a highly idiosyncratic reading of Arendt. On the spectrum running from methodism to decisionism, Cascardi locates her at the methodist end. Yet she is usually seen either as the avatar of a performative, agonistic public space (the decisionism end of the spectrum) or as the exponent of a middle ground between the extremes. In the latter interpretation, which is Lisa Disch's view, Arendt's conception of judgment is supposed to provide an alternative to untenable rationalist dreams of algorithmic decision procedures, on the one hand, and equally untenable irrationalist fantasies of blind leaps of faith, on the other. Rarely has Arendt been read as Cascardi reads her, as a proponent of normalization.

That said, I am not primarily interested in whether Cascardi has gotten Arendt right. I wish instead to assess the cogency of his argument. It relies on a series of apparently isomorphic conceptual oppositions or dichotomies: communication versus transformation, normativity versus genesis, the beautiful versus the sublime. These dichotomies are homologous to Richard Rorty's distinction between the normal political discourse of the social engineer, on the one hand, and the abnormal discourse of the strong poet, on the other hand.[1] They are also homologous to the distinction I have noted here between methodism and decisionism: between the view that warranted judgments are derivable via a specifiable method or decision procedure and the view that judgment is not susceptible to any warrants at all, but can only ever be a radical leap. (A good example of the latter view is Derrida's account of judgment in "Force of Law: The 'Mystical Foundation of Authority.'")[2]

Cascardi's case against Arendt relies on this structure of isomorphic dichotomies. It assumes a sharp contrast between two different pictures of politics. One picture embodies the communicative-normative-beautiful-normalizing-methodist pole of the structure. Associated by Cascardi with the Enlightenment norm of publicity, this is the picture of a rule-governed, constitutionally secured public space in which everyone shares at least a procedural "common sense"; they agree about what counts as a good reason for or against a given policy proposal and what counts as a legitimate procedure for settling disputes. In this public space as envisioned by Cascardi, all the fundamental questions of politics are already settled. Judgment proceeds smoothly from consensus to consensus without ever troubling the underlying presuppositions of the framework. Nothing ever happens that is genuinely new.

The second picture of politics embodies the opposite pole of Cascardi's structure of dichotomies. Here, at the transformative-generative-sublime-antinormalizing-decisionist pole, we find a politics of upheaval and revolution. With judgment radically unconstrained by any preexisting normative framework, transformative vision shatters every consensus, and sublime imagination transgresses every rule. Geniuses found states, simultaneously incarnating and betraying the spirit of revolution by establishing new constitutions, which necessarily devolve into normalization. The essence of politics is novelty and transformation, the refusal of communication-as-usual.

Presupposing and apparently endorsing this contrast, Cascardi faults Arendt for seeking to resolve the tension between the two poles. Aiming to close the gap between the politics of communication and the politics of transformation, Arendt is said to valorize the former at the expense of the latter, so that finally the transformative drops out. Kant, in contrast, is praised for keeping alive the tension between the two poles. Although not concerned with political judgment per se, he is credited nevertheless with preserving the sort of aporetic and antinomial space that Cascardi contends is required to nurture transformative political vision.

Cascardi's argument has a number of difficulties. First, his contrast between the politics of communication and the politics of transformation is misleading and overdrawn. The view of public space associated with the first pole caricatures the Enlightenment norm of publicity. Far from realizing that norm, it travesties it by insulating its own ground rules from public scrutiny. A democratic public space must allow for the possibility that even very deeply entrenched norms might be shown, at some point down the road, to exclude some voices from debate and might therefore become subject to change. Thus, contra Cascardi, a politics of *democratic* communication need not be a morass of normalization, nor must it preclude radical change.

If Cascardi's view of communicative politics is too bleak, then his view of transformative politics is too rosy. The latter valorizes novelty for its own sake, celebrating transgressive acts against community norms. Its underlying assumption, apparently endorsed by Cascardi, is that consensus is always bad and its disruption is always good, regardless of the substance of the case. This, however, is plainly false. It is one thing to disrupt a consensus that sees nothing unacceptable in, say, marital rape, and another to disrupt a consensus to the contrary. In the first case, the consensus is unjust and its disruption is a step toward justice; in the second, just the opposite is true. Thus, the politics of transformation that Cascardi seems to favor disregards both justice and democratic participation.

Contra Cascardi, then, some versions of the politics of communication could well be preferable to a politics of transformation. In the extreme forms he envisions, however, neither communication nor transformation is appealing; neither has much place for political judgment. In a politics of pure methodist communication, decisions would be fully calculable, plurality would be neutralized, and judgment would be rendered unnecessary. In a politics of pure decisionist transformation, in contrast, decisions would be sheer assertions of the will of the strongest, plurality would be suppressed, and judgment would be indistinguishable from will. In both cases politics would be lost.

What, then, should a political theorist conclude? The obvious conclusion is that one should try to do precisely what Cascardi faulted Arendt for attempting: namely, to construct a middle position between pure communication and pure transformation, a position that "resolves the tension" between them. Cascardi, however, offers two objections to such a project.

First, he contends that such an approach covers over Kantian aporias that nurture transformative vision. The aporia he wishes to preserve is rooted in an idea said to resist all possible representation, namely, an ultimate agreement at the end of history. But Cascardi fails to explain why and how this idea is at once aporetic and necessary for democratic politics. It is not clear to me that it is either. Construed as a regulative ideal, on the one hand, it does not seem aporetic. Construed as an expression of something that resists all possible representation, on the other hand, it is less a political resource than a mystification. To be sure, radical democrats ought to be interested in what (and who) can't be represented *within some given, historically and spatially located discursive regime.* An idea, in contrast, that resists *all possible* representation has an air of surplus paradox suited better to religion than to politics.

Second, Cascardi contends that Arendt's account of "community sense" is viciously circular. Unlike Kant, Arendt is said to make the claims of reflective judgment depend on the very *sensus communis* it is their task to create. But here Cascardi equivocates on "community sense," conflating two distinct senses of that expression. One is the tacit presumption of shared background norms and assumptions, including a shared language and a common world, a presumption that *could* turn out to be mistaken but that is nevertheless presupposed in making judgment claims; this "community sense" is pregiven and assumed. The other is the sort of achieved agreement, projected or real, that *could* result from the process of disputing judgment claims; this "community sense" is a possible outcome and achievement. There is no circularity, vicious or otherwise, in holding that judgment relies on the first meaning of community sense while simultaneously aiming to generate the second.

Thus, Cascardi's objections to the Arendtian project are not persuasive. He gives us no good reasons to reject the search for a middle ground between methodism and decisionism. Assuming, then, that we are willing to entertain such a project, we must now shift the inquiry to another level: does Arendt succeed in pulling it off?

This brings me to Lisa Disch's essay, which argues that Arendt *does* succeed. Disch proposes two lines of defense of Arendtian judgment. One the one hand, she claims to rescue Arendt from "a one-sided dialogue" that takes "Habermasian rational discourse as the template for . . . readings of [her] conception of judgment." On the other hand, she claims to demonstrate the value of that conception by using it to reinterpret feminist consciousness-raising so as to salvage the latter's emancipatory potential. This second line of defense is especially interesting and original; it will be the main focus of my discussion.

Arendtian judgment, according to Disch, constitutes a viable middle way between "radical skepticism" and "doctrinaire self-righteousness." If, therefore, it can be shown to be central to consciousness-raising (CR), then the latter can be defended against charges of epistemic arbitrariness, on the one hand, and moral authoritarianism, on the other. The trick is to show that consciousness-raising is an exercise in the sort of critical reflection that Arendt called "representative thinking." In that case, one could approve CR's characteristic reliance on storytelling, which offers exemplars in place of arguments. And one could also validate the resulting judgments as satisfying standards of "communicability" and "exemplary validity," if not those of "justification." The upshot would be twofold. First, consciousness-raising would be certified as a genuinely critical, democratic, and potentially emancipatory practice. And second, Arendtian judgment would be shown to have contemporary political relevance.

This, as I said, is an interesting and original thesis. To evaluate it, however, requires disaggregating two different claims. The first is that Arendtian judgment, as interpreted by Disch, really does constitute a viable alternative to both methodism and decisionism. The second is that consciousness-raising really does exemplify Arendtian judgment. Both claims depend, in the end, on how precisely one unpacks a series of key phrases, including "representative thinking," "thinking with an enlarged mentality," "community sense," "training the imagination to go visiting," "communicability," and "exemplary validity."

Let me begin with "representative thinking," "thinking with an enlarged mentality," and "training the imagination to go visiting." In Disch's account, the basic idea behind all three is the same: the way to avoid arbitrariness and rank subjectivism in one's political judgments is to engage in a thought experiment; one thinks successively via an act of imagination from the standpoints of various differently situated other people. The result of such imaginative "visiting" is an "enlarged mentality"; idiosyncrasy and bias get filtered out, and one's judgments become genuinely reflective.

This account of Arendtian judgment is intuitively appealing. It locates the problem of judgment in the "human condition" of plurality. I recognize that I judge matters that others also judge and that we all judge from different perspectives. By factoring this awareness into my judgment, I avoid parochialism and arrogant self-certainty. I do not negate plurality, however, by assuming that I can empathically imagine precisely how the others are judging. Rather, I imagine *myself* judging successively from their different vantage points. By appreciating that it always remains I who is "visiting," I avoid obliterating the line between self and other and I preserve the alterity of the others.

Notwithstanding its appeal, this account of judgment is not entirely satisfying. Let me raise three possible sources of difficulty. First, judging here remains a monological process wherein one goes visiting in imagination, as opposed to in reality. One imagines oneself judging from various different perspectives instead of going out and talking to and listening to other people. One elaborates an interior, not an exterior, dialogue. In this way, one avoids the risk of hearing others judge in ways that one could not imagine oneself judging in their situation.

As a result, one insulates oneself from the sort of provocation that could actually lead one to change one's perspective.

Second, the account Disch attributes to Arendt is silent on the crucial question of how one selects the perspectives one "visits." It cannot be that we are expected to visit the standpoint of every individual, whom the condition of "natality" distinguishes from every other. Rather, we must determine in each case what are the relevant *representative* standpoints. Here it seems necessary to supplement Arendt's understanding of individual plurality with something like the contemporary understanding of differently situated social groups. Perhaps in judging matters of reproductive health, for example, I need to think from the standpoint of the other gender. Or perhaps, more generally, in judging any matter of distributive justice I need to think, following John Rawls, from the standpoint of "the least advantaged."[3] But this opens whole new cans of worms. Can I be sure there really is such a thing as "the standpoint of the other gender"? And how do I decide in any given case who precisely is "the least advantaged"?

Finally, Disch's account of Arendtian judgment does not tell us whether or how visiting can lead me to change my own judgment. Suppose after judging some matter from my own standpoint, I go on and judge the same matter successively from some number of other relevant representative standpoints. Suppose, therefore, that by this process I accumulate in my imagination a plurality of different judgments concerning the matter. What happens next? How do I arrive at a resolution? Disch seems to deny that I integrate the various standpoints into a single higher standpoint, since that would mean transcending the condition of plurality. But presumably *something* happens or else there would be no point in enlarging my mentality. Without some account of how the process of representative thinking leads me somewhere, above all, to a better judgment, Arendtian judgment is, if not simply unacceptable, then radically incomplete.

If Disch's account of visiting is inconclusive, then her treatment of other key Arendtian themes threatens to return us to Cascardiesque dichotomies. She draws an overly sharp line between good Arendtian notions, such as "storytelling," "exemplars," "communicability," and "exemplary validity," on the one hand, and bad Habermasian notions, such as "arguments," "reasons," "principles," "deductions," and "justification," on the other. Like Cascardi, then, she polarizes the alternatives unnecessarily. Without getting embroiled in the subtleties of

Habermas interpretation and without rehearsing all the details, let me cut right to the crucial point: in political discourse telling a story or adducing an exemplar is not an alternative to advancing a reason. Rather, it is itself a form of argumentation in the broad sense, another way of advancing a reason or justifying a claim. In this respect it is entirely on a par with a deduction from principles. Both genres of reasoning must be "communicable" to persuade; both cannot help but rely on some pregiven "community sense." In addition, exemplary stories, like abstract deductions, must be defended by further reasons of some kind, if and when their appropriateness is challenged. If Arendt intended to deny this, she was simply mistaken. It does not help her larger case to deny it on her behalf.

In general, then, Disch has not yet persuaded me that Arendt has succeeded in finding the elusive third way. Can Arendt's account of judgment nevertheless help us vindicate consciousness-raising?

I remain dubious. In light of the previous discussion, let me raise four prima facie difficulties with Disch's argument. First, consciousness-raising is unlike Arendtian judgment in that it involves exterior, as opposed to interior, dialogue. In this respect one might prefer it to Arendtian judgment. In any event, it is unclear how the latter can help vindicate consciousness-raising. Second, consciousness-raising is unlike Arendtian visiting with respect to the process whereby attending to others' perspectives enlarges mentality. By listening to others, participants in CR came to appreciate that sufferings that had seemed wholly personal and psychological were widely shared and political because they were rooted in gender power differentials. Hearing the stories of fellow group members was less a matter of multiplying different perspectives than of encountering variants of a depressingly common single tale. It was the cumulative weight of the iterated testimony that led one to judge old "male-identified" self-understandings inferior to emerging new feminist ones. Thus, it is unclear that the process involved visiting in Arendt's sense.[4] And it is unclear that Arendtian judgment could or would serve to vindicate it.

On the contrary—and now I come to my third point—consciousness-raising might well be judged wanting by Arendtian standards of plurality. Most consciousness-raising groups were relatively homogeneous in composition with respect to education, age, class, and "race." That is why they could generate a relatively coherent feminist perspective on "personal politics." But this also made that perspective vulnerable to criticism. Insofar as many consciousness-raising groups failed to include women of color, poor and working-class women, career homemakers, religious women, and so on, they could be said to have failed to visit a sufficient plurality of different standpoints. Moreover, and this is my fourth point, the Arendtian model of judgment does not offer sufficient guidance for remedying that defect of CR. As we saw, it fails to advise us concerning which standpoints we ought to visit. Treating plurality solely as a matter of individual differences, it ignores group dominance and subordination.

Here it is worth emphasizing that Arendt was preoccupied with the image of the judge as an individual, unmodified. This preoccupation marks not only her theorizing but also her rhetorical practice. Although she herself occasionally spoke "as a Jew," she virtually never spoke "as a woman," and she overwhelmingly preferred to speak "as an individual," which is, of course, another mode of self-identification—as well as a mode of disidentification. She apparently assumed that to judge as anything more delimited than a human being was to compromise one's integrity.

Today, of course, all of us elect at times to judge from that position. And many of us detest the tendency of identity politics to degenerate into groupthink. Some of us nonetheless also seek to take seriously the inevitable positionality and locatedness of judgment. Contra Arendt, this is not simply a matter of individual differences in constitution and experience. It also concerns individuals' varying locations vis-à-vis salient axes of sociocultural differentiation, including gender, "race," class, sexuality, and nationality. Because these axes define relations of dominance and subordination, to be located vis-à-vis them is also to be implicated in injustice. Contra Arendt, therefore, the question of judgment is inextricably bound up with the question of justice. Not just individuality but also equality is at issue.

Unlike Disch, I conclude that Arendtian judgment is too dissociated from questions of dominance, subordination, and justice to deal adequately with the complex phenomenon of consciousness-raising. Only an account of political judgment that encompasses those issues, as well as issues of individuality, can vindicate the emancipatory moment in CR while also acknowledging legitimate criticisms of its shortcomings.

The point should be stated more generally. Only an account of judgment that simultaneously does justice to two moments—both the individuality of judgment and its structural locatedness in contexts of inequality—can possibly be acceptable today. But this means we must go well beyond Arendt's view. We must theorize political judgment in terms of two "conditions": first, only individuals judge; and second, they do so from specific positions that are discursively, institutionally, and sociostructurally constructed along axes of dominance and subordination.

This brings me to one final point, which is less a response to Cascardi and Disch than an observation about the current Arendt revival more generally. The current revival risks recreating and reinforcing what is most unsatisfying in Arendt's political theory, namely, the overburdening of concepts of action, judgment, and democratic process and their dissociation from justice and equality. In Arendt's thought, political process concepts are effectively fetishized, made to bear virtually the entire weight of normativity, a weight they cannot possibly bear. Insofar as the current Arendt revival repeats her gesture of overburdening action and judgment, it is in danger of symptomatically reflecting, instead of critically interrogating, the current "postsocialist" common sense. At a time when pundits speak glibly of "the end of equality," talk of judgment in abstraction from justice is an evasion, if not a fraud.[5]

Notes

1. Richard Rorty, *Contingency, Irony, and Solidarity* (Cambridge: Cambridge University Press, 1989). For a critique, see my "Solidarity or Singularity? Richard Rorty between Romanticism and Technocracy," in *Unruly Practices: Power, Discourse, and Gender in Contemporary Social Theory* (Minneapolis: University of Minnesota Press, 1989).

2. Jacques Derrida, "Force of Law: The 'Mystical Foundation of Authority,'" trans. Mary Quaintance, *Cardozo Law Review*, vol. 11 (summer 1990). For a critique, see my "The Force of Law: Metaphysical or Political?" *Cardozo Law Review* 13, no. 4 (December 1991): 1325–31.

3. John Rawls, *A Theory of Justice* (Cambridge: Harvard University Press, 1971).

4. Phenomenologically, at least, if another standpoint was visited, it was not that of somebody else but that of a different me, the standpoint of a self other than the one I had thought was mine, a self I might become. Thus, the appearance of a previously unseen commonality subtending a plurality of standpoints led to self disidentification and group solidarity. Nothing in Arendtian visiting, as I understand it, speaks to this sort of process.

5. Mickey Kaus, *The End of Equality* (New York: Free Press, 1995).

Part III

Seven

Hannah Arendt: Modernity, Alienation, and Critique

Dana R. Villa

*[German philosophy] is the most fundamental form . . . of home-
sickness there has ever been: the longing for the best that has ever
existed. One is no longer at home anywhere; at last one longs back
for that place in which alone one can be at home: the* Greek *world!
But it is in precisely that direction that all bridges are broken—
except the rainbow bridge of concepts.*
Friedrich Nietzsche, *The Will to Power*

*I did not want to cross the "rainbow bridge of concepts," perhaps
because I am not homesick enough, in any event because I do not
believe in a world, be it a past world or a future world, in which
man's mind . . . could or should ever be comfortably at home.*
Hannah Arendt, *The Life of the Mind*

In several recent essays and her new book, Seyla Benhabib characterizes Hannah Arendt as a "reluctant modernist."[1] From Benhabib's
perspective, Arendt's "homesickness" for the Greeks has been greatly
exaggerated. She views Arendt as a theorist of a deliberative democracy, one whose firsthand acquaintance with totalitarianism and the
agonies of statelessness led her to endorse (however grudgingly) the
primary tenets of Kantian universalism. Benhabib's reading hinges
upon placing Arendt's theory of action within a broadly discursive

conception of the public sphere. To accomplish this, she turns to the unfinished work on judgment, which enables her to de-emphasize the agonistic and theatrical elements of Arendt's "Greek" theory of action and bring the dimensions of intersubjectivity, dialogue, and democratic will formation to the fore.[2] Arendt's disturbing tendency to separate the moral from the political, Benhabib asserts, is overcome in her theory of political judgment, which displays a strong commitment to the "discursive redemption of validity claims" and a more or less explicit endorsement of the criterion of universalizability.[3] The "modernism" of Hannah Arendt, then, is manifest in her Kantian theory of political judgment, a theory that completes her previous thought on action by providing a set of "moral foundations" surprisingly reminiscent of Habermas's discourse ethics.

I am, for reasons I have discussed elsewhere, skeptical of this reading.[4] George Kateb's description of Arendt as a "great antimodernist" strikes me as more accurate.[5] The primary advantage of Kateb's description is that it conveys something of the ambition of Arendt's project: she provides far more than a theory of democratic deliberation. Kateb's characterization, unlike Benhabib's, implicitly recognizes Arendt's substantial debt to Nietzsche and Heidegger, the two greatest thinkers and critics of modernity.

Kateb's reading of Arendt as an "antimodernist" proceeds by situating her theory of action in terms of what he sees as her global critique of modernity. In his consideration of Arendt, Kateb stresses what he calls the "existential achievement" of political action. According to Kateb, Arendt affirms action, the "sharing of words and deeds" on a public stage, because it provides a source of meaning—a justification of existence—strong enough to withstand the tragic wisdom of Silenus.[6] Human beings can be reconciled to existence, made at home in the world, if they have access to such a stage and if their deeds and words have the opportunity to earn a place in public memory. The problem presented by modernity is that it destroys the conditions necessary if political action is to fulfill its existential vocation.

Modernity fans the flames of resentment of the human condition, mobilizing Faustian energies in the attempt to overcome finitude and limitation as such. Resentment of limitation leads to "extremist exertion" in all directions, the goal being to remake the world (or "complete it," in Kant's phrase). According to Arendt, resentment and extremist exertion can have only one result: a profound and pervasive alienation from the world. When "world alienation" reaches its apogee, as Arendt in *The Human Condition* argues it has, the frame of political action, of memorable deeds, is utterly devalued. If Arendt's theory of political action is motivated by "the hope . . . that humanity could be at home rightly," her antimodernism flows from the conviction that this hope has been dashed by the modern age.[7]

Neither Benhabib's nor Kateb's description of Arendt is innocent. Each is offered for reasons that are largely strategic: they are weapons in an interpretive battle. At stake is whether we should consider Arendt as "one of us"—as committed to a deliberative conception of democracy and universal rights—or as "one of them"—that is, as an anti-individualist thinker whose commitment to political action is so great that it leads her to wish modernity undone. Those sympathetic to Arendt (Habermasians, communitarians, and participatory democrats) will be attracted to Benhabib's account; those who are hostile, to Kateb's liberal critique.

I want to look more closely at what is at issue in the debate about whether Arendt is a "modernist" or an "antimodernist." It is my contention that this debate is poorly framed; that Benhabib and Kateb impose, quite violently, a conception of critique foreign to Arendt; and that the resulting characterizations obscure more than they reveal.

The assumption underlying both Benhabib's and Kateb's treatments of Arendt is that critique is either "immanent" or "rejectionist" in nature. This assumption has gained widespread currency thanks to the modern/postmodern debate and animates such recent discussions as Michael Walzer's *Interpretation and Social Criticism*.[8] According to Walzer, the social or political critic has, so to speak, a hermeneutic duty to identify with the basic hopes, values, and institutions of his or her society. All *responsible* criticism is a form of immanent critique, a variation on Marx's theme of whistling the bourgeoisie its own tune. The worst possible sin from this perspective is to engage in "totalizing" or rejectionist criticism—that is, to take a critical stance so distanced that it enables the critic to place these hopes, values, and institutions under suspicion. The relevant trope here is Nietzsche's "seeing things as if from another planet," a figure that both Walzer and Richard Rorty have deployed against Foucault to question the legitimacy of *his* critical project.[9]

If, in fact, the universe of critique is exhausted by the terms "immanent" and "rejectionist," we can expect interpretive quarrels concerning such "questionable" figures as Arendt or Foucault to conform to a preset pattern. The sympathetic reader (in this case Benhabib) will strive mightily to convince us that X is a democratic theorist, committed to questioning only aspects of modern political practice but not modernity *überhaupt*. The unsympathetic reader (Kateb) will take precisely the opposite tack and attempt to demonstrate that X's target is modernity or the modern project as such. Thus, Benhabib's and Kateb's readings of Arendt work in tandem: they both subject her thought to what Foucault called "the blackmail of Enlightenment."[10] Benhabib thinks that Arendt can and will pay up under these conditions and affirm her allegiance to Enlightenment, modernity, and liberal democracy. Kateb thinks that she can't and that our ultimate verdict on her political thought must therefore be harsh indeed.

In this essay I question not only the adequacy of the labels "modernist" and "antimodernist" as applied to Arendt but also the appropriateness of the immanent/rejectionist dichotomy. The case of Arendt demonstrates, I believe, just how nefarious this dichotomy has become as a policing mechanism in political theory.

My discussion proceeds as follows. In the first part of the essay, I show how Kateb's effort to portray Arendt as a rejectionist, "homesick" critic of modernity founders upon the recognition of the extraordinarily positive value she attaches to certain modes of alienation. In this connection I next look at Arendt's "expressivist" theory of action and the interpretations of her "Kantian" theory of judgment offered by Benhabib and by Ronald Beiner. In the third part I show how efforts, such as Benhabib's, to portray Arendt as an "immanent" critic bent on restoring a comprehensive public sphere fail to appreciate the central thesis of her critique of modernity. I conclude with a few remarks on the nature and place of that critique.

Whatever one's ideological commitments, Arendt's critique of modernity certainly appears, at first reading, to be a paradigm of rejectionist critique. What accounts for this impression? Partly, as Kateb notes, it is due to Arendt's unyielding focus on the downside of modernity: she describes its horrors and pathologies at length, but none of its greatness.[11] A less obvious but no less important explanation is that this critique moves on explicitly ontological terrain. This, of course, should come as no surprise: Arendt's rethinking of freedom as a mode of being and her disclosive conception of political action signal a theoretical perspective explicitly attuned to the ontological dimensions of politics. This attunement is manifest throughout her consideration of modernity, the focus of which is the decline of an authentically public reality. For Arendt, the modern age witnesses "the destruction of the common world."[12] It is this decidedly ontological slant that distinguishes her account of the "instrumentalization of the political" from parallel accounts (e.g., Habermas's) that depart from the Weberian concept of rationalization.

What does Arendt mean by "the destruction of the common world," and how does this idea shape her critique of modernity? Here I can only sketch what I have treated at greater length elsewhere.[13] When Arendt writes about the destruction, loss, or decline of the public world, she is not bemoaning the fragmentation wrought by the collapse of the religion/tradition/authority triangle and the advent of Weber's "warring gods."[14] Nor is she lamenting the loss of animating, shared public purposes, as contemporary communitarians are wont to do. Her concern, rather, is with the integrity and viability of a specific phenomenological realm—the public sphere, which she conceives as a theatrical "space of appearances." Arendt sees this space as undermined by an array of characteristically modern forces (including capitalism, the "rise of the social," and the "world-destroying" force of technological automatism). The viability of this stage for action depends upon the presence of relatively stable boundaries, boundaries that mark and preserve the "space of freedom" from the encroaching automatism of nature and labor. Modernity's release of Faustian, extremist energies overwhelms these boundaries, subsuming the realm of freedom within that of necessity. The essential theatrical dimension of the public world is denatured as this bounded whole is submerged in what Arendt calls a "process" reality (*HC*, pp. 296–304).

In thinking about the modern age, then, Arendt is concerned to isolate those factors that contribute most to the "de-worlding" of the public realm. Her efforts in this direction are greatly aided by the resources Heidegger makes available. Heidegger's thesis that the metaphysics of the moderns—our comprehension of what is—entails the "subjectification of the real" provides an essential touchstone for Arendt's reading of the modern epoch.

Heidegger argues (in the Nietzsche lectures, "The Age of the World Picture," and elsewhere) that the radical novelty of modernity resides in its reinterpretation of the being of what is, a reinterpretation that makes possible its projects of calculation and human mastery of the world. In contrast to the Greeks (whose understanding of the real moved entirely within the horizon provided by *physis*) and to medieval Christendom (which understood that which is as *ens creatum*), the moderns posit the human subject as "the relational center of all that is."[15] In Heidegger's view, the modern redrawing of the ontological horizon is manifest in the metaphysics of Descartes, Kant, and Nietzsche, and in the reduction of all realms of being to the generic category of experience. The aesthetic, the historical, the religious—all submit to the tyranny of the category of *Erlebnis*. For Heidegger the distinctiveness of the modern age is to be found in this reduction of the real to what the subject experiences, expresses, or can represent.[16]

Arendt's analysis of modernity in *The Human Condition* is also concerned with the subjectification of the real. She approaches this broad phenomenon, however, in terms of its implications for the *vita activa*. Thus, she concentrates on the modern reduction of freedom to will, property to the laboring subject (Locke), and the phenomenal world to the constructs of the knowing subject (Descartes, Kant, and modern science).[17] Throughout, her emphasis is on the way the theory and self-understanding of the modern age have consistently worked to undermine the durability and tangibility—the *worldliness*—of these phenomena. Hence, for the modern mind "freedom is never understood as an objective state of human existence"; nor is property understood to have any ground other than the living, laboring, individual; nor, finally, is the "objectivity" of the world—its common character—understood to have any ground other than the patterns of the human mind itself (*HC*, p. 70). Science, philosophy, economic and political theory—all conspire to conceal both the phenomenon of world and the worldliness of phenomena.

The effects of this pervasive subjectification cannot be undone by a revised self-understanding; for Arendt it is hardly a question of theorizing ourselves into a more "worldly" form of existence. Modern theory's reduction of freedom, property, and the phenomenal realm to subjective structures or capacities is not the problem so much as a symptom. The real problem, for Heidegger as well as Arendt, is the existential resentment that drives modern humanity to take itself so far out of the world, to ascribe to itself a position from which the world might be mastered, remade, and disposed of. Hence, the radical novelty of modernity consists in the fact that "now, for the first time is there any such thing as a 'position' of man."[18] Now, "for the first time," there is a distance, an alienation that encourages and makes plausible the Archimedean project of utterly transforming the conditions of human existence.[19] Hence Arendt's assertion that "world alienation, and not self-alienation as Marx thought, has been the hallmark of the modern age" (*HC*, p. 254). Such alienation leads to contempt for the world and worldly activities (such as politics); it weakens our attachment to existence for its own sake. Thus, in her essay on Lessing, Arendt writes that "Nothing in our time, it seems to me, is more dubious than our attitude towards the world."[20]

Kateb seizes upon the Arendtian themes of existential resentment and world alienation as the keys not only to her critique of modernity but to her political theory as a whole. Her attitude toward alienation is the giveaway, for although Arendt may dispute Marx's specific characterization of the pathology of the age, she shares his conviction that alienation is the problem and that an unalienated existence is both possible and desirable. Thus, from Kateb's perspective, Marx and Arendt are linked by the essentially *religious* idea that humanity exists to be at home in the world.[21] For Marx, as for Hegel, this goal is realized through the completed humanization of the world, a process that enables the collective subject of humanity to recover its alienated powers and capacities, to see itself in its world. Arendt, of course, sees the Marxian-Hegelian project as but one more formulation of the goal of human mastery. The Promethean desire for a completely anthropologized real is a pure expression of the kind of existential resentment that leads to alienation in the first place.[22] The overcoming of alienation requires not the completed humanization of the world (Arendt thinks *that* goal has largely been achieved) but the cultivation of an attitude of acceptance, or thankfulness for being. It is only through the cultivation of such existential gratitude that we will cease viewing the earth as a prison and finitude as lack, and will begin to be at home in the world once again.

Kateb's analysis of Arendt's "religious" presupposition puts her theory of political action in a peculiar light. Political action (the sharing of words and deeds in the public sphere) is, it turns out, the one form of extremist exertion that Arendt thinks does *not* contribute to our growing world alienation. However—and this is a key point for Kateb—if political action is to fulfill its existential vocation and provide a vehicle for reconciliation with an otherwise tragic condition, it is imperative that there exist groups of people—communities—who are "always already" at home in the world. Lacking a sense of place and shared identity, a society cannot give rise to a "frame for memorable deeds" that will have the illuminating quality Arendt demands from a genuine political sphere. Another way of putting this Katebian point is to say that Arendt's entire conception of the public realm presupposes a substantial degree of cultural rootedness and integrity. The modern age replaces the *heimlich* quality of *Gemeinschaft* with the alienation of *Gesellschaft*; the "frame for memorable deeds" becomes an instrumental structure filled by what Arendt deprecatingly refers to as "housekeeping" concerns. Political action loses its existential significance.

It is clear where Kateb has led us. Arendt is no modernist offering immanent critique; rather, her notion of worldliness, her antipathy to alienation, and her faith in the "existential achievement" of political action all point to an undeniable cultural conservatism, a yearning for the premodern. From Kateb's perspective, there is no question that Arendt is a communitarian, albeit a highly idiosyncratic one. Her greatest concern is for the public world illuminated by memorable deeds; yet the possibility of this theatrical space rests on the maintenance of firm boundaries and cultural integrity. The extremist energies of modernity dissolve the stable boundaries Arendt demands, replacing the "durable and tangible" world with something misty and particulate.[23] The modern (to say nothing of the postmodern) condition is one of blurred boundaries and the *Unheimlichkeit* they give rise to. Kateb, following the Heidegger of *Being and Time*, thinks that the only *authentic* response to such a reality is to learn to be at home in not being at home. Such a response demands, obviously, a revaluation of alienation (at least in its "moderate, everyday" forms): alienation becomes that which enables a looser, less resentful, aestheticized attachment to existence.[24] Against those such as Arendt who bemoan the alienation of modern life, we must learn to assert the value of alienation, of "homelessness" as existential condition. Inverting Gadamer, Kateb asserts that *alienation* is the basis of our openness to the world.

Kateb, then, would have us eschew the homesickness he sees as animating Arendt's critique of modernity. For Kateb it is the social or cultural critic's attitude toward alienation that provides the gauge of his or her basic modernism or antimodernism. The result in the case of

Arendt is never in question: the tight link she sees between resentment and alienation leaves little doubt that she views homelessness as pathological. She is a pure antimodernist, one who yearns for a "homey" *Gemeinschaft* not out of a nostalgia for authority but out of a desire to see the "frame of memorable deeds" do its thing, fulfill its redemptive role. The liberal modernist, in contrast, rejects not only the Arendtian path to reconciliation (political action, speech, and deeds on the public stage) but also the desire for reconciliation as such. This desire—even when found in modernists such as Marx—is deeply, unalterably antimodernist.

Of course, Kateb is right to emphasize the redemptive role political action plays for Arendt. Her desire for reconciliation flows from the tragic sensibility she shares with the Greeks, and it colors her entire approach to modernity. Yet Kateb's exclusive focus upon the "existential achievement" of political action yields a distorted view of her critique of modernity. For although Arendt, like Hegel, idealizes the Greeks as being uniquely at home in the world, she also shares his conviction that there is no going back; diremption cannot be undone (this, I take it, is one of the reasons for her fondness for René Char's aphorism and Tocqueville's epigram[25]). Moreover, Arendt knows that no "rainbow bridge of concepts" will succeed in recovering such wholeness.

Without the prospect of reconciliation, however, modernity looks like a downward spiral of increasing alienation. Arendt's political theory, then, would simply be another expression of the "unhappy consciousness" that, as Judith Shklar pointed out long ago, followed the implosion of utopian hopes.[26] It is, in fact, difficult to avoid this conclusion so long as we, like Kateb, insist upon seeing Arendt as driven by the desire to overcome alienation (a desire that transmutes into theoretical mournfulness with the demonstration of the impossibility of reconciliation). Kateb's story is complicated, however, when we balance the "religious" hope for reconciliation with the weight Arendt gives to the "pagan" value of worldliness. For Arendt modern existential resentment (what Heidegger calls the "will to will") is bad not because it blocks reconciliation but because it undermines worldliness. To be sure, "at-homeness" is one of the qualities Arendt attributes to a "worldly" (in Kateb's terms, unalienated) existence. Yet it is precisely the *artificiality*, the *reified* quality of this "home" that both Arendt's liberal critics and her communitarian admirers must ignore.

Full humanity does not require the absence of alienation or the availability of a *Gemeinschaft* in which one's group identity provides a form of metaphysical comfort. The "frame" Kateb speaks of is essentially a *stage*, and the worldly form of existence Arendt champions reserves an especially high place for *theatricality*. Kateb would have us elide the distinction between theatricality and community, the better to locate Arendt's "antimodernism" in terms of familiar categories. However, the history of political theory, from Plato to Rousseau and beyond (one could also include Heidegger in this regard), warns us against this move. From the beginning of *our* tradition, theatricality has been singled out as the enemy of community, artifice as the source of alienation.

In contrast to Kateb, I believe that any assessment of Arendt's critique of modernity must pause to consider the implications of her performance model of political action. As a crucial dimension of worldliness, theatricality exceeds—indeed, often stands in opposition to—the yearning for community, for an unalienated existence. This, in turn, reminds us of the specificity of Arendt's complaint: it is not alienation per se that she combats, but *world* alienation. One could go even further and say that to be *worldly* in Arendt's sense is to inscribe a certain modality of alienation at the heart of one's existence and to value this alienation positively. Arendt's emphasis upon agonism, performance, virtuosity, persona, and "alienated" representative thinking renders problematic, to say the least, Kateb's identification of worldliness with the *absence* of alienation. To be at home in the world in Arendt's sense means to be at home with the estrangement that permeates both her performative conception of action and her notion of "disinterested" judgment. I believe that Arendt is, in her idiosyncratic way, as much a champion of "moderate alienation" as is a liberal modernist such as Kateb.

The claim that Arendt valorizes alienation or estrangement appears, on the face of it, to be simply false. After all, doesn't Arendt's "disclosive" conception of political action rest upon an unabashedly expressivist vision of the self? Moreover, doesn't her idea of judgment (as "thinking without a rule") presuppose a shared set of practices, norms, and values as background? To put it in the Kantian terms Arendt prefers, doesn't the analogy of political judgment with reflective judgments of taste depend upon the presence of a strong, unproblematic *sensus communis*? If the primary value informing her theory of action is self-expression and her theory of judgment hinges on the availability of shared meanings and values, then it would appear that Kateb and the communitarians are right: Arendt is a romantic theorist of action and a neo-Aristotelian theorist of judgment (albeit one who inexplicably prefers Kantian drag).[27] However one approaches her political theory, there seems little desire on Arendt's part to make room for alienation. Let us take a closer look at Arendt's "expressivist" theory of political action and her Kantian/Aristotelian theory of judgment.

As Kateb rightly notes, Arendt values political action for its unmatched revelatory capacity.[28] The human condition of plurality has, according to Arendt, "the twofold character of equality and distinction" (*HC*, p. 175). The distinctness of the human individual is not reducible to the quality of otherness or alterity that he "shares with everything that is," nor to the quality of individuality that "he shares with everything alive." The form of being-together implied by the notion of plurality, by a *political* existence, enables the expression of a *unique* distinctness, a uniqueness that appears through the individual actor's words and deeds: "Speech and action *reveal* this unique distinctness. Through them, men *distinguish* themselves instead of being merely distinct; they are the modes in which human beings *appear* to each other, not indeed as physical objects, but *qua* men. This appearance, as distinguished from mere bodily existence, rests on initiative, but it is an initiative from which no human being can refrain and still be human" (p. 176).

A life without action and speech is "dead to the world," because it is through action and speech that persons disclose *who* they are. The "disclosure of who somebody is," according to Arendt, is "implicit in both his words and deeds." She hastens to add that "the affinity between speech and revelation is much closer than between action and revelation." Without the accompaniment of speech, "action would not only lose its revelatory character but, and by the same token, it would lose its subject," the agent (p. 178). Action without speech ceases to be action because "there would no longer be an actor, and the actor, the doer of deeds, is possible only if he is at the same time the speaker of words" (pp. 178–79).

In speaking and acting, then, "men show who they are, reveal actively their unique personal identities and thus make their appearance in the human world" (p. 179). If one reads this statement in conjunc-tion with Arendt's remarks on the "fiercely agonal spirit" that per-vaded the polis, one is indeed tempted to accuse her of holding an overtly romantic, expressivist view of the self.[29] The Arendtian politi-cal actor appears to be a self that externalizes, uncovers, or "defines" itself through the tangible medium of words and deeds. However, it is important to see that Arendt's agonistic conception of revelatory action is also essentially performative; like the agonism of Nietzsche, it is based on the *rejection* of anything like an expressivist conception of self.

What kind of self, then, *is* implied by the performance model of action? The expressivist conception assumes a core self, a basic or es-sential unity of innate capacities that are expressed, actualized, or con-certized in the world of appearances. The "disclosure of the agent in speech and action" implies, from this perspective, an abiding subject, a reality, *behind* appearances. In contrast, the performance model deployed by Arendt follows Nietzsche in seeking to unmask this "fiction," to escape the slavish, moralizing prejudice against action, a prejudice manifest in the "necessary" positing of such a subject as the causal ground of all deeds or "effects."[30] Arendt interprets freedom as virtuosity precisely to keep the actor *in* the world, to frame her identity qua actor as coextensive with, rather than prior to, her actions. From Arendt's point of view, the self that *precedes* action, the biological or psychological self (the self of needs, drives, motives), is an essentially dispersed, fragmented, and plural self; it is a self whose lack of ap-pearance deprives it of both unity and reality.[31] Like Nietzsche, Arendt challenges the assumption that a single, unified subject resides behind action; like him, she suggests that the unworldly self—the thinking as well as the biological and psychological self—is in fact a multiplicity of conflicting drives, needs, and faculties.[32]

The unity (coherence of identity) of the agent is, then, not a given; rather, it is an *achievement*, the product of action. But how does the performance of virtuosic action give rise to an identifiable self, a self possessed of perceivable unity and, thus, of "unique distinctness"? Ac-tion, according to Arendt, provides us with an escape from the inner, determining, multiple self. Freedom, as the spontaneous beginning of something new, is made possible by the transcendence of needs and psychology that entry into the public realm enables (because here nei-ther the needs of life nor purity of motivation are at stake). Such an escape from the divided self is not found in human beings' other free activity, thinking, which is the freedom of a "two-in-one," of a self engaged in internal dialogue.[33] The attempt of the philosopher to escape the realm of plurality through contemplative withdrawal "always remains an illusion," for in her solitude she is, according to Arendt, "more radically delivered to this plurality inherent in every human being than anybody else." Only entry into the public realm delivers us from such self-division: here the "companionship with others" calls "me out of the dialogue of thought" and "makes me one again—one single, unique, human being speaking with but one voice and recognizable as such by all others."[34]

Action, then, affords the self the chance to escape its "always changeable and somewhat equivocal" private nature, and to assume a "definite and unique shape."[35] This definite, recognizable shape signals the achievement of a distinct style of action, which is to say that it reflects the actor's virtuosity (*BPF*, p. 153). It is also created by the principles that inspire an agent's action and by the personae, the masks or roles that the actor assumes in public appearance (*OR*, pp. 106–7). Arendt's essential point is that if "the disclosure of 'who' in contradistinction to 'what' somebody is . . . is implicit in everything somebody says or does," then the achievement of identity is reserved for those whose words or deeds reflect a consistency of style. The performance of action in public provides the opportunity for stylization, and stylization is, in turn, the precondition for the kind of reification identity demands and for the transformation of a public life into a memorable narrative or story (*HC*, pp. 194–98).

The idea that identity is not given but is instead achieved through the creation of a distinctive style recalls again Nietzsche, who presented the problem of creating a self worthy of display and remembrance in a similar light. In *The Gay Science*, Nietzsche writes:

> *One thing is needful.*—To "give style" to one's character—a great and rare art! It is practiced by those who survey all the strengths and weaknesses of their nature and then fit them all into an artistic play until every one of them appears as art and reason and even weaknesses delight the eye. Here a large mass of second nature has been added; there a piece of original nature has been removed—both times through long practice and daily work of it. Here the ugly that could not be removed is concealed; there it has been reinterpreted and made sublime. Much that is vague and resisted shaping has been

saved and exploited for distant views. . . . In the end, when the work is finished, it becomes evident how the constraint of a single taste governed and formed everything large and small. Whether this taste was good or bad is less important than one might suppose, if only it is a single taste![36]

Nietzsche's conception of the self as a work of art is importantly different from Arendt's idea of the revelation of self that occurs in political action. Nevertheless, Nietzsche sees selfhood, "becoming who one is," as an achievement wrested from diverse materials, as consisting primarily in the attainment of style. Whether one has, in fact, attained this end is, as Nehamas notes, not something the *actor* can judge.[37] Nietzsche emphasizes that hardness toward oneself is necessary to bring coherence to welter, an emphasis Arendt echoes in stressing the discipline that playing a public role enforces (*OR*, pp. 106–8). But regardless of discipline, the final judgment whether style or coherence is achieved—and what *kind* of character is displayed—resides with others, with the audience. Style and character, the marks of an achieved unity, are essentially *public* phenomena, utterly distinct from whatever feeling of unity the agent may experience himself.[38]

This brings us to a third essential difference between the performance and expressivist models. The "disclosure of the agent in speech and deeds" implies, for Arendt, the absence of an underlying subject—identity as something achieved rather than given—as well as the *decentered* nature of such self-revelation. The disclosure of the agent—the "reward" of agonistic, individualizing action—is, Arendt stresses, nothing like a project. Intentionality has the most tenuous connection to the "who" that action reveals (*HC*, p. 184). Nor is the disclosure of the agent in words and deeds a process that necessarily increases self-knowledge or brings one closer to self-transparency. As Arendt states in *The Human Condition*, "disclosure can almost never be achieved by willful purpose, as though one possessed and could dispose of this 'who' in the same manner he has and can dispose of his qualities. On the contrary, it is more than likely that the 'who', which appears so clearly and unmistakably to others, remains hidden from the person himself . . ." (p. 179). We cannot be the authors of ourselves, of the stories that will be told about us (pp. 184–85). The audience—our peers and those who come after—decides what the masks we wear in public signify and define, the "who" that they reveal.

As political actors, then, we disclose our unique identities but we do *not* express ourselves. We do not express ourselves for two basic reasons: first, there is no unified self to express; second, although action can be said to achieve or make identity possible, at the same time it conceals that identity. Nietzsche again is apposite. In the preface to *The Genealogy of Morals*, he famously remarks that "we men of knowledge are unknown to ourselves. . . . [we] are not 'men of knowledge' with respect to ourselves."[39] If we substitute "men of action" for "men of knowledge" in the first phrase, we approach Arendt's position. "Nobody," she states, "knows whom he reveals when he discloses himself in word or deed"; nevertheless, "he must be willing to risk this disclosure" (*HC*, p. 180).

We see, then, how Arendt's "disclosive" theory of political action builds in estrangement at several levels. Arendt's goal is to break the romantic-idealist linkage of expression and revelation, authenticity and disclosure, once and for all. She does this by questioning the idea of a "core" self; by emphasizing the role of stylization, persona, and masks in the performance of political action; and, finally, by presenting the revealed public self as, in large part, a function of the "audience's" judgment. What is at stake is not the overcoming of alienation or estrangement (the goal of romanticism) but rather our inherited Cartesian-Rousseauian prejudices in favor of a "true" self behind the appearances.[40] The "worldliness" that inspires Arendt's theory of action is not the solidarity of group membership but a highly theatrical form of individualism, one that rests upon the *distance* that separates actor and audience (*HC*, p. 184).

In turning to consider Arendt's theory of political judgment, we confront an even greater interpretive quandary, for although most commentators agree with Ronald Beiner's assertion that Arendt's theory of judgment "completes" her theory of action, there is a good deal of disagreement over how, precisely, this completion takes place.[41] As I noted earlier, the matter is complicated by Arendt's idiosyncratic appeal to Kant's aesthetic theory rather than his practical philosophy. Moral and political judgment, she asserts, is analogous to the phenomenon of taste judgment as analyzed by Kant in the third *Critique*.

Beiner sees the completion effected by judgment as occurring at the level of ontology and meaning. Through its discriminating activity, judgment "confirms the being of that which has been disclosed" in political action.[42] By means of its reflective, nonsubsumptive operation, judgment recognizes the novel in its full particularity yet brings the new within the ambit of human understanding. In this broad manner, judgment contributes to the project of reconciliation: it makes it possible for us to be at home in an otherwise tragic world.[43] This power of judgment comes sharply into focus with the collapse and disappearance of the various "yardsticks" that traditionally guided it. Only when we are forced to "think without a bannister" (Arendt) does the faculty of judgment come into its own, and our reliance upon it announce itself.[44] From Beiner's communitarian perspective, this means that the shattered foundations of religion, tradition, and authority are to be replaced by a reconstructed moral horizon based on *shared* judgments.[45] It is only within such a reconstructed horizon that judgment can perform its existential task.

Beiner's communitarian interpretation of Arendt's views on judgment implicitly confirms Kateb's characterization. From my perspective this interpretation is notable for what it omits or suppresses, namely, the aesthetic character of judgment as theorized by Arendt. For Beiner, Arendt's appeal to Kant's *Critique of Judgment* is justifiable as a way of isolating that form of judgment which "saves the phenomena," which respects appearances as appearances. However, he thinks that Arendt's reliance upon the third *Critique* runs the risk of formalizing or aestheticizing judgment, a possibility with dire consequences. As Beiner puts it,

> [A]t some point one must ask: what is the *content* of the ends and purposes of political actors or historical agents that makes this set of political appearances, rather than that set, worth attending to? . . . What, substantively, characterizes someone as discriminating or knowledgeable or responsible in his judgments—apart from the *formal* conditions of disinterestedness and freedom from extraneous influences or heteronomous constraints? What are the *substantive* conditions that allow us to acknowledge wisdom and experience in the judging subject and appropriateness and relevance in the object of judgment? Without at some point introducing questions like these, the attempt to transpose a theory of judging as formal as Kant's into a theory of political judgment runs the risk of turning from a genuine appreciation of political appearances *qua* appearances into an unwarranted aestheticization of politics. It is at this juncture that Arendt would have done well to consult Aristotle, for he situates judgment firmly within the context of the substantive ends and purposes of political deliberation, rhetoric, and community.[46]

In other words, we need a lot less *Urteilskraft*, and a lot more *phronesis*. Beiner appropriates much of Gadamer's critique of Kantian aesthetics, including his suggestion that the *sensus communis* (which Kant had radically depoliticized) be reinjected with community-based "substance." Thus, although Beiner thinks Arendt is right to follow Kant in distinguishing the activity of judging from cognitive or technical exercises, he also thinks that "autonomous" judgment must be grounded in a concrete political community, a decidedly *heteronomous sensus communis*, if this faculty is to escape the aestheticism of Kant's disembodied spectators. When Arendt approvingly cites Kant's observation that taste judgments are redeemed persuasively (the judging person "can only woo the consent of everyone else" [*BPF*, p. 222]), Beiner reads this as an implicit demand for a "thick" community sense, one that can provide the basis for a robust deliberative politics in a way that a thinned-out "feeling for the world" cannot.

Benhabib approaches Arendt's theory of judgment from a different angle, but she too is troubled by the specter of aestheticism. The reason Arendt found Kant's analysis of reflective or taste judgment appealing, she argues, is that it provided the outline of a *procedure* necessary for ascertaining "intersubjective validity in the public realm."[47] Kant had argued that the specific validity of judgments of taste resided in our ability to strip such judgments of "subjective and personal conditions." This is accomplished, he thought, by "weighing the judgment, not so much with actual, as rather with the merely possible judgments of others, and by putting ourselves in the position of every one else."[48] This is the perspective of the "enlarged mentality," a notion Arendt seizes upon in "The Crisis in Culture." There, glossing Kant, she tells us that

> The power of judgment rests on a potential agreement with others, and the thinking process which is active in judging something is not, like the thought process of pure reasoning, a dialogue between me and myself, but finds itself always and primarily, even if I am quite alone in making up my mind, in an anticipated communication with others with whom I know I must finally come to some agreement. From this potential agreement judgment derives its specific validity. . . . This enlarged way of thinking, which as judgment knows how to transcend its individual limitations, cannot function in strict isolation or solitude; it needs the presence of others "in whose place" it must think, whose perspective it must take into consideration, and without whom it never has the opportunity to operate at all.[49]

Benhabib reads this passage as offering proof that what Arendt really sought in Kant's philosophy of judgment was a decision procedure that operated according to the criterion of universalizability. Kant's aesthetic theory proves superior to his practical philosophy in this regard, because it eschews the monology of the categorical imperative and places the quest for a "universal," objective judgment within the three-dimensionality of the public sphere and its plural perspectives. "Intersubjective validity" replaces a priori certainty or the subjectivism of mere preference.

Beiner's and Benhabib's "corrective" readings radically devalue the aesthetic dimension of Arendt's theory of judgment. Both see Arendt's appeal to Kantian taste judgment as a symbol for another (more palatable) ultimate concern. For Beiner the *sensus communis* betokens the centrality of community; for Benhabib the "enlarged mentality" points to an essentially intersubjective theory of judgment. In rescuing Arendt's theory of judgment from the charge of aestheticism, Beiner and Benhabib suppress the dimensions of distance, detachment, and alienation that so color Kant's philosophy of judgment. From the perspective of the communitarian or Habermasian, the problem with the Kantian judge-spectator is that she is *too* detached, unsituated, *independent*. Such detachment renders the judgments of such a spectator—especially her moral and political judgments—inherently dubious. Thus Beiner's desire to shore up this spectator's "feeling for the world," her *sensus communis*, with a healthy dose of shared ends and values: the spectator must become a *citizen*; thus also Benhabib's anxious desire to replace the *imaginative* role of "representative thinking" with an institutionalized decision procedure that produces the universal.

The irony in all this is that it is precisely the distance, disinterestedness, and alienation of Kant's aesthetics that attracts Arendt in the first place. She knew (obviously) what resources Aristotle held for thinking the nature of political judgment.[50] Nevertheless, she explicitly and self-consciously avoided deploying them. Indeed, just prior to her death, upon reading Ernst Vollrath's manuscript on judgment, she emphatically commented, "*Urteilskraft* is not *phronesis!*"[51] From Beiner's perspective, this insistence is inexplicable, bordering on the perverse. Yet Arendt had her reasons. The problem with *phronesis*, at least from the point of view of a theorist who identifies plurality as the *conditio sine qua non* of the public sphere, is that it collapses distance. The "thinking without a rule" proposed by Aristotle is exercised by citizens deliberating about the application or interpretation of generally subscribed-to universals in a particular situation. *Phronesis* provides a workable model of judgment only where the gods are *not* at war, where the *sensus communis* is indeed something thicker than a "mere" feeling for the world. Yet this is precisely why Arendt eschews it in thinking about judgment. What Kant offers (and Aristotle doesn't) is a way of conceiving judgment that does not subsume the individual under the community. Arendt's admiration for Socrates, Lessing, and Thoreau makes clear that the worldliness she has in mind is not reducible to the "situatedness" promoted by the communitarians.[52]

The examples of Socrates, Lessing, and Thoreau also cast suspicion on Benhabib's interpretation. For Benhabib the most important sentence in the passage I quoted is the first: "The power of judgment rests on a potential agreement with others, and the thinking process which is active in judging . . . finds itself . . . in an anticipated communication with others with whom I know I must finally come to some agreement." If we allow this sentence to define the problem of judgment in Arendt, then it certainly appears that she turns to Kant in quest of a decision procedure. However, if we allow that judgment is still exercised in those situations where agreement is not forthcoming—where, indeed, it may well be impossible—then a somewhat different emphasis is detected in Arendt's appropriation of Kant. What matters now is not the translation of the "enlarged mentality" into a concrete decision procedure, but the maintenance of the "thinking withdrawal," of the distance that makes judgment in Kant's sense possible. In this reading it is precisely the *imaginative* character of representative thinking that needs to be preserved if the autonomy or independence of judgment is to be maintained. Judgment demands thinking withdrawal, and such withdrawal makes it possible to hear the voice of conscience.[53] The "inner dialogue" does not substitute for representative thinking—Socrates and Thoreau remain committed, after all, to the project of persuasion[54]—but neither should "anticipated agreement" be treated as anything more than an "as if" (which is all it is for Lessing). Judgment, in other words, is not about the manufacture of consensus, the creation of rules of discourse that insure the triumph of "the force of the better argument." Yet, from Benhabib's perspective, it is the role of withdrawn thinking, the "as if" in representative thought, that makes Arendt's conception of *moral* judgment dangerously "intuitionist." One needs the discipline of the dialogue with others, not with oneself.[55]

The central role played by alienation in both Arendt's theory of action and her theory of judgment puts in doubt Kateb's reading of her "rejectionist" critique of modernity. What the modern subjectification of the real and the instrumentalization of politics have done is not to destroy *Gemeinschaft* but rather to render supremely problematic a certain kind of distance, a certain kind of estrangement. Where the instrumentalist considerations of *homo faber* or the needs of life dominate, the serious play of politics devolves into administration, coercion, or violence. Our capacity for spontaneous action and judgment resides, ultimately, upon a worldly form of estrangement (by no means the same as estrangement *from* the world), one that the "extremist exertions" of modernity has radically undermined. One can speak, in this regard, not only of our loss of feeling for the world but also of the world itself, for modernity's will to will overwhelms the dimension of artifice that "frames" genuine action, destroying mediation and contributing to the growing "naturalization" of human existence.

Arendt's antimodernism, then, is not totalizing, at least not in the sense of the cultural reactionary who abhors the alienation of modern life and yearns for the rootedness of a premodern existence (e.g., Heidegger at his most simplistic and loathsome, or Pope John Paul II). But if Arendt's critique of modernity is not "rejectionist" in this sense, is it perhaps immanent in nature? This is the view taken by many of her admirers who, like Benhabib, wish to give the widest possible currency to certain aspects of her thought.[56] What are we to make of the claims of communitarians, Habermasians, and participatory democrats in light of the *ontological* implications of Arendt's critique of modernity?

Speaking broadly, each of these three schools of thought wishes to enlist Arendt in the project of recovering a robust, comprehensive, and unitary public sphere. The explanations offered for how this sphere has been denatured, fragmented, or lost vary. For Benhabib and Habermas, the prerogatives of the public sphere have largely been usurped by the technocratic assertion of the "steering imperatives" of a complex political economy. For the communitarians, the fact that the public world has lost its power to "gather us together" is traceable to an undernourished sense of membership and to the absence of animating, shared public purposes (hence the view of the liberal public sphere as a proceduralist shell). For participatory democrats, the framework of liberal constitutionalism, combined with late capitalism and the rise of the national security state, conspires to undercut democracy and to render the title of citizen meaningless. The different diagnoses ought not conceal the fact that all agree that the res publica is in dire condition and that each sees Arendt as providing support for its particular program. Hence Benhabib's Habermasian appeal to Arendt's "intersubjective" concept of political action, the communitarian's appeal to her worldly, "rooted" conception of membership, and the participatory democrat's appeal to the echoes of civic republicanism in her text. Each school hopes that the pursuit of one of these "Arendtian" avenues will bring us noticeably closer to a genuine—more democratic, just, and meaningful—public sphere.

The notion of a unitary or comprehensive public sphere has recently come in for a good deal of criticism, as scholars working from Foucauldian, feminist, or neo-Gramscian perspectives draw attention to the irreducibility of mechanisms of exclusion in the constitution of any discursive community.[57] Arendt's Greek, hypermasculinist conception of the public sphere would appear to mark her as an extreme example of public realm theory's general insensitivity to such concerns. The fact that her work inspires Habermas, the communitarians, and participatory democrats has done little to endear her to champions of difference who wish to expose the disciplinary techniques by which "virtuous" (read docile) citizens are made, or the power relations implicit in the most resolutely intersubjective accounts of discursive rationality.

Interestingly, what binds together Arendt's contemporary critics and admirers is the unquestioned assumption that she stands for the recovery of a single, institutionalized public sphere. Of course, Arendt's work, with its idealization of the public realm of the polis and its invocation of the "lost treasure" of the revolutionary tradition, more or less invites this reading. But, it seems to me, her admirers and critics are a little too fixated upon the "models" of the public sphere they find in Arendt's text, models they decontextualize and treat as laudatory or suffocating normative ideals. One result of this fixation is a general disregard for the central argument of *The Human Condition*. As we have seen, this argument concerns the de-worlding of the public world manifest in modernity's relentless subjectification of the real. The upshot of this argument is that, in late modernity, Being cannot possibly equal appearance. Modern world alienation dissolves the *sensus communis*, with the result that the only things "seen and heard by all" are the false appearances (Heidegger's "semblances") offered up under the single aspect of mass culture (*HC*, p. 58). The mistake of the Habermasians, the communitarians, and the participatory democrats is to assume that there may be a late modern substitute for this feeling for the world. Arendt is under no such illusion.

We must, in other words, take seriously Arendt's various pronouncements about the "end of the common world." After this event—for Arendt, the defining event of the modern age—the prospects for an authentic, comprehensive, and relatively permanent public sphere fall to just about zero. This is not to say she gives up on action, politics, or "publicity" in the Kantian sense. Rather, it is to say that she is keenly aware of how the energies of modernity, which initially open the possibility of a groundless politics, wind up intensifying the paradox inherent in every revolutionary founding or spontaneous political action, namely, that the moment of "clearing" in which a space of freedom emerges is also the beginning of its disappearance.[58] The combination of modern world alienation with the late modern escalation of the automatism present in life itself renders the appearance of these "islands of freedom" an even more "miraculous" event (*BPF*, p. 168). Late modernity heightens their evanescence; such spaces lead a "fugitive" existence (to use Sheldon Wolin's term).[59]

It is not a question, therefore, of pretending that we can resurrect the agora or some approximation thereof by appealing to deliberation, intersubjectivity, or "acting in concert." What matters is our ability to resist the demand for "functionalized behavior" and to preserve, as far as possible, our capacity for initiatory, agonistic action and spontaneous, independent judgment. This project of preservation occurs in a "world" where, as Arendt constantly reminds us, the supports for these activities have been radically undermined.

It is here that Arendt's concerns intersect most sharply with those of certain "postmodern" theorists. An unlikely constellation appears when we view Arendt's emphasis upon agonism, plurality, and performance against the backdrop of her more Heideggerian thoughts concerning the destruction of the common world. Seen through this lens, Arendt's theory of political action, so clearly at odds with a Foucauldian politics of everyday life, links up with his concept of resistance, for where the space of action is usurped (as both Arendt and

Foucault argue it is), action in the strict sense is no longer possible. *Resistance* becomes the primary vehicle of spontaneity and agonistic subjectivity, a kind of successor concept to action.[60] Similarly, where the public sphere is fragmented and the *sensus communis* a thing of the past, the autonomy of judgment is preserved by efforts such as Arendt's and Lyotard's, which resist the temptation to ground this faculty in a theoretical discourse, and which struggle to provide a phenomenology of judgment "outside of the concept and outside of habit."[61] Finally, in an age that has witnessed the withdrawal of the political and its dispersion throughout the social body, Arendt's tenacious effort to think the specificity of the political is hardly an anachronism, as Lacoue-Labarthe and Nancy have recognized.[62] Where everything is political, nothing is political.

I raise these points of intersection merely as markers in order to question Habermas's overly neat dichotomization of public realm theory, on the one hand, and the concerns of postmodern or poststructuralist theory, on the other.[63] One indication of Arendt's originality and breadth as a thinker is the way her work clearly straddles this "abyss" that has been taken for granted by both sides of the modern/ postmodern debate. Arendt's public realm theory is too sensitive to modern forces of normalization, too self-consciously theatrical in conception, and too invested in the preservation of plurality to be easily assimilated to a political theory whose raison d'être is, in many respects, the enforcement of the boundary between performance and persuasion, communicative and world-disclosive speech. At the same time, she is too acutely aware of the modern de-worlding of the public world to subscribe to the belief that a politics of everyday life confined to "local" struggle and resistance can effectively prevent the further withdrawal of the political. In fact, as is the case with some versions of identity politics, such a politics may well contribute to this withdrawal. From an Arendtian perspective, the challenge of a "postmodern" politics is to maintain the link between action and publicity in a context where the institutionalized public sphere is deeply compromised and the definition of what is properly "public" is perhaps the most hotly contested issue of all. A slightly different way of putting this is to say that not all forms of resistance (or activism) are political and that resistance itself is, at best, a kind of displaced or second-best form of political action.

Arendt's critique of modernity, like her theory of political action, eludes easy classification. Too antinostalgic to be "rejectionist" yet too radical to qualify as "immanent," it fully displays Arendt's uncanny ability to combine an Olympian perspective on an epoch with a phenomenology of contemporary existence. Among recent theorists, only Foucault can be said to match her Nietzschean capacity to distance herself from the unquestioned assumptions of the age. This ability is the source of embarrassment and frustration for those theorists who think, with Walzer, that the first duty of the social or political critic is to identify with the hopes, fears, and basic values of his or her community.[64] It also clashes with the current prejudice, ironically perpetuated by Foucault, that insists upon viewing theory as a kind of toolbox, to be judged and deployed according to strategic considerations.

It is, of course, possible to appropriate Arendt in this way, to view her deconstruction of the traditional concept of action and her analysis of the "destruction of the common world" as somehow beside the point, as not *political* enough. The irony of this stance is that it reproduces the "technical" configuration of acting and thinking that she and Heidegger devoted so much energy to questioning. It is, moreover, extraordinarily shortsighted. Arendt's central theoretical works are of value not because they offer an edifying affirmation of human agency in an age of ideology or a vehement repudiation of docility[65]; what Arendt learned from the experience of totalitarianism was that all human capacities—particularly the capacity for action and judgment—crucially depend upon the conditions of their exercise and that it is indeed possible to uproot capacities that may appear to be part of our "nature." The urgency of her attempt in *The Human Condition* to "think what we are doing" flows from this insight, for what Arendt suggests is that the existential resentment underlying much of the modern project may yet succeed where totalitarian ideologies could claim only a temporary victory. The extirpation of the human capacity for action by "peaceful" means is the danger that looms "after Auschwitz." The light of the public can be extinguished by means other than terror.

Notes

Portions of this chapter originally appeared in my book *Arendt and Heidegger: The Fate of the Political* (Princeton: Princeton University Press, 1996).

1. See Seyla Benhabib, *The Reluctant Modernism of Hannah Arendt* (Thousand Oaks, Calif.: Sage Publications, 1996). See also her "Judgment and the Moral Founda-

tions of Politics in Hannah Arendt's Thought" and "Models of the Public Sphere" in *Situating the Self* (New York: Routledge, 1992).

2. Benhabib criticizes Arendt's agonism in "Models of the Public Sphere," contrasting her unfavorably with Habermas.

3. See Benhabib, "Judgment and Moral Foundations."

4. See Dana Villa, "Postmodernism and the Public Sphere," *American Political Science Review*, vol. 86, no. 3 (September 1992); and "Beyond Good and Evil: Arendt, Nietzsche, and the Aestheticization of Political Action," *Political Theory*, vol. 20, no. 2 (May 1992).

5. George Kateb, *Hannah Arendt: Politics, Conscience, Evil* (Totowa, N.J.: Rowman and Allanheld, 1984), p. 183.

6. Hannah Arendt, *On Revolution* (New York: Penguin Books, 1962), p. 281; hereinafter cited in text as OR.

7. Kateb, *Hannah Arendt*, p. 158.

8. Michael Walzer, *Interpretation and Social Criticism* (Cambridge: Harvard University Press, 1991), p. 89. See also Walzer's *The Company of Critics* (New York: Basic Books).

9. See Michael Walzer, "The Politics of Michel Foucault," and Richard Rorty, "Foucault and Epistemology," in *Foucault: A Critical Reader*, ed. David Couzens Hoy (New York: Blackwell, 1986).

10. Michel Foucault, "What Is Enlightenment?" in *The Foucault Reader*, ed. Paul Rabinow (New York: Pantheon, 1984).

11. Kateb, *Hannah Arendt*, chapter 5.

12. Hannah Arendt, *The Human Condition* (Chicago: University of Chicago Press, 1958), pp. 59–61, 257; hereinafter cited in text as HC.

13. See Dana Villa, *Arendt and Heidegger: The Fate of the Political* (Princeton: Princeton University Press, 1995), chapter 6.

14. See Hannah Arendt, "What Is Authority?" in *Between Past and Future* (New York: Penguin, 1968), hereinafter cited in text as BPF; and Max Weber, "Science as a Vocation," in *From Max Weber*, ed. H. H. Gerth and C. Wright Mills (New York: Oxford University Press, 1972).

15. Martin Heidegger, "The Age of the World Picture" in *The Question Concerning Technology and Other Essays*, ed. William Lovitt (New York: Harper and Row, 1977), p. 128.

16. Ibid., pp. 128–29.

17. Arendt, HC, pp. 70–71, 284; cf. "What Is Freedom?" in BPF.

18. Heidegger, "Age of the World Picture," p. 132.

19. Ibid., p. 132; Arendt, HC, p. 3.

20. Hannah Arendt, "On Humanity in Dark Times," in *Men in Dark Times* (New York: Harcourt Brace Jovanovich, 1968), p. 4.

21. Kateb, *Hannah Arendt*, p. 158.

22. Ibid., p. 162.

23. Ibid., p. 174.

24. See George Kateb, *The Inner Ocean* (Ithaca: Cornell University Press, 1992), especially essays 5 and 6.

25. Arendt quotes Char in the preface to BPF—"*Notre heritage n'est pas précédé d'aucun testament*" [Our inheritance was left to us by no testament] (p. 3)—and Tocqueville a few pages later: "Since the past has ceased to throw its light upon the future, the mind of man wanders in obscurity" (p. 7). Both quotations are deployed by Arendt to bolster her conviction that the "thread of tradition" has been cut and that the situation

of contemporary understanding is to be radically "on its own." See Stan Draenos's "Thinking without a Ground: Hannah Arendt and the Contemporary Situation of Understanding," in *Hannah Arendt: The Recovery of the Public World*, ed. Melvyn A. Hill (New York: St. Martin's Press, 1979).

26. Judith Shklar, *After Utopia* (Princeton: Princeton University Press, 1957), p. 110.

27. See Ronald Beiner, "Interpretive Essay," in Hannah Arendt, *Lectures on Kant's Political Philosophy* (Chicago: University of Chicago Press, 1983), pp. 136–38 (hereinafter cited in text as *LKPP*).

28. Kateb, *Hannah Arendt*, chapter 1.

29. This charge has been leveled by Martin Jay and Hanna Pitkin, among others.

30. See Friedrich Nietzsche, *The Genealogy of Morals*, vol. 1 (New York: Vintage, 1989), p. 13.

31. Thus, the "worldlessness" of the *animal laborans* is also a literal selflessness. See, in this regard, Arendt's discussion of the split Rousseauian "authentic self" in *OR*, pp. 96–98. Bonnie Honig includes a good discussion of this neglected aspect of Arendt's thought in her "Arendt, Identity, and Difference," *Political Theory* 16, no. 1 (February 1988). See also Kateb, *Hannah Arendt*, pp. 8–13.

32. See Friedrich Nietzsche, *The Will to Power*, trans. Walter Kaufmann (New York: Random House, 1968), nos. 490 and 488, for his conception of the subject as multiplicity (see also his *Beyond Good and Evil* [New York: Penguin, 1973], no. 12). Honig persuasively argues that Arendt shares Nietzsche's "political" conception of the self; Honig cites a passage from *The Life of the Mind* in which Arendt affirms "the obvious plurality of men's faculties and abilities" against the "implicit monism" of the tradition ("Arendt, Identity, and Difference," p. 485). Although her point is well taken, I think Honig valorizes the "fragmented" or multiple self in a way Arendt would find dubious. The "multiple" self Arendt celebrates (as Honig notes) is the performing self, the self capable of donning a number of different masks, of playing a number of different roles. It is important to maintain this distinction; otherwise, we give in to the temptation to read Arendt as a poststructuralist *avant la lettre*, which she certainly was not. For an excellent discussion of Nietzsche's "political metaphor for the self," see Alexander Nehamas, *Nietzsche: Life as Literature* (Cambridge: Harvard University Press, 1985), pp. 177–86.

33. Hannah Arendt, *The Life of the Mind*, vol. 1 (New York: Harcourt Brace Jovanovich, 1977), pp. 180–87.

34. Hannah Arendt, "Philosophy and Politics," *Social Research* 57, no. 1 (spring 1990), p. 86. See also her "Thinking and Moral Considerations," *Social Research* 51, no. 1 (spring/summer 1984), pp. 32–33.

35. Arendt, "Philosophy and Politics," p. 88.

36. Friedrich Nietzsche, *The Gay Science* (New York: Vintage, 1974), no. 290.

37. Nehamas, *Nietzsche*, p. 186.

38. Ibid. This is, of course, only one side of the matter, at least in the case of Nietzsche, who emphasized his own lack of audience and his reliance upon self-given standards.

39. Nietzsche, *Genealogy of Morals*, vol. 1, p. 15.

40. See Arendt, *OR*, pp. 98–109. Her primary objection to a Rousseauian politics of authenticity or compassion is that it "abolishes the distance, the worldly space between men" (102).

41. Beiner, "Interpretive Essay," p. 104.

42. Ibid., p. 111.

43. Ibid., p. 94. Beiner draws on Arendt's early essay "Understanding and Politics" (in her *Essays in Understanding, 1930–1954* [New York: Harcourt Brace, 1994]) in making this claim.

44. Beiner, "Interpretive Essay," p. 96.

45. Ibid., p. 112.

46. Ibid., pp. 137–38. A similar argument is made in Beiner's *Political Judgment* (Chicago: University of Chicago Press, 1984). For the expression of a similar communitarian perplexity regarding Arendt's turn to Kant, see Christopher Lasch, introduction to *Salmagundi* no. 60 (1983), p. xi.

47. Benhabib, "Judgment and Moral Foundations," p. 132.

48. Immanuel Kant, quoted in ibid., p. 133.

49. Arendt, *BPF*, pp. 220–21, quoted in Benhabib, "Judgment and Moral Foundations," p. 133.

50. Like Gadamer, Arendt was a student in Heidegger's famous 1924 seminar on Plato's *Sophist*, in which book 6 of Aristotle's *Nicomachean Ethics* received extended treatment. See Martin Heidegger, *Platon: Sophist*, vol. 19 of *Gesamtausgabe* (Frankfurt: Vittorio Klostermann, 1992).

51. Jerome Kohn, conversation with author.

52. See Arendt's "On Humanity in Dark Times," "Thinking and Moral Considerations," and "Philosophy and Politics" for her view of Socrates as a "citizen amongst citizens"; and *LKPP*, pp. 36–39. In her essay "Civil Disobedience" in *Crises of the Republic* (New York: Harcourt Brace Jovanovich, 1972), Arendt is critical of the politics of conscience in both Socrates and Thoreau. She views it as symptomatic of a kind of self-interest, a "care for one's soul" rather than for the world. Nevertheless, I think the alternative view of Socrates that she outlines in "Philosophy and Politics" and "Thinking and Moral Considerations" can also accommodate Thoreau. Indeed, Thoreau's "conscientious objection," which includes both his going to jail and the publication of *his* essay on civil disobedience is, like Socrates, highly theatrical in character and typifies a politics of gesture and doxastic appeal rather than mere withdrawal (as Arendt seems to think). In short, Arendt should have been more appreciative of the *political* character of Thoreau's action, despite the fact that it inspired many later resisters to cast their actions as *un*political.

53. Arendt, "Thinking and Moral Considerations," p. 37; cf. *LKPP*, p. 43.

54. Arendt, "Philosophy and Politics."

55. Benhabib, "Judgment and Moral Foundations," pp. 123, 138. Part of the reason for the tension between Arendt and Benhabib has to do with the *context* of judgment. Benhabib is interested in the ongoing process by which moral and political judgments are made within "normal" politics. Arendt centers her thinking about the relation between thought and judgment on those "rare moments when the chips are down" ("Thinking and Moral Considerations," p. 37). Nevertheless, it is instructive to contrast Benhabib's rendition of "enlarged mentality" with Arendt's. See *LKPP*, p. 43.

56. A typical statement in this regard is made by Jeffrey Isaac in his *Arendt, Camus, and Modern Rebellion* (New Haven: Yale University Press, 1992), p. 229, where he assimilates Arendt's stance toward modernity to Charles Taylor's.

57. For an overview of these criticisms, see Nancy Fraser, "Rethinking the Public Sphere," in *Habermas and the Public Sphere*, ed. Craig Calhoun (Cambridge: MIT Press, 1992).

58. Arendt, *OR*, p. 232. See, in this regard, Jim Miller's essay on the "Pathos of Novelty" in Arendt, in Hill, *Hannah Arendt*.

59. Compare this to Habermas's formulation in "On the German-Jewish Heritage," *Telos* 44 (summer 1980), p. 129.

60. See Villa, "Postmodernism and the Public Sphere"; cf. also Michel Foucault,

"The Subject and Power," in Hubert L. Dreyfus and Paul Rabinow, *Michel Foucault: Beyond Structuralism and Hermeneutics* (Chicago: University of Chicago Press, 1982).

61. Jean-François Lyotard, *Just Gaming* (Minneapolis: University of Minnesota Press, 1985), p. 82.

62. Philippe Lacoue-Labarthe and Jean-Luc Nancy, "Overture" to *Rejouer le Politique* (Paris: Editions Galilee, 1981).

63. See Jürgen Habermas, *Philosophical Discourse of Modernity* (Cambridge: MIT Press, 1987); and Villa, "Postmodernism and the Public Sphere."

64. Walzer, *Interpretation and Social Criticism.*

65. The former is Isaac's position (*Arendt, Camus, and Modern Rebellion*), the latter Honig's ("Arendt, Identity, and Difference").

Eight

Hannah Arendt and the Meaning of the Public/Private Distinction

Eli Zaretsky

Introduction

In considering Hannah Arendt, one must somehow comprehend the juxtaposition of sometimes bizarre and reprehensible ideas with others that are among the most progressive, innovative, and advanced of her—and our—times. Among the former ideas I don't mean indefensible but harmless obiter dicta such as her suggestion, in *The Human Condition*, that modernity witnessed the decline of architecture. Nor do I have in mind wrongheaded and harmful opinions such as her attempt, in *The Origins of Totalitarianism* and contradicted elsewhere in her work, to describe Marxism and Nazism as equally valueless theories. I do not mean even horrific formulations such as her description in *Eichmann in Jerusalem* of "the submissive meekness with which Jews went to their death—arriving on time at the transportation points, walking on their own feet to the places of execution, digging their own graves, undressing and making neat piles of their clothing, and lying down side by side to be shot," a description that is cold, distancing, and unconvincing.[1]

No, what I find most objectionable in Arendt is her central thesis: the "prepolitical," indeed prehuman, status of labor and the exalted role of speech and action, using these terms in her senses. Arendt's attempt to distinguish labor as a "biological" activity and politics as more truly "human" contradicts the scientific and democratizing thrust of much modern philosophy, notably pragmatism. One can only be appalled at her attack on what she called "social housekeeping" when one remembers that the issues she thought had debased politics involve such matters as wages and hours, industrial safety, or the abolition of child labor. Nor do her later attempts to allow such issues into politics so long as they do not take the form of "interests" really help matters, because the concerns of excluded groups always appear as "interests." Yet her essentially aristocratic, antidemocratic, and premodern prejudices are also the source of her continued relevance. This is the paradox I intend to explore.

A key to this paradox, I will argue, lies in situating Arendt in relation to the social democratic and the Marxist thought of her time. (Of course, Arendt was a profound and prescient critic of the social democratic tradition, but this does not exhaust her relation to it.) There are three further parameters along which I will examine this relationship. First, I will discuss the fact that there are Marxist and social democratic elements in Arendt's work, such as the theory of imperialism in *The Origins of Totalitarianism*, as well as the fact that she sometimes argues directly with Marx or with social democracy, as in *The Human Condition*. Second, I will show that much of Arendt's most creative thought developed from the aporias of Marxism, both its lack of understanding of nationalism (and, indeed, of group identity) and its failure to develop an understanding of the diversity of individual subjectivity and the consequent pluralism that distinguishes modernity. Third, I will show that certain currently neglected strengths of the Marxist and social democratic outlooks still provide an important way of criticizing Arendt. My concern throughout is to locate the *critical* elements in Arendt's thought and to distinguish them from the reactionary ones. The Arendt I mean to foreground is the woman who wrote enthusiastically to Jaspers, soon after her arrival in the United States, that "every intellectual here is a member of the opposition simply because he is an intellectual."[2]

Arendt's relations to Marxism and social democracy are not adequately appreciated in much contemporary Arendt scholarship. Of course, Arendt was anti-Marxist, but her well-known refusal to join "the company of detractors of a great man," referring to Marx, was more than a reaction to the McCarthyism of her time (*HC*, 79).[3] In addition, Arendt was influenced, sometimes reactively, in ways she was not always aware of. The complexity of her relationship to social democracy is sometimes obscured by descriptions of Arendt as "republican," a term hardly in use in her lifetime.[4] It is also missed by scholars who do not appreciate the near-universal anticapitalism of intellectuals in Arendt's time. Margaret Canovan, for example, describes Arendt as "strikingly prejudiced" against the bourgeoisie, whereas George Kateb describes her as displaying a "persistent animosity" toward it.[5] Finally, it is decisively obfuscated by contemporary interpreters who portray Arendt as a prophet of postmodern "surface" and "performance" and thus miss her preoccupation with aspects of the social democratic tradition other than distributive justice—for example, her critical preoccupation with the question of rights.[6] Arendt, in *The Human Condition*, did advance a nonteleological conception of politics, but this conception, I will argue, is best appreciated when seen as a development out of and beyond social democracy and not simply as a repudiation of it.

In arguing that Arendt's work should be seen to have a multifaceted and not merely a negative relation to social democracy, I do not mean to counterpose this approach to others, for example, those that stress her relation to German idealism and phenomenology (as Seyla Benhabib has done), feminism (Mary Jo Dietz), Greek thought (Hannah Pitkin), existentialism (Jeffrey Isaac), or Weberian action theory (Jürgen Habermas); of course, these and other readings are not mutually exclusive. But I do mean to suggest that Arendt's relation to Martin Heidegger is currently being overdone to the neglect of other influences and contexts, especially that of the Paris of the 1930s, which Richard Bernstein's recent work illuminates, and the New York Intellectual milieu of the 1940s and 1950s.[7]

New York in the 1950s was the first place Arendt lived where her genius, and her personality, was truly appreciated. As a woman, she could never have made a comparable career for herself in Germany or even in France. Even after her great accomplishments, she was never treated as a peer by her former teacher, Karl Jaspers, not to mention Heidegger. In spite of McCarthyism, Arendt frequently referred to the transformative effect that living in the United States had on her. In many ways it was most truly her home. This effect was intellectual as well as personal.

After fleeing Germany, Arendt lived—first in Paris and then in New

York—in left-wing milieus that were centrally concerned with the problem of how to move beyond Marx. Kurt Blumenfeld's Zionism, to which Arendt adhered in the 1920s and 1930s, defended the assertion of Jewish nationhood and identity against the Communist insistence on a universal class. The American milieu Arendt entered in the late 1940s is probably best described as Trotskyist. *Partisan Review*, one of her favored early venues, had broken with the Communists in 1937. As Edmund Wilson wrote, "[W]e in this country did our share in bringing out into the open" the fallacies of Marxism, by which Wilson meant its conservative and repressive features.[8] Dwight MacDonald's *Politics*, which ran from 1944 to 1949, originated the discourse about "totalitarianism" and published Albert Camus, Bruno Bettelheim, and Simone Weil, as well as Arendt. MacDonald's goal was to reject orthodox Marxism as an insufficient framework for the left, but not to reject the left itself.[9]

Arendt's central concern, "totalitarianism," was also central to the New York Intellectuals. These figures—Lionel Trilling, Alfred Kazin, Arthur Miller, Mary McCarthy, Sidney Hook, Irving Kristol, Ralph Ellison, Philip Rahv, Richard Wright, Irving Howe, Daniel Bell, even Philip Rieff, Richard Hofstadter, and C. Wright Mills a bit later—had all been associated with Marxism in the 1930s and were all moving away from Marxism, not only because they rejected Stalinism but also because they had come to question some aspects of New Deal "collectivism." Some, such as Hook and Kristol, kept moving toward the right, albeit with a libertarian slant. Kristol, for example, bought Friedrich von Hayek's argument in *The Road to Serfdom*—one of the key books published during World War II—and decided that capitalism was the prerequisite for liberty and ultimately, indeed, its equivalent.[10] But the others were engaged in posing what we can now see were the most important questions to challenge Marxism, those of identity, status, and culture and of the significance of individual uniqueness and diversity. Of course, these figures were anti-Stalinist, but they also rejected the Popular Front, not because it restricted the market but because they did not believe it was possible to reduce individual questions to social ones. Because of their dissatisfaction with the Marxist understanding of what I would term the personal—a term I will subsequently elaborate on—these figures turned to modernism, psychoanalysis, and, as in Arendt's case, to existentialism. Their purpose, however, was to advance a critique of capitalism and modernity that Marxism had monopolized, not to reject it. Without paying close attention to Arendt's years in Paris and New York, years when she was involved with people who were grappling with the inadequacies of social democracy from within, her relations to German thought will never be accurately understood.

What, then, was Arendt's relation to Marxism and social democracy, if not one of simple rejection? The key to answering this question in an overall way is the question of the public and the private. In part because of this emphasis, I am going to restrict myself to *The Origins of Totalitarianism* (1951) and *The Human Condition* (1958). I will argue that the concepts of state and society structure the former, just as the concepts of the public and the private structure the latter. The relation between state and society, as Arendt used it in *The Origins of Totalitarianism*, was familiar in the Marxist discourse of her time, as a critique of liberalism. Whereas liberal thinkers assumed that society was best understood as made up of moral persons and individual bearers of rights, the concepts of "state" and "society" had emerged among those who stressed the significance of peoples, classes, and transnational groups (such as the Slavs, Germans, or Jews) in understanding the modern nation-state. Thus, *The Origins of Totalitarianism*, although certainly brilliant and original, was also part of a preexisting discourse on nationalism and anti-Semitism that had been critical of liberalism.

Similarly, Arendt introduced the distinction between the public and the private in *The Human Condition* as a premise of classical political thought that moderns had "forgotten." Although there was some truth in her assertion, the concepts "public" and "private" had also been anticipated by the concepts "state" and "society" that had played such an important role in the debates about Zionism and other forms of nationalism. In reintroducing this distinction, Arendt was arguing for the significance of political theory in preference to sociological, functionalist, behaviorist, or economic determinist explanations. She was one in a line of thinkers who revitalized political philosophy as superior to the social sciences. Whereas some of these thinkers, notably Leo Strauss, had a wholly negative relation to the social sciences, others who were involved in the same revival of political philosophy, such as John Rawls, Jürgen Habermas, and Charles Taylor, had a *critical* relationship to the social sciences, not a one-sidedly negative one. In *The Human Condition*, Arendt portrays the public/private dichotomy as a transhistorical ideal, but I will argue that understanding this dichotomy in relation to the concepts of state and society as developed in *The Origins of Totalitarianism* can help historicize the public/private dichotomy and thus sharpen its critical dimension. My argument will thereby deepen the use of the public/private dichotomy that occurred in the feminist movement of the 1970s, and will show its relation to Arendt's rather different notion.

I will make my argument in three parts. First, I will look at the classical liberal conception of the public/private dichotomy and of the social democratic critiques of it with which Arendt was familiar due to her participation in the Zionist movement. Second, I will show how Arendt worked with the concepts of state and society and public and private in both of these works. Finally, I will suggest an alternative way of reading Arendt's public/private conception. I will suggest that rather than describing labor as a transhistorically inferior form of human activity, in Arendt's time it was becoming possible to transcend labor's historically encumbering role. This reading, I argue, preserves the nonteleological dimension of Arendt's concept of action while repudiating her deeply problematic disdain for "labor" and "social housekeeping."

The Role of the Public/Private Dichotomy in the History of Liberalism

The dominant modern conception of the division between the public and the private is the liberal one. Liberalism valorized the private sphere and sought to protect such "private" pursuits as economics, family, and religion from interference by the state. Thus, liberalism was premised on limiting the scope of politics. Its emphasis on rights secured this limitation. Although in private life people come from different national backgrounds or have different conceptions of the good life, these are irrelevant in the political sphere. Rights such as due process or equality before the law apply to individuals of any class, culture, or personal belief. By keeping the sphere of politics neutral in crucial respects, individuals were freed to pursue the diversity of their private pursuits.

Needless to say, there have been forms of liberalism, not to mention other tendencies, including republicanism, that rejected this version of the public/private distinction. Arendt's early work, however, came out of milieus that had been shaped by Hegel's and Marx's criticisms of classic liberalism. Hegel had argued in *The Philosophy of the Right* that individual freedom and subjectivity could be realized only in an ethical community (*Sittlichkeit*). Marx agreed but argued that Hegel had idealized the ethical community of his time. Within capitalism, formal equality was belied by socioeconomic relations of domination. Thus, the liberal distinction between the public and the private was actually a distinction between the *citoyen* and the bourgeois. All *citoyens* were equal, but as economic actors, individuals were divided into capitalists and laborers.[11] Only when the latter conflict was resolved could substantive, as opposed to merely formal, political equality be achieved.

Marx's critique of liberalism hinged on the distinction between state and society or public and private. Marx was criticizing the liberal insistence on keeping these spheres separate, arguing that this was impossible. Only after a period during which their interpenetrability was made explicit could true freedom or communism ensue. During the epoch when Marxism and social democracy dominated the critique of liberalism—roughly from the late nineteenth century to the 1960s—there were two further ways of criticizing the liberal insistence on distinguishing the public and the private. These emphasized first, nation, and second, gender and/or personal life. These subsequent criticisms of the liberal presumption of the public/private distinction were also criticisms of Marxism, but they arose within Marxism. They were immanent criticisms of Marxism for the inadequacies of its critique of liberal capitalism.

I will begin by discussing the significance of the nation. The liberal conception presupposed the irrelevance of nationality, but Arendt argued in *The Origins of Totalitarianism* that modern politics was organized through "nation-states," in which there were tensions between universal human rights and demands for national sovereignty. Her argument, in turn, was influenced by the long history of debates among and against Marxists concerning the relation of nation and class, a history in which the "Jewish question" had played an important role.

Marxists before World War II did not simply discount nationalism. In the nineteenth century they judged national questions by whether the nation had previously been autonomous as well as by whether the national struggle served the interests of the "international working class." Thus Poland was supported against Russia, and Ireland against England, whereas the claims of the "nonhistoric" nations, such as the

Slovaks or Ruthenians, were discounted. In the twentieth century the theory of imperialism complicated the Marxist theory of nationalism. Of course, in the Marxist tradition the assertion of national or cultural identity always had to defend itself against the assumed priority of class. In *The Origins of Totalitarianism*, Arendt was using familiar Marxist categories such as "imperialism," but in new ways, for example, by distinguishing the political rule of the bourgeoisie from the economic extension of capitalism.

In our time, a second way of challenging the liberal assumption of the public/private division has emerged: the challenge to the assumption that the family is "private." By the mid-twentieth century the idea that the "economic" sphere was relevant to politics was almost universally accepted; Arendt connoted this in the term "social." However, the family, or at least certain aspects of its sexual and gender relations, was considered a private sphere cut off from politics and economics. With the emergence of women's liberation a decade or so after *The Human Condition* appeared, the relation between the "political" and the "personal" moved to the forefront of politics, and this eventually took the form of the public and the private. The emphasis on gender and on "personal life," then, was a third challenge to the liberal dichotomy, following those based on class and nation. The emphasis on gender and personal life (and these need to be distinguished) that emerged in the 1970s did not reflect Arendt's *explicit* issues, but, as I will show, there is an important line of historical continuity. *The Human Condition* had a direct influence on the politics of the 1970s during which the "public" world was redefined to designate work outside the household. Hence, *The Human Condition* can be understood not only as a critique of social democracy and of the twentieth-century liberalism affected by it, but also as at least implying a critique of the liberal version of the "public/private" dichotomy.

Arendt's Use of the Public/Private Dichotomy

The Origins of Totalitarianism (1951)

The Origins of Totalitarianism was an attempt to locate the "elementary forms" of "totalitarianism." Before discussing this work, it is necessary to say a word about Arendt's method. She was not a Hegelian. She searched, she later explained, for "the elements which crystallized into totalitarianism," rather than attempting to write the history suggested by her title.[12] She used overdetermination in its Benjaminian, Nietzchean, and even Freudian senses. She searched for discrete elements and showed how they combined in unpredictable ways, based upon hidden and apparently unimportant similarities. In her 1946 proposal to her publisher, she promised to explain "full-fledged imperialism in its totalitarian form" as "an amalgam of certain elements which are present in all political conditions and problems of our time. Such elements are anti-Semitism, decay of the national state, racism, expansion for expansion's sake, alliance between capital and the mob." Anti-Semitism, in other words, became important when it became amalgamated with national passions, as in Poland or Austria, or in the Dreyfus affair. As such elements "crystallized," anti-Semitism became "the center of a whole outlook on life and the world."

Arendt's likening of Nazism and Stalinism in part 3 of her book led the left of her day to ignore the fact that parts 1 and 2 explain totalitarianism as the product of quintessentially capitalist trends. Part 3 was, in fact, an afterthought. In her original proposal Arendt envisioned four sections: "I. The Jewish road to the Storm-center of Politics; II. The Disintegration of the National State; III. Expansion and Race and IV. Full-Fledged Imperialism" of which "Race-Imperialism: Nazism" was to be the last part.[13] My reading of *The Origins of Totalitarianism* largely concentrates on parts 1 and 2 of the completed work.

Totalitarianism, according to Arendt, differs from tyranny in that it works upon private life. In tyranny, she wrote, "the whole sphere of private life with the capacities for experience, fabrication and thought are left intact . . . [whereas] the self-coercion of totalitarian logic destroys man's capacity for experience and thought just as certainly as his capacity for action" (*OT*, 474). According to Arendt, the groundwork for totalitarianism is laid through the isolation of the individual and the weakening of the juridical, ethical, and interpersonal relations that sustain individuality. She wrote that "The masses," one of the "elements" that crystallize into totalitarianism, "grew out of the fragments of a highly atomized society whose competitive structure and concomitant loneliness of the individual had been held in check only through membership in a class" (*OT*, 317). The purges, the use of the secret police, and the transformation of friends and family members into enemies continued a process of atomization that had been already launched: "Nothing proved easier to destroy than the privacy and private morality of people who thought of nothing but safeguarding their private lives" (*OT*, 338).

In placing anti-Semitism at the center of her account of totalitarianism, Arendt rejected the two reasons that, in her view, were normally given for its importance: the idea that Jews served as a scapegoat, and the idea that anti-Semitism is eternal. Instead, she explained the centrality of anti-Semitism to modern European history as a contradiction between society (reflected in such forms as nation, class, and race) and the state. She argued that the Jews received their citizenship from governments that pretended to be universal but were in fact based on nationality. After the Enlightenment, there was no longer room for a "nation within a nation." The ideal was equality, but the Jews were perceived as alien. Their early, close relation to the state as financiers and as mediators in the international balance of power proved to other nationals that the state did not really stand "above all classes and parties" in "splendid isolation," representing the "interests of the nation as a whole." The Jews were not a class, but their special relation to the state as both protectors and protected demonstrated that the state's claim to neutrality and universality was false.[14] Arendt summarized her thesis as follows: "The relationship between state and society was determined by the fact of class struggle, which had supplanted the former feudal order. Society was pervaded by liberal individualism which wrongly believed that the state ruled over mere individuals, when in reality it ruled over classes. . . . Nationalism, then, became the precious cement for binding together a centralized state and an atomized society, and it actually proved to be the only working, living connection between the individuals of the nation-state" (*OT*, 231).

Imperialism ended this unstable compromise. Arendt described imperialism as bringing about the "political emancipation of the bourgeoisie." By this she meant the direct entry of the bourgeoisie into politics as a class. Imperialism destroyed the fabric that wove together "nation" and "state." Politics became nakedly international and driven by capital accumulation. The new political role of the bourgeoisie rendered superfluous the special Jewish relation to the state. At the same time, a new kind of anti-Semitism arose in the form of mass anti-Semitic parties and as a component of Pan-Slavic, Pan-German, and other racialist movements. These movements rejected the state's claim to neutrality, as well as its claim to serve as the vehicle of national aspirations. Arendt explained the shift as follows: "[O]nly when the nation-state proved unfit to be the framework for the further growth of capitalist economy did the latent fight between state and society become openly a struggle for power" (*OT*, 123).

In using a state/society framework, Arendt sought to explain totalitarianism through the logic of capitalism. But capitalism, for her, meant a system of power and expansion, rather than the merely economic system described by Marxist reductionism. Hence, she wrote that the introduction of power as the only content of politics in the epoch of imperialism, "and of expansion as its only aim, would hardly have met with so little opposition, had it not so perfectly answered the hidden desires and secret convictions of the economically and socially dominant classes" (*OT*, 138). However, Arendt did not reduce capitalism to economic terms, as the Marxists of her day did; rather, she analyzed it as a political and ideological force. This is the point of her extended discussion of Hobbes. According to Arendt, "there is not a single bourgeois moral standard which has not been anticipated by the unequaled magnificence of Hobbes's magnificent logic. . . . He gives an almost complete picture, not of Man but of the bourgeois man"; "'Reason,' Hobbes wrote, 'is nothing but reckoning'"; "A free subject, a free will [are] words without meaning"; the value of a man is "his price." Hobbes's significance became clear in the imperialist epoch. He "foresaw that a society which had entered the path of never-ending acquisition had to engineer a dynamic political organization capable of a corresponding never-ending process of power generation."

Because Arendt understood capitalism in social and ideological rather than merely economic terms, she was able to link its history to that of race in ways that went beyond the reductionist Marxism of her day. Ignoring Hobbes's stress on the universality of reason, Arendt argued that Hobbes "provided political thought with the prerequisite for all race doctrines, that is, the exclusion in principle of the idea of humanity" (*OT*, 157). If, in fact, she argued, "we are imprisoned in Hobbes's endless process of power accumulation, then the organization of the mob" will inevitably take the form of race, "for there is, under conditions of an accumulating society, no other unifying bond available between individuals who in the very process of power accumulation are losing all natural connections with their fellow men." Race, Arendt wrote, is the death of "man," not its birth as racialist thinkers believed, and this idea is implicit in what Arendt considered to be Hobbes's attack on the idea that we share a common humanity. Not just race but a whole system of intertwined institutions could be explained in this way. Thus, the principle of race was "discovered" in South Africa, and the principle of bureaucracy in Algeria, Egypt, and India. But Rhodes in South Africa and Cromer in Egypt both "regarded the countries not as desirable ends in themselves but merely as means for some supposedly higher purpose."

The emphasis on race was the inevitable reaction to the inadequacy of power and self-interest as a basis of social organization. Racialist supplanted nationalist thinking because through race "a historical event . . . could be traced in the depths of one's own self" (*OT,* 175). In the imperialist epoch, the citizen of England, Germany, or France far from home became again an Englishman, German, or Frenchman: "In his own country he was so entangled in economic interests or social loyalties that he felt closer to a member of his own class in a foreign country than to a man of another class in his own" (*OT,* 154). The Jews too became a "nation" and a "race" or "people"; as Judaism declined as a religion, they moved from it to Jewishness. Like homosexuality, Judaism became "a psychological quality." This encouraged assimilation but also made it impossible: "Never did the fact of Jewish birth play such a decisive role in private life and everyday existence as among the assimilated Jews"(*OT,* 86).

Arendt's first book was brilliant, impassioned, loosely organized, and self-contradictory. But one idea that runs through it is her insight that the liberal presumption of a dichotomy between the public and the private was an ideological one. In a paragraph that summarized her thesis, she wrote that "the bourgeoisie's political philosophy was always 'totalitarian.'" The bourgeoisie "always assumed an identity of politics, economics and society, in which political institutions served only as the facade for private interests. The bourgeoisie's double standard, its differentiation between public and private life, were a concession to the [liberal] nation-state which had desperately tried to keep the two spheres apart." The bourgeois or liberal division between private and public, she continued, "had nothing to do with the *justified* separation between the personal and public spheres [a subject, I will argue, that was central to her next book], but was rather the psychological reflection of the nineteenth century struggle between bourgeois and citoyen, between the man who judged and used all public institutions by the yardstick of his private interests and the responsible citizen who was concerned with public affairs as the affairs of all" (*OT*, 336; emphasis added).

That Arendt was influenced by Marx is obvious to anyone who reads *The Origin of Totalitarianism*. Equally obvious is that she rejected the traditional Marxist explanations of the rise of totalitarianism and struggled to move toward an approach to modern history in which questions of identity and group belonging were given fuller due. My emphasis here is that what she took from Marxism, as well as the terms on which she departed from Marxism, centered on the question of the public and the private. Her next book made this clearer.

The Human Condition (1958)

The inner connection between *The Origins of Totalitarianism* and *The Human Condition* is this: when we cut ourselves off from others, we cut ourselves off from parts of ourselves. The nationalism, racism, and anti-Semitism at the center of *Origins* and the shrinking of the human soul at the center of *The Human Condition* are both manifestations of the same problem: the weakness of *social* supports (in the usual sense of that word, not Arendt's) for individuality, identity, and personal autonomy under modern conditions.

Totalitarianism was Arendt's formative experience and provided her with her central preoccupation, politics. By "politics" Arendt meant a distinctive human activity based on the human potential for freedom. Totalitarianism was its opposite. Politics was the central subject of *The Origins of Totalitarianism*, but this did not become clear until the publication of her next book, *The Human Condition*.

In formulating her conception of politics, Arendt once again engaged with the inadequacies of Marx's critique of liberalism. This time her engagement with Marx can be traced in Arendt's roundabout path to writing *The Human Condition*. Just as *The Origins of Totalitarianism* derived from Arendt's experience with Zionism and as a refugee, so *The Human Condition* resulted from nearly a decade of study.

In 1952, one year after the publication of *Origins of Totalitarianism*, Arendt applied for a Guggenheim Fellowship to write a book entitled "Totalitarian Elements in Marxism." She called the treatment of Marxism the weak point in *Origins*. Marx, she wrote in her application, "cannot be adequately treated without taking into account the great tradition of political and philosophical thought in which he himself stood."[15] "Totalitarian Elements in Marxism" was never completed to the point of publication, although the manuscript exists.

Margaret Canovan has suggested that Arendt became more anti-Marxist in the 1950s but kept her views to herself in order not to abet the McCarthyism that surrounded her.[16] Arendt was indeed horrified by McCarthyism, and she believed that ex-Communists had contributed to it. "Can you see how far the disintegration has gone," she queried Jaspers in 1953, "and with what breathtaking speed it has occurred? . . . Up to now, hardly any resistance. Everything melts away like butter in the sun. Most important . . . is the disintegration of the governmental machinery and the presumably quite conscious establishment of a kind of parallel government." The entertainment industry, schools, colleges, and universities had all been dragged in. Of special importance, she concluded, were the ex-Communists who "brought totalitarian methods into the thing (not methods of government but methods used within the party)."[17] Nonetheless, totalitarianism was not her main interest in Marx. Since Arendt's Guggenheim, there have been brilliant discussions of "totalitarian elements in Marxism" by Czeslaw Milosz, Milovan Djilas, Vaclav Havel, Leszek Kolakowski, Aleksandr Solzhenitsyn, and others. Arendt's main interest lay in the question of labor.

Arendt agreed with Marx that politics had to be rooted in a conception of the human condition. However, she disagreed that "labor," in Marx's sense, was the basis of that conception. She made her case by resurrecting yet another conception of the public/private: the idea that the "public" sphere was the realm of freedom, whereas the "private" sphere of labor, especially the family, was the realm of necessity. She ascribed this view to the Greeks. It also had a great deal to do with New York in the 1950s, but in that context the terms had become reversed: the private world had become the world of freedom. To make her case against Marx, she sought to distinguish two different kinds of exchange with the natural world: labor and work. We must consider this distinction before considering her basic conception of the public and the private.

According to Arendt, "labor is the activity which corresponds to the biological process of the human body," whereas work begins with an idea (*eidos*) and thus "corresponds to the unnaturalness of human existence" (*HC*, 7). Labor is subject to "the natural ruin of time" (*HC*, 55); work creates enduring objects.[18] Arendt introduced this distinction as a neologism and brought obscure linguistic evidence to bear in support of its usefulness. In fact, the distinction, though not the terms, was *doxa* for any educated European. Its most familiar form was the culture/civilization dichotomy, in which "culture" referred to such activities as cooking, home building, and child rearing, activities rooted in the family and village, whereas "civilization" referred to architecture and the high arts located in the *civitas*, or city. In the existentialist discourse of Arendt's time, immanence versus transcendence played on the same opposition. Many progressive thinkers of Arendt's time were uncomfortable with it. Freud, for example, wrote of his "scorn" to distinguish between culture and civilization.

When situated in relation to Marx, Arendt's distinction had a progressive element. This lay in her attempt to describe "economic" activity—work—as cultural, that is, as a realm of meaning. She quoted Marx: "[W]hat distinguishes the worst architect from the best of bees is . . . that the architect raises his structure in imagination before he erects it in reality." But she complained that the "all-important element of 'imagination' plays no role whatsoever in [Marx's] labor theory."[19] Arendt has more in common than is generally recognized with such contemporaries as E. P. Thompson and Raymond Williams, figures who were then demonstrating the ways in which economic activity is simultaneously cultural. The difference, however, is that Arendt described the distinction between labor (which she saw as meaningless) and work (which was meaningful but not fully social) as applying to different kinds of activities, whereas for Williams and Thompson, *all* work is both social and meaningful; what deprives both labor and work of meaning are conditions of subordination, such as slavery or capitalism.[20]

Arendt's attempt to maintain the distinction between labor and work involved her in many problems. She interpreted Marx's remark that "Milton produced *Paradise Lost* for the same reason a silk worm produces silk" to mean that Marx assimilated all human activity to metabolic processes. Marx's point was simply that it is natural for humans to produce culture. "Nothing," Arendt wrote, "can be mechanized more easily than the labor process" (*HC*, 146), an assertion that anyone who knows assembly lines would contest. She described works of art as the most "worldly of all tangible things; their durability . . . almost untouched by the corroding effect of natural processes," at the moment when "happenings"—earth and performance art, pop and video art—emerged. These, however, were minor failings compared to her contributions.

Arendt's great contributions lay in her concept of "action," by which she meant spontaneous, creative, unique, and visible acts, and in her linking of this concept to the public/private dichotomy. The purpose of the public/private dichotomy in Western culture had always been to affirm idealism and to degrade labor. In the ancient world the public realm was valorized because it was the realm of leisure and thereby of freedom. In the bourgeois world the "private realm" of the family was valorized for exactly the same reason. In contrasting "action" to both "labor" and "work," Arendt was participating in this tradition.

At the same time, there were elements in her formulation that made her thinking push beyond mere idealist prejudice. These elements reflected the changed historical circumstances of her time, especially the beginnings of the breakdown of the nineteenth-century public/private or family/economy dichotomy. Two of these elements were particularly important, though they remained latent or even contradicted in her work. The first was the large-scale entry of women into full-time careers. The second was the emergence of forms of "postindustrial" economic organization. Before discussing these, it is important to first grasp Arendt's argument in its own terms.

Arendt used the concept of "action" to criticize the trivialization of politics to which both the Marxism and the liberalism of her time had succumbed. The Human Condition resembles the "Port Huron Statement," written in 1962, in its rejection of both sides of the cold war.[21] According to Arendt, the valorization of labor alone, whether by capitalism or by Communism, could never bring about freedom. The emphasis on labor had degraded the public realm by making it a realm in which *interests* predominated over collective concerns. Marx's guiding hope, she conceded, had "doubtless [been] the Athens of Pericles," but the long-standing subordination of the public sphere to economic "housekeeping," which his philosophy sanctioned, destroyed the public realm, leaving "only private activities displayed in the open. The outcome is what is euphemistically called mass culture" (HC, 133–34). The loss of the public realm was the destruction of our humanity: a life without labor or work is still a human life, but "a life without speech and without action . . . has ceased to be a human life because it is no longer lived among men" (HC, 176).

What, then, is action? Its fundamental characteristics, according to Arendt, are that it is spontaneous, it is not predetermined, and it occurs in a "public"—that is, social—space. It is the fact of action in human life that renders nugatory all deterministic philosophies, whether of Hegelian or behaviorist provenance. Action cannot be subsumed by politics, as normally understood. The fundamental gain derived from action, though not its goal, is self-knowledge. According to Arendt, we do not know ourselves and then reveal to others what we know. Rather, we discover who we are in the process of revealing ourselves to others.[22] The need for others in the quest for the self points to the deep link between *The Origins of Totalitarianism* and *The Human Condition*: "Action and speech," Arendt wrote, "are so closely related because the specifically human act [of self-disclosure through action] must at the same time contain the answer to the question asked of every newcomer: 'Who are you?'" We can learn who we actually are only with and through others: "The revelatory quality of speech and action comes to the fore when people are with others and neither for nor against them" (*HC*, 180). Arendt's conception of action, when situated historically, can contribute to the process of breaking out of the liberal presumption of a public/private dichotomy as well as to the process of moving beyond the socialist, nationalist, and feminist criticisms of it.

Thus, Arendt's concept of action was located in relation to labor and work. True, she derogated both of these in contrast to action, but this is less important than the fact that she connected the three activities as "the human condition." Interpretations of Arendt that stress either her "republicanism" or her "existentialism" tend to miss the significance of this connection. In regard to Arendt's "republicanism," it is true that *The Human Condition* defended the importance of politics in a period that valorized the private realm. But Arendt's defense stressed individual diversity and creativity, not the importance of living one's life in terms of communal goals.[23] Readings that stress Arendt's "republicanism" almost always consider *The Human Condition* in isolation from *The Origins of Totalitarianism*. The latter book brings out the extent to which she was passionately involved with the question of rights and was complex and nuanced about group identity.

The real importance of Arendt's resurrection of the public/private dichotomy did not lie in the content of the dichotomy itself. In both its Greek and its later Victorian forms, the dichotomy was a self-serving tissue of clichés and deceptions. The real importance of her insistence on this dichotomy can be appreciated only when it is situated historically. Although Arendt upheld the traditional idealism of the dichotomy, her special contribution lay in using it to critique the Marxist and liberal approaches of her time. First, as we have seen, she used it—as "state and society"—to address the weak points in liberalism that had made totalitarianism possible. Then, in *The Human Condition*, she used it to demonstrate how pathetic and shrunken the social democratic conception of human life was, and how much it thereby shared with the capitalism it claimed to transcend. In this way she began to articulate a way of thinking about the world that transcended the long-standing conflict between liberalism and Marxism. This is one reason for her present appeal.

Arendt's Long-Term Influence

Arendt's characterization of the public and the private in *The Human Condition* bore many fruits, most of which she undoubtedly would have disowned. Some of the long-term meaning of her work, however, is best appreciated in light of the political effects launched by the New Left and the early women's movement, effects that are still under way.

The feminist understanding that the family can serve as a realm of "unfreedom" cut off from the larger public world can be read into *The Human Condition*, but it is not true to Arendt. Her traditional ideas about sex roles are well known but not really to the point, as there is probably room in feminism for some traditional ideals. More important is her attack on the "social" or "social housekeeping" in *The Human Condition*. This attack was directed against the women's movement at least as much as it was directed against social democracy. Indeed, viewed historically, it is almost impossible to separate social democracy from the twentieth-century women's movement. The term "social housekeeping" actually entered twentieth-century politics through the activities of women who gave the modern welfare state its raison d'être, such as Jane Addams and Charlotte Gilman in the United States, Beatrice Webb in England, and Helene Stocker in Germany. Even trade union issues, such as the wage, were then understood as family issues and supported by women reformers for this reason. As Addams explained, "A city is enlarged housekeeping." Thus, she wrote, "from the beginning of tribal life women have been held responsible for the health of the community, a function which is now represented by the health department; from the days of the cave dwellers, so far as the home was clean and wholesome, it was due to their efforts, which are now represented by the bureau of tenement-house inspection; from the period of the primitive village, the only public sweeping performed was what they undertook in their own dooryards, that which is now represented by the bureau of street cleaning."[24] Thus, Arendt's attack on the "social" was an attack on the historic women's movement, as her repeated use of the term "housekeeping," as well as the minimal value she applied to such activities as child raising, makes clear.

As I have noted, Arendt's attack on the social is untenable. For any oppressed group in modern society, economic issues are fundamental, and turning to the government is the only recourse against oppressive economic power in such forms as employers, landlords, or companies on whom individuals depend. Some of the great periods of economic reform, such as the New Deal era, were also periods of mass democracy and politicization.

Nonetheless, there is a further sense in which, for Arendt, private life, in the sense of personal life, was the true ground of freedom. She wrote, in *The Origins of Totalitarianism*, that "The more highly developed a civilization, the more [men] will resent everything they have not produced, everything that is merely and mysteriously given them." Hence, a "highly developed political life breeds a deep-rooted suspicion of this private sphere, a deep resentment against the disturbing miracle contained in the fact that each of us is made as he is—single, unique, unchangeable." The "alien" is merely one "frightening symbol of the fact of difference as such, of individuality as such" (*OT*, 300-1).

A fundamental question in interpreting *The Human Condition* is whether Arendt's conception of the public/private should be understood as applying to institutional spheres. By now the weight of opinion, with which I agree, is that Arendt's relegation of action, speech, and disclosure to a particular institution, "politics," if this was her meaning, is untenable. Even the polis incorporated a marketplace and schools. As Margaret Canovan notes, Arendt's "public realm" has much in common with what we today call "culture."[25] Jürgen Habermas distinguishes Arendtian processes, in which "those involved are oriented to reaching agreement," from strategic ones, whose participants are oriented "to their respective individual successes."[26] This distinction cuts across institutions.

Action has deep roots in labor and work, and Arendt's sometimes torturous distinctions bring this out. Arendt described the "physical, worldly in-between" of work as "overgrown with an altogether different in-between which consists of deeds and words and owes its origin exclusively to men's acting and speaking directly to one another." This "web," or "in-between," she continued, is not a facade or "an essentially superfluous superstructure." "The basic error of all materialism," she observed, "is to overlook the inevitability with which men disclose themselves as subjects, as distinct and unique persons, even when they wholly concentrate upon reaching an altogether worldly, material object" (*HC*, 182).

The sphere of private or familial life in developed capitalist society to some extent does overlap with the sphere of freedom in the Marxist sense, that is, life that is not determined by the social exigencies of production. The family remains a primary sphere of "personal life"—a form of life seen as cut off from and, in a sense, no longer defined by the sphere of production. "Personal life," the freedom that is made possible by alienated labor, that is, by the separation of the economy from the family, can be understood both institutionally and as a dimension of all activity. In suggesting the relevance of this reading of the "public/private" to Arendt, I can speak from personal experience. In the early 1970s when I attempted to understand, from a "neo-Marxist" point of view, both the emergence of the New Left and the emergence of the women's movement, it was Arendt's *The Human Condition* that pointed me to the significance of the public/private dichotomy. Indeed, at that time (1972) it was the only place where I found the terms "public" and "private" used, as opposed to the slogan "The personal is political."[27]

Situated in the context of the history of the public/private distinction, some of Marx's observations (for example, in the *Grundrisse*) are resonant with some of Arendt's formulations. There he wrote that "the ancient conception in which man always appears (in however narrowly national, religious, or political a definition) as the aim of production, seems very much more exalted than the modern world in which production is the aim of man and wealth the aim of production."[28] Marx praised capitalism not for creating *homo economicus* but for creating the conditions in which the species could pass beyond determination by production. "When the narrow bourgeois form has been peeled away," he asked, "what is wealth, if not the universality of needs, capacities, enjoyments, [and] productive powers, etc., of individuals."[29] Such formulations are not the same as Arendt's, but they share the view that economic activity is not the goal of the human species. Arendt, for her part, rightly noted that "the revolution, according to Marx, has not the task of emancipating the laboring classes but of emancipating man from labor" (*HC*, 104).

Understanding Arendt's conception of action as a democratic potential of modern society made possible by the advance of production seems to me to advance its value rather than to limit it, as Arendt presumably would have insisted. For me, Pablo Neruda's description of himself, in his Nobel Prize address, as writing poems in the same spirit in which bakers bake bread is more glorious than some of Arendt's hyperbolic descriptions of the Greeks. I want to be clear: In no way can Arendt be *assimilated* to the social democratic traditions that preceded her. She added an emphasis on the uniquely personal that was not present within that tradition and that is still at odds with progressive movements of the present, including some that honor her name. Nonetheless, the distinction between the public and the private gains immeasurably when it is situated historically and is linked to the distinction between necessity and freedom, for then, the values associated with "action" can be freed from being restricted to a particular sphere—"politics"—and instead can be developed recursively so that all spheres of life, including labor and work, can be informed by an appreciation of the human need to be recognized and known through engaging in meaningful, nondeterministic, personally creative, and ultimately "public" endeavors.

In conclusion, the liberal distinction between the public and the private has been the touchstone of a series of modern movements— socialism, movements for national liberation, and feminism. Some aspects of the distinction, such as the emphasis on rights and individual freedom, aspire to a universal and even foundational character, even as their concrete content is continually being redefined in the struggle of successive social groups today—the working class, Jews, African Americans and other national minorities, women, gays and lesbians. There is, however, a second aspect to this distinction. By seeking to "protect" the individual, it is linked to the promise of liberty and personal self-development with which the rise of capitalism has been inextricably, if conflictingly, linked. Thus, a succession of critical movements historically have focused on the latent social content of this distinction—what Arendt called "action"—and not merely on the question of rights. Arendt's place within a critical theory of modernity is better appreciated when it is situated in this context.

I conclude with two supplementary points. First, Arendt's relation to the idea of labor may supply a clue to another puzzle, her relation to psychoanalysis. Freud reigned with Marx in the New York circles in which Arendt lived, but Arendt despised psychoanalysis. In 1948 she described it to Jaspers as a "plague," a "madness." In 1953 she condemned the collaboration of analysts with McCarthyism.[30] The main reason for Arendt's antipathy was that she viewed analysis as reductionist and medicalized, as indeed the analytic practice in New York was. But she also criticized its content. In one of her few published discussions, she held that in "its working back toward the unconscious, psychoanalysis penetrates to that very realm over which human beings do not have, and never have had, control, i.e., to the realm of the ahistorical," the realm she was later to equate with labor.[31]

Nonetheless, *The Human Condition*'s stress on individual uniqueness also reverberates with the analytic culture of New York in the 1950s. It is hard to believe, for example, that Arendt did not think of the Freudian unconscious when she described "the 'who,' which appears so clearly and unmistakably to others, [yet] remains hidden from the person himself, like the *daimon* in Greek religion which accompanies each man throughout his life, always looking over his shoulder from behind and thus visible only to those he encounters" (*HC*, 179). Jacques Lacan's Heideggerian descriptions of the revelatory character of speech, which were actually contemporary to Arendt although unknown to her, often sound like her descriptions of action.

Finally, a focus on the public and the private may also shed light on Arendt's Judaism, which may eventually prove to be the deepest key to her thought. Arendt went to the Greeks for her idea of the public and the private. She might also have gone to the Hebrews. Unlike Greek thought, which is the thought of a sovereign people, Hebrew thought, like Arendt's own, was produced by a people in exile, a people who had to live in other people's lands, a people whose experience anticipates the "statelessness," the "homelessness," that Arendt presciently identified as a key to our time. At least since Ezekiel, who wrote in the time of the Babylonian captivity, the fundamental question for the Hebrew people was the question of the public and the private—that is, the question how one retains one's identity when the public authority is held by strangers.[32] The distinctive mark of the Hebrew attitude was that under conditions in which one is an alien, the private realm—family (including its labor), kashruth, circumcision, and Sabbath—was primary. Far from being a demeaned and prehuman realm, the family was the locus of transcendence. I wonder if this understanding was not latent but denied in *The Human Condition.*

Notes

I thank Rainer Forst, Nancy Fraser, John Judis, and Ted Koditschek for helpful comments and Craig Calhoun for the invitation to participate in the conference on Hannah Arendt at the University of North Carolina at Chapel Hill in 1995.

1. Hannah Arendt, *Eichmann in Jerusalem,* rev. ed. (New York: Viking Press, 1964), p. 11. See also Arendt's *The Human Condition* (Chicago: University of Chicago Press, 1958) and *The Origins of Totalitarianism* (New York: Meridian Books, 1958). The latter two works will hereafter be abbreviated *HC* and *OT,* respectively.

2. Arendt to Jaspers, January 29, 1946, *Hannah Arendt/Karl Jaspers Correspondence, 1926–1969* (New York: Harcourt Brace Jovanovich, 1992), p. 30.

3. "Not only are people afraid to utter the name Marx, but every little idiot thinks he has the right and duty to look down on Marx now." Arendt to Jaspers, June 3, 1949, *Arendt/Jaspers Correspondence,* p. 137. It is also true that in 1964 when Gerschom Scholem described her as someone "who came from the German Left," Arendt rejected the characterization. See "'Eichmann in Jerusalem': An Exchange of Letters between Gerschom Scholem and Hannah Arendt," *Encounter,* January 1964, p. 53, quoted in Margaret Canovan, *Hannah Arendt: A Reinterpretation of her Political Thought* (Cambridge: Cambridge University Press, 1992), p. 65. Certainly, Arendt had no sympathy for the critical theory of the Frankfurt School.

4. Seyla Benhabib, "Models of Public Space: Hannah Arendt, the Liberal Tradition, and Jürgen Habermas," in *Habermas and the Public Sphere,* ed. Craig Calhoun (Cambridge: MIT Press, 1992), pp. 73–75, is one of many descriptions of Arendt as "republican." In J. G. A. Pocock's *The Machiavellian Moment* (Princeton: Princeton University Press, 1974), from which most contemporary definitions of republicanism derive, Pocock cited Arendt as one of his inspirations.

5. Canovan, *Hannah Arendt,* p. 29; George Kateb, *Hannah Arendt: Politics, Conscience, Evil* (Totowa, N.J.: Roman and Allanheld, 1984), p. 66. Canovan notes: "If Arendt had been less prejudiced against capitalism, she might have noticed that joint stock companies are a striking instance of the creation of worldly entities by mutual contract" (p. 217). Other discussions include B. Parekh, "Hannah Arendt's Critique of Marx," in *Hannah Arendt: The Recovery of the Public World,* ed. Melvyn A. Hill (New York: St. Martin's Press, 1979), pp. 67–100; Jennifer Ring, "On Needing both Marx and Arendt: Alienation and the Flight from Inwardness," *Political Theory* 17, no. 3 (August 1989), pp. 432–38; and Wallis Arthur Suchting, "Marx and Hannah Arendt's *The Human Condition,*" *Ethics* 73 (October 1962), pp. 47–55.

6. As in Dana R. Villa, "Hannah Arendt: Modernity, Alienation, and Critique" (this volume).

7. See Richard J. Bernstein, *Hannah Arendt and the Jewish Question* (Cambridge, England: Polity Press, 1996).

8. Edmund Wilson, *Letters on Literature and Politics, 1912–1972* (New York: Farrar, Straus, and Giroux, 1977), pp. 359–60.

9. See Richard King, *The Party of Eros* (Chapel Hill; University of North Carolina Press, 1972).

10. Friedrich A. von Hayek, *The Road to Serfdom* (London: Routledge, 1944).

11. Marx made this argument in "On the Jewish Question" and elaborated on it in later works such as *The Class Struggles in France* and *The Eighteenth Brumaire*. See Karl Marx and Frederick Engels, *Collected Works* (New York: International Publishers, 1975).

12. Hannah Arendt, "A Reply," *Review of Politics*, January 15, 1953, pp. 77–78.

13. This quotation and those in the preceding paragraph are from Arendt's manuscripts, quoted in Canovan, *Hannah Arendt*, pp. 19, 28.

14. "In contrast to all other groups, the Jews were defined and their position determined by the body politic" (*OT*, 14).

15. Quoted in Canovan, *Hannah Arendt*, p. 66. See also Elisabeth Young-Bruehl, *Hannah Arendt: For Love of the World* (New Haven: Yale University Press, 1982), p. 276. Arendt's engagement with Marx is reflected in *Between Past and Future* (New York: Viking Press, 1968) and *On Revolution* (Westport, Conn.: Greenwood Press, 1982), as well as *The Human Condition* (1958).

16. Canovan, *Hannah Arendt*, p. 66.

17. Arendt to Jaspers, May 13, 1953, *Arendt/Jaspers Correspondence*, p. 210.

18. As Kimberley Curtis has pointed out, Arendt's attitude toward the biological shifted over time. In *The Life of the Mind*, she roots her arguments concerning appearance in biology and philosophical biology. Curtis, "Aesthetic Foundations of Democratic Politics in the Work of Hannah Arendt" (this volume).

19. Marx, *Capital*, Modern Library edition, p. 198, quoted in *HC*, pp. 133–35.

20. See E. P. Thompson, *The Making of the English Working Class* (New York: Pantheon, 1964); and Raymond Williams, *Culture and Society, 1780–1850* (New York: Columbia University Press, 1958).

21. See Students for a Democratic Society, "The Port Huron Statement" (New York: n.p. 1962).

22. According to Arendt, who writes of "the disclosure of the agent in speech and action" (HC, 175), "one discloses one's self without ever either knowing himself or being able to calculate beforehand whom he reveals" (192). Arendt's emphasis on speech calls out for a Derridean commentary.

23. It is sometimes said that the main value upheld in Arendt's work is that of "plurality." This is true, but only when plurality is deeply enough understood. There are at least three meanings of "plurality" already apparent in her work by 1958. First, she gave individual diversity and uniqueness—clichés of her world in the 1950s—new meaning. This was the basis of her critique of totalitarianism but also of her critique of economic society. In addition, she valued cultural diversity and would have been a critic of what is today called "identity politics." Third, Arendt was a "pluralist" in the usual sense: she understood that a democratic polity would incorporate different points of view.

24. Jane Addams, *Newer Ideals of Peace* (New York: Macmillan, 1907),pp. 192–97.

25. Margaret Canovan, "Politics as Culture: Hannah Arendt and the Public Realm," *History of Political Thought* 6, no. 3 (1985), pp. 617–42. Canovan discusses Oxford University as an example of the kind of public realm to which Arendt's descriptions apply. In the last year of her life, Arendt, rightly I think, declared that she herself was not a political animal. Hannah Arendt, "Sonning Prize Speech," cited in Canovan, *Hannah Arendt*, p. 154 n.

26. Jürgen Habermas, "Hannah Arendt's Communications Concept of Power," *Social Research* 44, no. 1 (1977), p. 5.

27. See my *Capitalism, the Family, and Personal Life* (New York: Harper and Row, 1976). This book was originally published as a series of articles in the journal *Socialist Revolution*, nos. 13–15 (January–April 1973).

28. Karl Marx, *Pre-Capitalist Economic Formations* (New York: International Publishers, 1964), p. 84.

29. Ibid., p. 85.

30. Arendt to Jaspers, May 28, 1948, and May 13, 1953, *Arendt/Jaspers Correspondence*, pp. 111, 210.

31. Hannah Arendt, "Psychoanalysis and Sociology," in *Hannah Arendt: Essays in Understanding*, ed. Jerome Kohn (New York: Harcourt Brace, 1994), p. 33. Arendt's essay was originally published in 1930. Psychoanalysis, she wrote, regards everything in the mental or intellectual realm as nothing but "repression," or "sublimation." As a general principle in all theory, Arendt criticized "the introduction of an invisible actor behind the scenes" (*HC*, 185).

32. On this topic, see the forthcoming work of Geza Kommarovsky on Ezekiel.

Nine

Plurality, Promises, and Public Spaces

Craig Calhoun

One of the annoying tendencies that postmodernists have picked up from modernist forebears is to think in simplistic binary oppositions. There were *the* moderns and *the* ancients. Today there are *the* modernists and *the* postmodernists. Apparently, the ideological and theoretical debates suggest, one must be either with modernity or against it. But of course there are critical positions on modernity that are hard to classify as postmodernist. Hannah Arendt offers one of these; Marx and Foucault offer others.[1]

Dana Villa is thus quite right to challenge both Benhabib's attempt to turn Arendt into a modernist and Kateb's rejection of her as an antimodernist. Benhabib's and Kateb's are serious and intelligent readings, but they are guided by sides taken in a quarrel that was not precisely Arendt's. Indeed, her work might better be read, as a resource for getting out of this particular, increasingly stifling argument in political theory.

In responding to Villa's and Eli Zaretsky's provocative engagements with Arendt, I will argue, first, that an Arendtian "way out" both of the frustrating postmodernist/modernist debates and of our present political predicament depends on faith in political action, not principled refusal. Second, I will suggest in this regard that we will do better to approach public life as the result of Arendtian political action rather than its precondition; this is, I think, the crucial lesson her work has to offer the discourse dominated today by Jürgen Habermas. Finally, as we think both with Arendt and in critique of Arendt about the troubled distinction of public from private, I will suggest that we keep in mind not only her crucial stress on plurality as both the heart of the human condition and the premise and point of public life, but also her less developed account of promises as means for plural human beings to bind themselves through action, creating solidarities rather than discovering them on the more deterministic bases of preexisting similarities. As Arendt wrote of political power, the most distinctively human sort of power,

> In distinction to strength, which is the gift and the possession of every man in his isolation against all other men, power comes into being only if and when men join themselves together for the purpose of action, and it will disappear when, for whatever reason, they disperse and desert one another. Hence, binding and promising, combining and covenanting are the means by which power is kept in existence; where and when men succeed in keeping intact the power which sprang up between them during the course of any particular act or deed, they are already in the process of foundation, of constituting a stable worldly structure to house, as it were, their combined power of action. There is an element of the world-building capacity of man in the human faculty of making and keeping promises.[2]

The Distinction of Spheres

Arendt's critical engagement with modernity centered on the ways in which emergent social conditions—notably what she called "the rise of the social," but also the related development of totalitarianism—undermined a needed distinction of public from private. The term "public," Arendt wrote, "signifies two closely interrelated but not altogether identical phenomena: It means, first, that everything that appears in public can be seen and heard by everybody and has the widest possible publicity. . . . Second, the term 'public' signifies the world itself, in so far as it is common to all of us and distinguished from our privately owned place in it."[3] Public space, thus, is the crucial terrain of the humanly created as distinct from the natural world, of appearance and memory, and of talk and recognition. It is open in precisely the way the household is closed; the two are complementary, as the human condition is complementary to the realm of things.[4] In private life, Arendt asserted, biological commonalities rule; in public life people appear as full individuals (*HC*, p. 41). The disclosure of "who" someone is, as distinct from "what," takes place through that person's public acts; "it can be hidden only in complete silence and perfect passivity" (p. 179). This is part of the significance of the idea of publicity (in the sense of the first preceding definition). Yet, Arendt thought, it is only in possessing specific private locations that people gain the distinction that, along with equality, is a condition of public life. This is crucially linked to her view that it is in public life that people are able to see (and create) the common world by looking at the things and relationships between them from their many different vantage points (p. 58). Arendt defined the public realm against what she saw as a viable private sphere of the household, especially in a smallholder economy. What she saw in the modern world was not a rise of the private but a collapse of the public/private distinction, and with it the basis for the kind of public life she so deeply valued. The rise of "the social," the instrumental organization of society to pursue material ends, was a challenge to both private and public. It tended, she argued, to "devour" even "the more recently established sphere of intimacy" (p. 45).

As Zaretsky suggests, the distinctive meaning of public and private shifted with changing institutional structures. The modern understanding of this dichotomy was shaped by the rise of states (especially states constructed according to the ideal of the nation-state), and public/private was widely construed as analogous to state/society. On the one hand, citizens claimed protection of their private affairs from undue state regulation or intervention. On the other hand, citizens outside the immediate apparatus of state rule claimed the right to enter collectively into public discourse and action aimed at shaping government. Both publicness and privateness became more significant. The modern idea of person requires both aspects (just as the private affairs of officeholders came increasingly to be distinguished from their public roles).

The notion of a realm of privacy protected from state interference reflected the growth of state power—and thus state potential to intervene in significant ways in the "private" lives of subjects or citizens. It also reflected a new valorization of "private" life. Treated often in both classical and Christian traditions as beneath public concern, the private domain was now, in a sense, raised above public interference. This happened in two ways that left the notion of a single private realm confused.

First, there was a moral revaluation of intimate relations and everyday life. This included both the realm of intimate relations (notably family and romantic love) and the realm of work (as in the famous Protestant ethic).[5] From this perspective, work, love, and family may seem closely related as dimensions of "personal" rather than public life; they were given new dignity as realms of meritorious human performance and were held up as domains of human satisfaction. Here "personal" connotes the involvement of the individual human being in face-to-face relations, as well as the realm of privacy.

Second, the new domain of privacy protected from state interference was extended to economic activity in general. Here the meaning changed, though in ways not immediately visible. Indeed, in the mid-twentieth century, Arendt would still feel comfortable lumping together as one domain of "housekeeping" both the intimate relations involved in the substance of life on a personal scale—cooking, making love—and the anything-but-intimate relations of the capitalist economy and corporate organizations. The latter sustained "life" in the sense that they produced its necessities, but they were (and are) qualitatively different as domains of human activity and relationship.[6] As Zaretsky makes clear, this account can be deeply misleading and is all the more surprising for the fact that others in Arendt's New York Intellectual milieu were coming to terms—often aided by Marxism—with the distinction of work as personal activity from impersonal economy.

The modern idea of "public" has been similarly multivalent. In particular, there has been slippage among references to (*a*) the state; (*b*) the political community, often defined as the nation; and (*c*) a domain of open discourse in which various understandings of collective identities and interests may be brought to the fore. The first two senses tend toward integralist, unitary conceptions of public life and the public good; the latter calls us back to the importance of plurality to publicness. But here the notion of "a" public may be misleading. As Arendt wrote (though her own usage was not consistent), "since the country is too big for all of us to come together and determine our fate, we need a number of public spaces within it."[7] This interpretation of plurality in the face of scale informs Arendt's affinity for the local council democracy as an alternative to statist regimes.

It is easy for the public/private distinction to be shaped by the powerful opposition of collective to individual. Part of the importance of Arendt's work is to remind us that it may be in public that people

can be most fully individual. At the same time, however, Arendt's attempt to delineate the importance of action in public appears to deni-
grate the possibility of comparably important action in private—or at
least in personal life. Here Zaretsky rightly points to the limits of a
conception of personal life as a realm of determined behavior focused
on economic production and biological reproduction.

Despite—or perhaps because of—its ambiguity, the public/private
distinction became a central feature of liberal political theory and ideology (with the difference between modern and classical versions too
seldom remarked). Liberalism was always a theory of the limits of politics as well as of political (and prepolitical) rights. As Zaretsky suggests, various forms of challenge to and reworking of this division became a staple of European social thought, with none more influential
than that incorporated in Marxism.[8] Zaretsky helpfully identifies
three major criticisms of this dimension of liberalism: (*a*) Marx's critique of the way economic activity and resulting class division viti-
ated the public/private dichotomy; (*b*) the point made from many directions that liberalism failed to attend to the significance of nation,
race, and other nonclass identity issues; and (*c*) the argument that "the
personal" either is intrinsically political or at least is so relevant to politics that it must not be treated as a separate realm. Though far from a
Marxist, Arendt accepted, as Zaretsky argues, the force of the first
criticism and engaged many of the same historical and sociological issues as Marx and some Marxists. Arendt was one of the major intellectual voices for the second line of critique. And she was at once engaged by the third and deeply troubled by it.

Arendt saw the weaknesses of liberalism but adamantly defended
the notion of a need for separate spheres.[9] As she stressed forcefully in
The Origins of Totalitarianism, the key feature distinguishing totalitarianism from mere tyranny is that the former works directly on private
life, not merely limiting public life. This is a matter not just of contrasting intentions but also of distinctively modern capacity. Modern sociological conditions offered rulers the possibility to reach deeply into the
family in particular and personal life in general, to engineer human life
(in both the everyday and the specifically Arendtian meanings of the
term) in ways never before imagined. This sociological capacity, this
new form of power (of which Foucault was to become a preeminent an-
alyst) was matched and abetted by changes in culture and philosophy
that also attended the infusion of the social into politics.

Arendt would never endorse social engineering and, against such threats, certainly would protect privacy. Even more, she would protect the personal and the distinctive from absorption into the impersonal. But she would not assimilate the notion of the personal to that of the private as Zaretsky does. We commonly think of politics as impersonal and of private life as the realm in which at least potentially we can be true to ourselves as individual persons. But Arendt is concerned to show us that this is not so; it is in public that we come fully into ourselves, that we achieve a fullness of personality, that we disclose our personal identities. On her account, we must not equate the personal with the psychological. This is why Arendt was ambivalent about the third line of critique of the liberal public/private distinction. Consider the term "identity politics," currently used to refer at once to public performances that create or disclose identity and to political struggles based on claims to identities settled in advance. The former fit with Arendt's vision, and the latter are sharply contrary to it. We need not agree with Arendt's claim that the realms of labor and biological reproduction are altogether determined and devoid of potential for real creativity and disclosure of personality, to grasp the force of this distinction. At the same time, we would do well to follow Zaretsky in questioning whether Arendt's argument about the importance of public life, especially politics, must be taken to refer to a distinctive institutional domain rather than to action itself (in her strong sense of the word). The language of "spheres" may mislead. If we are speaking about a mode of establishing relationships between human beings, then publicness can be instantiated in a variety of social spaces by no means all of which are institutionalized as political by their relationship to the state. Publicness can be created wherever people are related by their undetermined speech and action. Some public spaces may be institutionally supported or protected, but such institutionalization is not a precondition of publicness.

Public Activity

It is perhaps with such a broadened understanding in mind that, for all his distance from the Enlightenment, Villa appeals in the concluding line of his essay to "the light of the public." I want to push the potential inherent in this affirmation and, on this basis, to question Villa's suggestion that the conditions for politics are so diminished in the present era that resistance is the only responsible stance. The argument depends on keeping Arendt distinct from Habermas.

In his influential account of "the light of the public," Jürgen Habermas has made it almost synonymous with "the light of reason" by taking "the public" to refer to an institutionally protected and procedurally defined "sphere" that is the crucial setting for communicative rationality.[10] Such a reading has been widely contested, perhaps most especially on the grounds that no such integrated, comprehensive, unitary public sphere can exist under contemporary sociological conditions[11] and that it is not desirable, even as a regulative ideal, because of the inattention to difference and identity that it presumes.[12] Villa extends this critique.

In this regard, Villa rightly challenges Benhabib's reading of Arendt as "almost-Habermas." Though Habermas is perhaps not quite as Habermasian as Benhabib, the two converge on a conception of the public sphere challenged by a reading of Arendt that places more stress on plurality, on performative action, and on the possibility of making and remaking the common world by means of mutual commitments. The difference of such commitments from the kind of agreements posited by the notion of communicative action is significant. Arendt's "commitments" cannot be grasped entirely on the model of truth. They are acts of world making, not discovery or description. They do not depend on a prior establishment of "post-conventional" moral reason or on the triumph of rationality at an individual level. The American founders, Arendt says of her favorite example, grasped that they needed rely neither on the proposition that people were good outside society nor on a claim that they were already similar to each other or bound to each other as members of a nation: "They knew that whatever men might be in their singularity, they could bind themselves into a community which, even though it was composed of 'sinners,' need not necessarily reflect this 'sinful' side of human nature" (*OR*, p. 174).

Although Villa rightly challenges those of Arendt's critics and admirers alike who read her as advocating this sort of singular public sphere, he places much more emphasis on the obstacles she saw to recovering that kind of public life than on the openings she discerned for other kinds of public practices and public spaces. In particular, he reads her demonstration of the debased character of much modern public life as though publicness always came before politics in her arguments. It is at least equally plausible, however, to read Arendt as suggesting that public space cannot exist without politics, that it is called into being by politics as a specific kind of activity between people. Politics, in other words, can be about the making (and remaking) of public space as much as about what we do in it—let alone what we decide about matters of "the public good."[13]

In this respect Villa is surely right to present Arendt as a theorist of modernity, not only of politics in general. Her tone was, as he suggests, often tragic, though his sharpest conclusion—that her analysis led her to posit that modernity has brought an end to politics proper—is overdrawn. As much as Arendt admired the Greeks, she did not see real politics as something achievable only on their ground. Not only was she no simplistic advocate of a return to the classical polis, she found more to encourage her in modern political activity than Villa allows. It is not necessary to read the account of the French Revolution in *On Revolution* as describing a slippery slope leading inevitably to totalitarianism and to a postpolitical world in which the only responsible action must be resistance. Here Villa seems to accept a more integralist reading of the public sphere than Arendt requires (or, it seems, than his own political values encourage), only to turn it into a straw man to be knocked down by modernity so that political action in public is no longer a possibility for the postmodernist. This forfeits one of the advantages of the Arendtian account of public space (in contrast to the Habermasian language of *the* public sphere). Arendt's term more readily allows us to see the possibilities for political action instantiating multiple, overlapping, and sometimes conflicting public domains.[14] This does not mean that polities do not face the challenge of how to reconcile these multiple arenas of public activity in necessarily singular decisions (the issue to which Habermas's notion of the public sphere points), but this dimension of decision making—necessary to states—is distinct, Arendt suggests, from the broader domain of public action, which is not, for her, defined by the state.

On Revolution is, in this connection and indeed in general, a more important Arendtian text than either Villa or especially Zaretsky recognizes.[15] For all the pathos of its final pages and the romantic wistfulness of Arendt's admiration for council democracy, the book is not only an exposition of lost opportunities and tragedies. It is also an account of politics as action in which institution building is a central moment, and an available response both to chaos and to the supplanting of public life by social engineering. The Hungarian Revolution of

1956 failed, in Arendt's analysis, not because modernity doomed it but because the larger and more powerful Soviet Union invaded Hungary.

Villa rightly stresses Arendt's account of politics as performance and importantly distinguishes this from an expressivist view of politics (or of action generally). This performative view helps us see action—especially action in public space—as, in part, self-making.[16] This suggests problems for a sharp and easy distinction of public from private, with the production of identities and interests relegated to the latter. Here Zaretsky rightly notes that Arendt goes to the opposite extreme from most current theories. If it is common to see the truly "personal" as being presented or forged in private, Arendt sees action, speech, and disclosure as quintessentially public and, indeed, properly political. Her account troubles commentators by virtue of its apparently radical reduction of the significance of the private. Zaretsky has considerable company, then, when he suggests that private life is the true ground of freedom, but it is hard to see this as clearly Arendt's view. Private life is clearly a ground for free action (or better, a condition), but to privilege it as *the* ground is problematic. Along with Habermas, Zaretsky places the private very sharply prior to public life, as though people become full individuals in their private lives before entering the public realm. This is not Arendt's view. Given what Zaretsky suggests is contemporary society's lack of social support for individuality, identity, and personal autonomy, this account comes close to implying that we can only work to repair social conditions, and not act freely in public.[17]

Resistance and Action

Villa gets us only partway out of this radical limitation on political action, because (perhaps too much influenced by the rhetoric of postmodernism) he persists in a unitary understanding of modernity that is at odds with Arendt's more internally complex one. Influenced by Kateb's reading of Arendt as antimodernist, Villa presents Arendt as arguing that "The problem presented by modernity is that it destroys the conditions necessary if political action is to fulfill its existential vocation." We might equally argue, though, that it is precisely in such a crisis that political action is most crucially needed to create new "conditions."

Villa's concern is to avoid the "policing" of political theory by deployment of the notion that critique (and critical textual hermeneutics) is of necessity either "immanent" or "rejectionist." That is, he seeks to bring out the possibility—and indeed importance—of a mode of critique that does not rest on finding in the arrangements it challenges a "progressive element" or tendency that can be enhanced as the basis for change, and simultaneously does not evacuate the perspective of a critic-in-the-world in favor of some completely negative, disconnected, critical view from nowhere, from the past, or, with Nietzsche, "from another planet." For Villa, the primary exemplar of such an alternative mode of critique is Foucauldian "resistance" to existing conditions and tendencies. I have little doubt that Villa is right to see resistance as one of Arendt's critical strategies and to locate it in this tradition.[18] The question remains, however, whether she believed that modernity made resistance the only viable or responsible stance (either in general or after totalitarianism). Has more positive political action really lost its necessary conditions? Relatedly, we might ask whether in agreeing that "immanent" and "rejectionist" critiques do not exhaust the field of possibilities, resistance is the only other option.

Villa is not concerned only to widen the space of critical orientations beyond immanent and rejectionist. He would (it seems) like to rehabilitate the Nietzschean negative critique that is currently decried (and rejected) as "rejectionist." He does not agree that "The worst possible sin . . . is to engage in 'totalizing' or rejectionist criticism—that is, to take a critical stance so distanced that it enables the critic to place these hopes, values, and institutions under suspicion." But Villa seems here too quick to equate the notion of immanent critique with Michael Walzer's call for critics to identify with the basic hopes, values, and institutions of his or her society. Immanent critique is not just about finding common ground with at least some dimensions of the social or cultural formation one criticizes. It is also about recognizing the embeddedness of critique in historical and sociological settings—a point of which Arendt was intensely aware. The tradition of critical theory that praises immanent critique does so in part because it values the self-reflexive capacity to offer an account of its own conditions. The challenge to totalizing critique, accordingly, is that it cannot make sense of itself—including what it is in modern society, for example, that allows Nietzsche to try to take the critical stance of "seeing things as if from another planet." Totalizing critique courts the charges of (*a*) performative contradiction, (*b*) claiming to be without history, and (*c*) claiming to be literally disinterested and without meaningful motive.

Arendt finds little in her analysis of modernity that inclines her toward Habermasian optimism. She finds much that suggests that resistance is often the most responsible critical stance. But, I think, she refuses more firmly than Villa the stance of a totalizing critique of modernity; treats it as more complex; and sees more potential for meaningful political action than he avers. Whether this makes hers an "immanent" critique is another, and ultimately less interesting, question.

Villa's argument has two main moments. First, he shows nicely that Arendt does not subscribe to the relatively naive goal of ending alienation. She sees certain forms of worldly estrangement not only as inevitable but also as productive of positive goods and distinctive characteristics of human individuality and capacity for action. Being at home in the world is thus a problematic goal, and being altogether at home in the world without sacrificing crucial capacities for political action is something that perhaps only some of the Greeks achieved. Villa's exposition is admirable here and seems quite in tune with Arendt.[19]

The second moment in Villa's argument is the more problematic contention that distinctively modern "world alienation" is tied to an elimination of the prospects for authentic politics and public life because it eradicates the necessary feeling for a common world. Here Villa has some good points, but he overstates his case and makes Arendt too much of a postmodernist. Villa cites Arendt as observing "the destruction of the common world" and on this basis concluding that authentic public life and political action are no longer possible. As support for his claim, Villa cites two passages in *The Human Condition*, neither with detailed quotation. Both, in fact, bear out Zaretsky's point that Arendt ought often to be read with Marx in mind—or at least with a recognition that she, like Marx, is thinking through a critique of liberalism on historical and sociological grounds.[20] Both passages are worth exploring more fully.

The first passage comes from Arendt's discussion of property in the section on the public and the private realms. Arendt describes in this subsection how "private" originally meant not something positive but rather the deprivation of things essential to a truly human—and therefore public—life: "to be deprived of the reality that comes from being seen and heard by others, to be deprived of an 'objective' relationship with them that comes from being related to and separated from them through the intermediary of a common world of things, to be deprived of the possibility of achieving something more permanent than life itself" (*HC*, p. 58). This privacy—a privation of solid relations to others—leads to the loneliness of mass society in which individuation is as impossible as social solidarity (Arendt cites Riesman's *The Lonely Crowd*). Privacy does not sound very attractive in this passage, but Arendt goes on to single out one crucial feature of the private realm we must regret losing. This is property. By property, she says, she emphatically does not mean wealth, "because the wealth of any single individual consists of his share in the annual income of society as a whole." What she means is the ownership of a place in the world that is at once a basis for individuation and a solid location from which to act in public: "Originally, property meant no more or less than to have one's location in a particular part of the world and therefore to belong to the body politic, that is, to be the head of one of the families which together constituted the public realm" (p. 61).[21] It is therefore no accident that the "disappearance of the public realm should be accompanied by the threatened liquidation of the private realm as well" (p. 60).[22]

Villa's second citation is to the last paragraph of the section on world alienation that opens the concluding part of *The Human Condition*. Here Arendt has just described the great events that ushered in modernity, the further transformations that followed the French Revolution, and the entry of the social into the political realm. She has argued (congruent with Villa's emphasis on how much she shared Heidegger's critique of the subjectification of the modern world) that Marx was mistaken to see self-alienation (the ways in which capitalist labor dehumanizes people by turning them against themselves) as the hallmark of the modern age.[23] That hallmark is, instead, world alienation, the loss of a sense of integral relationship to and care for a common world. People had been integrated into the world when, through the family unit, they had owned individual pieces of it as property and had been enduringly identified with those pieces of property. Capitalist expropriation had ended this. Capitalism created a continuous process of "further expropriations, greater productivity, and more appropriation"(*HC*, p. 255). Capitalism thus extended the compulsion of "natural" life processes to all of society, whereas previously certain classes had had the opportunity to escape it. A key point here is that unlike action (though sometimes following from it), process, as Arendt understands it, simply proceeds and therefore undermines "world durability and stability." The rise of society involves not just the growth of capitalist economies and the entry of economic concerns (such as the eradication of poverty or the "wealth of nations") into the political realm, it involves also the collectivization of human beings. At least some people had hitherto been individuals supported as heads of family households, whereas now all people became nationals first and then simply humans. Society itself "became the subject of the new life process, as the family had been its subject before" (p. 256). But where the family supported proper individuals, nations and global humanity support undifferentiated, collective beings defined by and devoted to life processes. Now comes the passage in which Arendt suggests, to Villa, the destruction of the common world:

> [T]he process of world alienation, started by expropriation and characterized by an ever-increasing progress in wealth, can only assume even more radical proportions if it is permitted to follow its own inherent law. For men cannot become citizens of the world as they are citizens of their countries, and social men cannot own collectively a family and household men own their private property. The rise of society brought about the simultaneous decline of the public as well as the private realm. But the eclipse of a common public world, so crucial to the formation of the lonely mass man and so dangerous in the formation of the worldless mentality of modern ideological mass movements, began with the much more tangible loss of a privately owned share in the world. (p. 257)[24]

Clearly, Arendt is not in favor of these modern trends. But should she be read as asserting "the withdrawal of the political and its dispersion throughout the social body" such that, lacking a proper public, real political action must be replaced by mere resistance? Villa here is eliding Arendt's position with Lyotard's.

What Arendt has argued is that long-standing conditions for individuation and action in public have been undermined. But are the previous conditions the only conditions? Political action, for Arendt, can be both world making and self-making (though as Villa rightly observes with regard to the latter, not in ways subject to complete intentional control). Why should Arendt not be read as suggesting that the undermining of the traditional social sources of individuation and public life creates the occasion for a political project to found new such sources? Indeed, the crucial phrase in the quoted passage may be "if it is permitted to follow its own inherent law"; this surely suggests that action still has a chance to upset or alter ongoing social processes.

Villa takes his extreme position partly because he accepts from other interpreters of Arendt a conception of her emphasis on public space much too close to Habermas's account of the public sphere. "[W]hat binds together Arendt's contemporary critics and admirers," Villa writes, "is the unquestioned assumption that she stands for the recovery of a single, institutionalized public sphere."[25] Villa's essay helpfully brings out the problems Arendt sees posed for any such vision by the "de-worlding" of contemporary public life and by "modernity's relentless subjectification of the real." But he sets up something of a straw man when he tells us that after "the 'end of the common world' . . . —for Arendt, the defining event of the modern age—the prospects for an authentic, comprehensive, and relatively permanent public sphere fall to just about zero."

To his credit, Villa hastens to add that this is not to say that Arendt gives up on action, politics, or "publicity" in the Kantian sense. Indeed not (though his own subsequent elisions of her position with postmodernism nearly say as much). But why set up the standard that public life must be "comprehensive," "unitary," or "single"? Arendt does indeed give reasons why she thinks permanence is important—that deeds may be remembered—though this is a goal more than a condition. But it is not clear that she is, or on the basis of her theory would have reason to be, terribly worried about the loss of the other adjectives. She could, it seems to me, suggest that the Greek public sphere was able for various reasons (including scale) to be more comprehensive, single, and unitary (at the level of each polis), and that public space in other settings and on other bases have fewer of these characteristics. But even in Greece, or in the founding of America, Arendt does not praise singularity. On the contrary, she argues that the common world—the world that lies between people—of necessity must appear in multiple aspects and not be reduced to singularity (for example, by the triumph of economic, life-process definitions). "The end of the common world has come," she wrote just before taking up private property in the preceding section, "when it is seen only under one aspect and is permitted to present itself in only one perspective" (*HC*, p. 58). Precisely because of her agonistic approach to public life—her emphasis on contestation and plurality—Arendt has much less interest in the unity of a public sphere than, say, Habermas.

Plurality and Public Life

Much more clearly than Arendt, Habermas does think in terms of a unitary, bounded, and internally integrated public sphere. Arendt's usual term, "public space," leaves the "shape" of public life more open. This is partly because she emphasizes public action and agonistic, theatrical performance much more than Habermas does (as Villa rightly notes). Such public action can create institutions, as in the founding of the American Republic. But as action it is unpredictable. Its publicness comes from its performance in a space between people, a space of appearances, but it is in the nature of public action to be always forming and reforming that space and, arguably, the people themselves.

This conceptualization offers clear advantages for thinking about the place of plurality in the public sphere. By comparison, Habermas creates problems by placing identity formation prior to entry into the political public sphere and by denying importance to the "disclosure" of identity that Arendt regards as one of the most important features of public life. The public sphere of rational critical discourse can work, Habermas suggests, only if people are adequately prepared for it through other aspects of their personal and cultural experience. Habermas briefly discusses how the rise of a literary public sphere rooted in the rise of novel-reading and theatergoing publics contributed to the development of the political public sphere, but he does not follow through on this insight. He drops discussion of the literary public sphere with its eighteenth-century incarnation, that is, as soon as it has played its role in preparing for the rise of the Enlightenment political public sphere. He does not consider subsequent changes in literary discourse and how they may be related to changes in the identities people bring into the political public sphere. Neither does he consider the extent to which the best education for politics and public discourse takes place *in* politics and public discourse, not *before* either.[26]

More generally, Habermas does not adequately thematize the role of identity-forming, culture-forming public activity. He works mainly with a contrast between a realm of private life (with the intimate sphere as its inner sanctum) and the public sphere (of civil society), and assumes that identity is produced out of the combination of private life and the economic positions occupied in civil society. He offers little attention to or space for the performative dimensions dear to

Arendt (and described by Villa). He does not see public life as transformative of the individuals who participate in it or, indeed, as an occasion for them to be more fully individual than in the economy or in many other aspects of civil society. If anything, his public sphere calls on participants to leave their individuality behind in favor of deliberation on the putatively singular public good, relying only on universal rationality.

When we abandon the notion that identity is formed once and for all in advance of participation in the public sphere, however, we can recognize that in varying degrees all public discourses are occasions for identity formation and disclosure (that is, for doing things that reveal who we "really" are to others and how we matter to posterity in ways that are beyond our conscious intentions). This is central to the insight of Oskar Negt and Alexander Kluge in their appropriation of the phenomenological notion of "horizons of experience" as a way of broadening Habermas's approach to the public sphere.[27]

Experience is not something exclusively prior to and addressed only by the rational-critical discourse of the public sphere; it is constituted in part through public discourse and at the same time continually orients people differently in public life. We can distinguish public spheres in which identity formation figures more prominently and those in which rational-critical discourse is more prominent, but we should not assume the existence of any political public sphere where identity formation (and reformation) is not significant.

Excluding the identity-forming project from the public sphere makes no more sense than excluding those of "problematically different" identities. Few today would argue (at least in the broadly liberal public spheres of the West) against including in the public sphere women, racial and ethnic minorities, and virtually all other groups clearly subject to the same state and part of the same civil society. Yet many do argue against citizenship for those who refuse various projects of assimilation. It is not just Germans, with their ethnic ideas about national citizenship, who have a problem with immigrants. The language of the liberal public sphere is used to demand that only English be spoken in Florida, for example, or that Arabs and Africans conform to certain ideas of Frenchness if they wish to stay in France. For that matter, many other arguments—for example, that only heterosexuals should serve in the military—have much the same form and status. They demand conformity as a condition of full citizenship. Yet movement of people about the globe continues, making it harder to suppress difference even while provoking the urge. In a basic and intrinsic sense, if public performance has the capacity to alter civil society and to shape the state, then its own democratic practice must confront the questions of membership and the identity of the political community it represents.[28]

Habermas is, ultimately, a much more "liberal" thinker than is Arendt. His theory relies on the hope of transcending difference rather than on the provision of occasions for recognition, expression, and interrelationship. Habermas does not see plurality as basic to human life in general or, in particular, to the project of public life and therefore to democracy. Plurality is not a condition of private life or a product of quotidian personal tastes, in Arendt's view, but rather a potential that flowers in creative public achievements. Arendt accepted the classical Greek restriction on public participation precisely because she thought few people could rise above the implicit conformity imposed by a life of material production to achieve real distinction in the realm of praxis. But, given modern sociological conditions, Arendt did not support such exclusion (though neither was she in any sense "antielitist"): "The trouble lies in the lack of public spaces to which the people at large would have entrance and from which an élite could be selected, or rather, where it could select itself."[29]

Part of the point of linking the distinction between public and private to that between praxis and mere work or labor is to present the public sphere as something more than an arena for the advancement or negotiation of competing material interests. This image is carried forward in Habermas's account with its emphasis on the possibility of disinterested rational-critical public discourse and his suggestion that the public sphere degenerates as it is penetrated by organized interest groups. To presume that these are only different policies for achieving objectively ascertainable ends—let alone ends reducible to a lowest common denominator of interest—is to reduce the public sphere to a forum of Benthamite policy experts rather than to a vehicle of democratic self-government. This is clearly not something Habermas intends to praise. Yet it is not as sharply distant from his account of the public sphere as it might at first seem. One reason is that Habermas does not place the same stress as Arendt does on creativity. He treats public activity overwhelmingly in terms of rational-critical discourse rather than identity formation or expression; somewhat narrows the meaning and significance of plurality; and introduces the possibility of claims to expertise more appropriate to technical rationality than to communicative action. It is in this sense that Arendt suggests that modern intellectuals, unlike eighteenth-century *hommes de lettres*, are generally part of the social and are often agents of the state and of social engineering (*OR*, p. 122). Part of the background to this problem lies in the very manner in which public is separated from private in the eighteenth- and early-nineteenth-century liberal public sphere, which is the basis for Habermas's ideal-typical construction.

The liberal model of the public sphere pursues discursive equality by disqualifying discourse about the differences among actors. These differences are treated as matters of private, but not public, interest. On Habermas's account, the best version of the public sphere is based on "a kind of social intercourse that, far from presupposing the equality of status, disregarded status altogether."[30] It works by a "mutual willingness to accept the given roles and simultaneously to suspend their reality."[31] This "bracketing" of difference as merely private and irrelevant to the public sphere is undertaken, Habermas argues, to defend the genuinely rational-critical notion that arguments must be decided on their merits rather than according to the identities of the arguers. This is as important as was the fear of censors for anonymous or pseudonymous authors in the eighteenth-century public sphere. Yet it has the effect of excluding some of the most important concerns of many members of any polity—both those whose existing identities are suppressed or devalued and those whose exploration of possible identities is truncated. It makes politics much more a matter of deliberation on policy and much less an occasion for performative world making or disclosure of individual identity. In addition, this bracketing of differences also undermines the potential of public discourse for self-reflexivity. The plurality of participants, who appear precisely *as* different from each other, is a crucial spur to reflection on the identity of each and the significance of their interrelationships.

The conceptualization of public life as a singular sphere can also easily work in more immediately antidemocratic ways. Women, for example, were excluded from the now idealized public spheres of the early bourgeois era—ironically, more sharply excluded than in the era of absolutism.[32] The issue of "democratic inclusiveness" is not just a quantitative matter of the scale of a public sphere or the proportion of the members of a political community who may speak within it.

Although it is clearly a matter of stratification and boundaries (e.g., openness to the propertyless, the uneducated, women, or immigrants), it is also a matter of how the public sphere incorporates and recognizes the diversity of identities that people bring to it from their manifold involvements in civil society. It is a matter of whether in order to participate in such a public sphere, for example, women must act in ways previously characteristic of men and avoid addressing certain topics defined as appropriate to the private realm (the putatively more female sphere). Marx criticized the discourse of bourgeois citizenship for implying that it equally fitted everyone when it in fact tacitly presumed an understanding of citizens as property owners. The same sort of false universalism has presented citizens in gender-neutral or gender-symmetrical terms without acknowledging highly gendered underlying conceptions.

One alternative is to think of the public sphere not as the realm of a single public but as a sphere of publics. This does not mean that the flowering of innumerable potential publics is in and of itself a solution to this basic problem of democracy. On the contrary, democracy requires discourse across lines of basic difference. It is important that members of any specific public be able also to enter into others. This does not eliminate the need for a broader discourse concerned with, among other things, the balancing of different demands on states or different interests. But this discourse can be conceptualized—and nurtured—as a matter of multiple intersections among heterogeneous publics, not only as the privileging of a single overarching public.

Once we begin to think about such alternative understandings of publics, however, we confront resistance stemming from the way modern notions of the public sphere have been rooted in the discourse of nationalism. As Zaretsky suggests, Arendt rightly saw in nationalism a cement for binding central states to atomized societies. Ideas of the public commonly draw from nationalist rhetoric both the capacity to presume boundaries and an emphasis on the discourse of the whole.

It is one of the illusions of liberal discourse to believe that in a democratic society there is or can be a single, uniquely authoritative discourse about public affairs. This amounts to an attempt to settle in advance a question that is inextricably part of the democratic process itself. It reflects a nationalist presumption that membership in a common society precedes democratic deliberations, as well as an implicit belief that politics revolves around a single and unitary state. It is normal, however, not aberrant, for people to speak in a number of different public arenas and for these arenas to address multiple centers of power (whether institutionally differentiated within a single state, combining multiple states or political agencies, or recognizing that putatively nonpolitical agencies such as business corporations are loci of power and are addressed by public discourse). How many and how separate these public spheres are must be empirical variables. But each is likely to make some themes easier to address and simultaneously to repress others, and each will empower different voices to different degrees. That women or ethnic minorities carry on their own public discourses, thus, reflects not only the exclusion of certain people from the "dominant" public sphere but also a positive act of women and ethnic minorities. This means that simply pursuing their equitable inclusion in the dominant public sphere cannot be either an adequate recognition of their partially separate discourses or a resolution to the underlying problem. Recognizing a multiplicity of publics, none of which can claim a completely superordinate status to the others, is thus a first step.[33] It would be an exercise of force to authorize only one of these as properly "public," or some as more legitimately public than others that are held to be "private."

The Political and "the Social"

Because Arendt does not tie her idea of public space to the state in the way Habermas does his notion of public sphere, she does not stress any singular point of coming together. The occasions of public action may be multiple, each involving different mixes of people. What is most "comprehensive" is not any such space among concrete contemporaries, but the space of memory, in which the identities of individuals are disclosed in the stories told about them. Such identities require a field of common knowledge within which to be comprehensible, but there is no reason that that field must have strong institutional boundaries (in the way that, for example, an electorate must). To create such institutions is a potentially powerful public act, but public action—including the most authentic politics—is not conditioned on the prior existence of such institutions, boundaries, or internal integration. These come, if they come at all, afterward.

The Greeks, to whom Arendt turns for help in conceptualizing public life, sought permanence more in the stories told about them than in the institutions they created. Accordingly, as important as they are to her idea of public, they do not provide her with the model of a body politic, let alone a modern state. This, she tells us, was presaged by Rome, insofar as the Romans emphasized myths of founding in a way the Greeks never had—partly because the Romans worshiped their institutional framework as such, and partly because the foundation of a new body politic was "to the Greeks an almost commonplace experience."[34] But as much as he praised the glory that was Rome, Machiavelli crucially recognized that modern states were something new and different (*OR*, pp. 36, 39). They were institutions seeking stability, yet they were profoundly unstable. The ideal of the eternal nation conflicts with (and sometimes masks) this reality of profound political instability (p. 159). This is only partly because of the possibility of new attempts at founding, at revolution; it is also because of the variety of new pressures confronting modern states because they have taken on the challenge of attempting to provide social rather than only political goods.

These states—and the commensurate bodies politic conceptualized as nations—are necessarily different from ancient or Renaissance city-states. The republican project (which we now know ironically as the republican *tradition*) seeks, Arendt suggests, to regain some of the desirable features of such ancient publics within the institutional context of modern states. Crucially, this project seeks to recover a positive value on politics—participation in public deliberation about public goods. Indeed, Arendt is at pains to show that participation in public life can itself be a good, a source of pleasure and satisfaction: "[T]he Americans knew that public freedom consisted in having a share in the public business, and that the activities connected with this business by no means constituted a burden but gave those who discharged them in public a feeling of happiness they could acquire nowhere else" (p. 119). This distinguishes her view, and republicanism generally, from liberalism: "Thus it has become almost axiomatic even in political theory to understand by political freedom not a political phenomenon, but on the contrary, the more or less free range of non-political activities which a given body politic will permit and guarantee to those who constitute it" (p. 30).[35]

The great enemy of publicness and the foundation of stable republican institutions, Arendt suggests, is not instability or incoherence per se. It is, rather, "the social." Canovan points out two strands in Arendt's idiosyncratic usage of this term.[36] Most crucially, Arendt refers to the realm of "housekeeping," the *oikos* enlarged (even including very large-scale economic activity). Second, though, she also refers to "high society" and intends comment on the characteristic vices and overreliance on manners, and it is in this sense that society lives on in the general pursuit of social connection. Pitkin has extended these observations, showing further Arendt's criticism of the social vices of lying and hypocrisy, and the unfreedom imposed on someone who is forced by society to appear not for her own acts but as a representative (a woman, for example, or a Jew).[37] Above all, Pitkin suggests, Arendt's category of "the social" is cognate with Heidegger's "das Man." Both refer to people in general, as distinct from specific others. But whereas Heidegger's "das Man" is an ontological universal (not unlike George Herbert Mead's "generalized other"), Arendt's "social" is historically specific. It is the distinctive bearer of mass culture and desire as it emerged in the modern era: "Arendt's society was to be a historically variable phenomenon, humanly created and maintained in concrete, determinate ways at particular times, and humanly challengeable—not in the mind, by philosophical insight, but in the world created by joint political action."[38]

Arendt's usage of "the social" is also connected to the idea of civil society, however, and it shows such society in a much less flattering light than does most recent work. "Society," she writes, is "that curious and somewhat hybrid realm which the modern age interjected between the older and more genuine realms of the public or political on one side and the private on the other" (*OR*, p. 122). On this point Arendt is emphatically distinct from Habermas, who not only links politics more closely to the state but also situates the politically significant public sphere as "the public sphere of civil society."[39] The eighteenth-century salons and coffeehouses he idealizes elicit a much more ambivalent response from Arendt. It is not that Arendt fails to recognize the pleasures of sociability or that she never considers that successful public action such as that of the American founders might require social supports (any more than she thinks it would not be a good idea to ameliorate poverty). The issue, rather, is freedom. Civil society is first and foremost a realm of freedom *from* politics. But public freedom is freedom *in* politics. It is in this connection that Arendt praises Montesquieu for maintaining "that power and freedom belonged together; that, conceptually speaking, political freedom did not reside in the I-will but in the I-can" (p. 150).

Real freedom, then, consists of freedom to enter into public life. This is a space of appearances, and in this space, as Arendt echoes John Adams, people are motivated by "the passion for distinction." Republics thus share more spirit than Montesquieu suggested with respect to monarchies, in which honor is a driving pursuit. The virtue of the passion for distinction Adams called "emulation" or the "desire to excel another," and the vice he called "ambition," which aims at distinction on the basis of power (that is, domination by force) rather than achievement—these, Arendt suggested, are indeed the chief virtues and vices of political "man" (p. 119).

Living-Together

Emphasis on the pursuit of distinction immediately recalls Arendt's central argument, that the public is a realm of plurality, not sameness. For successful collective action, for solidarity achieved through public life, "homogeneity of past and origin, the decisive principle of the nation-state, is not required" (*OR*, p. 174). What is required, it would appear, is (*a*) the presence of other people, (*b*) the capacity for communication with those people, and (*c*) the eagerness to pursue distinction through achievement. Prior institutional arrangements of either private life (e.g., property) or public life (e.g., the agora) may facilitate public action, but it is hard to see Arendt regarding them as conditions. To do so would violate her basic understanding of action itself, as well as of natality.

Indeed, she argues that political action "may be started in isolation and decided upon by single individuals for very different motives," but it "can be accomplished only by some joint effort in which the motivation of single individuals . . . no longer counts. . . . The joint effort equalizes very effectively the differences in origin as well as in quality" (p. 174). In other words, the private (and social) characteristics of political actors lose their significance in those actors' shared public undertakings. The actors themselves—and certainly their motivations—may even be remade. At its most dramatic, their political action can found completely new political institutions that were not even foreseen by their creators at the beginning of their revolutionary action. This is the power of promises as a central component of political action, that—albeit only on extraordinary occasions—people may triumph over the reduction of politics to mere struggles and the consequent debasement of public life.

It is hard, then, to accept Villa's reading of Arendt's anxiety about the ways in which modernity compromises public life as an argument against attempting new beginnings or in favor of resistance as the only responsible political stance. Although political action takes place in the space of appearances between people and depends on publicness, it does not depend on the authority of any particular body politic or the coherence of any existing public sphere. Indeed, "no revolution ever succeeded [and] few rebellions ever started, so long as the authority of the body politic was truly intact. Thus, from the very beginning, the recovery of ancient liberties was accompanied by the [attempted] reinstitution of lost authority and lost power" (p. 155). But, in a stronger sense, "authority, as we once knew it, which grew out of the Roman experience of foundation and was understood in the light of Greek political philosophy, has nowhere been re-established"⁴⁰—not even, Arendt suggests, by the revolution that came closest, that in the United States. At the same time, however, she refuses to read this as a sign of closure but rather sees it as a return to a basic, if problematic, openness: "For to live in a political realm with neither authority nor the concomitant awareness that the source of authority transcends power and those who are in power, means to be confronted anew, without religious trust in a sacred beginning and without the protection of traditional and therefore self-evident standards of behavior, by the elementary problems of human living-together."⁴¹

We confront these "elementary problems of human living-together" with more or less help from our historical inheritance and sociological context. Confronting them, though, we always waive the opportunities to act in public, in communication and sometimes in contest with each other, and to give institutional form to the public life we achieve.

We achieve the power to act successfully, to create beyond our individual capacities or intentions, by our ability to make promises to each other. This is the elementary joining-together that confronts the elementary problems of human living-together: "The grammar of action: action is the only human faculty that demands a plurality of men; and the syntax of power: that power is the only human attribute which applies solely to the worldly in-between space by which men are mutually related, combine in the act of foundation by virtue of the making and the keeping of promises, which, in the realm of politics, may well be the highest human faculty" (*OR*, p. 175).

Notes

1. With deeper and richer conceptions of history, epochal change, and the modern era itself, these other critics suggest higher standards for what it would mean to transcend an epoch. See my "Postmodernism as Pseudohistory," in *Critical Social Theory: Culture, History, and the Challenge of Difference* (Oxford: Blackwell, 1995).

2. Hannah Arendt, *On Revolution* (1963; reprint, New York: Penguin, 1977), p. 175; hereafter cited in text as *OR*.

3. Hannah Arendt, *The Human Condition* (Chicago: University of Chicago Press, 1958), pp. 50, 52; hereafter cited in text as *HC*.

4. "The objectivity of the world—its object- or thing-character—and the human condition supplement each other; because human existence is conditioned existence, it would be impossible without things, and things would be a head of unrelated articles, a non-world, if they were not the conditioners of human existence" (*HC*, p. 9).

5. Max Weber, *The Protestant Ethic and the Spirit of Capitalism* (1904; reprint, New York: Scribner's, 1985). It is worth recalling that Weber's story here is not only one of rationalization, to which it is sometimes reduced both by followers (such as Habermas) and by critics (such as Villa in this volume), but also one of moral revaluation. See also Charles Taylor, *Sources of the Self* (Cambridge: Harvard University Press, 1989); and Arendt's scattered comments, especially her brief critical remarks on Rousseau and the Romantics in *HC*, pp. 38–39, 50.

6. This account is particularly pronounced in *HC* and contrasts somewhat to the greater attention to the scale of capitalist economic enterprise in *The Origins of Totalitarianism*, 2nd ed. (1951; reprint, New York: Harcourt Brace, 1973).

7. Hannah Arendt, *Crises of the Republic* (New York: Harcourt, Brace, Jovanovich, 1972), p. 232. Jeffrey C. Isaac's discussion of this dimension of Arendt's thinking about democracy is helpful; see chap. 5 of *Arendt, Camus, and Modern Rebellion* (New Haven: Yale University Press, 1992).

8. Zaretsky may somewhat overstress the dominance of Marxism in Arendt's Parisian and New York milieus and its centrality to her own intellectual orientation. Marburg and Berlin were also powerful shaping milieus and existentialism and a variety of other currents of thought were important alongside social democracy and Marxism in New York, as well as in Germany.

9. Though Arendt was no simple neo-Kantian, this aspect of her thought shares much not only with Kant but also with such neo-Kantian proponents of the necessary differentiation of value spheres as Weber and, later, Habermas.

10. Jürgen Habermas, *Structural Transformation of the Public Sphere* (1962; reprint, Cambridge: MIT Press, 1989).

11. In the present chapter I shall use "sociological" to refer to the broad domain of relationships, practices, and institutions often called "social," in order to maintain a distinction from Arendt's very different and somewhat idiosyncratic use of the term "social."

12. See Nancy Fraser, "Rethinking the Public Sphere: A Contribution to the Critique of Actually Existing Democracy," and other chapters in *Habermas and the Public Sphere*, ed. Craig Calhoun (Cambridge: MIT Press, 1992).

13. I do not want to suggest that this reading is in sharp contradiction to Villa. Villa stresses another side of Arendt to the near exclusion of the one I wish to bring out, but he does not deny it.

14. In making this claim I move in the opposite direction from the comparison Seyla

Benhabib offers in "Models of Public Space: Hannah Arendt, the Liberal Tradition, and Jürgen Habermas," in Calhoun, *Habermas and the Public Sphere.*

15. It is particularly unfortunate that Zaretsky ignores *On Revolution.* Surprisingly, he writes that "the key to [my reading] . . . is the question of the public and the private. In part because of this emphasis, I am going to restrict myself to *The Origins of Totalitarianism* (1951) and *The Human Condition* (1958)." *On Revolution* bears directly on the nature of public action and its relation to social and/or private concerns, and presents an importantly different side of Arendt's thinking on precisely the issues Zaretsky addresses.

16. This view is at the heart of Arendt's much-remarked "agonistic" account of politics. See especially Bonnie Honig, "Toward an Agonistic Feminism: Hannah Arendt and the Politics of Identity," in *Feminist Interpretations of Hannah Arendt,* ed. Bonnie Honig (University Park: Pennsylvania State University Press, 1995). The notion of performativity helps stress the dimension of "self-making"—which is clearly part of Arendt's concern—more than does the term "agonism," or competitive "showing" of oneself—in Arendt's words, "the passionate drive to show oneself in measuring up against others" (*HC,* p. 194). Arendt is, of course, intensely interested not only in disclosure and appearance (following Heidegger, as well as Greek guides) but also in creativity and individuation.

17. Here Zaretsky's account of the loss of basis for public life comes surprisingly close to Villa's, given their otherwise different orientations.

18. "Rebellion" is a close and at least equally apt term and rightly suggests a more active stance than does "resistance." See Isaac, *Arendt, Camus, and Modern Rebellion.*

19. It is worth noting, though, that this more complex account of alienation does not set Arendt altogether apart from other theorists. Hegel pursues not a simple end to alienation—and certainly not a merging of boundaries into some manner of undifferentiated at-homeness—but a complex sort of transcendence. Marx worked with a variety of different terms in his effort to describe the necessity and creativity of certain forms of objectification or estrangement while retaining critical purchase on alienation; see John Torrance, *Alienation, Objectification, Estrangement* (London: Methuen, 1975).

20. Villa is sufficiently far from an interest in Marx (not to mention Hegel and others) that he can describe Nietzsche and Heidegger simply and without question as "*the* two greatest thinkers and critics of modernity" (emphasis added).

21. In claiming the basis of "original meaning" for her interpretation of the significance of property, Arendt employs one of her favorite rhetorical tropes. Her claims about the "original" meanings of words are sometimes dubious and, in any case, carry little weight in determining whether her interpretations and conceptualizations are helpful. She often makes good points by means of bad claims about what words originally meant.

22. Arendt is here engaged in a somewhat tendentious argument with Marx, interpreting his hope for a "withering away" of the state as a call for the withering away of the public realm (see my remarks at the outset about the multiple meanings of public and private and the potential for confusion and/or manipulation).

23. With this in mind, we can see more clearly some of the reasons for the work/ labor distinction in Arendt. As Zaretsky notes, the issue is partly one of the importance of cultural meaning to work—work makes culture, in a sense, as well as making things. It is perhaps overoptimistic, however, to suggest that it is only subordination that sometimes deprives work of meaning—and, I think, a somewhat problematic assertion to put in the mouths of E. P. Thompson and Raymond Williams. Both (like Marx) idealized craft production, which fits Arendt's category of work rather well. Both saw the rou-

tinization of craft production, deskilling, and similar trends as links to the subordination of workers and, even further, as challenges to the meaningfulness of work. For this
reason, an end to simple subordination in itself does not restore to work its full potential as a meaningful mode of human productivity. Moreover, as important as cultural
meaning is to work, it is in action that cultural performativity flowers as the making of
a common world. World alienation, the loss of this common world or estrangement
from it, is thus a loss of human connection profoundly distinct from the alienation that
reduces work to mere labor.

24. The reason that men cannot be citizens of the world as they are of their countries
is tied to Arendt's understanding of the nation as a substitute for the family. Whereas
families supported "real" individuation, nations offer participation in an individuated
collectivity (a bad substitute but at least offering some individuation); the world of humanity as a whole must be defined by what all people have in common—which is only
material life processes—rather than by what differentiates them.

25. This claim is a bit extreme in the late 1990s. It is true of Benhabib, perhaps, and
of some communitarians who seek to adopt Arendt; but it is certainly no longer an unquestioned assumption. See, for example, the essays by Mary G. Dietz, Honig, and
Susan Bickford in Honig, *Feminist Interpretations of Hannah Arendt*.

26. Arendt, in "On Authority," in *Between Past and Future* (1961; reprint, New
York: Penguin, 1977), pp. 118–19, asserts that education is not an appropriate stance
for rulers toward the public, because members are adults and are ready for discourse.
But this is a matter of minimal criteria. Her performative approach suggests clearly how
participants in public life may seek more excellent identities and capacities.

27. Oskar Negt and Alexander Kluge, *The Public Sphere and Experience* (Minneapolis: University of Minnesota Press, 1993).

28. Habermas addresses these questions to some extent in his account of "constitutional patriotism" inspired by the problems of post-1989 German unification, but this
tends to presume nationality as a backdrop and to amount to an idealization of "civic"
against "ethnic" nationalism and, in general, of the *rechtsstaat*. See his "Citizenship and
National Identity: Some Reflections on the Future of Europe," *Praxis International* 12,
no. 1 (1992); and his "Struggles for Recognition in the Democratic Constitutional
State," in *Multiculturalism: Exploring the Politics of Recognition*, rev. ed., ed. Amy
Gutman (Princeton: Princeton University Press, 1994).

29. *OR*, p. 277; note the plural "spaces."

30. Habermas, *Structural Transformation of the Public Sphere*, p. 36.

31. Ibid., p. 131.

32. See Joan Landes's *Women and the Public Sphere* (Ithaca: Cornell University
Press, 1989) and "*Novus Ordo Saeculorum*: Gender and Public Space in Arendt's Revo-
lutionary France," in Honig, *Feminist Interpretations of Hannah Arendt*; and Geoff
Eley, "Gender, Class, and Nation," in Calhoun, *Habermas and the Public Sphere*.

33. See Geoff Eley, "Nations, Publics, and Political Cultures," in Nicholas B. Dirks,
Geoff Eley, and Sherry B. Ortner, eds., *Culture/Power/History* (Princeton: Princeton
University Press, 1995); and Fraser, "Rethinking the Public Sphere," in Calhoun,
Habermas and the Public Sphere.

34. Arendt, "On Authority," p. 121.

35. This is the insight Bonnie Honig follows up in her helpful *Political Theory and
the Displacement of Politics* (Ithaca: Cornell University Press, 1993).

36. Margaret Canovan, *The Political Thought of Hannah Arendt* (New York: Harcourt Brace, 1974), esp. pp. 105–9; see also her *Hannah Arendt: A Reinterpretation of
Her Political Thought* (Cambridge: Cambridge University Press, 1992), which revises

the earlier book on some particulars but not this one, and which offers a helpful reading of how the problems Arendt addressed in *The Origins of Totalitarianism* were central to Arendt's later work.

37. Hanna Pitkin, "Conformism, Housekeeping, and the Attack of the Blob: The Origins of Hannah Arendt's Concept of the Social," in Honig, *Feminist Interpretations of Hannah Arendt.*

38. Ibid., p. 73.

39. Habermas, *Structural Transformation of the Public Sphere.*

40. Arendt, "On Authority," p. 141.

41. Ibid.

Part IV

Ten

Must Politics Be Violent?
Arendt's Utopian Vision

John McGowan

This essay had its origins in my puzzling over the classic problem facing Arendt's readers: Why is her understanding of the political so narrowly circumscribed?[1] Following others (Margaret Canovan for one), I take the political, as defined in *The Human Condition, Between Past and Future,* and *On Revolution,* to be a response to the distopic reality of totalitarianism.[2] If we read the political as a utopian space characterized by the absence of violence, Arendt's distinctive and troubling division between the "political" and the "social" makes more sense. Violence is associated with necessity, with the material-biological needs that Arendt links to "life" and "the social question." The political can be nonviolent and free only insofar as it is uncoupled from necessity. Arendt's pursuit of this utopian politics leads her to imagine ways of founding a polity (constitutions and compacts), ways of acting in concert (performatives in the space of appearances before others), and a phenomenology of relatedness (including the crucial acts of promising and forgiving) that offer appealing images of human arrangements and actions that foster what politics at its best can achieve. Much of my essay is devoted to delineating the features of Arendt's hopeful, nonviolent politics.

There is, however, a political violence in Arendt's work—a violence that cannot be linked to necessity. Or, it would be more accurate to say that there are at least two political violences in Arendt. The first is associated with totalitarianism, with that radical evil which aims at the obliteration of "plurality." The second form is that described in the late essay "On Violence," in which violence is connected to the frustration within a polity of groups too weak to construct performatively an adequate space for action. Faced with the violence of the Civil Rights and student movements of the 1960s, Arendt for the first time explicitly addresses the topic of violence (which has been a persistent but never foregrounded theme in all her previous work), and the result is an essay that departs from much of her earlier thinking on the topic.

This essay, then, charts the vicissitudes of Arendt's thoughts on violence, paying tribute to the imaginative possibilities opened up by her attempt to construct a nonviolent politics, while also indicating that a political violence that Arendt can never completely banish troubles her vision of the political from start to finish. I will start with *The Origins of Totalitarianism*, because it sets forth the grim reality that generates the compensatory idealizations of the later work.[3]

Totalitarian terror is the institutionalization of permanent violence, a nightmare version of the dream of a permanent revolution. Terror can be the idea of violence—showing the victim the instruments of torture—as much as its actual enactment. The keys to terror are that it never ends and that there is no reason, logic, or pattern to its choice of victims. "Dictatorial terror" is somewhat predictable because "it threatens only authentic opponents" (*OT*, 322), but totalitarian terror achieves an "unheard-of unpredictability" (*OT*, 347) in its random attacks on "harmless citizens without political opinions"(*OT*, 322). The ever-present threat of violence against each and every citizen is required to achieve the "mass atomization" (*OT*, 323) that is the goal of totalitarianism. Earlier tyrannies strove to make each citizen equally subject to the state, "yet such equalization [if not accompanied by terror] is not sufficient for totalitarian rule because it leaves more or less intact nonpolitical communal bonds between the subjects, such as family ties and common cultural interests." Totalitarianism can come into being only when the "absolutely atomized elements in a mass society" are formed into a "completely heterogeneous uniformity" (*OT*, 322), each individual relating to the state, and to the state only, on his or her own.

Random terror achieves atomization by making all association with others dangerous. If the other is picked as a victim, one may be guilty by association if too close and will only be able to save oneself by rushing to denounce the onetime friend. In such a situation "it is obvious that the most elementary caution demands that one avoid all intimate contacts." This severance of all ties among citizens complements totalitarianism's "demand for total, unrestricted, unconditional, and unalterable loyalty of the individual member," because "such loyalty can be expected only from the completely isolated human being" (*OT*, 323).

Totalitarianism, then, goes hand in hand with mass society. Various developments in European history since the French Revolution (developments traced in parts 1 and 2 of *The Origins of Totalitarianism*) foster mass society. (Tocqueville's description of a modern world in which individuals face the state one-on-one without benefit of intermediary "voluntary associations" comes closest to Arendt's understanding of mass society.) Totalitarian movements focus the forces of mass society to insure its complete triumph over other elements in the complex web that is any modern nation-state. If this is the scenario Arendt has in mind, then terror ("the very essence of [the totalitarian] form of government" [*OT*, 344]) only completes a process of atomization that began long before terror was instituted.

What is the relation of terror to violence? The answer is hardly clear, but I think the final criterion is existential, even ontological. Violence, as Arendt finally says outright in "On Violence," is always understood as "instrumental" in her work.[4] Violence is a means by which to achieve a certain end—a means that always stands in need of justification but that can be justified when I convince others and myself that no other means was available or effective and that the end was sufficiently worthwhile. As we have seen, terror can be understood as a means for producing atomization and the resultant fierce loyalty of citizens to state—a means, then, to gain the "total domination of the total population . . . , the elimination of every competing nontotalitarian reality" (*OT*, 392). Terror and violence can both be linked to creation, as they are in Elaine Scarry's work.[5] But Arendt appears to distinguish between terror and violence on the grounds of their relation to reality. Violence, on the one hand, successfully creates because it realistically assesses the obstacles it faces and adopts or adapts its means accordingly. (Note: Success is not justification; to have succeeded in creating something still leaves the task of justifying that act of creation.) Terror, on the other hand, is unceasing and un-predictable precisely because, eventually, it must be unavailing. Its act of creation can never be completed because terror is, at base, a protest against the very terms of existence. What terror tries to create is a "fic-titious world" (*OT*, 391) that supplants the real one.

Arendt paints herself into two corners here, neither of which she manages to handle completely adequately. The first involves the issue of whether totalitarianism is, in the long run, self-defeating. An appeal to the nature of things, to the facts that totalitarianism tries to negate, suggests that the totalitarian project *must* fail; and much in Arendt's book supports that conclusion. But Stalin is still in power as Arendt writes, and there is nothing to suggest a "natural" time limit to totali-tarian regimes; her aim is hardly to console us with an assurance of eventual, inevitable failure or to suggest a quietist reliance on that eventual ending. Yet the triumph of totalitarianism in the West has been so complete that she has no human agency to poise against it, no human power to explain its collapse.[6] The totalitarian, we might say, exceeds the political, if we understand the political to be the arena where various options contend with one another for the power to be implemented. Totalitarianism succeeds in so utterly destroying the po-litical space of contention, so utterly eliminating all contention, that only its running up against natural, existential forces could explain its inability to sustain itself forever.

The second corner into which Arendt paints herself influences, I believe, everything she subsequently writes. Arendt's notion of the po-litical is, in many ways, a construct meant to guard against all that is wrong in totalitarianism: "The totalitarian ruler is confronted with a dual task which at first appears contradictory to the point of absur-dity: he must establish the fictitious world of the movement as a tangi-ble working reality of everyday life, and he must, on the other hand, prevent the new world from developing a new stability." Why this fear of stability? Because totalitarianism aims for the uniformity of total sameness, for complete harmony and solidarity, thus setting its face against the existential and ontological fact of *plurality*, "a plurality which *ipso facto* refutes every contention that any specific form of government is absolutely valid" (*OT*, 391). Because the condition of plurality is constituted by the uniqueness of every individual, totalitar-ian hostility to plurality takes the form of rendering the individual su-perfluous, the form of indifference to difference.[7]

The political in Arendt, then, must derive stability from plurality; counterintuitively she argues that contention and difference yield stability, whereas attempts to achieve harmony yield terror and instability. (Arendt thus makes arguments similar to those found in Madison's famous *Federalist* paper number 10 on "factions.") The problem raised by taking this position is that some conflicts obviously yield violence, not stability; the examples of civil war are all around us. Arendt's response is to try to differentiate between two different kinds of conflict; conflict concerning matters of "life" does yield violence, whereas the agonistic competition for distinction does not. And she exiles the potentially violent conflicts from politics.

In other words, Arendt derives from her understanding of totalitarianism the lesson that what she later calls "the space of appearances"[8] must attain enough stability to promote precisely the kinds of innovation and spontaneity that she associates with action. Why does she think that the achievement of stability generates plurality? First, stability ("normalization" after a period of revolutionary or transitional upheaval) allows "a new way of life to develop—one which might, after a time, lose its bastard qualities and take its place among the widely differing and profoundly contrasting ways of life of the nations of the earth" (*OT*, 391). To eschew world domination, to live at peace with other nations, to declare the revolution over would be to accept (at least implicitly) that this fictitious world created here is not *the* world, but only one world among others. The totalitarian drive to create just one world is endless and justifies constant turmoil; stability can be achieved only in establishing relations to what is different, relations that allow it to endure even as one pursues one's own way. Stability thus acknowledges plurality.

Second, stability (the acceptance that the transformations that a regime has achieved are satisfactory) means a turning of attention away from the single task of creating the fictitious world to the myriad tasks that characterize ongoing existence. The exhilarating (and annihilating) solidarity experienced in performing that single work must now yield to the differentiation experienced when various people focus on a variety of tasks. It is to prevent this return of plurality after the experience of solidarity that totalitarianism moves from violence to terror. (We might also add that plurality is not without its longueurs, even its own quiet desperation, which is one way to explain totalitarianism's attractiveness. Totalitarianism does offer a kind of ersatz action

that is bound to be attractive, both because action itself is difficult—
requiring courage—in Arendt and because the conditions for action
are attenuated in the modern world.) Violence was one of the means
used to overcome the obstacles to revolutionary transformation. A by-
product of violence, it turns out, is the kind of uniformity in a mass to
which totalitarianism aspires. (Or is totalitarianism just the appropriate political form for those who would sacrifice all else for the dizzying
experience of that wonderful solidarity?) When obstacles to the totalitarian movement are overcome, only the unceasing and random creation of fictional obstacles can continually restage the unity found in
violence. Thus, Arendt insists, "terror increased both in Soviet Russia
and Nazi Germany in inverse ratio to the existence of internal political
opposition" (OT, 393). Violence is a means used to overcome real obstacles; terror is a preemptive strike against society's ever settling into
a stability in which plurality can emerge once more.

Singularity and natality are dependent on a stable political space
forged out of an equality that acknowledges plurality. But, to put it
bluntly, the achievements at stake in the political sphere cannot be
matters of life and death, cannot be matters of "necessity," because
such matters lead to violent conflicts that disrupt the very stability that
must underwrite political action. So Arendt seems to achieve stability
and nonviolence in the political sphere by trivializing that sphere. Of
course, one response to such a view—a response Arendt often makes—
is that we moderns have the wrong priorities; by placing all the emphasis on matters of "life," we have produced the consumer society we
now inhabit, where the only way we know how to respond to abundance is to produce even more goods, despite the very obvious eco-
logical dangers and the less obvious danger of reducing all measures of
distinction and worth to economic ones, a course sure to exacerbate
conflict. To put it another way, Arendt thinks the good of plurality
(which makes each individual life precious, nonsuperfluous) is so over-
riding that it must be carefully insulated from the threat to stability
(which is needed to underwrite plurality) represented by group conflicts about the allocation of resources.

I will have more to say about Arendt's descriptions of the violence
that she carefully places outside the political. For now, it is important
to see that totalitarian terror presents us with one model of violent political founding. Totalitarianism is the evil twin of the Arendtian political. It represents not behavior in another realm but wrongheaded ac-

tion in the political realm. Arendt is at pains to stress that totalitarian regimes are not utilitarian, and we might even go so far as to say that totalitarian terror is an action guided by "principle" as Arendtian action must be: the principle of nonplurality.[9] If violence is a means used to overcome real obstacles and as such is not self-reliant but dependent on its ends, terror attacks the conditions in which plurality might emerge and so is the very action that constitutes a nonplural world. Whereas political action sustains and embodies (continually recreates) plurality, terror continually produces the negation of plurality.

Plurality has more than a little of the deus ex machina about it in Arendt. She insisted throughout her career that plurality is simply a fact of the human condition and that it will, it must, triumph in the long run. Yet, as she argues throughout *The Origins of Totalitarianism*, some historical conditions are more favorable to the preservation and (would Arendt go this far?) the production of plurality, whereas there exist strong human impulses that fear plurality and try to stamp it out.[10] Plurality, in other words, is hardly a constant; it appears dependent on human efforts to foster it (if not quite to create it) and vulnerable to human efforts to wipe it out. If plurality is a fact, not everyone values it as Arendt does, so that an account of why humans dread and fear plurality seems called for when trying to describe the fascination of totalitarianism. In place of such an account, Arendt offers us only an image of political action posed against "the perplexity of radical evil." Crucially, "evil" is violent action meant to negate plurality and is not to be confused with violent actions taken in the realm of necessity; these latter actions threaten the political, especially if they come to be all of human activity, but they are not "evil" because they are understandable, in some cases even justifiable, in terms of necessity.

Arendt consistently refused throughout her career to attempt any explanation of evil, while persistently calling our attention to the relevance of its existence as a political fact. Even *Eichmann in Jerusalem*, despite its famous subtitle—*A Report on the Banality of Evil*—is not "a theoretical treatise on the nature of evil," as Arendt insists in her postscript (*EJ*, 285). Eichmann "had no motives at all"; the "banality" of his deeds derived from their "sheer thoughtlessness" (*EJ*, 287): "That such remoteness from reality and such thoughtlessness can wreak more havoc than all the evil instincts taken together which, perhaps, are inherent in man—that was, in fact, the lesson one could learn in Jerusalem. But it was a lesson, neither an explanation of the phenomenon nor a theory about it" (*EJ*, 288).

Evil happens. Arendt has little more to say about it. But her conception of politics can be read as an attempt to rehabilitate the political sphere that twentieth-century totalitarianism has taught us to associate with evil, a "radical evil previously unknown to us." Totalitarian evil "enforces oblivion" on its victims, both the oblivion of being hidden away in concentration camps during life and the oblivion of having all traces of one's ever having existed erased after death. As a result, "something seems to be involved in modern politics that actually should never be involved in politics as we used to understand it, namely all or nothing—all, and that is an undetermined infinity of forms of human living-together, or nothing, for a victory of the concentration-camp system would mean the same inexorable doom for human beings as the use of the hydrogen bomb" (*OT*, 443). In our times, politics has been asked to carry so great a burden because politics has also been the site of the greatest evils.

Arendt's stress on the "*polis* [as] . . . a kind of organized remembrance" through which immortality is conferred on "passing existence and fleeting greatness" (*HC*, 198) responds directly to the oblivion that totalitarianism tries to impose. But Arendt's definition of the political, as many commentators have complained, often seems constructed primarily through negations. Arendt consistently links with violence what she wishes to exclude from politics. In regard to positive values, Arendt tries to recall for us a set of principles, goals, and motives apart from "life." Because we moderns have lost almost all access to this alternative set, we have "extraordinary difficulty" in "understand[ing] the decisive division between the public and private realms, . . . between activities related to a common world and those related to the maintenance of life. . . . In our understanding, the dividing line is entirely blurred, because we see the body of peoples and political communities in the image of a family whose everyday affairs have to be taken care of by a gigantic, nation-wide administration of housekeeping" (*HC*, 28).

To regain a sense of non-life-maintenance principles and goals would be to revive the political actions through which a common world of appearances is created and through which individual distinction, virtuosity, glory, and immortality are sought in performances before and competitions against one's peers (see *HC*, 41 and 198). The political has positive value because it offers a unique locale for the accomplishment of distinctively human actions that are other to the struggle for life. Arendt believes that only such actions are "free," because they are not performed under the compulsion of biological necessity. What politics can make available to us is freedom, not prosperity or justice. Politics cannot secure freedom, but it can strive to create the conditions of its availability and to protect freedom where it does exist. Only with freedom can we enjoy the opportunity to act in such ways as to pursue distinction and immortality.

Arendt does not try to locate any psychological or other cause below or behind freedom. It is crucial to her notion of action that freedom is a good in and of itself and that actions are undertaken solely for the sake of the goods that the political can offer—freedom, distinction, and remembrance: "The root of the ancient estimation of politics is the conviction that man *qua* man, each individual in his unique distinctness, appears and confirms himself in speech and action, and that these activities, despite their material futility, possess an enduring quality of their own because they create their own remembrance" (*HC*, 207–8). Arendt never uses the Hegelian vocabulary of "recognition," but her attempt to designate a noneconomic set of motives is not completely foreign to that vocabulary. For Arendt, the individual can be recognized as a distinct individual only in the space of appearances, where "in acting and speaking, men show who they are, reveal actively their unique personal identities" (*HC*, 179). Crucially, this revelation of identity is as much to the self as to others; the self does not know itself except insofar as it enacts itself before others—a process of unfolding or of creation that coincides with the self's life span.

Political activity does not only reveal the identity of the individual, it also reveals the humanity of political agents. Here, in the space of activities not compelled by necessity, we find the distinctively human, "man *qua* man." Arendt, like King Lear, deems men's lives cheap as beasts' if they are not elevated by activities that are not necessary. Politics, action, and even freedom are not quite for their own sake in Arendt. They offer a form of recognition, although Arendt, unlike Hegel, does not consider just how passionate the need for recognition can be, just how psychologically and politically vulnerable that need can make us.[11] For Arendt, our very humanness is also at stake; to forsake the political is to forsake what distinguishes us from the beasts.

There is much more to say about Arendt's "positive" account of the political, but I want to concentrate on the "negative" side of the ledger, on those things she excludes and her reasons for excluding them. Here is where violence enters the picture continually. The innocence of Arendtian politics is marked by the absence of all violence; the negative sign of her utopian politics is its nonviolence: "[M]ost political action . . . remains outside the sphere of violence" (HC, 26). Because the ancients understood violence instrumentally, "glorifications of violence as such are entirely absent from the tradition of political thought prior to the modern age" (HC, 228). Only with the modern confusion of "making" with "action" does violence enter political theory. Much of *The Human Condition* can be understood as definitionally enforcing a set of distinctions that separate politics from violence. Everything that is political is nonviolent; everything that is not political is violent.

On Revolution enacts the separation of the political from the violent most consistently of all Arendt's works, as she tries to undo the modern association of revolutionary action with violence. The political power Arendt identifies in the soviets, the revolutionary councils, the Mayflower Compact, and the actions of Jefferson, Adams, and Madison is categorically nonviolent. And, insofar as revolutionary fervor and virtue is violent, Arendt insists that it is nonpolitical. She sees in Melville's *Billy Budd* a fable that could have been written only after the French Revolution, a fable about the attraction (because it alone can counterbalance evil) and violence of goodness: "[O]nly the violence of . . . goodness is adequate to the depraved power of evil."[12] Goodness, however, because "it shares with 'elemental evil' the elementary violence inherent in all strength," is "detrimental to all forms of political organization" (OR, 87).

Are various activities violent because they are nonpolitical, or is politics erected as a "ring-wall" ("the word *polis* originally connoted something like a 'ring-wall'"[HC, 64 n. 64]) to escape the prevalence of violence in human affairs? Arendt appears to incline toward the second option, because she certainly understands the political as belated, as coming into existence only when there is a surplus that gives some men (it is always men in the examples she provides) the chance to do something other than labor (defined as the activity bound to producing the vital necessities required by the biological processes of the human body [see HC, 7 and 100]). Politics, thus, supplements labor; apparently, it supplements violence as well, offering a unique experience of nonviolence. But to put it this way is to offer a rationale for politics—escape from violence—that Arendt does not explicitly offer. Insofar as violence is consistently tied to necessity and politics is linked to freedom from necessity in her work, then an escape from violence through politics would follow. So my next step will be the tracing of this link of violence to necessity in Arendt; to anticipate my conclusion, there is a violence—such as the violence of totalitarian terror—that is not tied to the necessities of life and hence is not so easy to exclude from politics.

In the Arendtian trinity of labor, work, and action, labor is the "primordial violence with which man pits himself against necessity" (*OR*, 114). The violence here is not only the violence that laboring humans do to natural things but also the violence they do to one another. The violence done to things (the material alteration and/or destruction of things to be used or consumed by humans) is accompanied by another violence, the violence (the threat or use of force to cause bodily harm and pain) that compels certain humans to labor for others. Thus, violence is used not only to satisfy needs but also to allow some of its users to escape need altogether. The first condition of freedom, of having a polis at all, is transcendence of necessity—and such transcendence can be achieved only by violence against others: "All rulership has its original and its most legitimate source in man's wish to emancipate himself from life's necessity, and men achieved such liberation by means of violence, by forcing others to bear the burden of life for them. This was the core of slavery, and it is only the rise of technology, and not the rise of modern political ideas as such, which has refuted the old and terrible truth that only violence and rule over others could make some men free" (*OR*, 114). Political freedom is not just freedom from necessity, freedom from being ruled over by others (within the polis or ring-wall all are equal), and freedom from violence. Political freedom begins when these basic freedoms are made possible by conditions of abundance.

Modern technology, Arendt seems to believe, may give us abundance for all; otherwise, abundance is a good enjoyed only by a few, and they gain that good by "means of violence" against the others, who are forced to produce that abundance. Under conditions of scarcity, violence is inevitable, and the very possibility of politics rests on the prior existence of that violence. For Arendt, we moderns have either tried to deny the fact of this inevitable violence (a denial that modern technology may justify) or have declared that, given the choice between such violence and having a politics at all, we will choose not to have politics. But she argues vehemently that the second choice does not represent an actual option. Offering a variant of what Albert O. Hirschman calls "the perversity thesis," Arendt insists that all attempts, motivated by pity for *les misérables*, to eschew the violence whose sign is the poverty of some but not of all leads neither to increased well-being nor to a lessening of violence.[13] Precisely the contrary is true: the attempt to solve politically the problem of poverty destroys the political and leads to a generalization of violence throughout the society, a violence tending toward terror. Nowhere else does Arendt so starkly confront the unthinkable, the unacceptable, for modern sensibilities. Arendt thinks we lie to ourselves when we say that poverty can be alleviated by political action, and "all . . . lies . . . harbor an element of violence," because they lead the liar to try "to destroy whatever [the lie] has decided to negate" (*BPF*, 252). Trying to negate the necessary limits of political action leads to the destruction of the political and the utter triumph of what Arendt calls "the social."

Work, defined as the production of lasting artificial (nonnatural, human-made) objects, is also violent: "Material is already a product of human hands which have removed it from its natural location, either killing a life process . . . or interrupting one of nature's slower processes. . . . This element of violation and violence is present in all fabrication, and *homo faber*, the creator of human artifice, has always been a destroyer of nature" (*HC*, 139). Arendt aims for a Nietzschean affirmation of this violence as contrasted to the violence of labor: "The experience of this violence is the most elemental experience of human strength and, therefore, the very opposite of the painful, exhausting effort experienced in sheer labor" (*HC*, 140).

Still, even joyful violence must be carefully distinguished from politics and from action. (On the modern mistake of failing to distinguish fabrication from action, see *BPF*, 216–19.) Arendt takes some pains to insist that the founding and maintenance of the polis is work, not action, and as such is not itself political: "[T]he Greeks . . . did not count legislating among the political activities. In their opinion, the lawmaker was like the builders of the city wall, someone who had to do and finish his work before political activity could begin. . . . To them, the laws, like the wall around the city, were not the results of action but products of making. Before man began to act, a definite space had to be secured and a structure built where all subsequent actions could take place, the space being the public realm of the *polis* and its structure the law" (*HC*, 194–95).

The insistence that founding a polis is prepolitical is surely linked to Arendt's attempt to sidestep the Machiavellian insistence "on the necessity of violence for the founding of new political bodies and for the reforming of corrupt ones," an insistence that makes Machiavelli "the ancestor of modern revolutions": "Like the Romans [but unlike Arendt's Greeks], Machiavelli and Robespierre felt founding was the central political action, the one great deed that established the public-political realm and made politics possible; but unlike the Romans, to whom this was an event of the past, they felt that for this supreme 'end' all 'means,' and chiefly the means of violence, were justified. They understood the act of founding entirely in the image of making" (*BPF*, 139).

In *The Human Condition*, Arendt wants to shift the focus of political action away from the act of founding. But in the essay just quoted she goes off onto another tack, the one she later pursues in *On Revolution*: "The American Revolution," alone among modern foundings, "has been successful: the founding fathers as, characteristically enough, we still call them, founded a completely new body politic without violence and with the help of a constitution." A few sentences later, Arendt qualifies "without violence," writing of the "relatively nonviolent character of the American Revolution, where violence was more or less restricted to regular warfare." And she mentions that "the surprising stability of [the] political structure" the founding fathers established is surely related to the relative nonviolence of this origin (*BPF*, 140). At this point, the argument begins to rely less on insulating the polis from the violence inherent in fabrication than in presenting a model of relatively nonviolent fabrication.

I cannot do justice here to the full complexity of Arendt's description of what the founding fathers achieved and how they managed to pull it off. But I want to highlight certain moments in her story. Arendt begins by noting that Machiavelli, Locke, Rousseau, Robespierre, and John Adams all are "driven to ask for divine assistance and even inspiration in legislators":

> This "recourse to God," to be sure, was necessary only in the case of "extraordinary laws," namely of laws by which a new community is founded. We shall see later that this latter part of the task of revolution, to find a new absolute to replace the absolute of divine power,

is *insoluble* because power under the condition of human plurality can never amount to omnipotence, and laws residing on human power can never be absolute. Thus Machiavelli's "appeal to high Heaven"... was not inspired by any religious feelings but exclusively dictated by the wish to escape this difficulty; by the same token, his insistence on the role of violence in politics was due not so much to his so-called realistic insight into human nature as to his futile hope that he could find some quality in certain men to match the qualities we associate with the divine. (*OR*, 39; emphasis added)

Violence, then, is the way humans attempt to become like God, imitating in violent fabrication the absolute creator. Machiavelli and Hobbes both dream of transcending factional violence by gathering all violence into a leader so fearsome that order can be secured. But Arendt has already shown in her work on totalitarianism that dreams of such omnipotence lead from violence to terror. The trick now is to find some way of establishing the body politic within an acceptance of the "conditions of plurality," that is, within the limits of human finitude.

And a trick it must be, given that Arendt deems the problem "insoluble." Against "the fictitious world" that totalitarianism tries to create and maintain through terror is poised the equally fictitious world that the American revolutionaries try to create out of words. It's a trick not just because it's all smoke and mirrors, but also because the revolutionaries themselves must be unclear about the extent to which their words lack a referent. The founding fathers offer a founding without foundations; they are bringing something new into the world, but the burden of such absolute novelty is too great. They keep appealing to past precedent; they keep dressing their novelties in the clothes of the past. The authority of the past is substituted for divine authority. Models of action and decorum come from the republican tradition (especially the Roman republic), whereas legitimation of the new rests on claims of preserving or restoring "the ancient liberties" of freeborn Englishmen. Whether Adams, Madison, or Jefferson see through their own subterfuge is unimportant. What is crucial is that their act of founding is linguistic. In J. L. Austin's terms, they use language that might appear denotative (indicating referents from the past) but is actually performative.[14]

The question is what allows the founding fathers' performative to succeed. How can we explain its being taken up by the populace as constituting an adequate foundation for a new body politic? Arendt insists that the appeals to the authority of the past could hardly have been enough, because competing interpretations of that past were readily available. Of course, the founding fathers had almost no existing institutional authority to rely upon. This is precisely the dilemma of revolutionaries: how to establish a legitimate order when the existing order labels that act of establishment as fundamentally illegitimate. And Arendt rules out, although not explicitly, Weberian charisma as playing any significant role in the American founding. Arendt offers two explanations for the founding fathers' success: nonviolence and the instrument of a constitution (*BPF*, 140).

Nonviolence must be linked directly to plurality, a link that establishes the key difference between the fictions of totalitarian terror and the fictions of the founding fathers. Arendt's definition of action invokes plurality: "Action, the only activity that goes on directly between men without the intermediary of things or matter, corresponds to the human condition of plurality" (*HC*, 7). Barring "intermediary things or matter" separates action from the violence of fabrication. What is left? The two examples of action most frequently offered are the "incessant talk" in the Athenian agora (*BPF*, 51) and virtuoso performance (see *HC*, 206, and *BPF*, 153). And, as we should expect by now, violence figures as talkative action's opposite: "Only sheer violence is mute, and for this reason violence alone can never be great" (*HC*, 26); "Marx's glorification of violence therefore contains the more specific denial of speech, the diametrically opposite and traditionally most human form of intercourse. Marx's theory of ideological superstructures ultimately rests on this anti-traditional hostility to speech and the concomitant glorification of violence" (*BPF*, 23).

The founding fathers' fiction is nonviolent because it is a speech act that acquires power only insofar as it manages to draw others into dialogue with it: "The political realm rises directly out of acting together, the 'sharing of words and deeds.' Thus action not only has the most intimate relationship to the public part of the world common to us all, but is the one activity that constitutes it. . . . [A]ction and speech create a space between the participants." Prior to any consideration of the speech act's persuasiveness comes the speech act's reliance on the auditor, its invitation to the other to listen and respond. This radical dependence on the participation of the other elicits "the space of appearances . . . where I appear to others as others appear to me" (*HC*, 198). Acceptance of plurality, of an other whose difference is a necessary component of the very possibility of my acting, is embedded within the speech act. Debate, competitive striving for distinction, and conflict are all possibilities within the space of appearances; what is not possible is violent action to obliterate the other, for such action destroys the very terms of relationship that allow self and other to come into existence. The paradox that totalitarian terror fails to recognize is that total victory in the agonistic striving with others is equivalent to total defeat, because both insure the exile of the self from the space of appearances in which the outcome of the agon matters.

The preceding two sentences make Arendt's position look fairly similar to Hegel's presentation of the master/slave dialectic. If we stress, instead, how an acknowledgment of the other is embedded in the speech act and how the speech act creates the space of appearances, Arendt looks like a forerunner of Habermas. Having offered a description of the fully creative speech act, Arendt inevitably has to distinguish it from linguistic utterances that accomplish far less: "This space does not always exist, and although all men are capable of deed and word, most of them . . . do not live in it" (*HC*, 199). Heidegger's distinction between "full speech" and "empty chatter" lives on in Arendt's need to disqualify some speech from the honorific status of "action." Arendt can seem, then, to offer a transition between Heidegger's existential version of this distinction and Habermas's more directly political version of the nonfull word in his notion of "systematically distorted speech." Certainly, Habermas's understanding of the public sphere and of the crucial distinction between violence and persuasion are indebted to Arendt's formulations: the "Greeks, living together in a polis, conducted their affairs by means of speech, through persuasion, and not by means of violence, through mute coercion" (*BPF*, 23).

The nonviolence of linguistic action links Arendt and Habermas, but in his essay "Hannah Arendt: On the Concept of Power" (1977), Habermas distances himself from the other feature of the founding fathers' speech act: the making and ratification of a constitution. He complains that "in the end [Arendt] puts more trust in the venerable figure of the contract than in her own concept of communicative praxis. So she retreats into the tradition of natural right."[15] As I will indicate, the last point is just dead wrong; there is nothing in Arendt that corresponds to "natural right." Something that looks a lot like "the contract" is present, however, in Arendt, and Habermas is right to locate it within her understanding of power. But the Arendtian contract is significantly different from that found in the classic texts—by Hobbes, Locke, Rousseau, and Kant—in the contract tradition, so we should not assimilate her to that tradition too readily.

The creation of the space of appearances out of the action between humans yields the distinctively Arendtian understanding of power, an understanding that radically separates power from violence, an understanding in which power is defined precisely to provide a counterweight to violence: "Power is what keeps the public realm, the potential space of appearances between acting and speaking men, in existence" (*HC*, 200). Power is the name for the creative side effects that attend acting. The space of appearances, like a language or a cultural practice, is "utter[ly] dependent upon further acts to keep it in existence" (*BPF*, 153). One cannot preserve a language by fiat nor even by getting it all down in a dictionary and a grammar. The language exists only insofar as people use it. It is very hard to compel use, especially to keep a language alive. In other words, it is not easy to succeed in using a language for the direct purpose of keeping it alive. Keeping a language alive is a side effect of using it for all kinds of other reasons. (On the other hand, one can kill a language by forbidding its use, a strategy that involves compelling the speaker of the forbidden language to use another one. But the continued existence of that second language will be in danger if its survival is dependent on the person who uses it under compulsion. The usual scenario in such cases, of course, is that the speaker of the forbidden language is forced to speak the language spoken by the enforcer of the edict, so compulsion in this case is not aiming at preserving a language whose existence seems threatened.)

In short, power is not easy to enact directly. To make quilts just to keep the practice alive, rather than for the myriad reasons the practice arose in the first place, rarely works. For Arendt, the very indirection of power marks its distinction from the subjective and, in particular, from anything like "will." Power, for her, has nothing to do with what a self can or may try to impose on others and the world; such unilateral action would always be violence in her terms (and, strictly speaking, would not be "action"). Power in Arendt is radically and fundamentally intersubjective, not within the control of any individual. Power denotes what happens—the space of appearances exists—so long as "the sharing of words and deeds" continues: "[P]ower cannot be stored up and kept in reserve for emergencies, like the instruments of violence, but exists only in its actualization" (*HC*, 200). No one can possess power. Power is intersubjectively produced through the activities that create a public world.

The founding fathers' words, then, are a gambit, a step into the unknown through which, by eschewing the violent eradication of opposition, they call forth the responses that will engender the political realm they are trying to create. In one sense, to avoid violence the political actor must value form more than content. To want to achieve something in particular, to desire to carry this or that point, would mean placing commitment to some good above commitment to the ongoing form within which commitments are articulated. This fear of all content as disruptive, this elevation of form over matter, makes Arendtian politics empty (the primary and recurrent complaint against her theory of the political) and marks its close connection to Kant's (and, hence, a certain modernist) aesthetic.

In another sense, however, Arendt's politics is not empty and formal at all. Her championing of a particular form is in fact the commitment to two very specific goods—relatedness and freedom—for which she argues strenuously and in a variety of ways. For starters, she argues that freedom is possible only within a polis that highlights relatedness. She also argues that these two goods, as distinct from the alleviation of poverty and other desirable ends, are the only goods that the political can successfully deliver. She also tries in various places to convince us that her chosen goods are superior to other possible goods and thus should be granted priority. (These last arguments are offered forthrightly as flying in the face of everything "modern," which values "life" above all else.) And, as we would expect, she argues that only a commitment to politics in the form she advocates can protect us from violence.

The argument from violence is, to some extent, smuggled into Arendt's work, both because it introduces a different, negative good (protection from violence) distinct from the positive goods she tries to stress, and because admitting such a benefit from the political mars her Kantian association of freedom with that which is done purely for its own sake, that is, with "purposelessness" (see *HC*, 177 and 229). But the fact that stateless persons, noncitizens, are utterly vulnerable to the violence and terror of modern states was one of the unforgettable lessons Arendt derived from her own flight from the Nazis—and she retains that conviction even where it jars with her theory. If power creates the space of appearances, it also creates whatever "rights," whatever purchase against violence, that humans have. Rights are entirely political for Arendt, not natural as Habermas supposes. To reduce "primary positive rights" from "politics to nature" was one of the great mistakes of the French Revolution, one that entails losing the awareness that rights exist only as "given and guaranteed by the body politic" (*OR*, 108). That the state can itself become a means of violence does not mean that some other source of protection should or can be found outside the political. Freedom and rights are both political creations, both products of power, and their ability to resist violence—like the ability of the space of appearances to remain in existence—is a matter of the collective action that is power. In short, freedom and rights, like the state violence they are poised against, are human through and through, with no sanction apart from the human purposes they serve and no effectiveness beyond the human power they can muster.

It is fatal, Arendt argues, to fear power, because that leaves the way clear for violence. Rather, power should be multiplied and decentralized, which explains Arendt's commitment to federalism and to the soviets and revolutionary councils that precede state formation. Within states, multiplication of the sites where power arises and sustains itself requires the separation of powers advocated by Montesquieu and practiced by the Americans:

> For Montesquieu's discovery actually concerned the nature of power, and this discovery stands in so flagrant a contradiction to all conventional notions on this matter that it has almost been forgotten, despite the fact that the foundation of the republic in America was largely inspired by it. The discovery . . . spells out the forgotten principle underlying the whole structure of separated powers: that only "power arrests power," that is, we must add, without destroying it, without putting impotence in the place of power. For power can of course be destroyed by violence; this is what happens in tyrannies, where the violence of one destroys the power of many. (*OR*, 151)

The power of many, flowing from the plurality of interactions among the plurality of actors, is the only bulwark against the violence of the one, with its dreams of an absolute and divine omnipotence.

But why a constitution? What is this "trust" that Habermas claims Arendt places in the contract? As far as trust goes, I read Arendt as a thoroughgoing pragmatist. The rights articulated in a bill of rights, or the claims advanced by Habermasian speakers on the basis of universal norms implicit in the speech situation, are worth only what others in the polity here and now are willing to make them worth—no more, no less. Constitutional traditions, like normative ones or canons of reasonable argumentation or of established precedents for legitimate claims, are not insignificant; they all influence greatly decisions and actions made in the present. But none of these things guarantees anything; none of them has a status that, once and for all, allows it to trump positions justified in relation to other considerations. In other words, claims to ethnic superiority or to religious righteousness have, as a matter of fact, the same potential for garnering agreement as claims made in the name of norms that favor persuasion over force, inclusiveness over exclusiveness. The state, as a product of political activity, is open to capture by a "many" that is hardly every one. In fact, given plurality, it would be surprising if the "many" whose actions sustain the state were anything close to the whole population living within the state's geographic boundaries. It is precisely for this reason that the proliferation of associations, of power sites involving different groups, is crucial, just as it is crucial that selves participate in more than one of these associations. There is no safeguard against tyranny, violence, and totalitarianism except relatedness, the embodiment of plurality in as many political, institutional settings as possible. Citizenship is the mark of relatedness on the level of the state; outside citizenship, the individual is especially vulnerable to violence. Power emanates from each site of relatedness—the power that can arrest power—but twentieth-century totalitarianism shows that such power can be destroyed by "force, which indeed one man alone can exert against his fellow men and of which one or a few can possess a monopoly by acquiring the means of violence" (HC, 202).

Power "dependent upon the unreliable and only temporary agreement of many wills and intentions" (HC, 201) may seem a slim reed against the force that utilizes violence, but Arendt insists that it is all we've got. The reference to "agreement" here seems to place her firmly on the ground of contract. Furthermore, her discussion of the Mayflower Compact and of the U.S. Constitution in On Revolution specifically invokes the notion of a "mutual contract by which people bind themselves together in order to form a community . . . based on reciprocity and presuppos[ing] equality" (OR, 170). Founding is nonviolent when a presumption of equality among all the possible members of the polity leads to a call for the participation of those members in the endorsement of the linguistic act or document that establishes their relatedness. Habermas insists that we need a "standard of criticism" that is beyond or outside the agreement itself, and he sees, correctly, that "this possibility is just what Arendt disputes."[16] Habermas wants a standard by which to judge the terms of the established relatedness, whereas Arendt tells us that our only safeguard against violence and evil is the fact of the relatedness itself. We live and judge not by standards but by the commitments and affections and "goodwill" that relatedness engenders. This may not be much, but it is all we have. What makes us think there could be anything more—or that this something more would be effective where affection and goodwill are lacking? "If morality is more than the sum total of *mores*, of customs and standards of behavior solidified through tradition and valid on the ground of agreements, both of which change with time, it has, at least politically, no more to support itself than the good will to counter the enormous risks of action by readiness to forgive and be forgiven, to make promises and to keep them" (*HC*, 245).

Promises and forgiveness are the hallmarks of the Arendtian contract—and indicate its distance from the contracts found in the classic authors of that tradition. The classic contract involves an exchange of freedom for security, emphasizes consent, and (at least in Locke and Kant) considers legitimate grounds for deeming the contract violated. Arendt takes some pains to explain her version of the contract as a "mutual promise," which is distinct from "consent" (see *OR*, 170–71). Furthermore, her contract is motivated not by the desire to attain security but by an attempt to enable action, which is risky and does not take life as the highest good; hence "courage" is the requisite virtue for existence within the political (see *BPF*, 156). Given her understanding of action, the contract in Arendt is not an exchange of anything for anything, and it is certainly not something to which we consent only so long as we receive benefits stipulated in advance. Because action is spontaneous and because it constitutes the way that something new comes into the world, Arendt's contract does not provide protection and the negative liberty of rights, but instead creates the public space in which the new can emerge. Thus, the better image for the agreement that Arendt has in mind is a "mutual promise" and not a "contract." The contract's "actual content is a promise, and its result is indeed a 'society' or 'cosociation' in the old Roman sense of *societas*, which means alliance. Such an alliance gathers together the isolated strength of the allied partners and binds them into a new power structure by virtue of 'free and sincere promises'" (*OR*, 170). It is this "act" to which Arendt wants to call our attention in praising the U.S. Constitution, by which she refers less to the "written document" than to "the constituting act, 'antecedent to government,' by which a people constitutes itself into a body politic." What is remarkable about the American experience, as Arendt interprets it, is that the founding fathers offered "solely the act itself" (*OR*, 203), sending it out naked into the world, unsupported by the violence that usually accompanies attempts at founding, and that act proved capable on its own of calling a polity into existence. That act was not the offer of a bargain, not a contracting to give this in exchange for that, but a call to establish relatedness through mutual promises:

> Power comes into being only if and when men join themselves together for the purpose of action, and it will disappear when, for whatever reason, they disperse and desert one another. Hence, binding and promising, combining and covenanting, are the means by which power is kept in existence; when and where men succeed in keeping intact the power which sprang up between them during the course of any particular act or deed, they are already in the process of foundation, of constituting a stable worldly structure to house, as it were, their combined power of action. There is an element of the world-building capacity of man in the human faculty of making and keeping promises. . . . The grammar of action: that action is the only human faculty that demands a plurality of men; and the syntax of power: that power is the only human attribute which applies solely to the worldly in-between space by which men are mutually related, combine in the act of foundation by virtue of the making and keeping of promises, which, in the realm of politics, may well be the highest human faculty. (*OR*, 175)

Crucially, these promises are excessive, extravagant. Arendt's politics appear distopian insofar as she repudiates the dreams of social and economic justice that have motivated most radical politics of the past two hundred years. But, in her own terms, her politics are profoundly utopian in that she calls for the creation of a space beyond and apart from need, a space that to a certain extent defies the facts of necessity through the performance of an alternative mode of existence, the mode of action. Whereas the liberal contract secures life and property, the Arendtian contract resolutely turns its back on material goods and creates a purely human realm in which all that matters is the relation among people. The very extravagance of the promises involved here, the fragility of the attempt to turn our backs (even for a little while) on necessity, requires Arendt's pairing of "forgiveness" with promises. If the contract she imagines were to reside in a legal world where issues of the fulfillment of its letter dominated, the political realm would quickly disappear. If humans try to overcome unpredictability by offering each other promises, forgiveness must embody our awareness that human action can never fully succeed in such an effort. Promises are hubristic; they strive to create a world answerable to human desires under the eyes of that jealous god, necessity (*Ananke*).

Thus, forgiveness is human too, not divine as the adage claims. Forgiveness, the opposite of vengeance, is, like the promise, a performative in J. L. Austin's sense of that term. Unlike violent revenge, forgiveness is also an act in Arendt's terms because it sustains the relationship initially established by the promise. Forgiveness affirms the effort to keep a space of human relatedness open, whereas vengeance shuts down that space, repudiates the relation to the other. In short, the contract theorists envisioned a wary peace—secured by legal means of redress—between individuals who mostly want to be left alone to pursue their own ends. Arendt envisions an excessive, even foolhardy, binding of humans together by acts of promising and forgiving that sacrifice almost everything (including security and property) for the sake of relatedness. The realm created by "mutual promises" offers no guarantees, beyond its simply existing, that violence will not overwhelm it and the lives of those who are related through it. All it offers is the one space where relations are not relations of violence. Only humans who value this nonviolent, political space have the power to keep it open through their continuing acts of promising and forgiving.

It is fair to say, then, that necessity is the realm of violence in Arendt, and freedom (which always begins as freedom from necessity) is found only in the realm of nonviolence. The equation is most simply expressed when she says of "the people" in revolutionary France, "their need was violent" (*OR*, 91). The discussion of the relation between violence and historical necessity in *On Revolution* is fascinating because, in anatomizing a confusion she finds prevalent in all political thought since Hegel, Arendt seems blind to her own slightly different elision of the two terms. Violence, Arendt tells us, would seem to be required precisely when an outcome is in doubt. Only if we act violently, we tell ourselves, can we achieve this end. Thus, violence would be linked to contingency; unless we act violently, this will not happen. To be paradoxical about it, contingency would necessitate violence. But the responsibility for violence is too great to bear (except, perhaps, in the perplexing case of radical evil). Violence is always justified after the fact by an appeal to necessity; we *had* to act violently, given the circumstances. Thus, in systems such as Hegel's and Marx's, violence ends up being folded back into necessity, which then yields a final paradox: if necessity admits of only one option, why act violently (or in any other way), because necessity will bring about the only possible result by itself?

True, Arendt's absolute severing of action from necessity does not lead her into the paradoxical quietism that could result from stressing the fatalistic strains in Hegel and Marx. But if we consider violence, not action, then Arendt does mix violence inextricably with necessity in exactly the way that leaves the most crucial question begging. Arendt faults Marx for "persuading [the poor] that poverty itself is a political, not a natural phenomenon, the result of violence and violation rather than of scarcity." As a result, he encourages a kind of false consciousness about "their daily needs and wants, the force, in other words, with which necessity drives and compels men and which is more compelling than violence" (*OR*, 63).[17] But Arendt simply makes Marx's error in reverse: she makes poverty all natural, whereas he made it all political. Arendt's peculiarity is how much she deems nonpolitical; the very fact that she places so many human concerns within the realm of the necessary means that she cannot simply say we should ignore those concerns because we cannot change them. Instead, she has to say that those concerns are a source of continual and unending struggle as we try to wrest life from necessity. We are compelled to such violence all the time, but she is determined to shelter the political from violence's omnipresence.

I am not advocating that we should—or could expect to—figure out once and for all what is natural (inevitable, unchangeable) and what political (amenable to human action). But we should recognize that we make decisions all the time about what is best addressed by collective action and what is best left alone. Where we draw that line—what we relegate to the category of the necessary—will be where we draw the boundaries of the political, what we deem can be acted upon effectively by humans. Arendt's understanding of action as performative speech clashes with her tendency to advance her argument via definition. Again and again she tells us what "properly" belongs to the political and what "properly" belongs to the prepolitical or the nonpolitical.[18] Despite all her emphasis on the dynamism of action, what she never considers is that the boundaries of the political itself shift according to speech acts that define those boundaries. Yet it follows fairly straightforwardly from her own conception of power that the "space of appearances" will include and exclude different considerations at different times in response to the interactions which constitute that space. Contestation cannot be limited in advance, by definition. Words and actions will set the parameters of the public sphere in ways that cannot be predicted. The only limit point is where relatedness ends and civil war begins.

Arendt appears to half recognize this; in some ways, she presents Marx as a powerful storyteller, one who has altered the modern understanding of the political.[19] As a new storyteller, she can contest his story only by offering another one and, like him, throwing herself upon an audience she strives to persuade. In this mode she argues mostly from consequences; Marx's views lead to violence, both because he glorifies violence as the epitome of political action and because he has the revolutionary promise what cannot be delivered. We get better results from a different version of the political. But juxtaposed to this way of seeing that different ways of constituting the political are possible is Arendt's tendency to declare simply that views other than her own are wrong, because they are based on a failure to grasp the actual nature of the political, of action, of power, and the like. Arendt's stress on the need for a stable backdrop against which the agonistic competition for distinction is played out leads her to withdraw the constitution of the polity from the contestation that otherwise marks the political for her. She seems to believe that only the existence of that firm agreement which creates "cosociation" keeps the rest of the competition nonviolent; where contestation includes the constituting agreement itself, the threat of violent confrontation is too close.

So where does this leave violence between humans? As we have seen, Arendt explains that violence as some humans wresting freedom from necessity by making other humans bear the burden of life for them. With the advent of improved technologies of production, the modern world might be able to move beyond this kind of interhuman violence (see *OR*, 114). Hence, the solution to the violence done to the poor is technological, not political. One problem, of course, is that poverty amidst plenty is hard to explain as anything but political—the Marxian point that Arendt seems to miss or to sidestep in her claims that "social" issues cannot "be solved by political means, [but are] . . . matters of administration, to be put into the hands of experts" (*OR*, 91).

Another problem is that, although in *On Revolution* she appears to forget this fact, Arendt herself, in *The Origins of Totalitarianism*, had examined interhuman violence that has nothing to do with the means of securing life. What is oddly missing in Arendt's discussion of revolutions is the fact that certain groups oppose—and oppose violently—the coming together of another group to form the space of the political. If power is the constitution and maintenance of the political realm, then humans can be seen to struggle violently about which political associations are allowed to come into being and to continue to exist. The totalitarian urge—supported by its accompanying terror—is to deny existence to all associations except one. But violence can arise anywhere and anytime if any particular association is fought by another group.

This kind of political violence—violence not referable to necessity but to the struggle between different groups—is the topic of "On Violence," the meditation sparked by the student and civil rights activism of the sixties. This essay's version of violence is quite distinct from the violence of totalitarian terror, but the violence it discusses is clearly political. Arendt treats violence as a means in this text, a means always in need of justification and always justified by appeals to necessity: "Violence is by nature instrumental; like all means, it always stands in need of guidance and justification through the end it pursues" (*OV*, 150). (This sentence is a good example of Arendt's definitional mode, theorizing by fiat.) It makes sense to see that act of justification as a performative whose success depends on convincing one's interlocutors that violence really was necessary. There is not some discernible fact of the matter here. Rather, there are a set of circumstances and the explanation offered for what was done in those circumstances, and the plausibility of that explanation depends on the judgment of the audience. There is no a priori moral calculus here, so it is not surprising that judgment comes to occupy Arendt's attention more and more in her later work.

Besides bringing judgment to the forefront, treating violence as a means sometimes necessitated by circumstances (although the burden of persuasion always lies with the violent agent) has the crucial consequence of erasing the strict boundary between the nonpolitical as violent and the political as nonviolent in Arendt's work from 1952 to 1964. Although she retains her strict definitional distinction between power and violence—a distinction that places her at odds with almost everything written on the topic (OV, 136)—Arendt tells us that "nothing . . . is more common than the combination of violence and power, nothing less frequent than to find them in their pure and therefore extreme form" (OV, 145–46). Such a statement appears to reverse much of her earlier work—or, as I have suggested, indicates that the earlier work so radically separates violence from the political and from power precisely to present an alternative, even utopian, politics to pose against actual conditions. Even though violence and power are almost always combined in the world as we find it, they "are opposites; where the one rules absolutely, the other is absent" (OV, 155). Why, then, do they usually appear together?

Arendt's thesis in "On Violence" is that violence is a symptom of weakness. "Violence appears where power is in jeopardy" (OV, 155). Violence is the attempt to impose the communal conditions of relatedness when their maintenance by power is no longer succeeding. (This violence is not like terror, which tries to destroy relatedness altogether, but is an alternative means for achieving the ends Arendt associates with power. Hence, violence is power's "opposite" only in relation to means, not to ends, whereas terror is power's opposite both in ends and in means.) At such moments violence can be expected to appear on both sides of the conflict between the weak, constituted (legal) powers and those who (for whatever reasons) deem or position themselves outside the constituted powers. The government's recourse to violence marks those places where its promises fail to bind citizens to its distinctive way of constructing the political realm; the citizens' violence marks their lacking enough power to constitute a new political realm vis-à-vis the one now in place. For this reason Arendt argues that "violence, contrary to what its prophets try to tell us, is more the weapon of reform than of revolution." Violence in this case "can serve to dramatize grievances and bring them to public attention" (OV, 176), especially when that attention has not been gained through any more-sanctioned channels. Political violence, then, marks the place where government tries to deny access and citizens try to gain it within a society in which neither faction can constitute a polity by itself. Because nonviolent civil disobedience requires "organized minorities, bound together by common opinion" whose "concerted action springs from an agreement with each other," Arendt finds such action potentially more revolutionary than violent demonstrations.[20] The experience of civil disobedience gives its participants a taste of power, of the constitution of a group that then acts together. This turning inward toward the interrelations among the group's members, as distinct from a violence directed toward grabbing the attention of the powers that be, marks the difference for Arendt, although, of course, she realizes that civil disobedience also begins with a desire to "dramatize grievances."

Arendt argues in "On Violence" that civil violence has both specific causes (racism and the war in Vietnam) and structural causes. The latter, as we might expect, involve the disappearance in modern societies of the sites of political participation, the sites of power. Modern societies are rife with the kinds of weakness that generate violence because they do not proliferate power in the way Montesquieu recommended. The sign of the disappearance of power is the growth of government and of bureaucracy. As governments become bigger, more complex, and more hermetically sealed within their own processes, "the channels for action, for the meaningful exercise of freedom" shut down: "The greater the bureaucratization of public life, the greater the attraction of violence" (OV, 178). Arendt insists that this is not merely a question of access to the bureaucracy or to interest groups' having to resort to violence to get a hearing. In addition, there is the lack of public spaces in modern life where one can be free and can act in concert with others. "Voluntary associations have been the specifically American remedy for the failure of institutions" (CD, 102), but "the disastrous shrinkage of the public realm" (OV, 178) has caused an almost complete collective amnesia about that remedy. Like the revolutionaries discussed in "The Revolutionary Tradition and Its Lost Treasure" (OR, 215–81), the American student protesters have to a certain extent— and ignorant of all prior historical examples of this phenomenon— rediscovered the secret of power, the joy of "acting together in a way that they rarely can" (OV, 180). But the iron cage of modern bureaucratization, the colossus of the modern state, overwhelms the students as it did the soviets and the revolutionary councils formed in 1956 Hungary: "Monopolization of power causes the drying up or oozing away of all authentic power sources in the country" (OV, 182), and "every decrease in power is an open invitation to violence—if only because those who hold power and feel it slipping from their hands, be they government or be they governed, have always found it difficult to resist the temptation to substitute violence for it" (OV, 184).

Violence here is political through and through, insofar as it aims for political ends—for the ability to participate in the constitution and in the ongoing activities of the space of appearances, the only space in which freedom is possible. The intermingling of violence and power in this text undoes Arendt's earlier linking of violence to labor and fabrication and hence to the prepolitical in distinction to power: "Neither violence nor power is a natural phenomenon, that is, a manifestation of the life process; they belong to the political realm of human affairs whose essentially human quality is guaranteed by man's faculty of action, the ability to begin something new" (OV, 179). Violence is now presented as a flawed form of action but a form of action nonetheless. After Arendt's persistent efforts to tie violence entirely to necessity, this late text admits—as did *The Origins of Totalitarianism*—that there is a violence done by humans to humans that exceeds necessity, just as political action exceeds necessity.

The source of that violence can, in some cases, be tied again to necessity by seeing the violent group as aiming to divert the power of the political toward the attainment of some specific goal, some "interest" of an economic or other sort. But the source of violence can also be disinterested, in Arendt's understanding of that term; either it can be the sign of a struggle to create the space of appearances in a conflictual situation in which no group has enough power to make its performative constitutive act acquire the authority needed to succeed, or it can be a sign of the sheer refusal of relatedness to this or that other. In this last case, violence is a sign not so much of weakness as of sheer cussedness, of radical evil: "[W]e can neither punish nor forgive such offenses [of radical evil]. . . . [T]hey therefore transcend the realm of human affairs and the potentialities of human power, both of which they radically destroy wherever they make their appearance" (*HC*, 241). If the political is the human construct that attempts to create a nonviolent space of relatedness, then that construction is utopian, because some trace of violence commonly appears within the realm of power and because no permanent inoculation against a nonnecessary violence that is human, all too human, is forthcoming.

That Arendt herself recognized that her vision of a nonviolent founding of America (as presented in *On Revolution*) was more an exemplary fable than another triumphant insistence on American exceptionalism is suggested by the brief meditation she published in the *New York Times Magazine* in response to the question Is America by nature a violent society?[21] Reminding her readers "that American society is artificial 'by nature,'" Arendt locates within the American polity both forms of political violence that I have found in her work. Radical evil in America takes the form of racism, the persistence of which offers the major reason to be pessimistic about American political reality: "The factor of racism is the only one with respect to which one could speak of a strain of violence so deeply rooted in American society as to appear to be 'natural.' 'Racial violence was present almost from the beginning,' the splendid Report on Civil Disorders has put it." And this racism generates another violence: the violence of the impotent, which figures so largely in "On Violence." Interestingly, however, at this point another source of violence enters. "[R]acism," Arendt tells us, "always insists on absolute superiority over all others. Hence, racism is humiliating 'by nature,' and humiliation breeds even more violence than sheer impotence." Here, in the only instance I know of in Arendt's work, the suggestion is made that inequality itself—as contrasted to the ideal equality of the participants who, acting in concert, create the space of appearances—can generate violence. Impotence, of course, is a kind of inequality, but impotence can have a variety of causes. In pointing toward humiliation, Arendt appears to be thinking about an inequality that results from being deemed categorically unfit for full and equal participation with others. The novelty of this concern in her work reminds us that she has not understood totalitarian anti-Semitism in this way; she has elaborately read anti-Semitism as symptomatic of an assault on citizenship, the assault that renders all individuals (not just the individuals belonging to a specific group) superfluous. Faced now with an American society that is selectively dismissive of individuals, Arendt points here toward the issues of differentiation and inequality that commentators have often felt are inadequately addressed in her work.[22]

Arendt's attention to the multiple causes of violence, to the mixture of violence with power, and generally to the violence within the political in those works where she focuses on human political and nonpolitical activity in the twentieth century highlights, in my view, the extent to which we should take the theoretical works of the middle period as offering an idealized, utopian vision of the political. The stringent separation of violence from politics in those middle works enables the extended descriptions of the nonviolent foundation of the polis in intersubjective promises, of the agonal yet peaceful actions within that polis, and of the requisite virtues required to foster that polis: courage, goodwill, the ability to make promises, and the ability to forgive those whose promises are not fulfilled. In a polis thus constituted, not only necessity but also evil itself is, at least temporarily, in abeyance. Freedom reigns undisturbed, albeit circumscribed.

Arendt's utopian vision is itself a judgment of the present. But her thoughts on violence can also be seen to raise issues about the conditions in which judgments can and must be made. Walter Benjamin wrote that the question of violence always "bears on moral issues,"[23] a sentiment Arendt echoes when she tells us that violence always stands in need of justification. The difficulties of making judgments cannot be sidestepped by definitional categorizations. Kant's and Arendt's and our own interest in judgment stems from the experience of confronting particulars in which elements are "mixed" in ways that render pre-existing categories inadequate. Arendt's last work on judgment veers, in my view, more toward her performative side, recognizing that politics as we experience and live it has continually to be made anew, because the definitions, solutions, and institutions of the past do not fully serve our perceptions and needs in the present. This fact that the definition of the political constantly changes does not get us off the hook of having to produce such definitions. Judgments in Arendt take a firm, if fallible, stand.

Two things in Arendt's middle work seem to me particularly relevant to this ongoing work of judgment. Her utopian vision highlights the extent to which judgments are guided by visions of what is desirable; it helps to imagine what we want in order to judge what we encounter. And her insistence on necessity and on evil highlights the extent to which judgments have to decide what is possible. Even abstracted from her particular judgments about modernity, Arendt's middle work suggests that all judgments take place in the context of crucial commitments to certain ends and to a certain take on human possibility. Violence holds a central place in our political thought (which, for Arendt, is our thought about human action) precisely because it represents what many images of the desirable aspire to avoid and because it represents the resistant, even the intractable, in the world and in ourselves with which action has to contend.

Notes

This essay incorporates (through both inclusion and excision) reactions to an earlier version that were offered by Richard Bernstein, Susan Bickford, Craig Calhoun, Lisa Disch, Joe Gerteis, Steve Leonard, Jim Moody, and Jeff Weintraub. I plead their indulgence for not having identified individually each place where they influenced my thinking and each insight I have gratefully appropriated.

1. See Martin Jay, "The Political Existentialism of Hannah Arendt," in *Permanent Exiles* (New York: Columbia University Press, 1985), 237–56, for a useful (and dissenting) overview of Arendt's narrow version of the political. Jay also devotes several pages to violence in Arendt. "In [Arendt's] lexicon," Jay writes, "violence is understood as inherently nonpolitical because of its instrumental character" (247), but he concludes that "the watertight separation between violence and politics proves in the end to be porous" (249). I think Arendt's seeming contradictions become less debilitating if we distinguish between the theoretical (utopian and exemplary) middle works and those works, such as *The Origins of Totalitarianism* and "On Violence," that offer analyses of twentieth-century political experience. Admittedly, this distinction is hardly airtight itself. The Arendtian distinction that has most exercised her commentators is the one between politics and the social. Thus, even a writer as sympathetic to Arendt as Richard Bernstein, in *Beyond Objectivism and Relativism: Science, Hermeneutics, and Praxis* (Philadelphia: University of Pennsylvania Press, 1983), insists "that the 'social' and the 'political' are much more intimately interrelated than Arendt at times leads us to think" (213).

2. Margaret Canovan, in *Hannah Arendt: A Reinterpretation of Her Political Thought* (Cambridge: Cambridge University Press, 1992), premises her "reinterpretation" of Arendt's work on the insistence that "virtually the entire agenda of Arendt's political thought was set by her reflections on the political catastrophes of the mid-century" (7).

3. Hannah Arendt, *The Origins of Totalitarianism* (New York: Meridian Books, 1958); all quotations from this work are marked by the abbreviation *OT*.

4. In "On Violence," in *Crises of the Republic* (New York: Harcourt Brace Jovanovich, 1972), Arendt writes: "Violence is by nature instrumental; like all means, it always stands in need of guidance and justification" (150). Subsequent references to "On Violence" are marked by the abbreviation *OV*.

5. See Elaine Scarry, *The Body in Pain* (New York: Oxford University Press, 1985).

6. I should not be so bleak here. It would be more accurate to say that Arendt has nothing *but* human agency to poise against the totalitarian—a human agency that appears next to impotent but is all that we have. Such agency is "miraculous," inexplicable, and individual, a witness to plurality and to human potential. Arendt's *Men in Dark Times* (New York: Harcourt Brace Jovanovich, 1968) considers a number of examples, but the most striking example in Arendt's work is Anton Schmidt, the German sergeant who is counterbalanced with Eichmann in her *Eichmann in Jerusalem* (New York: Penguin Books, 1977). Arendt makes two comments about Schmidt's actions to save Jews from the Nazis: "How utterly different everything would be today in this courtroom, in Israel, in Germany, in all of Europe . . . if only more such stories could have been told" (231); and "[Schmidt's story indicates] that under conditions of terror most people will comply but *some people will not*. . . . Humanly speaking, no more is required, and no more can be reasonably asked, for this planet to remain a place fit for

human habitation" (233). Subsequent references to *Eichmann in Jerusalem* are abbreviated *EJ*.

7. See Richard Bernstein's essay in this volume for a fuller account of Arendt's connection of totalitarianism with the rendering of individuals superfluous.

8. See Hannah Arendt, *The Human Condition* (Chicago: University of Chicago Press, 1958), especially 199–207. Subsequent references to this work are marked by the abbreviation *HC*.

9. For Arendt's rather mysterious notion of "principle," see her *Between Past and Future* (New York: Penguin Books, 1977), 152–54. Subsequent references to this work are marked by the abbreviation *BPF*.

10. Kimberley Curtis puts this point extremely well in her essay in this volume. "[A]esthetic provocation under conditions of plurality," she writes, "is far from secure" in Arendt's work, because "although it is a feature of ourselves as appearing beings that, Arendt believes, can never be conditioned away absolutely, its effective force in our lives is extremely mutable, subject to varying conditions, institutions, sensibilities, practices."

11. I have discussed the notion of recognition at some length in *Postmodernism and Its Critics* (Ithaca: Cornell University Press, 1991), 217–23. See also the essays collected in Charles Taylor et al., *Multiculturalism and "The Politics of Recognition"* (Princeton: Princeton University Press, 1992).

12. Hannah Arendt, *On Revolution* (New York: Penguin Books, 1977), 84. Subsequent references to this work are marked by the abbreviation *OR*.

13. See Albert O. Hirschman, *The Rhetoric of Reaction* (Cambridge: Harvard University Press, 1991).

14. J. L. Austin, "Performative Utterances," in *Philosophical Papers* (Oxford: Oxford University Press, 1961), describes a performative as "a kind of utterance which looks like a statement . . . and yet is not true or false. . . . Furthermore, if a person makes an utterance of this sort we should say that he is *doing* something rather than merely *saying* something. . . . [I]n saying what I do, I actually perform the action. When I say, 'I name this ship the *Queen Elizabeth*,' I do not describe the christening ceremony, I actually perform the christening" (235). Bonnie Honig, *Political Theory and the Displacement of Politics* (Ithaca: Cornell University Press, 1993), chap. 4, and Frederick M. Dolan, *Allegories of America* (Ithaca: Cornell University Press, 1994), chaps. 1 and 5, offer extensive discussions of the performative in Arendt, and my comments here are indebted to their work.

15. Jürgen Habermas, "Hannah Arendt: On the Concept of Power," in *Philosophical-Political Profiles* (Cambridge: MIT Press, 1983), 185. Habermas later evidences a much more favorable view of constitutions, although he still ties them to universal principles, not local agreements. In 1984 (seven years after the initial publication of the essay on Arendt), Habermas states in an interview: "Of course I also think that such transformations of political institutions should only be carried out in light of the constitutional principles recognized today—by drawing on the universalist content of those principles. The whole wretchedness of so-called actually existing socialism can basically be traced back to a reckless disdain for the principles of the constitutional state" (Peter Dews, ed., *Habermas: Autonomy and Solidarity* [London: Verso, 1986], 186).

16. Habermas, "Hannah Arendt," 184.

17. In focusing on the connection between violence and necessity in Marx (as Arendt portrays his thought), I have not adequately differentiated the violence of those revolutions that emphasize the "social question" from the violence of a totalitarian revolution, which focuses on creating a fictitious world that obliterates plurality. *On Revolution* shows that the two are not the same for Arendt; a discussion of the distinction would

have to begin with a consideration of why Arendt believes "compassion," although it is perfectly understandable and even admirable, is so disastrous politically. Thus, the sources, motives, and goals of a violence connected to the effort to alleviate poverty (not properly a political violence at all for Arendt) are quite different from the sources of totalitarian violence. What is less clear is whether Arendt believes the results of these two violences are much different, that is, whether she believes terror, finally, comes in only one form.

18. If I may be allowed an overstatement for dramatic effect, one gulf between contemporary intellectual discourse and Arendt's discourse stems from Arendt's belief that the very existence of the political is dependent on a strict understanding of its proper content, compared to our understanding of the political as a process that can be understood apart from its subject matter and that can be put into action no matter what the particular concern. In other words, for us anything is potentially political.

19. On the theme of storytelling in Arendt, see Seyla Benhabib, "Hannah Arendt and the Redemptive Power of Narrative," and David Luban, "Explaining Dark Times: Hannah Arendt's Theory of Theory," both in *Hannah Arendt: Critical Essays,* ed. Lewis P. Hinchman and Sandra K. Hinchman (Albany: State University of New York Press, 1994), 111–37 and 79–109. See also Lisa Disch, "More Truth than Fact: Storytelling as Critical Understanding in the Writing of Hannah Arendt," *Political Theory* 21, no. 4 (1993): 665–94. Their work has influenced my reading of Arendt's middle works as exemplary fable more than historical analysis. On the distinction between "exemplary truth" and the truth associated with "factual statements," as well as the conclusion that "this teaching by example is, indeed, the only form of 'persuasion' that philosophical truth is capable of without perversion or distortion," see *BPF,* 247–49.

20. Hannah Arendt, "Civil Disobedience," in *Crises of the Republic,* 56; see also 76–77. Subsequent references are marked by the abbreviation *CD.*

21. All quoted passages in this paragraph are from Hannah Arendt, "Is America by Nature a Violent Society?" *New York Times Magazine,* April 28, 1968, 24. My thanks to Richard Bernstein for calling this article to my attention.

22. Thus Susan Bickford, in *The Dissonance of Democracy: Listening, Conflict, and Citizenship* (Ithaca: Cornell University Press, 1996), writes that Arendt, like Aristotle, fails to "investigate the forces that screen political attention, deflecting it from some voices and opinions, focusing it on others" (118). All actions in the public sphere do not have the same impact, and a theory of the political would do well to attend to these differences and the "forces" that cause them.

23. Walter Benjamin, "Critique of Violence," in *Reflections* (New York: Schocken Books, 1986), 277.

Eleven

"The Banality of Evil" Reconsidered

Richard J. Bernstein

On February 16, 1963, the first installment of Hannah Arendt's five-part report on the Eichmann trial was published in the *New Yorker*. Following the *New Yorker's* policy, the series was entitled "A Reporter at Large: Eichmann in Jerusalem." But even before the installments began to appear, they had created a scandal. It was rumored that Arendt exonerated Eichmann and blamed the Jews for their own extermination. She was anti-Zionist and anti-Semitic. She was "soulless," "malicious," "arrogant," and "flippant." She distorted the facts. She trivialized the entire Holocaust with her catchword "the banality of evil." There were those who accused her of making Eichmann seem much more attractive than the Jews that he murdered. Arendt was attacked, threatened, vilified, and excoriated. Some of her closest friends "broke" with her. The Eichmann controversy raged for years. Even today, more than thirty years after the appearance of *Eichmann in Jerusalem: A Report on the Banality of Evil*, there are those who cannot forgive her for what she wrote.[1]

I want to clarify my intentions for reexamining Hannah Arendt's report and her understanding of the banality of evil. I am not concerned with putting Hannah Arendt on trial nor with condemning or exonerating her. I want to understand what she is saying and why. I want to follow some of the basic "thought-trains" that arose from her encounter with Eichmann in Jerusalem. There is a great deal that can be legitimately criticized about her book—both what she says and how she says it. One of the central themes in Arendt's writing is the inescapability of personal responsibility. I believe Arendt herself bears some of the responsibility for how her book was read and why it caused so much pain and anguish.

I also believe that the reason Arendt's report is so troubling is that it compels us to face up to painful questions about the meaning of evil in the contemporary world, the moral collapse of respectable society, the ease with which mass killing becomes "normal" acceptable behavior, the feebleness of the so-called voice of conscience, and the subtle forms of complicity and cooperation that "go along" with murderous deeds. These, unfortunately, are not issues restricted to Nazi horrors. They are still with us, and they demand that we struggle with them again and again.

Arendt constantly stresses how the unprecedented event of twentieth-century totalitarianism has ruptured our traditional moral and political concepts and standards. These are no longer adequate for understanding or comprehending what has happened. In the preface to *The Origins of Totalitarianism*, she writes: "Comprehension does not mean denying the outrageous, deducing the unprecedented from precedents, or explaining phenomena by such analogies and generalities that the impact of reality and the shock of experience are no longer felt. It means, rather, examining and bearing consciously the burden which our century has placed on us—neither denying its existence nor submitting meekly to its weight. Comprehension, in short, means the unpremeditated, attentive facing up to, and resisting of, reality—whatever it may be."[2] This drive for comprehension—even when what we encounter appears to be thoroughly incomprehensible—underlies *Eichmann in Jerusalem*.

It is important to remember that although Arendt was critical—even scornful—of the chief prosecutor, Gideon Hauser, and the case he presented, she expressed the highest admiration for the three judges who tried the case against Eichmann. She completely endorsed their judgment concerning Eichmann's responsibility. She writes: "What the judgment had to say on this point was more than correct, it was the truth." She cites the following passage from their judgment:

> "In such an enormous and complicated crime as the one we are now considering, wherein many people participated, on various levels and

in various modes of activity—the planners, the organizers, and those executing the deeds, according to their various ranks—there is not much point in using the ordinary concepts of counseling and soliciting to commit a crime. For these crimes were committed en masse, not only in regard to the number of victims, but also in regard to the numbers of those who perpetuated the crime, and the extent to which any one of the many criminals was close to or remote from the actual killer of the victim means nothing, as far as the measure of his responsibility is concerned. On the contrary, in general *the degree of responsibility increases as we draw further away from the man who uses the fatal instrument with his own hands."*[3]

This is one of the main points that Arendt emphasizes throughout her report. She did not think that the prosecution had proved "beyond a reasonable doubt" that Eichmann had committed an overt act of murder with "his own hands." She strongly objected to what she took to be the prosecutor's melodramatic attempt to demonize Eichmann, to portray him as a "sadistic monster" who was possessed by an "insane hatred of the Jews." By relying on such conventional categories, the prosecutor (unlike the judges) obscured the character of this "desk criminal" and his crimes. Eichmann was neither "perverted nor sadistic." He was "terrifyingly normal." Eichmann was a "new type of criminal, who is in actual fact *hostis generis humani*, [and who] commits his crimes under circumstances that make it well-nigh impossible for him to know or to feel that he is doing wrong" (*EJ*, 276). This is what Arendt thought was so unprecedented and what needed to be squarely confronted in order to understand Eichmann's deeds and responsibility. As Arendt tells us, "That Eichmann had at all times done his best to make the Final Solution final was therefore not in dispute. The question was only whether this was indeed proof of his fanaticism, his boundless hatred of Jews, and whether he had lied to the police and committed perjury in court when he claimed he had always obeyed orders" (*EJ*, 146).

But if it is true, as I will argue, that Arendt's judgment of Eichmann is far more damning than the "monster" that the prosecutor portrayed, why was Arendt so severely and bitterly attacked? Many of her critics claimed that her report was filled with factual errors—errors so egregious that they undermined her claims and judgments. But this was not the main reason for the scandal. In his open letter to Arendt, Gershom Scholem spoke for many when he questioned the tone of her book. Scholem accused her of being "malicious" and "flippant." She lacked any sense of love for her people and lacked "*Herz-enstadt*" in dealing with the sufferings of the Jewish people. He also questioned her account of the role of the Judenräte, the Jewish councils appointed by the Nazis to organize Jewish communities and to carry out Nazi directives. This was the part of her report that caused the greatest uproar—especially among the Jewish community. Scholem claimed that Arendt was guilty of "a kind of demagogic will-to-overstatement." He questioned whether "our generation is in a position to pass any kind of historical judgment" on what the Jews under the Nazis had suffered and done. Finally, Scholem expressed his disdain for Arendt's "thesis concerning the 'banality of evil,'" a phrase that he said was a slogan and a catchword. He chided her for abandoning her earlier analysis of "radical evil" to which she "bore such eloquent witness" in *The Origins of Totalitarianism*.[4]

By taking up Scholem's key objections, we can begin to probe the basic issues with which Arendt was struggling. Consider the basis for what became the most vehement attacks on Arendt—her discussion of the Judenräte (Jewish councils). Although she discusses the role of the Jewish councils in a few brief pages, it is here that she *seems* to be soulless and heartless, apparently blaming the victims for their own destruction. The Jewish councils were created by the Nazis to administer local Jewish communities and ghettoes. Members of these councils were typically selected from local Jewish leaders who were given the responsibility to police and to regulate their own communities. There is extensive documentary evidence detailing the Nazi directives for establishing these councils, who was selected, and what they did and did not do. Despite objections, protests, and even suicides by some council members, the Nazis were remarkably successful in organizing these councils and seeing that they functioned properly. Arendt begins her discussion of the Jewish councils by writing, "To a Jew this role of the Jewish leaders in the destruction of their own people is undoubtedly the darkest chapter of the whole dark story" (*EJ*, 117). The statement that many critics found most offensive and outrageous is the following: "Wherever Jews lived, there were recognized Jewish leaders, and this leadership, almost without exception, cooperated in one way or another, for one reason or another, with the Nazis. The whole truth was that if the Jewish people had really been unorganized and leaderless, there would have been chaos and plenty of misery but the total number of victims would hardly have been between four and a half and six million people" (*EJ*, 125). Because this claim is so provocative and disturbing, it is important to scrutinize carefully what Arendt is saying and what she is not saying. She is *not* passing moral judgment on the reasons or motives of the members of the Jewish councils. She is not even denying that millions of Jews would have been murdered even if there were no Jewish councils. She herself reports the "effectiveness" of the SS Einsatzgruppen (mobile killing units) in murdering Jews even where there were no councils. One of the ironies of the accusations brought against Arendt is that, quite early in her report, she castigates the prosecutor for "asking witness after witness—'Why did you not protest?'" She says that this question was "cruel and silly." It ignored the dire consequences of any protest or resistance, the totality of Nazi terror. To emphasize her point, she writes that one need only permit "his imagination to dwell for a few minutes on the fate of those Dutch Jews who in 1941 . . . dared to attack a German security police detachment. Four hundred and thirty Jews were arrested in reprisal and they were literally tortured to death. . . . For months on end they died a thousand deaths. . . . There exist many things considerably worse than death, and the S.S. saw to it that none of them was ever very far from the victims' minds and imagination" (*EJ*, 12).

But Arendt did think that many Jewish leaders in the councils crossed an "abyss" when they cooperated in the selection of Jews to be sent for "resettlement," that is, to be deported to forced-labor camps and death camps. Her brief discussion does not do justice to the ways in which some leaders sought to subvert Nazi directives. In this context she does not mention what she shows later in her report. When Jews found themselves in a situation in which their plight was supported by the larger surrounding population, Jewish leaders acted quite differently. In Denmark, Jewish leaders, with the cooperation of Danes, were able to save most of the relatively small Danish Jewish population, which escaped to Sweden.[5] In claiming that "if the Jewish people had been unorganized and leaderless" there would have been far fewer victims of Nazi murder, Arendt is making one of those strikingly counterfactual historical judgments that is almost impossible to confirm or deny by an appeal to hard evidence. Nevertheless, one should not obscure the kernel of truth in her discussion of the Jewish councils. Although Arendt was one of the first to reach a wide public on this topic, much of what she says was already well known to scholars of the Holocaust. There is considerable scholarly support for her judgment. The evidence amassed by Isaiah Trunk in his detailed study dedicated exclusively to the Judenräte in Eastern Europe (written, in part, to refute Arendt) actually supports the core of Arendt's claim:

> The situation became morally unbearable when, during the mass "re-settlement actions," the Germans forced the Councils and the Jewish police to carry out the preparatory work and to participate in the initial stages of the actual deportation. The latter task was forced mainly upon the Jewish police. The Councils then faced a tragic dilemma never before experienced by a community representative organ. Cooperation then reached the morally dangerous borderline of collaboration. The Councils were called upon to make fateful decisions on the life and death of certain segments of their coreligionists.[6]

Even Walter Z. Laqueur, who was among Arendt's sharpest critics, concludes his article "Hannah Arendt in Jerusalem: The Controversy Revisited" with a statement that might have been written by Arendt herself: "But if in many cases mitigating circumstances can be found, if some leaders in fact behaved heroically, the *Judenrat* phenomenon, as a whole, has acquired a negative connotation, and rightly so. From the moment at the very latest that the Jewish Councils were used by the Nazis to help in the 'final solution' their action became indefensible."[7]

But why does Arendt raise the question of the Jewish councils in her report? What did this "darkest chapter of the whole dark story" (at least for the Jewish people) have to do with Eichmann? Paradoxically, this question—the rationale for discussing the Jewish councils—has rarely been considered in the "Eichmann controversy." Yet Arendt is quite explicit: "I have dwelt on this chapter of the story, which the Jerusalem trial failed to put before the eyes of the world in its true dimensions, because it offers the most striking insight into the totality of the moral collapse the Nazis caused in respectable European society—not only in Germany but in almost all countries, not only among the persecutors but also among the victims" (*EJ*, 125–26). This is the crucial point for Arendt—"the totality of the moral collapse" among "respectable society." Arendt was damning in her judgment of the moral collapse of respectable German society. She was scornful of what she called the "post-war fairy-tale," repeated by many Nazis as well as other Germans, that they were always "inwardly opposed" to Hitler and were only trying to "mitigate" worse horrors. It was the *totality* of moral collapse "among the persecutors but also among the victims" that she wants us to confront.

This moral collapse is something that Arendt personally experienced when she fled from Germany in 1933. Reflecting on this period in her life, she said, "the problem, the personal problem, was not what our enemies did but what our friends did. In the wave of *Gleichschaltung* (coordination), which was relatively voluntary—in any case, not yet under the pressure of terror—it was as if an empty space formed around one."[8]

Consider the context in Arendt's report where she discusses the Jewish councils. She is examining Eichmann's claim that "Nobody . . . came to me and reproached me for anything in the performance of my duties" (*EJ*, 131). The question of the "voice of conscience" and Eichmann's conscience had become an important issue in the trial. Arendt did not think that Eichmann, as the court's judgment phrased it, had "closed his ears to the voice of conscience." On the contrary, his "conscience" was like an empty cipher that spoke with the voice of "respectable society." And what he heard was that there is nothing intrinsically wrong with murdering millions of innocent victims: "His conscience was indeed set at rest when he saw the zeal and eagerness with which 'good society' everywhere reacted as he did" (*EJ*, 126).

The issues for moral reflection raised by this "totality of moral collapse" continued to haunt Arendt for the rest of her life. In her 1965 course of lectures delivered at the New School, "Some Questions of Moral Philosophy," she began by discussing the "basic experiences" that lay behind her concern with moral questions. She said that the dominant belief of her generation had been that "moral conduct is a matter of course." But, she states, "no one in his right mind can any longer [believe] this."[9] For Arendt the most intractable moral questions arose not from the Nazis' behavior but from the behavior of ordinary, respectable people. Margaret Canovan succinctly summarizes what so troubled Arendt: "Although these [ordinary, respectable] people would never have dreamed of committing crimes as long as they lived in a society where such activities were not usual, they adapted effortlessly to a system in which blatant crimes against whole categories of people were standard behaviour. In the place of 'thou shalt not kill' which had seemed the most indisputable rule of civilian existence, such people had no difficulty in accepting the Nazis' rule according to which killing was a moral duty for the sake of the race."[10] According to Arendt, totalitarian domination called into question the very presuppositions of traditional moral philosophies. Despite Arendt's indebtedness to Aristotle, she felt that we could no longer accept the classical understanding of virtue and character whereby, with a proper education and training, a virtuous disposition becomes constitutive of what we are: "Only habits and customs can be taught, and we know only too well the alarming speed with which they are unlearned and forgotten when new circumstances demand a change in manners and patterns of behavior."[11] Aristotle himself realized that virtuous activity presupposes a polis or community in which the virtues can flourish. But the event of totalitarianism showed how terror and violence could so rapidly obliterate the very conditions required for such an ethos.

Furthermore, for all Arendt's esteem for Kant, she was skeptical about his "official" moral philosophy. Arendt did not think that telling right from wrong or distinguishing good from evil was based solely on the faculty of practical reason. The type of reflective judgment—judgment of particulars—analyzed in Kant's *Critique of Judgment* was required to distinguish not only the beautiful from the ugly but also right from wrong. Mores, customs, habits, rules, traditional standards could all change "effortlessly"; they provided no barrier to committing evil deeds. This was the horrible "lesson" of twentieth-century totalitarianism. Arendt stresses how little questions concerning good and evil have to do with what have traditionally been called morals and ethics: "The fact that we usually treat matters of good and evil in courses in 'morals' or 'ethics' may indicate how little we know about them, for morals come from *mores* and ethics from *êthos*, the Latin and the Greek words for custom and habit, the Latin word being associated with rules of behavior, whereas the Greek is derived from habitat, like our 'habits.'"[12]

Arendt's study of totalitarianism and especially the concentration camps—"the most consequential institution of totalitarian domination"—led her to question what she called "the optimistic view of human nature," which "presupposes an independent human faculty, unsupported by law and public opinion, that judges anew in full spontaneity every deed and intent whenever the occasion arises."[13] There are strong reasons for *wanting* to believe that there is such an independent faculty. Such a belief underlies most traditional understandings of morality and legality. But even if we have reasons for believing that there is such a human faculty, twentieth-century totalitarianism, with its ideological conviction that "everything is possible," has taught us that such a capacity can be eliminated. In *The Origins of Totalitarian-*

ism, Arendt tells us that the ultimate aim of totalitarianism is to transform "human nature"—to eliminate the very conditions required to live a *human* life: spontaneity, individuality, natality, and plurality. This is what she originally characterized as "radical evil"—the evil that emerges in connection "with a system in which all men have become equally superfluous." These are the "crimes which men can neither punish nor forgive," crimes which can no longer be understood and explained by evil motives.[14]

Increasingly, Arendt came to believe that the capacity to distinguish right from wrong, good from evil, presupposes the exercise of the mental activities of thinking and judging. These are the very capacities that Eichmann lacked. This is how Arendt sought to account for the phenomenon that she called "the banality of evil." But what precisely does Arendt mean by this provocative phrase that so deeply offended many of her readers—the phrase that Scholem calls a "slogan" and a "catchword"?

If we turn to the main text of *Eichmann in Jerusalem,* there is scarcely any explicit discussion of what she means by evil or the banality of evil. As I have already indicated, the subtitle, *A Report on the Banality of Evil,* did not even appear in the *New Yorker* articles. There are only two passages in her report that explicitly mention evil. The first is directly relevant to the discussion of the so-called voice of conscience:

> And just as the law in civilized countries assumes that the voice of conscience tells everybody "Thou shalt not kill," even though man's natural desires and inclinations may at times be murderous, so law in Hitler's land demanded that the voice of conscience tell everybody: "Thou shalt kill," although the organizers of the massacres knew full well that murder is against the normal desires and inclinations of most people. Evil in the Third Reich had lost the quality by which most people recognize it—the quality of temptation. (*EJ,* 150)

The expression "the banality of evil" appears only once in the final sentence of her report (just before her epilogue). Arendt comments on "the grotesque silliness" of Eichmann's final words before being hanged. Eichmann is reported to have said, "After a short while, gentlemen, *we shall all meet again.* Such is the fate of all men. Long live Germany, long live Argentina, long live Austria. *I shall not forget them.*"

Arendt comments:

In the face of death he had found the cliché used in funeral oratory. Under the gallows, his memory played him the last trick; he was "elated" and he forgot that this was his own funeral.

It was as though in those last minutes he was summing up the lesson that this long course in human wickedness had taught us—the lesson of the fearsome, word-and-thought-defying *banality of evil.* (*EJ,* 252)

That is it! There is no further commentary or explanation of what she means by "the banality of evil." When her critics attacked her, Arendt made several attempts to clarify her meaning. But these "clarifications" introduce further problems. In her postscript to the 1965 edition of the book, she writes: "[W]hen I speak of the banality of evil, I do so only on the strictly factual level, pointing to a phenomenon which stared one in the face at the trial. Eichmann was not Iago and not Macbeth, and nothing would have been farther from his mind than to determine with Richard III 'to prove a villain.' Except for an extraordinary diligence in looking out for his personal advancement, he had no motives as all. . . . He *merely,* to put the matter colloquially, *never realized what he was doing"* (*EJ,* 287). It simply is not clear in what sense Arendt is speaking "on the strictly factual level." This is precisely what is contested, for to speak of the banality of evil is not simply to report a fact but—in Arendt's terms—to make a *judgment* about the character of Eichmann's motives (or rather his lack of motives).[15] Furthermore, at the very least it is misleading to say that "Eichmann never realized what he was doing," for Eichmann certainly knew—as Arendt acknowledges—that his actions led to the murder of millions of innocent victims.

Arendt's reply to Scholem gives a hint about the meaning of "the banality of evil," but this is still not completely satisfactory. She writes: "It is indeed my opinion now that evil is never 'radical,' that it is only extreme, and that it possesses neither depth nor any demonic dimension. It can overgrow and lay waste the whole world precisely because it spreads like a fungus on the surface. It is 'thought-defying,' as I said, because thought tries to reach some depth, to go to the roots, and the moment it concerns itself with evil, it is frustrated because there is nothing."[16] The clearest and most judicious statement about the meaning of "the banality of evil" occurs in her 1971 essay "Thinking and Moral Considerations":

Some years ago, reporting the trial of Eichmann in Jerusalem, I spoke of "the banality of evil" and meant with this no theory or doctrine but something quite factual, the phenomenon of evil deeds, committed on a gigantic scale, which could not be traced to any particularity of wickedness, pathology, or ideological conviction in the doer, whose only personal distinction was a perhaps extraordinary shallowness. However monstrous the deeds were, the doer was neither monstrous nor demonic, and the only specific characteristic one could detect in his past as well as in his behavior during the trial and the preceding police examination was something entirely negative: it was not stupidity but a curious, quite authentic inability to think.[17]

This claim is repeated in the introduction to *The Life of the Mind*, in which Arendt reports that the Eichmann trial was one of the sources for her preoccupation with mental activities.[18]

Arendt's portrait of Eichmann is damning and frightening but not because he was a "sadistic monster" or exhibited demonic or "satanic greatness." It was his "ordinariness" and "normality" that she found so troubling. His primary motivations seemed to be petty ambition, a desire to please his superiors, and a desire to show how dedicated he was in carrying out orders and fulfilling his "duty."

What was so thought-defying for Arendt was Eichmann's inability to think and to judge. The phenomenon that needed to be confronted was how "an average 'normal' person, neither feeble-minded nor indoctrinated nor cynical, could be perfectly incapable of telling right from wrong" (*EJ*, 26). Eichmann was incapable of uttering anything but clichés and stock phrases. Without the slightest difficulty he could switch from one set of rules to an entirely different set of rules. When he was brought to trial, "he knew what he had once considered his duty was now called a crime, and he accepted this new code of judgment as though it were nothing but another language rule."[19] Arendt agreed with the judges when they declared that what Eichmann said was "empty talk," but she did not think that this "emptiness" was feigned to cover up "hideous" thoughts. There was no depth to be plumbed here, there was only thought-defying shallowness and superficiality: "Clichés, stock phrases, adherence to conventional, standardized codes of expression and conduct have the socially recognized function of protecting us against reality, that is, against the claim on our thinking attention which all events and facts arouse by virtue of their existence. If we were responsive to this claim all the time, we would soon be exhausted; the difference in Eichmann was only that he clearly knew of no such claim at all."[20]

To understand the phenomenon that Arendt seeks to describe when she speaks of the banality of evil, I want to step back and reflect on something that Heidegger wrote. One of the many shocking revelations in the controversy about Heidegger and the Nazis has been the discovery of a sentence from the unpublished version of one of Heidegger's most famous and influential essays, "The Question Concerning Technology." In this 1953 essay Heidegger characterizes *Gestell* (enframing), the essence of modern technology, as a mode of revealing that he calls "challenging-forth." He then contrasts "challenging-forth" with a mode of revealing that he calls "bringing-forth." To illustrate what he means by *Gestell,* Heidegger's published text reads: "But meanwhile even the cultivation of the field has come under the grip of another kind of setting-in-order, which *sets upon* nature. It sets upon it in the sense of challenging it. Agriculture is now [motorized] food industry."[21] In the original manuscript of this lecture, there is a clause that was deleted from the published version. The original sentence reads: "Agriculture is now motorized food industry—in essence the same as the manufacturing of corpses in gas chambers and extermination camps, the same as blockading and starving of nations, the same as the manufacture of hydrogen bombs."[22] When Thomas Sheehan brought this passage to the attention of the English-speaking public, he declared that it is characterized by a rhetoric, a cadence, a point of view that is damning beyond commentary.[23] But Sheehan is overlooking something that is extremely important here and that is relevant for understanding what Arendt means by the banality of evil.

This passage in Heidegger's essay occurs where he begins his characterization of *Gestell.* He is graphically portraying what he takes to be the essence (*Wesen*) of modern technology, a "setting-in-order" in which everything becomes "standing-reserve" (*Bestand*)—something to be manipulated, ordered, and transformed. Even human beings are treated as "human resources." So when Heidegger writes the preceding disturbing sentence, he is describing what is happening in the mode of revealing that he names *Gestell*—"the supreme danger." But what does this have to do with the "banality of evil"? Heidegger's crucial phrase here is "in essence the same" (*im Wesen das Selbe*).[24] Heidegger is describing a type of *mentalité* in which motorized agriculture, arranging for the shipment of human material to death camps, and manufacturing corpses in gas chambers are "in essence the same." This is what is characteristic of the way in which Eichmann conceived of what he was doing. From the perspective of common sense—traditional conceptions of morality and conscience—this is shocking and scandalous. We may find it almost incomprehensible to imagine how someone could "think" (that is, not think) in this manner, how manufacturing food, bombs, or corpses could be "in essence the same," and how this could become "normal," "ordinary" behavior.[25] Yet this is the *mentalité* that Arendt believed she was facing in Eichmann and that she claims we must confront if we are to understand the new type of criminal that he represents.[26] There is no suggestion here of exonerating Eichmann from his crimes and responsibility. Rather, Arendt is trying to comprehend what appears to be so incomprehensible. She completely rejects all versions of what she calls "the cog theory" as an evasion of personal responsibility. In response to the claim that one was merely a cog or a wheel in a system, it is always appropriate to ask (in matters of law and morality), "And why did you become a cog or continue to be a wheel in such circumstances?"[27]

Concerning the banality of evil, it is helpful to distinguish two issues that have frequently been confused. The first might be called the conceptual issue: showing that individuals can commit evil deeds on a gigantic scale without these deeds being traced back to evil or monstrous motives. This is the primary issue for Arendt. But there is a second issue: whether Eichmann fits this description. I think that Arendt tends to overstate her case about Eichmann. Ironically, Arendt herself was always deeply skeptical about the ability to penetrate into the "darkness of one's heart"—to say with confidence what are someone's "real" motives. So on her *own* grounds it is a bit extreme to say that "Except for an extraordinary diligence in looking out for his personal advancement, he had no motives at all." Furthermore, some of the evidence suggests that Eichmann was far more fanatical in carrying out his duties than Arendt indicates.[28] But even if we have doubts about the adequacy of Arendt's depiction of Eichmann's motives or lack thereof, we still have to face the conceptual issue she so forcefully raises.

Arendt claims that what was most striking about Eichmann was something negative, "his total absence of thinking." He was trapped in his own clichés, stock phrases, and conventional language rules. He seemed incapable of that "enlarged mentality," the *imagination* to think from "the standpoint of somebody else." This is what led Arendt

to ask a series of questions concerning the relationship of evil, thinking, and judging:

> Is evil-doing, not just the sins of omission but the sins of commission,
> possible in the absence of not merely "base motives" (as the law calls
> it) but of any motives at all, any particular promoting of interest or
> volition? Is wickedness, however we may define it, this being "deter-
> mined to prove a villain," *not* a necessary condition for evil-doing? Is
> our ability to judge, to tell right from wrong, beautiful from ugly, de-
> pendent upon our faculty of thought? Do the inability to think and a
> disastrous failure of what we commonly call conscience coincide?
> The question that imposed itself was: Could the activity of thinking
> as such, the habit of examining and reflecting upon whatever hap-
> pens to come to pass, regardless of specific content and quite inde-
> pendent of results, could this activity be of such a nature that it "con-
> ditions" men against evil-doing?[29]

Arendt was inclined to answer all these questions—especially the last
one (which sums up the others)—in the affirmative. These questions
are some of the primary sources for *The Life of the Mind*. I cannot
fully explore here Arendt's rich, suggestive, yet inconclusive reflections
on thinking and judging. She never wrote the last part of *The Life of
the Mind*, "Judging" (although I think that her lectures on Kant's *Critique of Judgment* and her occasional remarks about judgment provide essential clues for what she would have written). I want to focus
on a single strand in her questioning—the relation between thinking,
judging, and evil. The more tenaciously we follow the pathways of her
thinking, the deeper the perplexities that we encounter. To anticipate, I
do not think Arendt ever gives a fully satisfactory answer to the questions she raises about the relation of thinking and evil.

The problem Arendt seeks to address is whether there is an "inner
connection between the ability or inability to think and the problem
of evil."[30] Thinking must not be confused with knowing. The radical
distinction between thinking and knowing was anticipated by Kant's
distinction of *Vernunft* and *Verstand*. The type of thinking Arendt is
speaking about is not something limited to philosophers or to "professional thinkers" but a thinking that can be practiced by everyone.
Thinking involves an internal dialogue, what Arendt calls a "two-in-
one," in which there is an intercourse between me and myself: "The
business of thinking is like the veil of Penelope: it undoes every morn-
ing what it had finished the night before."[31] In "Thinking and Moral
Considerations," Arendt uses "a man as [a] model who did think with-

out becoming a philosopher, a citizen among citizens, doing nothing, claiming nothing that, in his view, every citizen should do and had a right to claim."[32] Her model is Socrates. The thinking he exhibited has "a destructive, undermining effect on all established criteria, values, measurements for good and evil, in short on those customs and rules of conduct we treat in morals and ethics."[33] Thinking in this Socratic sense is dangerous: it has this "destructive" and "undermining effect on all established . . . values." But if this is so, then our perplexity about "the inner connection between the ability or inability to think and the problem of evil" only increases. To understand what Arendt means by this "inner connection," we need to introduce the crucial "third term"—judging. It was this ability to judge, to tell right from wrong in particular, concrete circumstances, that was lacking in Eichmann—as it was lacking in those members of respectable society who switched from one set of mores and customs to another with such ease. Arendt emphasizes that "those few who were still able to tell right from wrong went really only by their own judgments, and they did so freely; there were no rules to be abided by, under which the particular cases with which they were confronted could be subsumed. They had to decide each instance as it arose, because no rules existed for the unprecedented" (*EJ*, 295).

The preceding characterization of judgment provides the clue as to why Arendt was drawn to Kant's *Critique of Judgment*. Kant's analysis of the *sensus communis* and reflective judgment, whereby we have the ability to judge a particular without subsuming it under a general or universal rule, provides Arendt with a model for what she wants to claim about judgment. Arendt acknowledges that Kant was primarily concerned with aesthetic judgments (that is, "this is beautiful," "this is ugly"), but Arendt claims that his analysis is also applicable to such reflective judgments as "this is right," "this is wrong."

Still, we may ask what the precise relation is between thinking and judging. At times Arendt seems to think of judging as itself a form of thinking:

> The presupposition for this kind of judging is not a highly developed intelligence or sophistication in moral matters, but merely the habit of living together explicitly with oneself, that is, of being engaged in that silent dialogue between me and myself which since Socrates and Plato we usually call thinking. This kind of thought, though at the root of all philosophical thinking, is not technical and does not con-

cern theoretical problems. The dividing line between those who judge and those who do not strikes across all social and cultural or educational differences.[34]

But in *The Life of the Mind*, Arendt emphasizes that thinking and judging are independent mental activities. What, then, is the relation between thinking and judging? The closest we come to an explicit answer in Arendt is in the final paragraph of her lecture "Thinking and Moral Considerations" (which is repeated in *The Life of the Mind*):

> The faculty of judging particulars (as Kant discovered it), the ability to say "this is wrong," "this is beautiful," etc., is not the same as the faculty of thinking. Thinking deals with invisibles, with representations of things that are absent; judging always concerns particulars and things close at hand. But the two are interrelated, in a way similar to the way consciousness and conscience are interconnected. If thinking, the two-in-one of the soundless dialogue, actualizes the difference within our identity as given in consciousness and thereby results in conscience as its by-product, then judging, the by-product of the liberating effect of thinking, realizes thinking, makes it manifest in the world of appearances, where I am never alone and always much too busy to be able to think. The manifestation of the wind of thought is no knowledge; it is the ability to tell right from wrong, beautiful from ugly. And this indeed may prevent catastrophes, at least for myself, in the rare moments when the chips are down.[35]

What Arendt says here is at once extremely suggestive and unsatisfactory. The very intelligibility of her claims depends on the assertion that thinking has a liberating effect on the faculty of judgment. But Arendt does not really provide any arguments to justify this assertion. At times it seems that Arendt is at war with herself, that she never quite reconciles the tensions in her own internal dialogue. On the one hand, she insists that thinking by itself does not yield moral knowledge and "does not produce usable practical wisdom," yet on the other hand, it has an all-important "indirect" practical by-product—for it presumably liberates the faculty of judgment.[36] But why should we think that there is such a liberating relation between thinking and judging in moments of crisis? Even if we return to her example of Socrates, Arendt herself notes that the perplexities he aroused in Alcibiades and Critias did not liberate their faculties of judgment: "What they had been aroused to was license and cynicism."[37] Much more damaging to Arendt's thesis is her own blindness concerning Heidegger's "error" in supporting Hitler and the Nazis. Ironically, in the same year that she published "Thinking and Moral Considerations," she also published her tribute to Heidegger on his eightieth birthday. Recalling her experience in the 1920s, she tells us: "[T]he rumor about Heidegger put it quite simply: thinking has come to life again. . . . There exists a teacher; one can perhaps learn to think."[38] So Arendt actually proposes two models or exemplars of thinking: Socrates and Heidegger. The thinking performed by Socrates, who is at once a "gadfly," "electric ray," and "midwife," is a thinking that has "political and moral significance . . . in those rare moments in history when 'Things fall apart; the centre cannot hold; / Mere anarchy is loosed upon the world.'" Arendt further tells us:

> At these moments, thinking ceases to be a marginal affair in political matters. When everybody is swept away unthinkingly by what everybody else does and believes in, those who think are drawn out of hiding because their refusal to join is conspicuous and thereby becomes a kind of action. The purging element in thinking, Socrates' midwifery, that brings out the implications of unexamined opinions and thereby destroys them—values, doctrines, theories, and even convictions—is political by implication. For this destruction has a liberating effect on another faculty, the faculty of judgment, which one may call, with some justification, the most political of man's mental abilities.[39]

These remarks take on a bitter irony when we juxtapose them with the actions of Heidegger, whom Arendt considers to be the thinker par excellence of the twentieth century. Although one may disagree about what Arendt euphemistically call's Heidegger's "error," I do not see how anyone can claim that *his* thinking had a "liberating effect" on his faculty of judgment. Heidegger in 1933 completely failed to *judge* accurately what was happening. One might try to get around the disparity in Arendt's portraits of Socrates and Heidegger by claiming that the type of thinking Arendt ascribes to Heidegger is categorically different from Socrates' thinking. But there is no evidence that Arendt makes any such distinction. Like Heidegger, Arendt sharply distinguishes professional philosophy from thinking. The way in which she characterizes thinking, including the thinking of Socrates, is heavily indebted to Heidegger's characterization of thinking.[40] Arendt desperately wants to show that thinking does have moral consequences—at least "indirectly," by liberating the faculty of judgment by which we judge "this is right" and "this is wrong" in moments of crisis. But although she asserts this categorically, she never gives us adequate reasons to show this connection.

It may be objected that posing the issue as I have misses Arendt's main point, for it is misleading to ask what precisely the relation is between the mental activities of thinking and judging such that in crisis situations the "manifestation of the wind of thought . . . is the ability to tell right from wrong, beautiful from ugly." Posing the question in this way makes it seem as if we are looking for some general criterion or standard that would enable us to understand how thinking achieves such a result. But (a defender of Arendt might object) this is to ignore Arendt's critique of the search for such a general criterion or standard; it is to fail to appreciate the importance that Arendt places on *exemplars*, that is, the rationale for her selection of Socrates as the model of a person whose thinking prevents him from doing evil. Furthermore, in "Some Questions of Moral Philosophy," she writes:

> These considerations perhaps may explain why Socratic morality with its negative, marginal qualities has revealed itself as the only working morality in borderline situations, that is, in times of crisis and emergency. When standards are no longer valid anyhow—as in Athens in the last third of the fifth and the fourth centuries or in Europe in the last third of the nineteenth and twentieth centuries—nothing is left but the example of Socrates, who may not have been the greatest philosopher but who still is the philosopher par excellence. Whereby we must not forget that for the philosopher, who not only thinks but is extraordinarily and in the opinion of many of his fellow citizens inordinately fond of thinking, the moral by-product of thought is itself of secondary importance. He does not examine things in order to improve either himself or others.

Even if we accept Arendt's claim that "the example of Socrates" is the model on which we should focus, we can still ask, what precisely is it about Socrates' thinking that results in this "moral by-product"? And what precisely is it about Heidegger's thinking that accounts for his disastrous "error"? In her unpublished lectures titled "Basic Moral Propositions," Arendt says that "our decisions about right and wrong will depend upon our choice of company. . . . And this company [in turn] is chosen through thinking in examples, in examples of persons dead or alive, and in examples of incidents past and present."[41] But this still does not help to resolve the issue. Arendt herself "chose" Socrates *and* Heidegger as exemplars of thinkers. Yet, for her, it is Socrates (and not Heidegger) who shows us how thinking can liberate the faculty of judgment—and "prevent catastrophes . . . in the rare moments when the chips are down."

My primary point is *not* to draw an invidious comparison between the example of Socrates and the example of Heidegger, but rather to expose a "gap" in Arendt's thinking—to show that Arendt's appeal to exemplars is not sufficient to answer the central question she poses for herself: "Could the activity of thinking as such, the habit of examining and reflecting upon whatever happens to come to pass, regardless of specific content and quite independent of results, could this activity be of such a nature that it 'conditions' men against evil-doing?"

There are further problems. We can see that the faculty that is most important in preventing catastrophes for the self is the faculty of judgment—"the ability to tell right from wrong, beautiful from ugly." One must be cautious about reconstructing or second-guessing what Arendt would have said if she had completed the final, culminating part of *The Life of the Mind*. But there are perplexities in what she does say. The reason Arendt was so drawn to Kant's analysis of reflective judgment is that Kant analyzes a type of judgment of particulars in which the judgment is made without subsuming the particulars under a universal principle or general rule. Unlike Kant, who is primarily concerned with aesthetic judgments, Arendt seeks to extend his analysis to such particular judgments as "this is right," "this is wrong." In her Eichmann report Arendt was struck by those few who resisted evil, who could discriminate between right and wrong, and who "went really only by their own judgments" because there were "no rules to be abided by, under which the particular cases with which they were confronted could be subsumed. They had to decide each instance as it arose, because no rules existed for the unprecedented" (*EJ*, 295). If we grant Arendt's point that "this is beautiful," "this is ugly," "this is right," and "this is wrong" are all examples of reflective judgments, we still want to understand the differences among these types of reflective judgment. What precisely are we asserting when we say "this is *right*" and "this is *wrong*"? She seems to gloss over and obscure two separate questions. The first issue is how we are to characterize the *type* of judgment we are making when we judge something to be right or wrong. Arendt tells us that this type of judgment is a reflective judgment. But if we agree with Arendt that this is a reflective judgment, by which we judge particulars directly without subsuming them under a universal or general rule, we may still ask what we mean by "right" and "wrong" and how these predicates are to be distinguished from "beautiful" and "ugly." Arendt never seems to answer *this* question.

But perhaps the most troublesome perplexity in Arendt's attempt to account for the banality of evil—the phenomenon she claimed to have witnessed in Eichmann—is what she has left unsaid. On the one hand, she tells us that thinking and judging are faculties that can be ascribed to everyone, in the sense that everyone *potentially* has the capacity to think and to judge. This is a crucial presupposition in her attempt to show that there is an "inner connection between the ability or inability to think and the problem of evil."

On the other hand, Arendt claims that Eichmann's specific characteristic was "a curious, quite authentic inability to think." Presumably this is also true of the members of "respectable society" who so effortlessly could switch from one set of mores to another—from the conviction that one ought not kill to the conviction that killing was permissible or even required for racial reasons. Suppose we accept Arendt's claim about Eichmann's inability to think. The primary question that then confronts us is, how are we to *account* for this lack? More generally, if indeed every human being has the potential to be able to think and to judge, how are we to account for Eichmann (and all the others) who did not think and judge? Moreover, despite Arendt's constant references to "total moral collapse," she believed that there were those few (all too few) who did *not* lose their ability to judge and to act accordingly.[42]

In one of the most moving chapters of *Eichmann in Jerusalem*— almost in counterpoint to her unrelenting portrayal of Eichmann— Arendt tells the story of Anton Schmidt, a sergeant in the German army who helped Jewish partisans by supplying them with forged papers and military trucks until he was arrested and executed by the Germans. She relates that when the story of Anton Schmidt was told in the Jerusalem court, those present observed two minutes of silence in honor of this man who helped to save Jewish lives. Arendt comments: "And in those two minutes, which were like a sudden burst of light in the midst of impenetrable, unfathomable darkness, a single thought stood out clearly, irrefutably, beyond question—how utterly different everything would be today in this courtroom, in Israel, in Germany, in all of Europe, and perhaps in all countries of the world, if only more such stories could have been told" (*EJ*, 231). Despite what Arendt tells us about thinking, judging, and evil, the question she does not answer—and it may indeed be unanswerable—is, how can we account for the differences between Adolf Eichmann and Anton Schmidt? Why is it that there are so few stories to be told about those like Anton Schmidt who, under conditions of totalitarian terror, did not lose their ability to judge, to distinguish right from wrong, and to act decisively in light of their judgment?

I have been arguing that Arendt never satisfactorily answers the questions that she raises concerning the "inner connection of thinking and the problem of evil." She asserts that our ability to judge, to tell right from wrong, is "dependent upon the faculty of thought"—"the habit of examining and reflecting upon whatever happens to come to pass"—but she never *justifies* the crucial claim that thinking has this liberating effect on the faculty of judgment. When she turns to judgment and shows the relevance of Kant's analysis of reflective aesthetic judgments and the *sensus communis*, she does not really explain what we are *asserting* when we judge a particular deed to be right and distinguish it from what is wrong. Finally, she leaves us with a profound and unsettling perplexity. Even if we accept the role she assigns to thinking and judging in preventing evil in moments of crisis, we are left with no account of why—even in instances of extreme totalitarian terror—some persons lose or show no signs of the ability to think and (a few) others still maintain their ability to judge.

Arendt, in her own dialogue with herself, was pulled in opposite directions. The unprecedented event of twentieth-century totalitarianism taught a terrifying lesson. Totalitarian domination is based on the "principle" that everything is possible, and this reveals that there is nothing about human nature or the human condition that cannot be altered or destroyed. Totalitarian terror aims at "the transformation of human nature itself." Even our ability to think and to judge can be obliterated. Indeed, Arendt thought that one of the major threats of modern society was that the capacity for independent thinking and judging might be eliminated. We can no longer believe that traditional mores, customs, or habits are sufficient to prevent evil. Under extreme conditions there is nothing that can prevent "total moral collapse." We may desperately want to believe that there is something about human beings that cannot be transformed, something deep about the human self, the voice of conscience, or our sense of responsibility that cannot be obliterated. After totalitarianism, we can no longer hold on to this belief. This is the specter that now haunts us, the all too real possibility of this danger. As she tells us in "Some Questions of Moral Philosophy," "the greatest evil perpetuated is the evil committed by Nobodies, committed, to be sure, by human beings but by human beings who refused to be persons." Arendt herself was critical of what she once called the "optimistic view of human nature," which presupposes "an independent human faculty, unsupported by law and public opinion, that judges anew in full spontaneity every deed and intent whenever the occasion arises." Yet, ironically, it is Arendt herself who seems to *want to believe* that there is such a human faculty. This is what she calls the faculty of judgment. I emphasize that she "wants to believe" because this is where she is at war with herself, for she claims that Eichmann did *not* possess this ability to judge. It would seem that this ability was also lacking in all those members of "respectable society" who adapted so effortlessly to Nazi ideology.

Yet we do know that even under conditions of the most extreme terror, some individuals are capable of resisting, judging what is right and wrong, and acting according to their consciences. The question that eludes Arendt—and it may be impossible to answer—is how we are to explain (in a noncircular way) what accounts for the differences between those who are still capable of judging what is evil and acting according to their consciences, and those who have lost or never had this ability.

Arendt's conclusion of the story of Anton Schmidt, the German sergeant who was executed for helping Jewish victims, is a fitting conclusion to this essay. After she contrasts his behavior with "the hollowness of respectability" of those Germans who argued it was "practically useless" to oppose the Nazis, she tells us: "For the lesson of such stories is simple and within everybody's grasp. Politically speaking, it is that under conditions of terror most people will comply but *some people will not*, just as the lesson of the countries to which the Final Solution was proposed is that 'it could happen' in most places but *it did not happen everywhere*. Humanly speaking, no more is required, and no more can reasonably be asked, for this planet to remain a place fit for human habitation" (*EJ*, 233).

Notes

A revised version of this essay was published as "Evil, Thinking and Judging," in my *Hannah Arendt and the Jewish Question* (Cambridge: MIT Press, 1996).

1. The subtitle, *A Report on the Banality of Evil*, did not appear in the *New Yorker* articles; it appeared when the articles were published as a book in May 1963.

2. Hannah Arendt, *The Origins of Totalitarianism*, 3d rev. ed. (New York: Harcourt Brace Jovanovich, 1968), viii.

3. Hannah Arendt, *Eichmann in Jerusalem: A Report on the Banality of Evil*, 2d ed. (New York: Viking Press, 1965), 246–47; Arendt's emphasis. All further citations from this text will be noted parenthetically with the abbreviation *EJ*.

4. Gershom Scholem and Hannah Arendt, "'Eichmann in Jerusalem': Exchange of Letters between Gershom Scholem and Hannah Arendt," *Encounter* 22, no. 1 (January 1964): 51–56, repr. in *The Jew as Pariah*, ed. Ron H. Feldman (New York: Grove Press, 1978), 240–51.

5. Concerning Denmark, Arendt writes: "The story of the Danish Jews is *sui generis*, and the behavior of the Danish people and their government was unique among all the countries of Europe. . . . One is tempted to recommend the story as required reading in political science for all students who wish to learn something about the enormous power potential in non-violent action and in resistance to an opponent possessing vastly superior means of violence" (*EJ*, 171).

6. Isaiah Trunk, *Judenrat* (New York: Stein and Day, 1972), 570.

7. Walter Z. Laqueur, "Hannah Arendt in Jerusalem: The Controversy Revisited," in *Western Society after the Holocaust*, ed. Lyman H. Legters (Boulder: Westview Press, 1983), 118.

8. Hannah Arendt, "What Remains? The Language Remains: A Conversation with Günter Gaus," in *Essays in Understanding, 1930–1954*, ed. Jerome Kohn (New York: Harcourt Brace, 1994), 10–11. The German word *Gleichschaltung* can be literally translated as "coordination" or "cooperation," but this does not convey its ugly racist overtones of complicity and "cleansing."

9. Hannah Arendt, "Some Questions of Moral Philosophy," Arendt Archives, Library of Congress. These 1965 lectures are now being edited by Jerome Kohn. The first lecture has been published in *Social Research* 61, no. 4 (winter 1994): 734–64.

10. Margaret Canovan, *Hannah Arendt: A Reinterpretation of Her Political Thought* (Cambridge: Cambridge University Press, 1992), 158.

11. Hannah Arendt, *The Life of the Mind* (New York: Harcourt Brace Jovanovich, 1978), 5.

12. Ibid.

13. Hannah Arendt, "Personal Responsibility under Dictatorship, " *Listener*, August 6, 1964, 187.

14. Arendt, *The Origins of Totalitarianism*, 458–59. For a detailed analysis of what Arendt means by radical evil and its relation to the banality of evil, see chapter 7, "From Radical Evil to the Banality of Evil: From Superfluous to Thoughtlessness," in my *Hannah Arendt and the Jewish Question* (Cambridge, England: Polity Press, 1996).

15. Arendt stubbornly maintained that her Eichmann report was "strictly factual." She repeated this in public and in private. In a letter (dated September 20, 1963) to her good friend Mary McCarthy, she insists: "As I see it, there are no 'ideas' in this Report, there are only facts with a few conclusions, and these conclusions usually appear at the end of each chapter. . . . In other words, my point would be that what the whole furor is about are *facts*, and neither theories nor ideas. The hostility against me is a hostility against someone who tells the truth on a factual level, and not against someone who has ideas which are in conflict with those commonly held." Hannah Arendt and Mary McCarthy, *Between Friends: The Correspondence of Hannah Arendt and Mary McCarthy, 1949–1975*, ed. Carol Brightman (New York: Harcourt Brace, 1995), 148.

16. Scholem and Arendt, "'Eichmann in Jerusalem,'" 250. See my discussion of this response in "From Radical Evil to the Banality of Evil." There is a passage from "Some Questions concerning Moral Philosophy" that helps to clarify the sense in which the banality of evil is "thought-defying." Arendt writes:

> Thinking and remembering, we said, is the human way of striking roots, of taking one's place in the world into which we all arrive as strangers. What we usually call a person or a personality, as distinguished from a mere human being who can also be a nobody, is actually what grows out of this root-striking process which is thinking. . . . If he is a thinking being, rooted in his thoughts and remembrances, and hence knowing that he has to live with himself, there will be limits to what he can permit himself to do, and those limits will not be imposed from the outside upon him but be as it were self-set; these limits can change considerably and uncomfortably from person to person, from country to country, from century to century; but limitless, extreme evil is possible only where these self-grown roots, which automatically limit the possibilities, are entirely absent; they are absent wherever men skid only over the surface of events, where they permit themselves to be carried away without ever penetrating into whatever depth they may be capable of, and this depth, of course, changes again from person to person, from century to century, in its specific quality as well as its dimensions.

17. Hannah Arendt, "Thinking and Moral Considerations: A Lecture," *Social Research* 38, no. 3 (fall 1971): 417.

18. See Arendt, *The Life of the Mind*, 3–16.

19. Arendt, "Thinking and Moral Considerations," 417.

20. Ibid., 418.

21. Martin Heidegger, "The Question concerning Technology," in *Basic Writings*, ed. David F. Krell (New York: Harper & Row, 1977), 296. For a critical discussion of this essay, see my "Heidegger's Silence: *Êthos* and Technology," in *The New Constellation: The Ethical-Political Horizon of Modernity/Postmodernity* (Cambridge: MIT Press, 1992), 79–141.

22. This passage is cited in Wolfgang Schirmacher, *Technik und Gelassenheit* (Freiburg: Alber, 1983), 25. The German original is, "Ackerbau ist jetzt motorisierte Ernährungsindustrie, im Wesen das Selbe wie die Fabrikation von Leichen in Gaskammern und Vernichtungslagern, das Selbe wie die Blockade und Aushungerung von Ländern, das Selbe wie die Fabrikation von Wasserstoffbomben." The passage was translated by Thomas Sheehan in "Heidegger and the Nazis," *New York Review of Books*, June 16, 1988.

23. See Sheehan, "Heidegger and the Nazis," 41.

24. See my discussion of the significance of this phrase in "Heidegger's Silence."

25. Although I think that the *mentalité* that Heidegger graphically portrays in his characterization of *Gestell* enables us to understand what Arendt means by "the banality of evil," Arendt strongly diverges from Heidegger concerning the issue of personal responsibility. Arendt maintains that Eichmann is personally responsible for his deeds. Heidegger, I have argued, obscures the issue of personal responsibility. See ibid.

26. Seyla Benhabib suggests that "A better phrase than the 'banality of evil' might have been the 'routinization of evil' or its *Alltäglichung* (everydayness). Analogical thinking governs the logic of the everyday, where we orient ourselves by expected and

established patterns and rules." "Hannah Arendt and the Redemptive Power of Narrative," *Social Research* 57, no. 1 (spring 1990): 185. Although Arendt did focus on how evil deeds became routinized, the phrase "the routinization of evil" does not capture her striking claim that such deeds lacked not only "evil motives" but any motives at all. Furthermore, it was not the orientation by "established patterns and rules" that she emphasized, but rather the ease with which such patterns and rules could be exchanged for new ones.

27. Arendt, "Personal Responsibility under Dictatorship," 186. See her discussion and rejection of "cog" theories in this article.

28. To cite one notorious example, I find it difficult to reconcile Eichmann's actions in Budapest during the spring and summer of 1944 with Arendt's portrait of him as someone who had "no motives at all" and who "never realized what he was doing." By 1944, the only important European Jewish community that had been unaffected by deportation was in Hungary, where there were 750,000 Jews. When Eichmann and his staff went to Budapest in March 1944 to organize a Jewish council, it was well known (even by Jewish leaders) what "deportation" and "resettlement" meant. Yet Eichmann was able swiftly to organize a Jewish council and initiate mass deportations. Raul Hilberg, in *The Destruction of the European Jews* (Chicago: Quadrangle Books, 1961), tells us:

> Under the command of Eichmann himself, the top deportation specialists of the RSHA had been concentrated into a single, devastatingly hard-hitting unit. These men had barely arrived, and the German regime in Hungary had barely been established, when the destruction process was set into motion with a speed and efficiency which displayed the accumulated experience of several years of European-wide deportations.
>
> In two lightning moves the Germans [primarily Eichmann] maneuvered the Jewish community leadership into absolute submission and mobilized the Hungarian government for instantaneous destructive action. (823)

Arendt herself reports that after Budapest was bombed by the Allies on July 2, Horthy gave the order to stop the deportations. Nevertheless, Eichmann did not obey "'the old fool's' order but, in mid-July, deported another fifteen hundred Jews." Eichmann even schemed to keep Jewish leaders from informing Horthy about this deportation. Arendt says this is "one of the most damning pieces of evidence against Eichmann" (*EJ*, 201), yet she fails to see this as evidence of Eichmann's fanaticism.

29. Arendt, "Thinking and Moral Considerations," 418.

30. Ibid., 425.

31. Ibid., 427. Arendt uses the following quotation from Heidegger as an epigraph for the introduction to *The Life of the Mind*:

> Thinking does not bring knowledge as do the sciences.
> Thinking does not produce usable practical wisdom.
> Thinking does not solve the riddles of the universe.
> Thinking does not endow us directly with power to act.

32. Arendt, "Thinking and Moral Considerations," 427. Arendt explains here (and repeats in *The Life of the Mind*) her use of Socrates as a model.

33. Ibid., 434.

34. Arendt, "Personal Responsibility under Dicatorship," 205.

35. Arendt, "Thinking and Moral Considerations," 446.

36. Robert Bernasconi detects a similar tension in Arendt. She never quite justifies

her claim that thinking has a moral side effect or by-product. Furthermore, he notes that in regard to evil deeds, Arendt was ultimately concerned not with thinking but with judging. See Robert Bernasconi, "Habermas and Arendt on the Philosopher's 'Error': Tracking the Diabolical in Heidegger," *Graduate Faculty Philosophy Journal* 14, no. 2–15, no. 1 (1991): 3–24.

37. Arendt, "Thinking and Moral Considerations," 434. Arendt notes that Alcibiades and Critias were not content with being taught how to think "without being taught a doctrine, and they changed the non-results of the Socratic thinking examination into negative results." But even if we accept her interpretation, this underscores how thinking is not sufficient to liberate the faculty of judgment. There is a further perplexity when Arendt, in characterizing Socrates as a thinker, tells us, "Ugliness and evil are excluded by definition from the thinking concern, although they may occasionally turn up as deficiencies, as lack of beauty, injustice, and evil (*kakia*) as lack of good" (437).

38. Hannah Arendt, "Martin Heidegger at Eighty," in *Heidegger and Modern Philosophy*, ed. Michael Murray (New Haven: Yale University Press, 1978), 295.

39. Arendt, "Thinking and Moral Considerations," 445–46.

40. Margaret Canovan perceptively illuminates the tensions exhibited in Arendt's appeal to Socrates and Heidegger as thinkers. She relates this to the larger theme of philosophy and politics. See "Socrates or Heidegger?" in *Hannah Arendt*, 268–74. See also my discussion of Arendt's understanding of judgment in "Judging—The Actor and the Spectator," in *Philosophical Profiles: Essays in a Pragmatic Mode* (Cambridge, England: Polity Press, 1986).

41. Hannah Arendt, "Basic Moral Propositions," Arendt Archives, Library of Congress.

42. In "Some Questions of Moral Philosophy," Arendt expresses the issue succinctly:

> The total collapse of conscience and morality, or rather of the age-old laws according to which men in our civilization ought to behave, suggest that what we are talking about is indeed nothing but mores—customs and manners, adjustment to society: Conscience is nothing but the voice of society, of those who are around us.
>
> Against this: There were always a few with whom it did not work. And we are concerned in this course with these: What prevented them from acting as everybody else did? . . .
>
> Those who resisted could be found in all walks of life, among poor and entirely uneducated people as among members of good and high society. They said little: The argument was always the same: No *conflict*, no struggle, the evil was no temptation . . . they simply said I can't; I'd rather die; for life would be not worthwhile when I have done it.
>
> Hence we are concerned with the behavior of common people, not of Nazis or convinced Bolsheviks, not with saints and heroes, and not with born criminals. For if there is any such thing as what we call morality for want of a better term, it certainly concerns such common people and common happenings.

Twelve

Evil, Violence, Thinking, Judgment: Working in the Breach of Politics

Stephen T. Leonard

I do not believe that we can stabilize the situation in which we have been since the seventeenth century in any final way.
                                                                    Hannah Arendt

Called upon toward the (unforeseen) end of her life to articulate the intended effects of her work, Hannah Arendt said that her aim was not to "indoctrinate" her students to adopt a specific set of concepts and categories—let alone some kind of theory! Rather it was her "hope" that the effect of her teaching would be to instill a commitment to "act" in the face of "certain extreme things which are the actual consequence of non-thinking."[1]

This attitude is at once an inspiring pedagogical ideal and a puzzling, frustrating, perhaps even saddening practical commitment.[2] Arendt's assertion that the "question" of her success is "how [her students] might act" in situations "when the chips are down" (OHA, p. 309) defines a test of teaching that most of us would surely aspire to pass. Yet, considering her lifelong effort to help us see how we might mark and live the distinction between beast, human being, and (ideally) citizen,[3] the fact that she understood the practical intent of her pedagogical efforts to be relevant only in moments of dire emergency is a disappointing testament to the ideal of "the public space."

Moments of emergency are not the times when human beings together articulate that glorious space of appearances where we find expression as *zoon politikon*. Rather, they are the moments when our humanity itself is subject to full assault, when moral, ethical, and (therefore) political standards fail. These are moments of last resort, of life and death—when evil shapes the world, violence rules, courage does not bring glory, contestation does not bring the immortality of remembrance, and virtue (sadly enough) is reduced to being truly its own reward.

Of course, Arendt's legacy, as this volume attests, goes well beyond her minimal—some might say overly modest—hopes. Yet after considering the essays by Richard Bernstein and John McGowan (and others in this collection), it is difficult to avoid the conclusion that Hannah Arendt herself never found good grounds for hoping that the "political life" could be realized in the modern (let alone the postmodern) age. Among other things, I suggest that much of Arendt's work assumes a radical breach of the possibilities of politics.

Recognizing this does not make her any less suggestive, any less enlightening, or any less provocative (even if it makes her suggestive, enlightening, and provocative *in different ways*). And there is no evidence to suggest that Arendt herself felt debilitated by what might be called the hopelessness of politics; there are a vigor and an enthusiasm that infect all her writing, right up to the last. Moreover, there are interpretive advantages to reading Arendt as working in the breach of politics, where the corruption is so deep that recovery is improbable, if not impossible.[4] It may help explain what makes her so difficult for us. And, at the very least, it may steer us away from the temptation to find in Arendt some plan "to retie the broken thread of tradition or to invent some newfangled surrogates with which to fill the gap between past and future."[5]

All this said, it is still well worth asking about the relationship of Arendt's practical and pedagogical intentions to her normative ideals. It does not seem unreasonable to ask whether her normative ideals are appropriate if she herself cannot find good grounds for defending them. And it does not seem unreasonable to ask whether her pedagogical and practical intentions are appropriate in light of questions about her ideals.

Complicated as these objections might seem, we needn't travel far to find the organizing themes their analysis would require. In fact, I argue, John McGowan's essay shows that Arendt's account of the modern breach of politics renders problematic her own account of "politics." And, as I think Richard Bernstein's essay implies, Arendt's concern with "the life of the mind," especially the human capacities of thinking and judging, is a retreat into the breach of politics, not a means of grounding the creation of "the public space." Put the two together and it begins to seem that "the life of the mind" is Arendt's Maginot Line, an impermeable (one hopes) defense of last resort in the struggle to sustain the ideal of the polis. But we all know the problems of Maginot Lines; in Arendt's case there simply wasn't much left of the republic to defend when she fell back on "thinking" to take up its defense.

Locating the Breach of Politics

Hannah Arendt's classical conception of politics is, I think, familiar enough to warrant only elliptical treatment in this limited space. For my purposes it is important to note that her positive appraisal of antiquity is rare among moderns for the compelling reasons that she articulated in her various reflections on the character and content of what she might have called that offensive oxymoron "modern political theory."

The upshot of Arendt's appreciation for the life of the polis and her reading of modern political thought is that her ideological contemporaries are actually those who, at the birth of the modern age, looked to antiquity as a source of insight for the new "independent, secular, political realm such as had been unknown since the fall of the Roman Empire" (*BPF*, p. 160). It is Montesquieu, to whom she is referring in the quoted passage, and his followers who should be counted as Arendt's ideological contemporaries. Like them, she found in antiquity a source for thinking about politics in secular modernity. But there is more: it is from Montesquieu, "the last political thinker to concern himself with forms of government," that Arendt draws her analysis of tyranny's corrosive effects on what she calls "politics" and "power."[6] It is Montesquieu, she says, who was the only modern to speak to the differences between political liberty (or freedom) and freedom of the will.[7] And it is with Montesquieu (and "pre-Christian antiquity") that the founding fathers of the American Republic—apparently, for Arendt, one of the few groups of moderns who were able to create a "body politic"— shared a clear understanding of what political liberty requires.[8]

Undergirding all this, and most crucial for the issues at hand, Arendt shared with Montesquieu and his followers a belief in a fundamental distinction between the activities of politics and the demands of necessity. When matters of necessity—such as economic status— become matters of politics, the fundamental distinction between the two collapses, and the space of politics is overwhelmed. Thus, Arendt, like Montesquieu and his followers, was well aware of the corrosive effects of what Adam Ferguson called "the spirit which reigns in a commercial state" and what Benjamin Constant called "the commercial tendency of the epoch."⁹ The effect of this subversion of politics is that, in words that Arendt herself could have written, moderns have become concerned with "security in private enjoyment" rather than with "an active and constant participation in the collective power";¹⁰ or, as Adam Ferguson argued, moderns are unable to "rise above considerations of mere subsistence, and the regards of interest."¹¹

Here is that dimension of modernity marked by the rise of *political economy* as a mode of political thought and practice, and here are the preoccupations of what Arendt called *homo faber*.¹² As John McGowan shows, this sphere of necessity was, for Arendt, hardly a suitable measure of "man *qua* man." Moreover, and importantly, it was a sphere of activity marked by violence, albeit necessary violence. In antiquity the struggle to be free of natural necessity meant that some ruled and some were ruled, but "social" concerns did not taint "political" relations. For moderns the preoccupation with necessity has allowed the violence of necessity to undermine the public space.

Of course, many critics have pointed out that this distinction between the political and the social removes social inequalities from political consideration. And, of course, we might simply dismiss Arendt's conceptual and practical distinction as merely another instance of her practice of securing what McGowan calls "theorizing by fiat." But, as I hope to have suggested and as she herself insisted, Arendt's definition of the political is not idiosyncratic—except, perhaps, for twentieth-century moderns.¹³ Nor was her account of the polis an idealized one; she knew that the polis was not perfect, and she would have agreed with Adam Ferguson that in antiquity "the honours of one half of the species were sacrificed to those of the other. . . . In the midst of our encomiums bestowed on the Greeks and the Romans, we are, by this circumstance, made to remember, that no human institution is perfect."¹⁴

The imperfections of the polis having been noted, it should also be noted that imperfection was hardly a curse for Arendt. In fact, McGowan argues, it was the reality of human imperfection that led her to insist that promising and forgiveness were critical to sustaining human relations without resort to violence. Additionally, it seems that Arendt's willingness to accommodate imperfection was merely the flip side of her opposition to the hope for human perfection and to the "conformism" it often entailed, an illusion that she found in Marx and other revolutionaries of modernity. Together, imperfection and opposition to conformity are also important conceptual components in Arendt's ontology of relations, which she encompassed with the experiences of natality and plurality (*HC*, pp. 38–49). Natality recognizes how the limitations of birth and death make us fallible and vulnerable; plurality recognizes how the differences of our experiences make us fundamentally unique individuals.

From the recognition and the embrace of imperfection, to the opposition to conformism in thought and practice and the celebration of fallibility and difference embodied in natality and plurality, Arendt easily expands upon the classical model of politics. Indeed, as John McGowan demonstrates, it is the ontological qualities of natality and plurality that Arendt believes "the political" (by definition) cultivates. In this sense, accusing Arendt of subscribing to a cramped or narrow account of the political is really beside the point. Within a conceptual universe where the violence of necessity cannot perfect humankind, "politics" excludes "social" questions.

But in another sense the objection is exactly on the mark. For there is much in Arendt to suggest that the greatest threats to human excellence today do not come from the difficulties of transcending necessity nor even from forms of government (such as tyranny) that arise from the desire to transcend necessity yet fail to enable the realization of "political power." Rather, they come from forms of activity that have nothing to do with the struggle against necessity. These are activities that involve violence, but it is violence entailed in the struggle against, or the struggle for, natality and plurality. These activities and forms of violence are embodied in totalitarianism and the modern struggle for equality.

What totalitarianism and the modern struggle for equality point out is that even if Arendt, like Montesquieu and his followers, might praise the idea of the polis, the fact is that her experience of modernity was different from theirs. And this is no small matter. Experience, she says, is that from which "thought itself arises" and to which it "must remain bound as . . . its bearings" (*BPF*, p. 14). She interpreted her experiences as requiring "thinking without bannisters" (OHA, p. 336). By contrast, I think, her ideological contemporaries still had bannisters to use, or at least the remnants of a handrail and a few intact balusters. Even if the structure of thought was by their time beginning to come apart, they could still assume much of what made their reverence for antiquity a relevant, rather than merely antiquarian, exercise. Without these remnants, and in light of the challenges of totalitarianism and the modern struggle for equality, Arendt's defense of "politics" falls apart.

On the cusp of modernity, where tyrants could not be totalitarians and inequality was in many quarters accepted as a given fact of existence, the enactment of a classically informed model of politics must have seemed a real possibility. First, the reach of tyrants was severely limited. One could still escape or avoid mechanisms of state discipline, and the tyrant, unlike the totalitarian, did not have the capacity to erase individuality. This can happen only in mass societies, and on the cusp of modernity there were no mass societies. Resistance to tyranny did not, therefore, mean resistance to attacks on the very ontology of human being, as it does in the case of totalitarianism. Resistance to tyranny need only involve trying to reopen the public space. Tyranny was not an assault on humanity, even if it hampered the full realization of human potential.

Likewise, resistance to the "commercial tendencies of the epoch," the subversion of politics by concerns of necessity, could have been easily conceptualized as a process of normative inversion. Reverse the relative influences of social and political concerns, and the public space could then reappear. It needs to be said, however, that this public space required as its presupposition not only the ontological distinction between necessity and politics, but also an ontological distinction between citizens and others.

In antiquity the real equality of citizens was made possible by real, conceptually well articulated social inequalities. At the cusp of modernity, advocates of the classical model certainly had a more expansive conception of who might qualify for membership in the body politic, but social inequalities still remained. For some—perhaps for most—

these social inequalities could be screened by continuing to conceptualize politics and citizenship without reference to social inequalities.

In a generous interpretation we could certainly admit that the violence of necessity remains a real threat in modern life. But, as McGowan suggests, it strains the limits of credibility when Arendt argues (like her ideological contemporaries) that poverty and want are "natural," especially when she dismisses these concerns in contexts where there is wealth in abundance. Indeed, such claims begin to point out how Arendt's "bannisterless" defense of the polis cannot be sustained. If Arendt could continue to conceptualize the realm of necessity as it might have been at the cusp of modernity, her account of politics might make more sense. But the simple fact is that for a classical conception of politics to work, not only must, as Adam Ferguson put it, "the honours of one half of the species [be] sacrificed to those of the other" (and this is a rather conservative estimate), but also *the humanity* of those who suffer most from existing relations of power have to be sacrificed. Women, slaves, and those who lived the life of *homo faber* were not sacrificed because of scarcity (the concept itself is a modern one); rather, they were sacrificed because it was assumed that that is their lot "by nature." To repeat, those confined to the realm of necessity and excluded from the realm of political equality were there *not* because of "scarcity" but because it was assumed they belonged there "by nature."[15]

In other words, the necessity/politics opposition is an ontological distinction, in two related senses. One sense is that these are different spheres of life, different spheres of activity; the other is that these spheres of life are occupied by fundamentally different creatures— politics by "man" and necessity by human "nonman." What I think makes Arendt's defense of a classical conception of politics so difficult to accept is her failure to recognize the mutually constitutive character of this ontological pairing. Bluntly put, if you're going to exclude "social" demands from "politics," then you'd better be prepared to exclude a large part of the species from the category of "man *qua* man." And if you can't exclude part of the species from the category of citizen, you'd better be prepared to admit their concerns for recognition— even if they are only "social"—as potentially "political."

What is most striking—and telling against her conception of politics—is that Hannah Arendt was an eloquent defender of the idea that we all share, as members of the same species, the ontological characteristics of natality and plurality. Against the ontologically given inequalities that enabled the ready distinction between the social and the political, Arendt argues that natality and plurality are what make it possible for us to become "man *qua* man," *and they are qualities that belong to every member of the species.* Thus, engaging totalitarianism and the modern struggle for equality in terms of a concern for natality and plurality is to move beyond and radically expand the boundaries of the "political."

Totalitarianism seeks complete domination, a goal made more or less realizable to the extent that plurality can be diminished and uniformity and conformity strengthened. The struggle for equality, especially in the struggle against racism (and one could readily add here sexism, gender exclusions, ethnic discriminations, and exclusions that derive from age, education, physical disabilities, and other characteristics) is a struggle against the "humiliation" of, in McGowan's words, "an inequality that results from being deemed categorically unfit for full and equal participation with others." This is a struggle for recognition but not merely for material or economic equality. It is not a struggle for the means of subsistence, but a struggle for the means of expression. It is, in short, a struggle for the acknowledgment and respect of one's humanity, or, as Richard Bernstein put it, for "the very conditions required to live a *human* life."

I suppose the point here is that if the same concerns Arendt expresses in her analysis of totalitarianism and racism had been applied to her reconstruction of "politics," she might have told a different story. This other story may well have been predicated on the indefensibility of the distinction between "politics" and "the social." But, unfortunately, the only story we have is the one that Arendt chose to tell—and it is not a story we should find compelling.

What do we make of this and of Arendt's response to the breach of politics in modernity? McGowan suggests we read her account of the political as "utopian"; even her defense of the American Revolution would, on this account, be "utopian." Thus, for Arendt, the political is a "utopian space characterized by the absence of violence."

This is a generous and sympathetic interpretation, but it works— as McGowan himself shows—only so long as one is willing to ignore the way that Arendt's account of modernity undercuts her account of politics, for if the evil of totalitarianism and humiliating inequalities is that they diminish natality and plurality, *in what sense can a defensible conception of politics excuse forms of human relations that are also antithetical to plurality and natality?* To insist on a distinction between the social and the political when some are excluded for reasons having nothing to do with the necessity of scarcity is to perpetuate a model of politics that should have collapsed when the traditions that supported it disappeared.

But perpetuate that model is exactly what Hannah Arendt did. And what I take to be her response to the apparent dissonance that arises out of trying to make sense of "politics" where there are no grounds for doing so—namely, in examining the life of the mind—doesn't help matters much. As McGowan says, Arendt's "thoughts on violence can . . . be seen to raise issues about the conditions in which judgments can and must be made," especially when "preexisting categories" are "inadequate." The question is, which categories are inadequate? I am arguing that Arendt became concerned with judgment and thinking precisely because the concepts and categories in her account of "politics" proved inadequate in the face of totalitarianism and the modern demand for equality. John McGowan's essay intimates that Arendt's considerations of evil and violence themselves evince doubts about her account of politics. Richard Bernstein's essay on Arendt's account of the relationship of evil, thinking, and judgment further advances these doubts.

Judgment without Bannisters?

"Arendt constantly stresses how the unprecedented event of twentieth-century totalitarianism has ruptured our traditional moral and political concepts and standards," says Richard Bernstein. And it is "the totality of moral collapse" he says she wanted us to confront.

One aspect of this confrontation was trying to recover the grounding of judgment, but in a way that did not rely on the now discredited "bannisters" of tradition. The work that was published as *The Life of the Mind* was not, of course, Arendt's first foray into what she called "thinking without bannisters" (*M*, p. 336). A decade and a half earlier, Arendt wrote that "we seem to be neither equipped nor prepared for [the] activity of thinking," and she offered the essays of *Between Past and Future* as "exercises" that would enable the gaining of "experience in *how* to think; they do not contain prescriptions on what to think or which truths to hold" (*BPF*, pp. 13–14).

All of this fits readily with some of Arendt's claims that I have noted here: that she thought totalitarianism had definitively demonstrated the collapse of standards for judgment; that in the face of this collapse she thought it necessary to consider how to "think without bannisters"; that her pedagogical intention was not to "indoctrinate." Indeed, her fear of replacing one set of standards for judgment with another was palpable. Perhaps more than anything else she was concerned that if "thinking" did not find its place in the modern world, the loss of tradition would be replaced by the utter and radical contingency of values. And the effect, she believed, was that "the moment that you give anybody a new set of values—or this famous 'bannister'—you can immediately exchange it" (OHA, p. 314).

But what her concern with "thinking" does not fit is the hope that her students—not by indoctrination but by being "roused" or "awakened"—would *act* in the face of "certain extreme things that are the actual consequence of non-thinking" (OHA, p. 309), for if thinking and judging (along with willing) are merely what Arendt calls "mental activities," in what sense might they secure a particular mode of action, even one as desperate as facing "the actual consequence of non-thinking?" Indeed, she even used as an epigraph Heidegger's assertion that mental activities "do not endow us directly with the power to act" (*LM*, p. 1; see also p. 71 ff.).

Nonetheless, she still clung to the hope that she might be able to determine whether and how thinking "is of such a nature that it 'conditions' men against evil-doing."[16] And it was the tension produced by noting the "invisibility" and impotence of thinking, on the one hand, and hoping for its efficacy, on the other, that lay behind what Richard Bernstein called "the conceptual issue [Arendt] so forcefully raises," namely, "the relation between thinking, judging, and evil"—a relationship that, Bernstein argues, Arendt never establishes in any convincing way.

Arendt's defenders might respond that much of what informs her concerns about thinking, willing, and judging is the recognition that, in her words, "although [mental activities] can never directly change reality . . . the principles by which we act and the criteria by which we judge and conduct our lives depend ultimately on the life of the mind" (*LM*, p. 71). It is this assumed connection, however, that is in question. Bernstein's reconstruction of the gaps, inconsistencies, and tensions in Arendt's argument is compelling and clear, and I will not rehearse it here. But I do want to suggest how some of the faults he identifies can be turned against Arendt's "politics."

My opening comes in the form of Arendt's characterization of the importance of remembrance for politics. Remembrance, she says, is the means by which human beings preserve the "treasure" of "that public space between themselves where freedom could appear." It is through "tradition," "which selects and names, which hands down and preserves, which indicates where the treasures are and what their worth is," that remembrance is made possible, "for remembrance . . . is helpless outside a preestablished framework of reference" (*BPF*, pp. 4–6). Put another way, remembrance, through tradition, makes it possible to identify those *exemplars* which Richard Bernstein rightly notes are critical for Arendt's method of argument and crucial for her understanding of judgment.

Recognizing the importance of remembrance, many troubling problems with Arendt's ideas now begin to emerge. First, there is the obvious, but not trivial, objection that if politics requires remembrance, and remembrance tradition, in what sense could we have "politics" in the face of totalitarianism—where traditions that could ground judgment are missing—or in the face of modernity in general—where the thread of tradition is all but lost? Perhaps this objection might be answered by noting (again) that for Arendt, the challenge of the present was precisely the challenge of thinking without the "bannisters" of tradition.

There is more than a mere logical difficulty or conceptual tension at stake here. The problem is a practical, even a political, one, for Arendt's thoughts about the life of the mind must themselves be read as an attempt to construct (or perhaps reconstruct) a "tradition." *The Life of the Mind* may be about "thinking without bannisters"—that is, the suspect and weak bannisters of modernity—but it is not devoid of an appeal to a "tradition," even one of its own making, for if Arendt is going to make good the connection between thinking, judging, and, ultimately, acting, she too must take up the task of remembrance.

Thus, Arendt assumes that she is engaged in thinking without bannisters, yet her own account of the conditions of thinking and judging requires, by definition, the constitution or reconstitution of a tradition from which remembrance might proceed. The practical problems in this logical or conceptual inconsistency become readily evident when we consider the exemplars of thinking that Arendt cites.

On this matter Bernstein subjects Arendt to a withering critique. As he argues, Arendt's exemplary "thinkers," Socrates and Martin Heidegger, are at best problematic and at worst ill-conceived models, particularly in light of concerns about the relationship of thinking and judging. Arendt herself said that Socrates had the effect of arousing "license and cynicism," and as I. F. Stone (among others) has argued, Socrates was hardly a model citizen.[17] "Much more damaging to Arendt's thesis," says Bernstein, "is her own blindness concerning Heidegger's 'error' in supporting Hitler and the Nazis." If these are exemplars of thinking-judging human beings, thoughtlessness might not be so bad.

Of course, Arendt would not have abided such a conclusion, for it was against the "thoughtlessness" of people like Adolph Eichmann and the "consequence of non-thinking" that was totalitarianism that she took up the problem of thinking and judging (hence Bernstein's coupling of evil, thinking, and judgment). Yet one cannot help but be uncomfortable if given the Hobson's choice Arendt presents us: either Eichmann-like "thoughtlessness" or Socratic or Heideggerian "thinking." These are not, in fact, the only choices; we might still consider as exemplars those who refused to act thoughtlessly or to withdraw into the "invisibility" (and apparent impotence) of thought.

Here we arrive at the last piece of Arendt's puzzling account of the relationship of evil, thinking, and judgment. Bernstein notes that one of the critical deficiencies of Arendt's argument is that she could not "account for the differences between Adolf Eichmann and Anton Schmidt."

Arendt's apparent inability to produce a plausible account of how totalitarianism can erase the capacity for thinking and judging in one man while another suffers no such loss, makes the project contained in *The Life of the Mind* appear politically irrelevant. Schmidt's actions demonstrate that, in fact, totalitarianism did not eliminate the capacity for judgment from the world. In light of what Bernstein calls "the bitter irony" that Heidegger's actions produced for Arendt's assertion that "thinking" is "political by implication" (TMC, pp. 445–46), Schmidt's actions also suggest that Arendt may have been grasping at straws in trying to secure judgment by an appeal to thinking.

How might we explain her misplaced concerns? Arendt herself said that it is "when men are deprived of the public space—which is constituted by acting together and then fills of its own accord with the events and stories that develop into history—they retreat into their freedom of thought."[18] Anton Schmidt apparently felt no such need, yet Hannah Arendt did.

Now it seems that we have to ask whether Arendt's retreat to thinking about thinking, to thinking "without bannisters" and with Socrates and Heidegger, marked the loss of the public space. I think not. A more plausible explanation is that it was the inadequacies of Arendt's conception of the political that prevented her from seeing how the Anton Schmidts, the Rosa Parkses, and millions of other (in her words) "common people" in modernity still found a place to resist the modern assault on humanity, to act to secure the space for the re-alization of natality and plurality—to act, in short, *politically*. There is no small irony in the fact that she praised the courage and judgment of these people even while she fell back on "thinking" in her struggle against modernity. What's more, without a myopic vision of the politi-cal, Arendt might have even given these people credit for helping to create the public space that today allows us to debate whether Hannah Arendt's conception of the political is appropriate for contemporary life. This fact, it seems to me, is the most powerful argument against that conception and against the temptation to believe that "thinking" is the place of last resort where our humanity can be secured.

Lessons

The problem with Arendt, if I may be a bit flip, is her "post-Heideg-gerian recovery of republicanism."[19] Failing to find the resources for her republic, Arendt turns to find the (Heideggerian) moment of being in thinking that can underwrite a renewal of hope. Thankfully, her own analysis of totalitarianism and the modern struggle for equality shows that our political concerns ought to be quite other than those that fill the space of her "politics."

What does the challenge posed by totalitarianism and by justified violence in the struggle against inequality tell us about a classical con-ception of politics? It tells us that among the "bannisters" we no longer need and the "traditions" we can do without are those which presuppose a conceptually well founded reality of social inequality. And thinking without bannisters today may well require us to find a way of thinking the political that does not require us—as Arendt's concept of the political does—to be blind to the social and to construct a purely formal, and practically illusory, equality. As Arendt herself shows, such illusory equality in an age without bannisters cannot and should not be sustained.

Arendt said that "action as beginning . . . is the actualization of the human condition of natality, [and] speech . . . is the actualization of the human condition of plurality" (*HC*, p. 178). But if this is so, then anything that prevents—or enables—the actualization of natality and plurality is, by definition, political, if by politics we mean the activities through which we express our natality and plurality and thereby become "man *qua* man." Even if we shouldn't follow Arendt in seeking the kind of politics that can insulate "the social" and "the political" to preserve the privileged status of the "citizen," we still might be able to follow her in seeking the kind of politics that can make good the promise of freedom in the actualization of natality and plurality for each and every human being.

And so, for us, one of the lessons of Arendt's work in the modern breach of "politics" should be that, as John McGowan rightly puts it, "anything is potentially political." Another lesson is that the capacity for judgment is still alive in the world and that if we are going to engage the kind of remembrance that can make freedom possible, we ought not retreat or withdraw into thinking about thinking but honor the tradition of those who acted to realize humanity itself. And no account of "politics" should delay us from that task.

Notes

1. Hannah Arendt, "On Hannah Arendt" (hereafter, OHA), in *Hannah Arendt: The Recovery of the Public World*, ed. Melvyn A. Hill (New York: St. Martin's Press, 1979), p. 309.

2. Here I follow Arendt's interlocutors in ibid., pp. 303–15.

3. The three-part distinction is intentional. My reasons for using it should become clear shortly, but, to anticipate, I assert that Arendt's own arguments lend themselves to recognizing that between "beasts" and "citizens" there are human beings. Moreover, the concerns of human beings could well be considered "political." Thus, although I agree with John McGowan that Arendt seems to argue that political activity is what makes us human and distinguishes us from beasts, what is at issue here is whether Arendt's conflation of the human and the citizen can be sustained. I think not.

4. In this I recognize my differences with many of Arendt's students and disciples. Whereas Arendt's followers may see her work as intending "the recovery of the public world" (to use the title of Melvyn Hill's edited volume), Bernstein and McGowan have pushed me to read Arendt as intending "the recovery of humanity," which I take to be a political activity, but not precisely in Arendt's sense of the term.

5. Hannah Arendt, *Between Past and Future* (hereafter, *BPF*)(New York: Penguin, 1954), p. 14.

6. See Hannah Arendt, *The Human Condition* (hereafter, *HC*) (Chicago: University of Chicago Press, 1958), especially pp. 199–204. The quoted passage is on p. 202.

7. See Hannah Arendt, "Willing," in *The Life of the Mind* (hereafter, *LM*) (New York: Harcourt Brace Jovanovich, 1978), especially pp. 198–200.

8. See especially ibid., pp. 199–201. John McGowan's discussion of Arendt's analysis of the American Revolution elaborates on the conceptual and practical dimensions of "the political."

9. Adam Ferguson, quoted in Paul Rahe, *Republics Ancient and Modern* (Chapel Hill: University of North Carolina Press, 1992), p. 55. Benjamin Constant is quoted on p. 15.

10. Constant, quoted in ibid., p. 15.

11. Ferguson, quoted in ibid., p. 16.

12. See Arendt, *HC*, especially chapter 18.

13. Arendt was sensitive to this charge, as is evident in OHA, pp. 322–24. Her response here seems to miss the point of C. B. Macpherson's comment. Macpherson wanted to discuss how Arendt's conceptual distinctions screen out class conflict, whereas it seems that Arendt was concerned that Marx believed in human perfectibility.

This difference is important. Arendt might be read as trying to preserve a classical conception of politics *against* the modern tendency to believe in human perfectibility. By contrast, those who are critical of Arendt's conception of politics might be read as attacking the idea that the exclusion of "social" concerns from politics actually perpetuates inequalities that *assume* the more pronounced imperfectibility of some persons (those confined to "the social") while preserving the privileges of others ("citizens") who suffer from a less pronounced imperfectibility. By seeing only the threat of perfectibility, Arendt misses the crucial ontological distinctions that support inequality, or so I argue.

14. Ferguson, quoted in Rahe, *Republics Ancient and Modern*, p. 16.

15. Arendt offers an anachronistic reading of classical politics when she makes "scarcity" the explanation for exclusion from politics. The Greeks never believed that scarcity explained the need for subordination. For them, some were natural rulers, others naturally ruled.

The problem with an appeal to scarcity—as Marxists have discovered—is that it is a highly contested concept, both philosophically and historically. It is surprising that Arendt adopts it so readily, especially given her criticisms of modern thought. In a sense, the concept of scarcity enables Arendt to ignore what makes the social/political distinction work in conditions of inequality, namely, the dehumanization of the excluded.

16. Hannah Arendt, "Thinking and Moral Considerations: A Lecture" (hereafter, TMC), *Social Research* 38, no. 3 (fall 1971), p. 417.

17. See I. F. Stone, *The Trial of Socrates* (Boston: Little, Brown, 1988).

18. Hannah Arendt, *Men in Dark Times* (Harmondsworth, England: Penguin, 1968), p. 17.

19. I purloined this phrase—which inspired this essay—from my friend James Farr. For those who find my flippancy offensive or my arguments weak, I take full responsibility for use of the phrase. For those who find the phrase insightful or my arguments here compelling, Professor Farr must be given due credit.

Afterword

Reflective Judgments by a Spectator on a Conference That Is Now History

Martin Jay

To the consternation of certain of her admirers, near the end of her life Hannah Arendt unexpectedly posited a principled opposition between the exercise of judgment and direct participation in the realm of politics. Not those who act, she followed Kant in arguing, but those who come after them have the final word, because only they have the ability to see the whole for what it is, "the miserable story of mankind's eternal ups and downs, the spectacle of sound and fury,"[1] a mere farce that the actors—who are in Kant's word "fools"—naively take to be meaningful. "The spectator, not the actor," she insisted, "holds the clue to the meaning of human affairs."[2]

But to avoid being bored by the melancholy spectacle he sees, Arendt then added, the spectator must himself invent a pattern, tell a story that wrests intelligibility out of chaos. Judgment, therefore, is ultimately an ironic and unhappy business, for unlike the actors, who genuinely think their stories are true, the spectator knows on some level that his are aesthetic concoctions, artful secondary elaborations that wrest form from formlessness. He must thus eschew any empathetic identification with actors themselves, any pretense of faithfully reexperiencing their own experiences, and must judge, to use her colorful metaphor, "without bannisters."

Such judgments, whether we call them historical, political, or perhaps even moral, are, however, more than merely *post facto* subjective or even intersubjective impositions fashioned entirely out of whole cloth, even if they are never true to the course of events as they actually were, for the judge, Arendt insisted, is not the same as a fabricator of fictions, a *homo faber* or creative genius who makes things up out of thin air. Instead, judgment involves a kind of selection of what is presented, albeit one that involves the ability to demolish the set configurations that may prevail. Thus, when Seyla Benhabib in a frequently cited essay refers to the "redemptive power of narrative" in Arendt, she explicitly intends the blasting of the false historicist continuum of history and the willful reconfiguration of its ruins into new constellations that Arendt's great friend Walter Benjamin posited as the only way to undermine an ideological relation to the past.[3]

Although disturbing to those who remember Arendt's apparent privileging of the *vita activa* over the *vita contemplativa* in all of her previous work, these thoughts on both the necessity and the burden of *post facto* judgment can provide modest comfort to those, like myself, in the awkward position of having to comment on an entire volume in which the intellectual activity to be sure, has been anything but foolish. If I have any advantage, it is that of the latecomer, who can survey the field from afar and make out—or rather blast and then reconstellate—patterns that the contributors may have been too close to their endeavor to discern. As a spectatorial judge commenting on a broad collection of voices, I have the privilege of telling what it means, or at least I can do so until someone else plays the role at a later date—for as Arendt herself emphasized, her essentially Kantian notion of spectatorship, unlike that of Hegel's, was irreducibly pluralist; there is no final judge who gets the last word, no audience who occupy the same seats at the spectacle forever.

From the thus admittedly tentative vantage point of this temporarily final spectator, let me first say how rich and suggestive the essays in this volume have been. It is clear that despite a generation of vigorous debate about the import of her work, Arendt still has the power to provoke fresh and challenging readings. What also seems evident is that the time for either pious defensiveness or unrelieved hostility is now thankfully past, allowing a more dispassionate distance I will try to emulate.

If the book as a whole has had any center of gravity, it has been the vexed issue of the relationship between politics, aesthetics, and ethics in Arendt's work. Several of the essays have defended her version of the aestheticization of politics against previous critics. Arguing against the claim that she is either a nostalgic communitarian pining for the lost world of the Greek polis or a Habermasian modernist hoping for a consensual public sphere, Dana Villa presents us with a protopostmodernist Arendt who willingly embraces a certain version of alienation, that from a putatively natural or fully realized state of Being, and denies an expressivist notion of authentic selfhood. His Arendt is the celebrant of a performative politics of appearances in which the coherence of the self is a theatrical artifact, an achieved fiction, whose paradoxically unintended coherence can be appreciated— indeed can be said to be fashioned—only by spectators after the fact. Restoring the Greek agora or realizing the possibility of "acting in concert," which most commentators take to be Arendt's goal, Villa claims in fact was not; what mattered for her instead was preserving "our capacity for initiatory, agonistic action and spontaneous, independent judgment." As such, her ideas can be fruitfully integrated with those of postmodern theorists of resistance, such as Foucault, who also reject any dream of a renewed realm of positive communal meaning in the name of individual aesthetic self-fashioning. Although in his earlier works cited in his notes Villa resists a simple assimilation of Arendt to postmodernism, in his contribution to this volume his qualifications are far less evident.

Villa's ingenious reading of Arendt against the grain as a frankly aesthetic thinker, insulated from attempts to integrate her ideas with Gadamer's resurrection of the Greek *phronesis* or Habermas's intersubjective *Öffentlichkeit*, is seconded by Anthony Cascardi but with certain important qualifications. Although an aestheticizer of politics, Cascardi's Arendt is not yet a postmodernist, not yet, we might say, a reader of Kant through Lyotardian lenses. As a result, the aesthetics she privileges is still, alas, that of the beautiful rather than the sublime, which Cascardi claims is "part of her larger passion to save politics from irrationalism." To do so, however, she neglects those moments in Kant's work when humans stand alone in the face of an awesome and majestic nature, in favor of those when we are together in a society. This bias then produces a slippage from questions of aesthetic judgment to those of social or political solidarity. Or, as Cascardi claims in one of his notes, the problem is that Arendt depends on covert and undefended analogies between taste and morality through the Kantian notion of an "enlarged mentality," and then between morality and politics based on a flabby belief in the *sensus communis*.

Cascardi instead prefers a nonanalogical aesthetic politics of the sublime, which he identifies in somewhat melodramatic fashion with a "politics of radical transformation" that "relies on the feelings generated by those things that stand beyond the available limits of representation." He wants to disentangle what he sees as Kant's support for an aesthetics of "free particulars" outside any system of criteria for judging, and Arendt's attempt to subordinate such incommensurable particulars to regularity and rules, which implies the dreaded universality Cascardi associates with rationality. This vision is not all that far from the one Villa attributes to Arendt, although Cascardi thinks Arendt herself failed to attain it, being drawn, as he puts it, "to those moments when Kant himself seemed to recoil from its pain and power." Both Villa and Cascardi are anxious to discredit any crypto-Habermasian attempt to harness her thoughts on reflective judgment for the purposes of communicative rationality. Where they part company, however, is on the question of appearances: Villa's stress on theatricality implies that politics is an arena of such appearances in which spectators can judge the "initiatory, agonistic action" of actors, whereas Cascardi's sublime transformations somehow happen beyond any positive representation.

One way to explain the difference is that Villa seems to stress what might be called normal politics, the politics of an already created world that can be only perpetually resisted rather than radically transformed, whereas Cascardi is interested in the possibility of radical transformation, those unusual moments of actual foundation that Arendt herself found so fascinating. Such moments Cascardi compares to the sublime, because they are never beholden to prior rules or dependent on a prior consensus; their very arbitrariness and contingency is a sign of their radical freedom. Although one might perhaps call such moments of founding prepolitical, at least from the point of view of the normal politics of theatrical appearance and spectatorial judgment in the agora, they remain admittedly remote possibilities, even in the midst of the most regularized and desiccated of public realms. Like the phenomena of natality and forgiveness, to which Arendt gave so much attention, they indicate the openness of the world to the *novum*, the absolutely new.

Whether, however, they are best understood under the sign of the sublime, as Cascardi suggests, is not so clear. In his own essay on Arendt, entitled "The Survivor," Jean-François Lyotard notes that "what is at stake in this reflective judgment is the birth of a subject and thus of a community, but only of a promised birth. With the beautiful, it is pure happiness, the miracle of promise; but with the sublime, it is its impossibility, the imminent threat of non-being. The beautiful is an event of birth; the sublime, one of death."[4] Although himself urging the melancholic acceptance of nonbeing and the opening of oneself to death,[5] Lyotard acknowledges that as a survivor of the Holocaust, Arendt had the right to side with natality, life, and the beautiful instead.

In fact, as the mention of the Holocaust suggests, the link between the sublime aestheticization of politics—indeed, any purely aesthetic reading of politics—and violence has to be posed more seriously than it is in either Villa's or Cascardi's essay. Arendt, as John McGowan skillfully shows, struggled throughout her career to find a way to untangle political action from violence. One of her most persistent ploys was to insist that whereas "sheer violence is mute,"[6] action and speech are equivalent. Her model of action was thus less the violent warrior-hero of, say, Homer's *Iliad*, than the deliberative citizen exercising her practical wisdom in the public realm. However much one may want to disentangle Arendt's stress on performance from a belief in Aristotelian *phronesis*, it is difficult to deny that by equating, on the one hand, action and speech and, on the other, violence and silence, she makes it hard to see how an aesthetics of sublime unrepresentability can produce anything very liberating, for although Arendt was notoriously hostile to representative government, preferring the direct democracy she saw in councils, she could not have been opposed to other modes of representation. In fact, she explicitly wrote that "political thought is representative. I form an opinion by considering a given issue from different viewpoints, by making present to my mind the standpoints of those who are absent; that is, I represent them."[7] Moreover, the recounting of great deeds, which provides the only immortality we humans can hope for, also depends on representation. Indeed, her whole theory of spectatorial judgment as redemptive narrative implies a faith in the power of such representation. To the extent that the sublime makes us silent in the face of what we cannot say or represent, it comes uncomfortably close to the violence that Arendt wants to distinguish from the political.

As McGowan points out, Arendt was not always successful in keeping them entirely apart. "[I]t is important to see," he tells us, "that totalitarian terror presents us with one model of violent political founding. Totalitarianism is the evil twin of the Arendtian political." How, we have to ask, can we distinguish the sublime transformation advocated by Cascardi, with its disdain for "a democratic politics of common sense, of the *sensus communis*, of (good) taste," from its malign twin? How is the making ex nihilo, the creation without any prior criteria that characterizes the interruption of normal politics, to be kept from turning into a warrant for violence and terror? According to McGowan's skeptical account, Arendt herself failed to find an answer to this question, however much she sought to defend the founding of America as an example of nonviolent foundation.

To be sure, if McGowan is right, Arendt's more ambitious desire to confine violence solely to the realm of necessity and to identify political action entirely with freedom also breaks down in practice, as do most of her attempts to set up watertight definitional oppositions. Another way to say the same thing is to note that even a nonviolent performative notion of making or founding, which initiates the polity, must of necessity presuppose an intersubjective community able to respond to the illocutionary force of the performative act itself. When Cascardi complains of Arendt's *sensus communis* that "the mechanism of reflection she describes in fact *presupposes* the totality of sense that it is the task of judgment to create," and asks, "How can one put oneself in the place of *everyone else*, if that all-inclusive community is yet to be formed?" the same might be said of the performative act that is the sublime gesture of radical transformation, for it too must be situated in a context that is always already intersubjective and social (if not fully political) and, thus, is not the same thing as standing alone in the face of nature's awesome power, a condition that reproduces the isolation that Arendt thinks is by definition antipolitical.

If this is correct, then neither can the beautiful and the sublime be neatly separated, which means that other categories will have to be introduced besides those of aesthetic judgment to save Arendt from the charge of unintelligibility. Here the reader of this collection is able to find a possible answer in the return of the moral to center stage, the realm that the postmodern celebrants of aestheticism want to push to the margins. Although he doesn't develop it, the moral comes back in McGowan's concluding remarks, where he cites Benjamin's observation that violence always "bears on moral issues." It is even more at the center of Kimberley Curtis's bold attempt to defend an ethical impulse in the very aestheticism others have found inherently amoral, and in Richard Bernstein's ruminations on Arendt's banality of evil and the controversy it unleashed.

Arguing against Villa's notion that Arendt was satisfied only to redeem appearances, Curtis claims that what she calls Arendt's "ontology of display" has a strong ethical imperative. Self-display requires an audience to appreciate it and to intensify our awareness of the reality that comes into being only through spectatorial witnessing, just as a play is only realized in a theater. "This is a profoundly ethical need," she contends, "in the sense that without such an awareness we can neither belong well to a world of others nor care for them well." Such ethical caring has an epistemological source as well, which is produced by the fact that the only impartiality granted to us mortals comes from the capacity to look on the world from the standpoint of others.

Curtis thus claims that Arendt moves from a description of ontological and epistemological realities and needs, to a prescriptive imperative to care for others. Such a move, however, is far more difficult to sustain than she suggests, implying as it does the naturalist ethics that has been witheringly debunked by theorists from Kant and G. E. Moore to Levinas and Lyotard. You can't get so easily from an ontological description of what is to an ethical command of what should be; you can't get from a need "to cultivate our tragic pleasure—our pleasure in the feeling of reality intensified through the presence of particular others and through the recalcitrant and plural quality of the world thus engendered" to an obligation to care for the pleasure of others. Like Bentham, who famously failed in his attempt to derive from his individual pleasure/pain calculus a general deontological principle of the greatest happiness of the greatest number, Curtis's version of Arendt provides no real guidance on ethical issues.

Bernstein comes to similar conclusions. Aware of the suggestive parallels that Arendt drew between reflective judgments about aesthetic, political, and moral questions, he nonetheless charges that she obscures two fundamental questions: (1) "how we are to characterize the *type* of judgment we are making when we judge something to be right or wrong. . . . [I]f we agree with Arendt that this is a reflective judgment, by which we judge particulars directly without subsuming them under a universal or general rule, we may still ask what we mean by 'right' and 'wrong' and how these predicates are to be distinguished from 'beautiful' and 'ugly.'"; and (2) if there is a crucial link between the inability to do what she called "thinking" and the failure to tell right from wrong, how can we account for the fact that some people seem to lack the capacity to think, which she claims is a human faculty per se?

Answering the second question, Bernstein admits, is beyond his powers, and I have no suggestions how to help him. But his essay does provide an interesting approach to the first in its citation of Arendt's reply to Scholem's question about her reasons for replacing the idea of the "radicality" of evil in *The Origins of Totalitarianism* with its "banality" in *Eichmann in Jerusalem*. Evil, Arendt tells Scholem, "possesses neither depth nor any demonic dimension. It can overgrow and lay waste the whole world precisely because it spreads like a fungus on the surface. It is 'thought-defying,' as I said, because thought tries to reach some depth, to go to the roots, and the moment it concerns itself with evil, it is frustrated because there is nothing." Villa's definition of Arendt's theatricalized politics, it will be recalled, was the valorization of a nonexpressive self that was nothing but appearances, a self that lacks any essence or depth prior to its revelation in the public realm. Such a self, he claims, cannot be its own author; the identity it may achieve is solely a function of the *post facto* storytelling of the spectators who witness its performance.

If evil is precisely the lack of depth and substance, the thoughtless superficiality of an Eichmann who had no internal moral resources with which to judge the role he was so ruthlessly playing in the public sphere, how, we must wonder, was he different from the postmodern aesthetic, nonexpressivist self revealing nothing but what his audience reads into his performance? When Villa entitles an earlier essay on Arendt "Beyond Good and Evil," in which he compares her with Nietzsche and contemporary French Nietzscheans,[8] he is telling us more about his own agenda than about that of Arendt herself; it is not coincidental that *Eichmann in Jerusalem* and the controversy it unleashed are entirely absent from his discussion, for by banishing morality entirely from the realm of politics, by rejecting as an inappropriate introduction of teleology and instrumentality any purpose outside the action itself, all that is left is a celebration of performance, difference, plurality, transformation, and resistance for their own sake, with no ability whatsoever to distinguish meaningfully one version from another. The result is an implicitly quantitative rather than qualitative politics, in which more of those things is assumed to be better than fewer despite the substance of what is being performed, transformed, or resisted. It's as if James Dean in *Rebel without a Cause* has become the model of a postmodern politics that eschews the depths of thought and moral distinction for the superficial narcissism of self-fashioning through infinite negation.

A quantitative rather than qualitative measure is also implied in the defense of Arendt's use of the Kantian idea of "enlarged mentality" as an antidote to subsuming particulars under universals in several of the essays. It is evident, for example, in Lisa Disch's ingenious attempt to interpret women's consciousness-raising groups as an example of the imaginative "visiting" that Arendt thought was an alternative to rational argumentation. This anti-Habermasian approach claims that the inclusion of more and more positions is a better road to impartiality than arguing about their respective validity. As Arendt once put it, "The more people's standpoints I have present in my mind while I am pondering a given issue, and the better I can imagine how I would feel and think if I were in their place, the stronger will be my capacity for representative thinking and the more valid my final conclusions, my opinion."[9]

There are several serious problems with this claim, both theoretical and practical. Why should a greater number of standpoints produce a more valid or impartial conclusion or opinion than fewer, especially when irreconcilable and adversarial positions resist mediation? Like Karl Mannheim's ill-fated attempt to coordinate ideologies through a harmonious notion of relationism,[10] Arendt's visiting is simply not sufficient to produce a more impartial position, let alone a more valid one. What does it mean, moreover, to have such differing standpoints present in one's mind at the same time? How many can any one mind entertain at once? How do you know when you have enough to become impartial? Can, moreover, women's consciousness-raising groups be considered a model of impartiality-producing visiting when they excluded on principle half of the human race, the men whose opposing viewpoints and practices were assumed to be the source of women's oppression? What kind of impartiality flows from such an a priori exclusion of the other side of the question? What kind of toleration of plurality is only extended to 50 percent of the population?

Kirstie McClure's subtle and unexpected defense of Arendt's infamous essay on Little Rock unintentionally provides another troubling example of the difficulty of realizing Arendt's antinormative agenda. McClure insightfully explains that the controversy it generated was, at the deepest level, between believers in abstract norms such as justice and equality and Arendt's faith in particular examples and specific narrations, the "odor of judgment," as Arendt calls it. Then, like Lisa Disch, McClure notes that Arendt tried to put herself in the place of the participants, which Arendt defined as white mothers and black mothers in the South.

Imaginatively visiting these participants seems to me useful and perhaps even necessary as a way to avoid the abstractions of a priori reasoning and to distinguish concrete from abstract others, but it is nonetheless insufficient for three reasons. First, why did Arendt stop with only those two ideal typical participants, failing to consider others who were also indirectly involved, other victims of racism such as, say, Native Americans or Northern black men, or white politicians such as Governor Faubus and President Eisenhower? How, after all, does one know when the proper number of visits is completed and impartiality achieved? How enlarged must our mentality be before we can reach a defensible conclusion? Second, how could Arendt know that her thought experiment in imaginative visiting was more than the imposition of her own prejudices onto the others whose position she claimed to inhabit? A recent debate between Iris Marion Young and Seyla Benhabib addresses precisely this question and comes to uncertain conclusions; even Benhabib, who defends the Arendtian position against Young's deconstructionist suspicion of any reciprocity, acknowledges that one should take the perspective of others into account but not pretend to a full substitution or reversibility.[11]

Third, and even more problematic, why did Arendt's approach produce a result that was, by her own later acknowledgment—and I would suppose by that of every contributor to this volume—palpably inferior to that arrived at by the defenders of such abstract moral principles as equality? Maybe, in short, in this case a few normative bannisters would have been useful to prevent her from falling over the edge. Or rather, they might have induced her to make explicit and to question her own implicit abstract principles, such as the belief that state rights should always be defended against federal intervention because they intrinsically privilege diversity above uniformity.

The recent publication of Arendt's correspondence with Mary

McCarthy provides ample evidence of how a priori her attitude to equality actually was. Responding to McCarthy's own fear that "the worm of equality is not only eating away at the old social and economic foundations but at the very structure of consciousness, demolishing 'class distinctions' between the sane and the insane, the beautiful and the ugly, the good and the bad," Arendt advanced the familiar Nietzschean claim that "the chief vice of every egalitarian society is Envy—the great vice of free Greek society. And the great virtue of all aristocracies seems to me to be that people always know who they are and hence do not compare themselves with others. This constant comparing is really the quintessence of vulgarity. If you are not in this hideous habit you are immediately accused of arrogance—as though by not-comparing you have decided to be on top."[12] Was this assumption really a lesson produced by the odor of judgment and an enlarged mentality, or rather by a priori principles of her own? Was it actually the product of imaginative "visiting" with those on the bottom of the social or economic ladder, whose motivations may have been a little less reducible to "vulgar" envy and resentment than Arendt seemed to think? Can one, in fact, ever argue only from paradigmatic cases without any general principles lurking in the background? Can one simply base decisions only on exceptions and never on rules? And if so, how can one really avoid the arbitrary decisionism that radically antinormative politics always courts?

Remembering Arendt's misjudgment of the Little Rock case provides some caution against the claim frequently made in these essays that her position should be zealously protected against any Habermasian infusion of rational argumentation or universal normativity. It also reminds us that the Arendt who may be relevant in the 1990s is not merely the antifoundationalist, postmodernist celebrant of politics as aesthetic performance. There is also a neoconservative Arendt who emerges when we give her formulations a certain, not entirely unjustified spin; for who today embodies a performative notion of politics, scornfully rejects universal principles, loudly prefers agonistic opinion to consensus-building reason, cynically assumes that truth telling is an antipolitical intrusion, and truculently denies the power of government to bring about social justice and economic equality—who does all these things better than that paragon of the non-Habermasian public sphere, that sublime resister to the docile subjectivity called political correctness, Rush Limbaugh? Arendt, to be sure, would have clearly preferred Lessing to Limbaugh, whose gnawing resentment is all too palpable, but when you privilege initiatory, agonistic action and spontaneous, independent judgment above principles, norms, logical arguments, and substance, you don't always get what you bargained for. Were this the only outcome of Arendt's mixed legacy, here is at least one spectator who could judge the spectacle only as unedifying indeed. Arendt herself, however, gives us at least some of the resources to resist this version of that legacy, as a number of contributors to this volume have clearly demonstrated. Tempering her position with that of Habermas, *pace* Villa, Cascardi, Curtis, and Disch, would help to reinforce the resistance, but this would be the subject of another book. There is, it seems to me in conclusion, clear reason to remain in the audience and to keep the show going for a long time to come. Arendt, for good or ill, has herself become one of the most prominent bannisters of political theory at the end of the twentieth century, who is likely to continue guarding the stairs we clumsily seek to climb for some time to come.

Notes

1. Hannah Arendt, *The Life of the Mind*, vol. 1, *Thinking* (New York: Harcourt Brace Jovanovich, 1978), p. 95.
2. Ibid., p. 96. Arendt cites the epithet "fools" from Kant's "Uber den Gemeinspruch," in *Werke*, vol. 6 (Berlin: de Gruyter, 1968), p. 166.
3. Seyla Benhabib, "Hannah Arendt and the Redemptive Power of Narrative," *Social Research* 57, no. 1 (spring 1990), p. 189.
4. Jean-François Lyotard, "The Survivor," in *Toward the Postmodern*, ed. Robert Harvey and Mark S. Roberts (Atlantic Highlands, N.J.: Humanities Press International, 1993), pp. 154–55.
5. "I still wonder," Lyotard writes, "whether 'birth' (the ability to judge, the vocation to begin) makes 'administered life' just a survival in comparison with the true life of the soul. I wonder if, from this still possible miracle, we can expect any alternative to the system?" (ibid., p. 162).
6. Hannah Arendt, *The Human Condition* (Chicago: Doubleday, Anchor, 1958), p. 25.
7. Hannah Arendt, *Between Past and Future* (New York: Meridian, 1977), p. 241.
8. Dana Villa, "Beyond Good and Evil: Arendt, Nietzsche, and the Aestheticization of Political Action," *Political Theory* 20, no. 2 (May 1992), pp. 274–308.
9. Arendt, *Between Past and Future*, p. 241.
10. Karl Mannheim, *Ideology and Utopia: An Introduction to the Sociology of Knowledge*, trans. Louis Wirth and Edward Shils (New York: Harcourt, Brace, 1936). Ironically, Arendt attacked this book from a Heideggerian perspective when it was published. See her review in *Die Gesellschaft* 7 (1930), pp. 163–76.
11. Iris Marion Young, "Comments on Seyla Benhabib, *Situating the Self*," and

Seyla Benhabib, "In Defense of Universalism—Yet Again! A Response to Critics of *Situating the Self*," *New German Critique* 62 (spring/summer 1994), pp. 165–89.

12. Mary McCarthy to Hannah Arendt, June 19, 1964; and Arendt to McCarthy, June 23, 1964, in *Between Friends: The Correspondence of Hannah Arendt and Mary McCarthy, 1949–1975*, ed. Carol Brightman (New York: Harcourt Brace Jovanovich, 1995), pp. 164 and 167. See also Arendt's diatribe against affirmative action in her letter of December 21, 1968:

> The general civil-rights enthusiasm led to integrating larger numbers of Negroes who were not qualified and who understood much quicker, of course, than the others, full of good will, that they were in an intolerable competitive situation. Today the situation is quite clear: Negroes demand their own curriculum without the exacting standards of white society and, at the same time, they demand admission in accordance to their percentage in the population at large, regardless of standards. In other words they actually want to take over and adjust standards to their own level. This is a much greater threat to our institutions of higher learning than the student riots. (pp. 230–31).

In the current climate of "political correctness" bashing, these blunt judgments may no longer seem to some (although I am not among them) as obnoxious as they might have a few years ago, but they do little to suggest that Arendt's mentality was very enlarged when it came to the issue of race in America.

Contributors

Richard J. Bernstein is Vera List Professor of Philosophy at the New School for Social Research. His most recent book is *Hannah Arendt and the Jewish Question.*

Susan Bickford is assistant professor of political science at the University of North Carolina at Chapel Hill. She is the author of *The Dissonance of Democracy: Listening, Conflict, and Citizenship* and of articles on Aristotle, Arendt, and feminist theory.

Craig Calhoun is chair of the Department of Sociology at New York University. His most recent books include *Neither Gods nor Emperors: Students and the Struggle for Democracy in China* and *Critical Social Theory: Culture, History, and the Challenge of Difference.* Calhoun is the current editor of the American Sociological Association journal, *Sociological Theory.* He is presently engaged in comparative historical research on nationalism, identity politics, and democracy.

Anthony J. Cascardi is professor of comparative literature, Spanish, and rhetoric and chair of the Department of Rhetoric at the University of California at Berkeley. His latest books are *The Subject of Modernity* and *Ideologies of History in the Spanish Golden Age* (forthcoming). He is currently at work on a project entitled "The Consequences of Enlightenment."

Kimberley F. Curtis is assistant professor of the practice of political science and women's studies at Duke University. She specializes in political theory, with particular concentration in contemporary Continental work and feminist theory. She is completing a book entitled "Aesthetics and Ethics in the Political Theory of Hannah Arendt." She is also engaged in research on the public debate about the ethics of new reproductive technologies.

Lisa Disch is associate professor of political science at the University of Minnesota. She has published *Hannah Arendt and the Limits of Philosophy*, and her recent articles have appeared in *Signs* and the *Journal of Health Politics, Policy, and Law*. She is currently researching theories of narrative and working to revive the practice of electoral fusion.

Nancy Fraser is professor of political science at the New School for Social Research. Her latest book is *Justice Interruptus: Critical Reflections on the "Postsocialist" Condition.*

Martin Jay is professor of European intellectual history at the University of California at Berkeley. His most recent work includes *Force Fields*; *Downcast Eyes*; *The Weimar Republic Sourcebook* (coedited with Anton Kaes and Edward Dimendberg); and *Vision in Context* (coedited with Teresa Brennan). He is currently working on a book on the discourse of experience in recent European and American thought.

Stephen T. Leonard is associate professor of political science at the University of North Carolina at Chapel Hill. He is the author of *Critical Theory in Political Practice* and coeditor of *Political Science in History* and *Intellectuals and Public Life*. His most recent work is on civic education in the history of the academic disciplines.

Kirstie M. McClure is associate professor of political science and humanities at Johns Hopkins University.

John McGowan is professor of English and comparative literature at the University of North Carolina at Chapel Hill. He has taught at the

University of Michigan and the University of Rochester and is the author of *Representation and Revelation: Victorian Realism from Carlyle to Yeats, Postmodernism and Its Critics,* and *Hannah Arendt: An Introduction.*

Dana R. Villa teaches political theory at Amherst College, where he is assistant professor of political science. He is the author of *Arendt and Heidegger: The Fate of the Political* and of many articles on contemporary political thought.

Eli Zaretsky is associate professor of history at the University of Missouri at Columbia. He is the author of *Psychoanalysis: From the Psychology of Authority to the Politics of Identity* and *Capitalism, the Family, and Personal Life,* and the editor of William I. Thomas and Florian Znaniecki's *The Polish Peasant in Europe and America.*

Index

world, the: Arendt's conception of, 18, 21, 31–32, 43–44, 63, 78, 91, 92, 125, 183, 184, 187–88, 193, 198, 200, 233, 238, 243–44, 284, 345

Wright, Richard, 210

Young, Iris Marion, 347

Zaretsky, Eli, 11, 12, 21, 22, 232, 234, 235–37, 239, 240, 242, 250

Zionism, 210, 211, 212